Study Guide

to accompany

LIPSEY/PURVIS/STEINER

ECONOMICS

AND MICROECONOMICS AND MACROECONOMICS

Seventh Canadian Edition

prepared by

E. Kenneth Grant
University of Guelph

William J. Furlong
University of Guelph

Richard G. Lipsey
Simon Fraser University

Douglas D. Purvis
Queen's University

◼ HarperCollins*Publishers*

The seventh Canadian edition is dedicated to our children: Mara, Mark, Liam, and Dylan.

Senior Editor: John Greenman
Project Editor: Claire M. Caterer
Art Direction: Teresa Delgado
Cover Design: Jaye Zimet
Cover Photos: *Clockwise from top left position* : Grain elevator, Thunder Bay, Thomas Kitchin/First Light; Oil upgrader, Regina, Saskatchewan, Thomas Kitchin/First Light; Bay & King Streets, Toronto, Alan Sirulnikoff/First Light; Ford plant, Lorraine C. Parow/First Light; Farming, Quebec, Joe Viesti/Viesti Associates. *Center photo*: Parliament Building, Ontario, Joe Viesti/Viesti Associates.
Production: Jimmy Spillane
Compositor: L&F Technical Composition
Printer and Binder: Malloy Lithographing, Inc.
Cover Printer: Malloy Lithographing, Inc.

Study Guide to accompany Economics, and Microeconomics and Macroeconomics
Seventh Canadian Edition
Copyright © 1991 by HarperCollins Publishers Inc.

ISBN: 0-06-500032-3

91 92 93 94 9 8 7 6 5 4 3 2

Contents

To the Student

The content of this *Study Guide* tests and reinforces the student's understanding of the concepts and analytical techniques stressed in each chapter of *Economics*, Seventh Canadian Edition, by professors Lipsey, Purvis, and Steiner. Our own teaching experience has led us to believe that students have the most trouble understanding technical information and applying theoretical concepts to particular situations. Consequently, most multiple-choice questions and exercises are technical and numerical in nature. We feel that policy issues and specific applications of theory to real-world examples are primarily the responsibility of the textbook. You will find excellent discussions of issues and applications in the body of the text, especially in the policy "boxes" that appear in each chapter.

Each chapter in this *Study Guide* corresponds to a text chapter and is divided into three basic sections. The Learning Objectives briefly summarize the important concepts and analysis covered in the textbook and *Study Guide*. It might be useful for you to compare this section with the summary section appearing at the end of each text chapter.

The Multiple-Choice Questions test your comprehension of definitions, analytical concepts, and numercial techniques. When you answer these, avoid the temptation to leap at the first answer that seems plausible. There is one best answer for each question. You should be able to explain why any other answer is not as satisfactory as the one you have chosen.

In some ways the greatest reinforcement to learning economics comes from doing the questions in the Exercises section. You are usually asked to demonstrate numerically and/or graphically the sense of what has been expressed verbally. You may wish to refresh your understanding of high school algebra before attempting some of the questions. In addition, you are often asked to explain your method of analysis and your results. The ability to solve problems and to communicate and interpret results are important goals in an introductory economics course.

Do not be discouraged if you have difficulties with certain questions. Those marked with an asterisk (*) are quite challenging for the beginner, and a full appreciation of the points involved can be achieved only after you have participated in lectures and have carefully read the text.

Unlike other study guides, answers are provided for all questions in this one. However, we caution that our answers are brief. Your instructors often require much fuller explanations on midterm and final examinations.

Acknowledgments

The seventh Canadian edition and the ninth U.S. edition (by Menz, Mutti, and Forbush) of the *Study Guide* share certain materials. We thank the constructive comments of several anonymous referees and professors Leon Sydor and Peter Burrell of the University of Windsor. All errors and omissions are our responsibility.

E. Kenneth Grant

William J. Furlong

PART ONE

The Nature
of Economics

Chapter 1

The Economic Problem

Learning Objectives

After studying this chapter, you should be able to:

—understand the problem of scarcity and the need for choice

—illustrate the relationship between scarcity, choice, and opportunity cost with a production possibility boundary

—understand why resource allocation is a key economic problem

—explain why unemployed resources force the economy inside its production possibility boundary

—describe how growth in productive capacity makes it possible to have more of all goods and services

—explain how alternative economic systems differ in terms of public versus private ownership of resources, market versus command systems for decision making, and incentive structures

Multiple-Choice Questions

1. The fundamental problem of economics is, in short,
   (a) too many poor people
   (b) finding jobs for all
   (c) the scarcity of resources relative to wants
   (d) constantly rising prices

2. The use of goods and services to satisfy wants is called
   (a) consumption
   (b) production
   (c) the making of commodities
   (d) economic scarcity

3. Scarcity is a problem that
   (a) efficient production will eliminate
   (b) is nonexistent in wealthy economies
   (c) exists because of finite amounts of resources and unlimited human wants
   (d) arises when productivity growth slows down

4. Which of the following is *not* an example of a factor of production?
   (a) a bulldozer   (c) a manicure
   (b) the services of an engineer   (d) downtown parking lots

5. The necessity of choice in production and distribution arises because of
   (a) unemployment   (c) scarcity
   (b) declines in productivity   (d) central planning

6. Opportunity cost measures the
   (a) different opportunities for spending money
   (b) amount of money that must be given up to purchase a commodity
   (c) amount of one good that must be forfeited to obtain a given amount of another good
   (d) alternative means of producing output

7. Assuming the alternative is employment, the opportunity cost of a university education is
   (a) tuition costs only
   (b) tuition and book costs only
   (c) the forgone salary only
   (d) tuition costs plus book costs plus the forgone salary

8. A production possibility boundary illustrates the concept of
   (a) scarcity   (c) opportunity cost
   (b) choice   (d) all of the above

9. A downward-sloping production possibility boundary that is also a straight line implies
   (a) constant opportunity cost   (c) zero opportunity cost
   (b) declining opportunity cost   (d) rising opportunity cost

10. If it costs $6 to buy a unit of good *A* and $2 to buy a unit of good *B*, the opportunity cost of good *A* in terms of good *B* is
    (a) 3   (c) ⅓
    (b) 4   (d) 12

11. If a 12-month membership in a fitness club costs as much as tickets for 24 Montreal Expos baseball games, the opportunity cost of a one-month membership in the fitness club is
    (a) ½ baseball game   (c) 2 baseball games
    (b) 1 baseball game   (d) 12 baseball games

12. A point to the right of an existing production possibility boundary might be attainable
    (a) if less of one good is produced
    (b) with full employment of resources
    (c) with economic growth
    (d) with a reallocation of the factors of production

13. Which of the following does *not* cause a shift in the production possibility boundary?
    (a) an improvement in production methods
    (b) an increase in the country's population
    (c) a decrease in unemployment
    (d) a flood that destroys agricultural land

14. If a commodity can be obtained without sacrificing the production or consumption of anything else,
    (a) its opportunity cost is zero
    (b) the economy is on its production possibility boundary
    (c) all factors of production are efficiently allocated
    (d) the economy must be a command system

15. Which of the following would *not* be a source of differences among alternative types of economic systems?
    (a) ownership of resources (public, private)
    (b) the process for making economic decisions
    (c) incentive systems
    (d) the need to determine what is to be produced and how to produce it

16. The process of determining the relative quantities of alternative goods and services to be produced is referred to by the term
    (a) resource allocation   (c) consumption
    (b) macroeconomics   (d) scarcity

17. Decisions on resource allocation are
    (a) necessary only in centrally planned economies
    (b) made by central planners in traditional economies
    (c) necessary only in command economies
    (d) decentralized but coordinated by the price system in market economies

18. The recent changes in Eastern Europe suggest that the majority of people in these countries view
    (a) decentralized markets as a superior means of increasing living standards than fully planned economies
    (b) completely free market economies as ends in themselves
    (c) the process of central planning as a relatively efficient way of coordinating economic decisions
    (d) private ownership of resources as an end

Exercises

1. Four key economic problems are identified in Chapter 1:
    (1) What is produced and how? (resource allocation)
    (2) What is consumed and by whom? (distribution)
    (3) How much unemployment and inflation are there? (total employment and the price level)
    (4) How is productive capacity changing? (economic growth)

After each of the topics listed next, place the appropriate number indicating which type of problem applies. Use each classification only once.
(a) Rises in oil prices during the 1970s induced a switch to alternative energy sources. _____
(b) The standard of living in Canada, measured by real output per capita, has risen steadily over the past century. _____
(c) Large harvests cause worldwide lower grain prices, helping consumers but hurting farmers. _____
(d) The unemployment rate increased in the early months of 1990. _____

2. The following data show what combinations of corn and beef can be produced annually from a piece of land of given acreage.

Corn (bushels)	Beef (pounds)
10,000	0
8,000	900
6,000	1,200
4,000	1,400
2,000	1,450
0	1,500

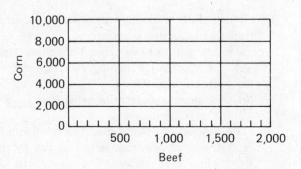

(a) On the graph, draw the production possibility boundary for this piece of land.

(b) Can this acreage produce the combination of 5,000 bushels of corn and 500 pounds of beef? What does this combination suggest about the use of this acreage?

(c) Can this acreage produce the combination of 8,000 bushels of corn and 1,200 pounds of beef?

(d) What is the opportunity cost of expanding beef production from 900 to 1,200 pounds per annum, assuming that the land is fully utilized?

(e) What would be the cost of producing 400 additional pounds of beef if this economy were currently producing 8,000 bushels of corn and 500 pounds of beef? Explain.

(f) What happens to the production possibility boundary if a growth hormone is developed that will allow more beef production?

(g) What happens to the production possibility boundary if some of the land is lost due, for example, to a flood?

3. A certain economy produces only two consumer goods, X and Y. Only labor is required to produce both goods, and the economy's labor force is fixed at 100 workers. The table indicates the amount of X and Y that can be produced daily with various quantities of labor.

Number of workers	Daily X production	Number of workers	Daily Y production
0	0	0	0
20	10.0	20	150
40	20.0	40	250
60	25.0	60	325
80	27.5	80	375
100	30.0	100	400

(a) Draw the production possibility curve for this economy, using the grid. (*Hint:* The labor force must always be fully employed.)

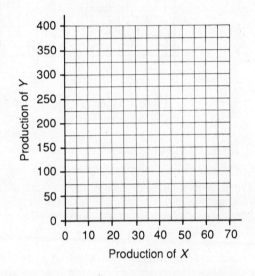

(b) What is the opportunity cost of producing the first 10 units of good X? What is the opportunity cost of producing the next 10 units of X (i.e., from 10 to 20)? What happens to the opportunity cost of X as its production is continuously increased?

(c) Suppose that actual production for a given period was 20 units of X and 250 units of Y. What can you infer from this information?

(d) Suppose that a central planner in this economy were to call for an output combination of $X = 35$ and $Y = 150$. Is this plan attainable? Explain.

(e) New technology is developed in X production, so that each worker can now produce double the daily amount of X indicated in the schedule. What happens to the production possibility curve? Draw the new curve on the graph. Can the planner's output combination in (d) now be met?

4. Junior gets a weekly allowance of $10. He spends all of his allowance on only two commodities: video games at the arcade and chocolate bars. Assume that the price of a video game is 50 cents and the price of a chocolate bar is $1.
    (a) Plot Junior's weekly consumption possibilities.

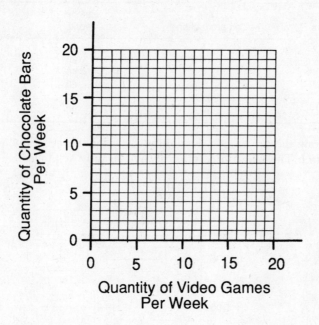

    (b) Can Junior attain the following consumption combinations?
         (i)   15 video games and 2 chocolate bars
         (ii) 4 video games and 8 chocolate bars
         (iii) 7 video games and 7 chocolate bars

    (c) What is the opportunity cost of Junior's first chocolate bar? his second? his third?

    (d) By visual inspection of Junior's consumption possibility boundary, what could you say about his opportunity cost of consuming each of these commodities?

*5. An economy's production possibility boundary is given by the mathematical expression $20 = 4A + B$, where A is the quantity of good A and B is the quantity of good B.
    (a) If all resources in the economy were allocated to producing good A, what is the maximum level of production for this good? What is the maximum level of production for good B?

(b) Suppose that the production of *B* is increased from 12 to 16 units and that the economy is producing at a point on the production possibility boundary. What is the opportunity cost per unit of good *B*? What is the opportunity cost per unit of good *B* if the production of this good was increased from 16 to 20?

(c) In what way is this production possibility boundary different from those in exercises 2 and 3 in terms of opportunity costs?

(d) In what way does the combination of four units of good *A* and five units of good *B* represent the problem of scarcity?

*6. Consider the production possibilities for two totally dissimilar goods, such as apples and machine tools. Some resources are suitable for apple production and some for the production of machine tools. However, there is no possibility of shifting resources from one product to another. In this case, what does the production possibility boundary look like? Explain and show graphically.

Answers

Multiple-Choice Questions

1. (c) 2. (a) 3. (c) 4. (c) 5. (c) 6. (c) 7. (d) 8. (d) 9. (a) 10. (a) 11. (c) 12. (c)
13. (c) 14. (a) 15. (d) 16. (a) 17. (d) 18. (a)

Exercises

1. (a) 1 (b) 4 (c) 2 (d) 3
2. (a)

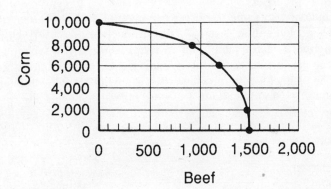

(b) Yes. In fact, this combination is inside the production possibility boundary, indicating that resources are either not being used efficiently or are unemployed.

(c)   No, this combination lies outside the production possibility boundary.

(d)   2,000 bushels of corn are lost.

(e)   The cost would be zero, since no corn would be forgone. The current production combination implies inefficient use of the land.

(f)   This technological improvement would increase the maximum amount of beef that could be produced, making the beef intercept greater than 1,500. The corn intercept would not be changed.

(g)   The intercepts for both corn and beef production decrease, or the production possibility boundary shifts inward.

3.   (a)

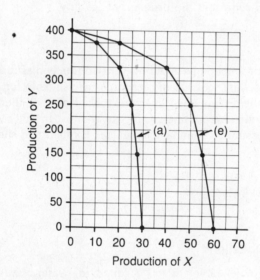

(b)   25 units of good Y (i.e., Y decreases from 400 to 375). 50 units of good Y. The opportunity cost of producing X is increasing—increasing X production by yet another 10 units from 20 to 30 would imply forgoing an additional 325 units of Y.

(c)   This production combination lies inside the production possibility boundary, so some resources are unemployed or inefficiently used.

(d)   This combination is outside the production possibility boundary and is therefore unattainable with current resources and technology.

(e)   The production possibility boundary shifts to the right as graphed in (a). The planner's output combination is now attainable but is inside the new boundary, implying that if it were indeed achieved, the economy would be inefficiently using its resources.

4. (a)

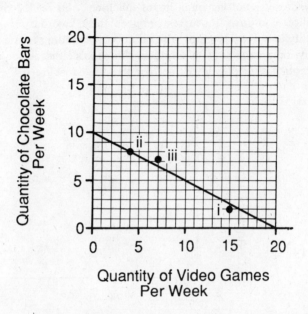

(b) (i) Yes, this combination lies inside his consumption possibility boundary and is therefore affordable with $10.

(ii) Yes, this combination is on his consumption possibility boundary and therefore costs exactly $10.

(iii) No, this combination lies outside his consumption possibility boundary and therefore costs more than a $10 allowance permits.

(c) To purchase the first chocolate bar, Junior must pay $1, which could have been used to purchase two video games. Thus the opportunity cost of the first chocolate bar is two video games. The opportunity cost of the second and third bars is also two video games each.

(d) Since the consumption possibility boundary is linear (i.e., a straight line), the opportunity cost is constant.

*5. (a) If all resources were allocated to the production of good A, there is no production of good B. Hence, according to the mathematical expression, the maximum production of good A is five units. If all resources were used to produce good B, then $B = 20$ and the production of good A is zero.

(b) The increase from 12 to 16 requires a loss in production of good A of one (from two to one). An increase in B from 16 to 20 requires a loss in production of good A of one (from one to zero).

(c) The opportunity cost is constant, whereas it was increasing for both exercises 2 and 3.

(d) According to the equation, four units of A and four units of B are possible. The combination of four units of A and five units of B is not feasible and indicates that more resources are required than are currently available.

*6. When all resources suitable to apple production are employed, the resulting apple output is A'. When all resources suitable to machine tool production are employed, the resulting quantity of machine tools is M'. Since there is no possibility of shifting resources between these two outputs, the production possibility boundary is simply the point corresponding to the coordinates (A', M'). Any combination of apples and machine tools either inside or on the dashed lines implies unemployed or inefficiently used resources.

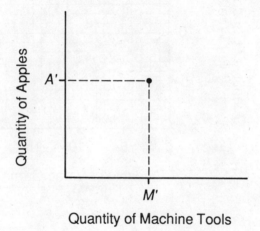

Chapter 2

Economics As a Social Science

Learning Objectives

After studying this chapter, you should be able to:

—distinguish between positive and normative statements

—explain how the "law" of large numbers allows successful predictions about group behavior

—understand the roles of variables, assumptions, and predictions in developing and testing theories

—distinguish between endogenous and exogenous variables and between stocks and flows

—give an example of a functional relation

—graph linear relationships and interpret graphs

Multiple-Choice Questions

1. Normative statements
   (a) concern what ought to be
   (b) are based on value judgments
   (c) cannot be subjected to empirical scrutiny
   (d) all of the above

2. "Capital punishment deters crime" is an example of a
   (a) positive statement   (c) normative statement
   (b) value judgment   (d) analytic statement

3. "Capital punishment should be reintroduced in Canada" is an example of a
   (a) positive statement   (c) analytic statement
   (b) normative statement   (d) testable hypothesis

4. Which of the following is the best example of a positive statement?
    (a) Equal distribution of national income is a desirable goal for society.
    (b) Foreign ownership is undesirable for Canada and should therefore be eliminated.
    (c) Although free trade causes some Canadians to lose their jobs, it will significantly increase the income of the average Canadian.
    (d) Taxes should be lowered.

5. Economic predictions are intended to
    (a) forecast the behavior of each consumer
    (b) forecast the behavior of groups of individuals
    (c) test normative statements
    (d) anticipate the irrational behavior of certain odd individuals

6. The "law" of large numbers basically says that
    (a) the greater the number of observations, the greater the sum of each variable
    (b) measuring error increases with the number of observations
    (c) a few observations are just as accurate as a large number of observations
    (d) erratic behavior by individuals tends to offset itself in a large group

7. In measuring the area of a room, the normal curve of error implies that
    (a) more people will make small errors than large ones
    (b) roughly the same number of people will understate the area as overstate it
    (c) the average error of all individuals is approximately zero
    (d) all of the above

8. With respect to agriculture, weather is an example of
    (a) an exogenous factor of production   (c) a dependent variable
    (b) an endogenous input   (d) an induced input variable

9. A variable that is defined with reference to a period of time is
    (a) a stock   (c) endogenous
    (b) a flow   (d) exogenous

10. The role of assumptions in theory is to
    (a) represent the world accurately
    (b) abstract from reality
    (c) avoid simplifications of the real world
    (d) ensure that the theory considers all features of reality, no matter how minor

11. If annual per capita consumption expenditure decreases as average annual income decreases, these two variables are then said to be
    (a) negatively related   (c) random
    (b) positively related   (d) all of the above

12. Which of the following statements about economic theories is most appropriate?
    (a) The most reliable test of a theory is the realism of its assumptions.
    (b) The best kind of theory is worded so that it can pass any test to which it is applied.
    (c) The most important thing about the scientific approach is that it uses mathematics and diagrams.
    (d) We expect our theories to hold only with some margin of error.

13. A theory may contain all but which of the following?
    (a) predictions about behavior that are deduced from the assumptions
    (b) a set of assumptions defining the conditions under which the theory is operative
    (c) hypotheses about how the world behaves
    (d) one or more irrefutable normative statements

14. A scientific prediction is a conditional statement because
    (a) it takes the form "if that occurs, then this will result"
    (b) it is conditional on being correct
    (c) it is impossible to test
    (d) it is true in theory but not in practice

15. Statistical analysis
    (a) is an exact science that eliminates all errors
    (b) treats the errors in acceptance or rejection as exogenous
    (c) can control the likelihood of making an erroneous decision
    (d) cannot make predictions with data drawn at random

16. Economic hypotheses are generally accepted only when
    (a) the evidence indicates that they are true with a high degree of probability
    (b) they have been proved beyond a reasonable doubt
    (c) they have been established with certainty
    (d) the evidence is consistent with them in all cases

Appendix Questions

The following multiple-choice questions are based on the material in the appendix to this chapter. Read the appendix before answering these questions.

17. The slope of a straight line is
    (a) always positive
    (b) calculated by dividing the variable measured on the horizontal axis by that measured on the vertical axis
    (c) zero
    (d) constant

18. The relationship between two variables on a scatter diagram
    (a) may be obscured by the movement of another variable
    (b) cannot be significant because of errors of observation
    (c) will show a wavelike pattern if the variables are related to time
    (d) will usually be a straight line

19. Suppose that a scatter diagram indicates that imports are, on average, positively related to national income over time. If in one year imports fall when national income increases, the observation
    (a) disproves the positive relationship between the two variables
    (b) suggests that other factors also influence the quantity of imports
    (c) proves a negative relationship between the two variables
    (d) suggests that a measurement error has necessarily been made

20. In statistical testing of a theory, choosing a random sample of observations is important because
    (a) it reduces the chance that the sample will be unrepresentative of the entire group
    (b) it allows the calculation of the likelihood that the observed characteristics of the sample do not exist for the whole group
    (c) economic theories cannot be tested using scientific methods
    (d) both (a) and (b)

21. The statement that the quantity produced of a commodity and its price are positively related is
    (a) an assumption economists usually make
    (b) a testable hypothesis
    (c) a normative statement
    (d) not testable as currently worded

22. Which of the following equations is consistent with the hypothesis that federal income tax payments (T) are positively related to family income (Y) and negatively related to family size (F)?
    (a) $T = -733 + 0.19Y + 344F$ (c) $T = -733 + 0.19Y - 344F$
    (b) $T = -733 - 0.19Y - 344F$ (d) none of the above

23. Suppose that regression analysis estimates the following relationship between imports (M) and national income (Y): $M = 100 + 0.15Y$. This means that
    (a) imports are negatively related to national income
    (b) when national income is zero, imports are zero
    (c) imports are 15 percent of national income
    (d) other things remaining constant, for every increase of $1 in national income, imports will rise by 15 cents

Exercises

1. After each phrase, write P or N to indicate whether a positive or a normative statement is being described.
   (a) a statement of fact that is actually wrong _____
   (b) a value judgment _____
   (c) a prediction that an event will happen _____
   (d) a statement about what the author thinks ought to be _____
   (e) a statement that can be tested by evidence _____
   (f) a value judgment based on evidence known to be correct _____
   (g) a hurricane forecast _____

2. Are the italicized variables endogenous (N) or exogenous (X) in these statements?
   (a) *Market price* and *equilibrium quantity* of a commodity are determined by demand and supply. _____
   (b) The number of sailboats sold annually is a function of *national income*. _____
   (c) The *condition of forest ecosystems* can be affected by regional air pollutants. _____
   (d) The quantity of housing services purchased is determined by the *relative price of housing, income,* and *housing characteristics.* _____
   (e) Other things being equal, *consumer expenditures* are negatively related to interest rates. _____

3. Are the following variables stocks (S) or flows (F)?
   (a) the federal government's current budget deficit _____
   (b) the money supply _____
   (c) the total capital in the form of plant and equipment _____
   (d) personal income tax payments _____
   (e) an economy's annual total output _____
   (f) your bank balance at the end of the month _____
   (g) quarterly sales of automobiles _____

Appendix Exercises

The following exercises are based on the material in the appendix to this chapter. Read the appendix before attempting these exercises.

4. Given the relation between saving (S) and income (Y), $S = -\$100 + 0.10Y$, what is the amount of S for each of the indicated values of Y? Plot S on the graph.

Y	S
0	_____
500	_____
1,000	_____
1,500	_____
2,000	_____

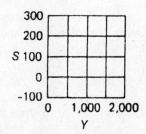

5. Suppose that two variables are related by the following equations:

$$(1)\ X = 5 + 0.5Y$$

$$(2)\ X = 50 - 0.5Y$$

(a) Complete the table using the X1 column for equation 1 and the X2 column for equation 2.

Y	X1	X2	X3
10	_____	_____	_____
20	_____	_____	_____
30	_____	_____	_____
40	_____	_____	_____
50	_____	_____	_____
60	_____	_____	_____

(b) Plot the relationship between Y and $X1$ and $X2$ in the graph.

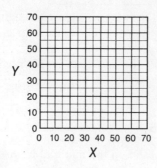

(i)   The straight line relating variables Y and $X1$ has a (positive/negative)
      _____ slope of _____ .
(ii) The straight line relating variables Y and $X2$ has a (positive/negative)
      _____ slope of _____ .

(c) Assume that the constant term in Equation 1 increases from 5 to 25.
     Complete column $X3$ in (a), and plot the new relationship on the graph
     in (b). The curve has shifted _____. The slope is _____ .

6. Suppose that an economist hypothesizes that the quantity demanded of
    television sets (Q_d) over some time period is determined by the price of each
    television (P) and the average income of consumers (Y). The specific functional
    relationship among these three variables is hypothesized to be the expression
    $Q_d = 1Y - 4P$.
    (a) Which of these variables will be determined in the market for televisions?
         Are these variables considered endogenous or exogenous?

    (b) Which of these variables will be determined outside the market for
         televisions? Are these variables considered endogenous or exogenous?

    (c) What does the negative sign before the term $4P$ imply about the relationship
         between Q_d and P? What does the implicit positive sign before the term
         $1Y$ imply about the relationship between income and quantity demanded?

    (d) Which of the three variables are stock variables and which are flow
         variables? Explain.

    (e) Suppose for the moment that average income is constant at a level of 8,000.
         Write the expression for the demand relationship.

    (f) Assuming that $Y = 8,000$, calculate the values of Q_d when $P = 500$, $P =$
         1,000, $P = 2,000$, and $P = 0$.

(g) Plot the relation between P and Q_d (assuming $Y = 8,000$) on the graph. Indicate the intercept values on both axes.

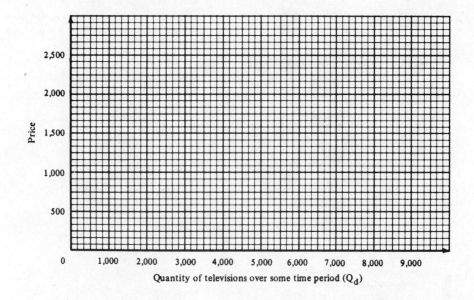

(h) Assuming that $Y = 8,000$, calculate the *change* in the quantity demanded when the price increases from 1,000 to 2,000. Do the same for a price increase from 500 to 2,000. Call the *change* in the quantity demanded ΔQ_d and the change in the price ΔP. Form the ratio $\Delta Q_d / \Delta P$. Is this ratio constant?

(i) Now suppose that the average income of consumers changes to $9,000 per month. Plot the new relationship between P and Q_d. What are the intercept values and the slope?

Answers

Multiple-Choice Questions

1. (d)   2. (a)   3. (b)   4. (c)   5. (b)   6. (d)   7. (d)   8. (a)   9. (b)   10. (b)   11. (b)   12. (d)
13. (d)   14. (a)   15. (c)   16. (a)   17. (d)   18. (a)   19. (b)   20. (d)   21. (b)   22. (c)   23. (d)

Exercises

1. (a) P (b) N (c) P (d) N (e) P (f) N (g) P
2. (a) N (b) X (c) N (d) X (e) N
3. (a) F (b) S (c) S (d) F (e) F (f) S (g) F

4. $S = -\$100; -\$50; 0; \$50; \$100$

5. (a)

Y	X1	X2	X3
10	10	45	30
20	15	40	35
30	20	35	40
40	25	30	45
50	30	25	50
60	35	20	55

(b)

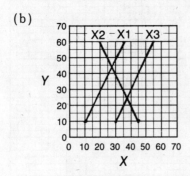

   (i)   positive; 1/2
   (ii) negative; 1/2

(c) rightward; unchanged (1/2)

6. (a) Q_d and P are determined in the market for television sets. They are endogenous variables.

(b) Average income, which is determined in many other markets, is not influenced to any significant extent by the market for televisions. It is exogenous to the market for televisions.

(c) Q_d and P are negatively related; as P increases, Q_d falls. Q_d and Y are positively related; as Y increases, Q_d increases.

(d) All three variables are flow variables. Q_d and P are determined over a period of time in the television market. To be consistent, average income, a flow variable, is measured over the same time period.

(e) The equation becomes $Q_d = 8,000 - 4P$.

(f) $Q_d = 6,000, 4,000, 0,$ and $8,000$.

(g) The intercept on the P axis is 2,000, and the intercept on the Q_d axis is 8,000. Your plotting should also indicate that the demand curve is a straight line that slopes downward.

(h) The change in quantity demanded is $-4,000$ when P increases from 1,000 to 2,000. When P increases from 500 to 2,000, quantity demanded falls by 6,000. In both cases the ratio $\Delta Q_d / \Delta P$ is equal to -4.

(i) The intercept on the P axis is 2,250, and the intercept on the Q_d axis is 9,000. The slope remains -4.

Chapter 3

An Overview of the Market Economy

Learning Objectives

After studying this chapter, you should be able to:

—understand how modern economies are based on the specialization and division of labor

—explain how three kinds of economic decision makers—households, firms, and government—interact in a market economy

—explain the distinction between market and nonmarket sectors and between the private and public sectors

—begin using economic reasoning to understand how the price system serves as a social control mechanism

—explain the relation between microeconomics and macroeconomics

—understand the circular flow of income

Multiple-Choice Questions

1. In economics, the term *market economy* refers to
   (a) institutions such as the Toronto Stock Exchange
   (b) a place where buyers and sellers gather on Saturday mornings
   (c) a society where individuals specialize in productive activities and enter voluntary trades
   (d) a society where most economic decisions are made by marketing analysts

2. In a barter economy, individuals
   (a) haggle over the price of each and every commodity
   (b) trade goods directly for other goods
   (c) use money to lubricate the flow of trades
   (d) must each be a "jack of all trades"

21

3. The introduction of production lines where individuals specialize in performing specific tasks is known as
   (a) the division of labor
   (b) the specialization of labor
   (c) the market economy
   (d) the advent of labor as a factor of production

4. In a market economy, the allocation of resources is determined by
   (a) the government and its marketing boards
   (b) the various stock exchanges in the country
   (c) a central planning agency
   (d) the millions of independent decisions made by individual consumers and firms

5. The "invisible hand"
   (a) can only be seen by economists
   (b) refers to excessive government taxation
   (c) refers to a market economy's price system
   (d) refers to the central planning agency of a command economy

6. Economic theory assumes that households
   (a) make consistent decisions as though each were comprised of a single individual
   (b) seek to maximize profits
   (c) are the buyers of the factors of production
   (d) all of the above

7. One reason for *not* assuming that governments behave in a consistent manner is that
   (a) different public officials have different objectives
   (b) governments have become too big
   (c) too many irresponsible policies have been introduced
   (d) by offering higher salaries, the private sector has attracted most of the smart university graduates

8. A central assumption in economic theory regarding firms is that they
   (a) are each owned by a single individual
   (b) must be incorporated
   (c) seek to maximize profits
   (d) must all be making profits

9. An example of a nonmarket activity is
   (a) volunteer coaching for Little League baseball
   (b) government provision of weather reports
   (c) police protection
   (d) all of the above

10. The distinction between the private sector and the public sector depends on whether the
   (a) product is sold or given away
   (b) company is listed on a stock exchange
   (c) organization is owned by individuals or the state
   (d) financial statements of the organization are available for public scrutiny

11. If households increase their desire to purchase fresh pasta, more resources will ultimately be allocated to the production of fresh pasta because
    (a) firms do not want dissatisfied consumers
    (b) fresh pasta has good nutritional content
    (c) the price of fresh pasta will be driven up and thereby permit profits to be made
    (d) consumer organizations will inform pasta manufacturers of the change in demand

12. If a hailstorm destroys a significant proportion of the Niagara Peninsula's peach crop, the average household in Ontario will desire to purchase fewer peaches because
    (a) of empathy for peach producers
    (b) of altruistic concern that all households get their fair share of peaches
    (c) the shortage will drive the price of peaches up
    (d) peach purchases will be rationed by supermarkets

13. Macroeconomics is concerned with aggregate flows within the entire economy, whereas microeconomics might study how
    (a) price is determined in a single market
    (b) resources are allocated across markets
    (c) total employment in the automobile industry changes in response to government policies
    (d) all of the above

14. Which of the following is *not* a component of aggregate demand?
    (a) investment
    (b) government expenditure
    (c) taxes
    (d) consumption

15. Which of the following is a leakage from the circular flow of income?
    (a) household savings
    (b) consumption expenditure
    (c) investment in plant and equipment
    (d) national defense expenditure

16. The two major types of markets in the circular flow of income are
    (a) public markets and private markets
    (b) product markets and factor markets
    (c) free markets and controlled markets
    (d) markets for goods and markets for services

17. The circular flow of income refers to
    (a) the flow of goods and services from sellers to buyers
    (b) the flow of money in and out of the banking system
    (c) the flow of money incomes from buyers to sellers
    (d) both (a) and (c)

18. The price system in a free market economy works in all but which of the following ways?
    (a) Price is a determinant of a firm's profits and therefore encourages or discourages production.
    (b) Prices signal to consumers how much they must sacrifice to obtain a commodity.
    (c) Prices indicate relative scarcities and costs of production.
    (d) Prices allocate resources equally among sectors of the economy.

Exercises

1. Indicate whether or not the following events would occur in a market economy with a shift in interest from snowmobiling to skiing. Explain.

    (a) Initially, a shortage of ski equipment and a surplus of snowmobiles will develop.

    (b) Prices of snowmobiles will be increased to maintain profit levels.

    (c) Profits of ski equipment producers and retailers will rise; profits of snowmobile producers and dealers will tend to fall.

    (d) Central authorities will shift resources from production of snowmobiles to production of skis.

    (e) Production of skis will be expanded.

    (f) Resources will shift from production of snowmobiles to production of skis.

    (g) Resources particularly suited to producing snowmobiles will earn more, obtaining a greater relative share of national income.

2. Indicate whether the following economic transactions are attributable (in Canada) to the market economy (M) or the nonmarket economy (NM) and to the private sector (PR) or the public sector (PU).

    (a) the provision of national defense _____

    (b) home repairs done by the homeowner _____

    (c) the sale of fresh produce at the local farmers' market _____

    (d) a government-operated toll bridge _____

    (e) tenants' rent payments to the landlord _____

    (f) Albertan beef sales to the Soviet Union _____

    (g) municipal all-volunteer fire brigade _____

3. Classify the following transactions in the circular flow of income. Specifically, identify each as a household consumption expenditure, factor payment, addition, or leakage.

    (a) government buys office equipment _____

    (b) households purchase automobiles _____

    (c) government receives business tax payments _____

    (d) firms borrow from banks for investment purposes _____

    (e) firms pay their workers _____

    (f) households deposit money with banks _____

    (g) governments purchase goods from firms _____

    (h) firms retain some profits and deposit these in banks _____

    (i) households pay butlers and maids _____

    (j) households pay income taxes _____

4. (a) Through a biological quirk, the avocado, regardless of when or where the tree is planted, yields crops that are far greater in odd years of harvest than in even years. Under a market system, we would predict that the potential gluts in good crop years would result in _____ prices and that the potential shortages in poor crop years would lead to _____ prices.

(b) In the period 1965–1977, the prices of avocados tended to increase more rapidly than the general price level. We would predict that this increase would result in _____ land and other resources being dedicated to avocado production.

(c) In fact, avocado production more than doubled. The reasonable inference is that consumer demand had substantially _____ .

(d) Relative prices of avocados dropped significantly in 1978 and 1979 as compared with the previous poor and good crop years. What could this signal mean to growers and potential growers?

Answers

Multiple-Choice Questions

1. (c) 2. (b) 3. (a) 4. (d) 5. (c) 6. (a) 7. (a) 8. (c) 9. (d) 10. (c) 11. (c) 12. (c) 13. (d) 14. (c) 15. (a) 16. (b) 17. (d) 18. (d)

Exercises

1. (a) likely to occur if shift takes place rapidly
   (b) No, lower prices are likely.
   (c) likely to occur
   (d) No, changing prices and profits will signal the shift automatically.
   (e) likely to occur as profits rise
   (f) likely to occur as profits rise in skis and fall in snowmobiles
   (g) No, exactly the opposite will occur.

2. (a) NM, PU   (e) M, PR
   (b) NM, PR   (f) M, PR
   (c) M, PR   (g) NM, PU
   (d) M, PU

3. (a) addition   (f) leakage
   (b) consumption   (g) addition
   (c) leakage   (h) leakage
   (d) addition   (i) factor payment
   (e) factor payment (j) leakage

4. (a) lower; higher
   (b) more
   (c) increased (increased popularity in salads, in Mexican food, and greater familiarity with an unusual fruit could be reasons)
   (d) to be wary of expanding output further; present and prospective profits have almost certainly been reduced

PART TWO

A General View of the Price System

Chapter 4

Demand, Supply, and Price

Learning Objectives

After studying this chapter, you should be able to:

—understand the concepts of quantity demanded, quantity supplied, and quantity exchanged

—appreciate and use demand schedules and demand curves as methods for showing the relation between quantity demanded and price

—indicate what factors are most relevant in determining the demand for a good

—appreciate and use supply schedules and supply curves as methods for showing the relation between quantity supplied and price

—indicate what factors are most relevant in determining the supply of a good

—explain the difference between movements along a curve and shifts in the curve

—distinguish changes in quantity demanded from changes in demand and changes in quantity supplied from changes in supply

—use comparative static analysis to show how equilibrium price and quantity are affected by demand and supply shifts

—use basic economic reasoning to explain the underlying behavior of consumers and firms by which price and quantity move to their equilibrium levels

—explain why price theory determines changes in relative prices, not absolute prices

Multiple-Choice Questions

1. The term *quantity demanded* refers to the
   - (a) amount of a good that consumers are willing to purchase at some price during some given time period
   - (b) amount of some good that consumers would purchase if they only had the income to afford it
   - (c) amount of a good that is actually purchased during a given time period
   - (d) minimum amount of a good that consumers require and demand for survival

2. An increase in quantity demanded refers to
    (a) rightward shifts in the demand curve only
    (b) a movement down a demand curve
    (c) a greater willingness to purchase at each price
    (d) an increase in actual purchases

3. The demand curve and the demand schedule
    (a) each reflect the relationship between quantity demanded and price, *ceteris paribus*
    (b) are both incomplete in that neither can incorporate the impact of changes in income or tastes
    (c) are constructed on the assumption that price is held constant
    (d) illustrate that in economic analysis, only two variables are taken into account at any one time

4. When the Multiple Listing Service (MLS) reports that in the month of April at an average selling price of $250,000, total sales of homes in Toronto were 2,000, they are referring to
    (a) quantity demanded
    (b) quantity supplied
    (c) equilibrium quantity
    (d) actual purchases, which may or may not equal quantity demanded or quantity supplied

5. A decrease in the price of VCRs will result in
    (a) an increase in demand for VCRs
    (b) a decrease in supply of VCRs
    (c) an increase in the quantity demanded of VCRs
    (d) a movement up along the demand curve for VCRs

6. An increase in demand means that
    (a) consumers actually buy more of the good
    (b) at each price, consumers desire a greater quantity
    (c) consumers' tastes have necessarily changed
    (d) price has decreased

7. A decrease in the price of compact disc players will induce
    (a) a leftward shift in the demand curve for record turntables
    (b) an increase in demand for records
    (c) a leftward shift in the demand curve for compact discs
    (d) a rise in demand for compact disc players

8. If goods *A* and *B* are complements, an increase in the price of good *A* will lead to
    (a) an increase in the price of good *B*
    (b) a decrease in the quantity demanded of good *B*
    (c) a decrease in demand for good *B*
    (d) no change in demand for good *B* because *A* and *B* are not substitutes

$P_A \uparrow$ $Q_B \downarrow$

$Q_A \downarrow$

9. Increased public awareness of the adverse health implications of smoking
    (a) is a noneconomic event that cannot be addressed in the model of demand
         and supply
    (b) is characterized as a change in tastes that leads to a leftward shift in the
         demand curve for cigarettes
    (c) will lead to an eventual increase in the price of cigarettes due to shifts in
         the demand curve for cigarettes
    (d) induces a fall in the supply of cigarettes

10. A change in demand could be caused by all but which one of the following?
    (a) a decrease in average income
    (b) an increase in the price of a substitute good
    (c) a decrease in the cost of producing the good
    (d) an increase in population

11. An increase in the supply of broccoli could be caused by all but which of the
    following?
    (a) an increase in the price of broccoli
    (b) a decrease in the price of labor employed in harvesting broccoli
    (c) an improvement in pesticides, thereby decreasing the variability in broccoli
         output
    (d) a change in the goals of producers

12. A movement along a supply curve could be caused by
    (a) an improvement in technology
    (b) a change in the prices of inputs
    (c) a shift in the demand curve
    (d) a change in the objectives of producers

13. Excess demand exists whenever
    (a) price exceeds the equilibrium price
    (b) quantity supplied is greater than quantity demanded
    (c) the equilibrium price is above the existing price
    (d) there is downward pressure on price

Questions 14 and 15 refer to the following diagram.

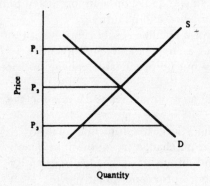

demand – the whole curve
quantity demanded – a single point on the curve.

14. At a price of P_1,
    (a) there is upward pressure on price
    (b) demand will rise to restore equilibrium
    (c) quantity supplied is greater than quantity demanded
    (d) the market has reached an equilibrium price

15. When price equals P_3,
    (a) quantity exchanged equals quantity demanded
    (b) there is excess supply
    (c) there is a tendency for price to rise
    (d) the market is in equilibrium

16. The "laws of demand and supply" are
    (a) federal statutes and are therefore enforced by the RCMP
    (b) enshrined in the Canadian Constitution
    (c) irrefutable propositions concerning economic behavior
    (d) predictions of economic behavior that have tended to withstand much, but
         not all, empirical testing

17. An increase in both equilibrium price and quantity is consistent with
    (a) an increase in supply   (c) a decrease in quantity supplied
    (b) a decrease in supply   (d) an increase in demand

18. Assuming a downward-sloping demand curve, an improvement in production
    technology for some good is predicted to lead to
    (a) a fall in supply
    (b) an increase in both equilibrium price and quantity
    (c) a decrease in equilibrium price and an increase in equilibrium quantity
    (d) a decrease in equilibrium price but no change in equilibrium quantity

19. Should bell-bottom jeans come back into fashion, economic theory predicts
    (a) a decrease in the price of bell-bottom jeans but an increase in the quantity
         bought and sold
    (b) an increase in both equilibrium price and quantity
    (c) a shift in the supply curve to the right
    (d) an increase in equilibrium price and a decrease in equilibrium quantity

20. Simultaneous increases in both demand and supply are predicted to result in
    (a) increases in both equilibrium price and quantity
    (b) a higher equilibrium price but a smaller equilibrium quantity
    (c) a lower equilibrium price but a larger equilibrium quantity
    (d) a larger equilibrium quantity but no predictable change in price

21. A decrease in input prices as well as a simultaneous decrease in the price of
    a substitute good will lead to
    (a) a lower equilibrium price and a larger equilibrium quantity
    (b) a lower equilibrium price but no change in equilibrium quantity
    (c) a lower equilibrium price and an uncertain change in quantity
    (d) an unpredictable change in both price and quantity

22. The price of steel and the quantity exchanged are most likely to fall when
    (a) income falls
    (b) the price of coal (an input) falls
    (c) the price of aluminum (a substitute) rises
    (d) steelworkers' wages rise

23. Comparative statics
    (a) refers to unchanged prices and quantities
    (b) is the analysis of demand without reference to time
    (c) is the analysis of market equilibria under different sets of conditions
    (d) describes the time path of equilibrium prices

24. Today the price of strawberries is 60 cents a quart, and raspberries are priced
    at 75 cents a quart. Yesterday strawberries were 80 cents and raspberries $1.
    Thus, for these two goods,
    (a) the relative price of raspberries has fallen
    (b) the relative price of strawberries has fallen by 20 cents
    (c) the relative prices of both goods have fallen
    (d) relative prices have not changed

25. In price theory, which of the following represents a relative price increase for
    strawberries, assuming that the average price level rises by 10 percent?
    (a) an increase in price from $1.00 to $1.05 per quart
    (b) an increase in price from $1.00 to $1.10 per quart
    (c) an increase in price from $1.00 to $1.15 per quart
    (d) both (b) and (c)

Exercises

1. The demand and supply schedules for good X are hypothesized to be as follows:

(1) Price per unit	(2) Quantity demanded (units per time period)	(3) Quantity supplied (units per time period)	(4) Excess demand (+) or excess supply (−) (units per time period)
$1.00	1	19	− 18
0.90	3	18	−15
0.80	5	17	−12
0.70	8	15	−7
0.60	12	12	0
0.50	18	9	+9
0.40	26	5	+21

(a) Using the grid, plot the demand and supply curves (approximately). Indicate the equilibrium level of price and quantity of X by P_x and Q_x.

(b) Fill in column 4 for values of excess demand and excess supply. What is the value of excess demand (supply) at equilibrium? _____

(c) Indicate and explain the likely direction of change in the price of X if excess demand exists. Do the same for excess supply.

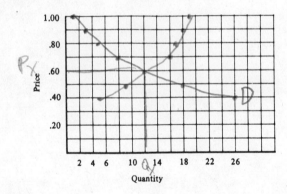

2. Read the description of certain events in the markets for selected commodities.
    Predict the economic impact of these events by drawing the appropriate shifts
    in the diagrams. Also, use + and − to indicate whether there will be an increase
    or decrease in demand (*D*), supply (*S*), equilibrium price (*P*), and equilibrium
    quantity (*Q*). If there is no change, use *O*. If the change cannot be deduced with
    the information provided, use *U* for uncertain

Market	Event		*D*	*S*	*P*	*Q*
(a) Canadian wine	Early frost destroys a large percentage of the grape crop in British Columbia.		___	___	___	___
(b) South African wine	A public campaign is organized to boycott South African−produced goods.		___	___	___	___
(c) Videocassette recorders (VCRs)	Technological advances reduce the costs of producing VCRs.		___	___	___	___
(d) Fast foods	The public shows greater concern over high sodium and cholesterol; also, there is an increase in the minimum wage.		___	___	___	___
(e) Bicycles	There is increasing concern about physical fitness; also, the price of gasoline rises.		___	___	___	___
(f) Prophylactics	Canada Health and Welfare announces that prophylactics (condoms) help prevent the spread of AIDS.		___	___	___	___
(g) Gold	Vast gold deposits are discovered in northern Ontario.		___	___	___	___

*3. The following diagram illustrates a hypothetical market for farm machinery in Canada.

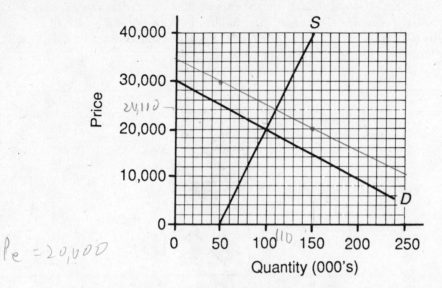

$P_e = 20,000$

The federal government has decided that output in this industry should increase by 50 percent. Since current industry output is 100,000 units, it therefore plans to purchase 50,000 units of farm machinery regardless of price. The government intends to give away these units to third-world countries as part of Canada's foreign aid.

(a) Draw the new demand curve for farm machinery that takes into account government demand. What are the new levels of equilibrium price and quantity?

(b) By how much does industry output increase in percentage terms? Why does this increase fall short of the government's target of 50 percent?

(c) How many units would the government have to purchase in order to satisfy its objective of increasing industry output to 150,000 units? What is the associated quantity demanded by the private sector (i.e., by nongovernment consumers in Canada)?

4. The purpose of this question is to encourage you to obtain the market equilibrium by algebraically solving a system of simultaneous equations. You may refer to Mathematical Note 5 in the text before attempting this exercise.

The demand for gadgets depends on the price of gadgets (P) and average household income (Y) according to the following relationship:

$Q^D = 30 - 10P + 0.001Y$

The supply of gadgets is positively related to own price and negatively dependent on W, the price of some input (e.g., labor) according to

$Q^S = 5 + 5P - 2W$

(a) Assume initially that $Y = \$40,000$ and $W = \$5$. Substitute these values into the equations to obtain the demand and supply curves.

(b) Now use the equilibrium condition $Q^D = Q^S$ to solve the demand and supply curves simultaneously for the equilibrium price.

(c) Finally, substitute the equilibrium price into either the demand or supply curve to obtain the equilibrium quantity.

(d) Graph the demand and supply curves for gadgets in (a), and label them D_0 and S_0, respectively. Confirm that your answers in (b) and (c) are correct.

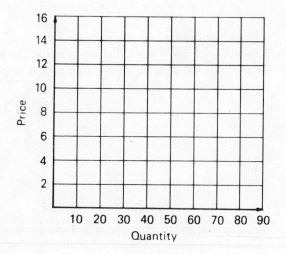

(e) Suppose that average household income increases to $\$55,000$ but W remains constant. What are the new levels of equilibrium price and quantity? Plot the new demand curve, label it D_1, and confirm your answer.

(f) Now assume that the input price W increases to $\$12.50$. Using the demand curve you derived in (e), determine the new levels of equilibrium price and quantity. Plot the new supply curve, label it S_1, and again confirm your answer.

5. The demand and supply of widgets are given by

$$Q^D = 30 - 1.0P$$

and

$$Q^S = 1.0P$$

(a) Plot the demand and supply curves on the graph, and label them D and S, respectively.

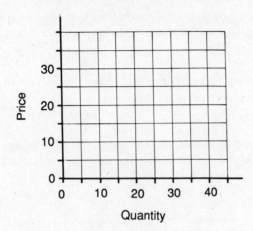

(b) Determine the equilibrium price and the equilibrium quantity. Do this using two methods. First interpret the diagram. Then impose the equilibrium condition that

$$Q^D = Q^S$$

and solve algebraically.

(c) Now suppose that the demand curve changes to

$$Q^D = 30 - 1.5P$$

but the supply curve is unchanged. Plot the new demand curve and label it D'. Before price adjusts from your answer in (b), is there excess demand or excess supply in the market? How much?

(d) Once price responds to market pressures created by the change in demand, what will be the new levels of equilibrium price and quantity?

Answers

Multiple-Choice Questions

1. (a) 2. (b) 3. (a) 4. (d) 5. (c) 6. (b) 7. (a) 8. (c) 9. (b) 10. (c) 11. (a) 12. (c)
13. (c) 14. (c) 15. (c) 16. (d) 17. (d) 18. (c) 19. (b) 20. (d) 21. (c) 22. (d) 23. (c)
24. (d) 25. (c)

Exercises

1. (a)

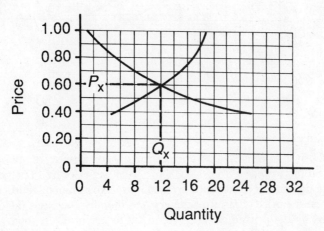

(b) It is zero.

Price	Excess demand (+) or excess supply (−)
$1.00	−18
0.90	−15
0.80	−12
0.70	− 7
0.60	0
0.50	+ 9
0.40	+21

(c) If excess demand exists, price is likely to rise; in the event of excess supply, price is likely to fall.

2.

	D	S	P	Q
(a)	O	−	+	−
(b)	−	O	−	−
(c)	O	+	−	+
(d)	−	−	U	−
(e)	+	O	+	+
(f)	+	O	+	+
(g)	O	+	−	+

*3. (a)

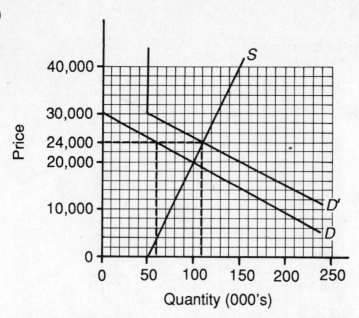

The equilibrium price is $24,000, and the equilibrium quantity is 110,000 units.

(b) Industry output increases from 100,000 to 110,000 units, or by 10 percent. The additional demand of 50,000 units created by the government exerts upward pressure on the price of farm machinery and thereby decreases the quantity demanded by the private or nongovernment sector of the economy. These private-sector consumers reduce their purchases from 100,000 to 60,000 units.

(c) The government would have to purchase all 150,000 units, which would be supplied only when the price reached $40,000. The quantity demanded by the private sector is reduced to zero when the price reaches $30,000.

4. (a) $Q^D = 30 - 10P + 0.001(40,000)$ $Q^S = 5 + 5P - 2(5)$
   $= 70 - 10P$ $= -5 + 5P$

(b) For equilibrium, $Q^D = Q^S$, so that
   $70 - 10P = -5 + 5P$
   which solves for the equilibrium price of $5.

(c) Substituting this value into either Q^D or Q^S, one obtains the equilibrium quantity of 20 units.

(d)

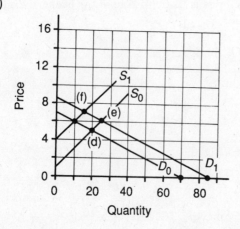

(e) Now $Q^D = 85 - 10P$. Setting $Q^D = Q^S$, or $85 - 10P = -5 + 5P$ yields $P = \$6$ and $Q = 25$.

(f) Now $Q^S = -20 + 5P$ and $Q^D = 85 - 10P$, so that $Q^D = Q^S$ solves for $P = \$7$ and $Q = 15$.

5. (a)

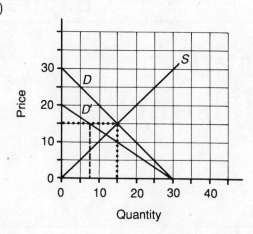

(b) $P = \$15$, $30 - 1.0P = 1.0P$, and $Q = 15$, $Q^S = 1.0(15)$.

(c) When price is $15, $Q^S = 15$ and $Q^D = 7.5$; thus there is excess supply of 7.5 units.

(d) The new equilibrium obtains at the intersection of D' and S where $P = \$12$ (i.e., $30 - 1.5P = 1.0P$), and $Q = 12$.

Chapter 5

Elasticity and
Market Adjustment

Learning Objectives

After studying this chapter, you should be able to:

—understand elasticity of demand and elasticity of supply and how they are measured

—explain the significance of elastic and inelastic demand and supply

—identify what factors determine whether demand or supply is elastic or inelastic

—recognize how the time available to adjust to a price change affects measured elasticity

—understand the relation between elasticity of demand and total expenditure (total revenue)

—distinguish between income-elastic and income-inelastic demand

—explain cross-elasticity of demand and why substitute commodities have positive cross-elasticities but complements have negative ones

—understand the distinction between arc and point elasticity

Multiple-Choice Questions

1. The price elasticity of demand measures
    (a) the responsiveness of quantity demanded of a good to changes in its price
    (b) the variation in prices due to a change in demand
    (c) the size of price changes caused by a shift in demand
    (d) the degree of substitutability across commodities

2. The price elasticity of demand is measured by
    (a) the change in quantity demanded divided by the change in price
    (b) the change in price divided by the change in quantity demanded
    (c) the slope of the demand curve
    (d) the percentage change in quantity demanded divided by the percentage change in price

3. If the price elasticity of demand for a good is 2 and price increases by 2 percent, the quantity demanded
    (a) decreases by 4 percent
    (b) decreases by 1 percent
    (c) decreases by 2 percent
    (d) cannot be determined with this information

4. If the percentage change in price is greater than the percentage change in quantity demanded, demand
    (a) is elastic   (c) is unit-elastic
    (b) is inelastic   (d) shifts outward to the left

Questions 5 through 8 refer to these figures.

5. The demand curve with an elasticity of zero is
    (a) a   (c) c
    (b) b   (d) d

6. The demand curve with an elasticity of unity is
    (a) a   (c) c
    (b) b   (d) d

7. The demand curve with an elasticity of infinity is
    (a) a   (c) c
    (b) b   (d) d

8. The demand curve with an elasticity that is variable is
    (a) a   (c) c
    (b) b   (d) d

9. An increase in the price of a good and a decrease in total expenditure on this good are associated with
    (a) inferior goods   (c) elastic demand
    (b) substitute goods   (d) normal goods

10. The price elasticity of demand for snowmobiles is estimated to be 1.2; thus an increase in price
    (a) always decreases quantity demanded by 12 percent
    (b) always decreases quantity demanded by 1.2 percent
    (c) increases total expenditure
    (d) decreases total expenditure

11. If the demand for some commodity has an elasticity of unity, a decrease in price
    (a) causes a 1 percent decrease in quantity demanded
    (b) induces no change in quantity demanded
    (c) results in no change in total expenditure
    (d) is matched by a unit increase in quantity demanded

12. The price elasticity of demand for a good will be greater
    (a) the less available are suitable substitutes for this good
    (b) the longer the time period considered
    (c) for a group of related goods as opposed to an element of that group
    (d) the greater is income

13. If the price elasticity of supply of a good is 0.1, this means that a
    (a) 0.1 percent increase in price is matched by a 0.1 percent increase in quantity supplied
    (b) 10 percent decrease in price is associated with a 1 percent decrease in quantity supplied
    (c) 10 percent increase in price will increase total revenue by 0.1 percent
    (d) 1 percent decrease in price induces a 10 percent decrease in quantity supplied

Questions 14 and 15 refer to the following schedule. (Consult Table 5-3 in the text for the precise calculation of elasticity. Use average prices and quantities in your calculations.)

Price per unit	Quantity offered for sale
$10	400
8	350
6	300
4	200
2	50

14. The supply curve implied by the schedule is
    (a) elastic for all price ranges
    (b) inelastic for all price ranges
    (c) of zero elasticity for all price ranges
    (d) variable, depending on the initial price chosen

15. As price rises from $6 to $10 per unit, the supply response is
    (a) elastic   (c) of zero elasticity
    (b) of unit elasticity   (d) inelastic

16. Which of the following pairs of commodities is likely to have a cross-elasticity of demand that is positive?
    (a) hockey sticks and pucks   (c) records and compact discs
    (b) bread and cheese   (d) perfume and garden hoses

17. Margarine and butter are predicted to have
    (a) the same income elasticities of demand
    (b) very low price elasticities of demand
    (c) negative cross-elasticities of demand with respect to each other
    (d) positive cross-elasticities of demand with respect to each other

18. Inferior commodities have
    (a) zero income elasticities of demand
    (b) negative cross-elasticities of demand
    (c) negative elasticities of supply
    (d) negative income elasticities of demand

19. Which of the following goods is more likely to have an income elasticity of demand that is less than one?
    (a) hamburger meat   (c) perfume
    (b) microwave ovens   (d) winter vacations

20. Which of the following commodities is more likely to have an elastic demand?
    (a) toothpicks   (c) heart pacemakers
    (b) cigarettes   (d) broccoli

21. A perfectly inelastic demand curve means that
    (a) a percentage decrease in price exactly increases quantity demanded by the same percentage
    (b) an increase in price reduces quantity demanded
    (c) the price elasticity of demand is infinity
    (d) quantity demanded does not change in response to any price change

22. A decrease in income by 10 percent leads to a decrease in quantity demanded by 5 percent; the income elasticity of demand is therefore
    (a) −0.5   (c) 2.0
    (b) 0.5   (d) 50.0

23. A commodity is classified as a normal good if
    (a) an increase in consumer income results in an increase in demand
    (b) it is consumed by a majority of the population
    (c) its price and quantity demanded are negatively related, *ceteris paribus*
    (d) an increase in its price leads to an increase in quantity supplied

24. Suppose that the short-run demand for a good is relatively more inelastic than its long-run demand. A given rightward shift in the supply curve will lead to a
    (a) smaller decrease in price in the long run than in the short run
    (b) smaller increase in quantity demanded in the long run than in the short run
    (c) larger decrease in price in the long run than in the short run
    (d) smaller decrease in both price and quantity demanded in the long run than in the short run

25. If an individual allocates $200 for his monthly expenditure on compact discs and decides to spend no more and no less regardless of price, this individual's demand for compact discs is
    (a) perfectly inelastic   (c) of unit elasticity
    (b) perfectly elastic   (d) less than one but greater than zero

26. A shift in demand would not affect price when supply is
    (a) perfectly inelastic   (c) of unit elasticity
    (b) perfectly elastic   (d) a straight line through the origin

Exercises

1. In each of the following scenarios, categorize the price elasticity of demand as elastic, inelastic, or unit-elastic. Where calculations are required, use average price and quantity. Note that categorization may not always be possible with the information provided.

   (a) The price of personal computers falls from $2,750 to $2,250, and the quantity demanded increases from 40,000 units to 60,000 units.

   (b) Canada Post increases the price of a stamp from 39 cents to 43 cents, but its total revenue remains the same.

   (c) The price of matchbooks doubles from 1 cent to 2 cents, but the quantity purchased does not change.

   (d) An increase in the demand for blue jeans causes the price to increase from $35 to $45 and the amount purchased to increase from 1 million to 1.1 million.

   (e) A sudden decline in the supply of avocados leads to an increase in price by 10 percent and a concomitant reduction in quantity demanded by 20,000 units from the original level of 90,000 units.

   (f) A 5 percent decrease in the price of gasoline results in a decrease in total revenue of 5 percent.

   (g) An increase in consumer income results in a 15 percent decrease in price as well as a 15 percent drop in purchases.

2. Two alternative demand curves are depicted in the upper panels of the following diagrams.

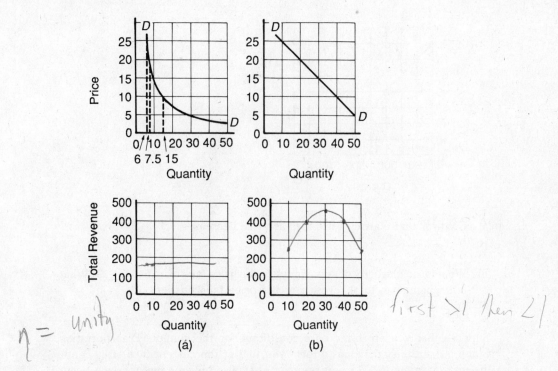

η = unity   (handwritten)

first >1 then <1   (handwritten)

(a)

(b)

(a) Calculate the total revenue associated with each demand curve at the following prices: $25, $20, $15, $10, and $5. Graph the respective total revenue curves on the lower panels.

(b) By inspection of these total revenue curves, what can you say about the price elasticity of demand along each of the demand curves?

3. Fill in the following table:

	Price elasticity	Change in price	Change in total revenue (up, down, none)
(a)	2.0	up	down
(b)	1.0	down	none
(c)	1.0	up	none
(d)	0	down	down
(e)	0.6	up	up

(handwritten right margin: ↓ 1.0 ↓ up?)

4. Calculate the numerical values of price elasticity along the following demand curve. Use the four price-quantity segments indicated by the dots on the demand curve.

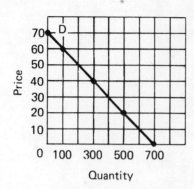

(a) Confirm that elasticity declines as price decreases.

(b) What is the elasticity of demand when the price falls from $40 to $30? What is happening to total revenue as the price falls further?

*5. Suppose that you are hired as a consultant for the Guelph Transportation Commission. Its statisticians inform you that at the current fare of 80 cents, the system serves 25,000 riders per day. They also indicate that for each 1-cent increase (decrease) in the fare, ridership decreases (increases) by 500 passengers.
   (a) What is the arc price elasticity of demand at the current fare? (*Hint:* Consider a change in fare from 1 cent below to 1 cent above the current fare.)

   (b) To consider raising total revenue for the transit system, the Guelph Transportation Commission has hired you to determine by how much it should increase the fare. What do you advise? Why?

   (c) What fare will maximize total revenue for the transit system? What is the associated ridership?

*6. The table provides data on income and demand for goods X and Y.

Period	Income	P_x	Q_{D_x}	P_y	Q_{D_y}
(1)	$10,000	$25	10	$10	42
(2)	10,000	28	9	10	40
(3)	10,000	28	8	15	35
(4)	11,000	28	9	15	36
(5)	11,500	34	7	20	32

(a) Why should no elasticities be calculated between periods 4 and 5?

(b) Calculate the following elasticities, selecting appropriate periods and using arc formulas: price elasticity for X_____; price elasticity for Y_____; income elasticity for X _____; income elasticity for Y_____; cross-elasticity for periods 1 to 2 _____; cross-elasticity for periods 2 to 3 _____.

7. (a) Given the supply curves shown, demonstrate that the elasticity of supply equals 1 along S_1 but falls as price increases along S_2. (Compute arc elasticities between the points indicated.)

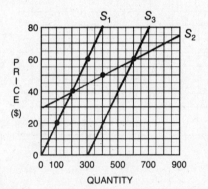

(b) How is the result for S_1 related to the fact that this supply curve passes through the origin?

(c) What does a supply curve such as S_3 imply about the willingness of firms to supply when the price received equals zero?

(d) Why is it that S_3 may be a reliable indicator of supply behavior for some price ranges but, particularly as price approaches zero, this straight-line curve may be misleading?

8. The six diagrams represent different combinations of elasticities of demand and supply at the equilibrium price P_E. Indicate which diagram corresponds to each of the following statements. (η_d refers to elasticity of demand, and η_s refers to elasticity of supply.)

(a) η_d is greater than one and η_s is unity   _____
(b) η_d is unity and η_s is infinity   _____
(c) η_d is unity and η_s is unity   _____
(d) η_d is greater than one and η_s is zero   _____
(e) η_d is zero and η_s is unity   _____
(f) η_d is infinity and η_s is unity   _____

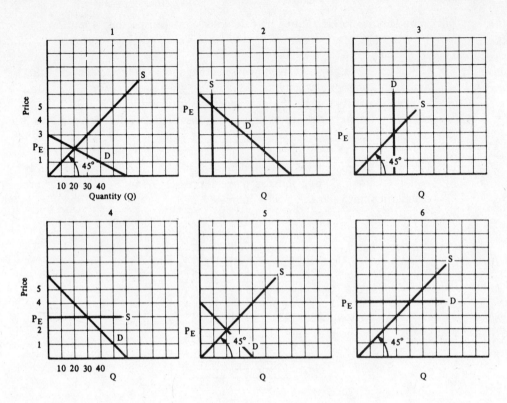

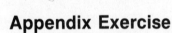

Appendix Exercise

The following exercise is based on the material in the appendix to this chapter. Read the appendix before attempting this exercise.

9. The appendix discusses the distinction between *point* and *arc* elasticity. Point elasticity measures elasticity at a particular point on the demand curve rather than over an interval (arc elasticity). This exercise requires you to calculate point and arc elasticities for the demand curve drawn in the following diagram. (*Note*: The demand curve is linear with a constant slope of $\Delta P/\Delta Q = -1/2$, or equivalently, $\Delta Q/\Delta P = -2$.)

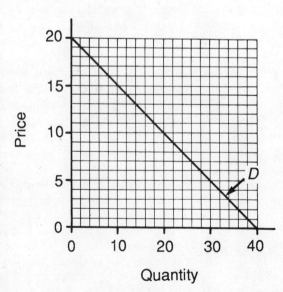

(a) Calculate the *point* elasticity of demand at a price of $10.

(b) Calculate the *arc* elasticity of demand for the following price changes (calculations should be to two decimal places).

Price Change   Arc Elasticity

$18 to $10   ____
$14 to $10   ____
$12 to $10   ____
$11 to $10   ____

(c) What happens to the difference between arc elasticity and point elasticity as the price change gets smaller? When is arc elasticity likely to be a good approximation of point elasticity?

Answers

Multiple-Choice Questions

1. (a)   2. (d)   3. (a)   4. (b)   5. (b)   6. (c)   7. (a)   8. (d)   9. (c)   10. (d)   11. (c)   12. (b)
13. (b)   14. (d)   15. (d)   16. (c)   17. (d)   18. (d)   19. (a)   20. (d)   21. (d)   22. (b)   23. (a)
24. (a)   25. (c)   26. (b)

Exercises

1. (a) $\eta = 2.0 = (20{,}000/500 \times 2{,}500/50{,}000)$; elastic demand
    (b) elasticity of unity
    (c) perfectly inelastic demand
    (d) η cannot be determined because the demand curve has shifted.
    (e) $\eta = 2.5 = (20{,}000/80{,}000) \times 100$ percent $\div 10$ percent; elastic demand
    (f) perfectly inelastic demand
    (g) η cannot be determined because the demand curve shifts.

2. (a)

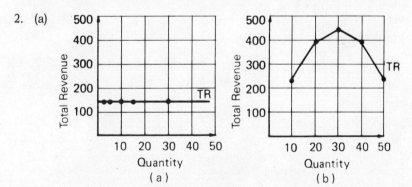

(a)   (b)

(b) Panel (a): Since total revenue does not change along the demand curve, the price elasticity of demand is equal to unity at every point along this demand curve.
Panel (b): Since total revenue increases as price falls from $25 to $20 to $15, demand is elastic over this range. Total revenue is at its maximum value of $450 when price equals $15; this corresponds to unit elasticity. For further price decreases from $15 to $10 to $5, total revenue decreases, and hence demand is inelastic along this portion of the demand curve.

3. (a) down; (b) none; (c) 1; (d) down; (e) up

4. (a) Elasticity measures are:

$$\frac{100/50}{10/65} = 13.0; \quad \frac{200/200}{20/50} = 2.5; \quad \frac{200/400}{20/30} = 0.75; \quad \frac{200/600}{20/10} = 0.167$$

(b) $\dfrac{100/350}{10/35} = 1.0$

Over this interval, total revenue is constant. With further declines in price, total revenue will decline as we move into the inelastic portion of the demand curve.

*5. (a) Calculate arc elasticity from 79 cents to 81 cents so that the average price corresponds to the current fare of 80 cents.

$$\eta = \frac{1,000}{0.02} \times \frac{0.80}{25,000} = 1.60$$

(b) Since demand is elastic, any increase in price only serves to decrease total revenue. Thus you should recommend that the price be decreased in order to increase total revenue.

(c) Try successively lower fares until total revenue begins to decrease. The maximum total revenue is found to be $21,125, which obtains at a fare of 65 cents and a ridership of 32,500 passengers.

*6. (a) Elasticity measures are calculated under the *ceteris paribus* assumption that other factors affecting demand are unchanged. Between periods 4 and 5, not only has income changed, but so have the prices of X and Y.

(b) (1) to (2), price elasticity for $X \quad = -\dfrac{9-10}{28-25} \times \dfrac{(28+25)/2}{(9+10)/2}$

$= 0.93$

(2) to (3), price elasticity for $Y \quad = -\dfrac{35-40}{15-10} \times \dfrac{(15+10)/2}{(35+40)/2}$

$= 0.33$

(3) to (4), income elasticity for $X = \dfrac{9-8}{11,000-10,000} \times \dfrac{(11,000+10,000)/2}{(9+8)/2}$

$= 0.13$

(3) to (4), income elasticity for $Y = \dfrac{36-35}{11,000-10,000} \times \dfrac{(11,000+10,000)/2}{(36+35)/2}$

$$= 0.03$$

(1) to (2), cross-elasticity $= \dfrac{40-42}{28-25} \times \dfrac{(28+25)/2}{(40+42)/2}$

$$= -0.43$$

(2) to (3), cross-elasticity $= \dfrac{8-9}{15-10} \times \dfrac{(15+10)/2}{(8+9)/2}$

$$= -0.29$$

7. (a)   Starting from the origin for S_1, the elasticities are

$$\frac{100/50}{20/10} = \frac{100/150}{20/30} = \frac{100/250}{20/50} = 1$$

For S_2 when price rises from 40 to 50, the elasticity is

$$\frac{200/300}{10/45} = 3$$

but when price rises from 50 to 60, the elasticity is

$$\frac{200/500}{10/55} = 2.2$$

   (b)   Because S_1 passes through the origin, P and Q always change in the same proportion, which gives an elasticity value of 1.
   (c) S_3 implies that firms are willing to supply the good even when the price they receive is zero.
   (d)   Ideally, we would like to know the actual range of price-quantity observations that provided the basis for this estimated supply curve. When we consider potential price changes outside of this range, our projected quantities supplied may be misleading. Especially as price received falls to zero, we might expect that some costs can be avoided if the producer reduces the quantity supplied or that alternative uses for some inputs may become attractive.

8. (a)   1 and 6 (b)   4 (c)   5 (d)   2 (e)   3 (f)   6

9. (a)   Point elasticity $= -1.00 = (-2 \times 10/20)$, or 1.00 neglecting the negative sign.
    (b)

Price Change	Arc Elasticity
$18 to $10	2.33
$14 to $10	1.50
$12 to $10	1.22
$11 to $10	1.11

   (c)   As the change in price gets smaller, the values of arc elasticity and point elasticity converge. Thus arc elasticity serves as a good approximation of point elasticity for small changes in price.

Chapter 6

Supply and Demand in Action: Price Controls and Agriculture

Learning Objectives

After studying this chapter, you should be able to:

—understand that for many commodities, domestic and international markets are linked

—explain how the relationship between a given world price and domestic demand and supply determines whether a country imports or exports a good

—recognize the types of market fluctuations and elasticity conditions that lead to government intervention

—understand and explain the effects of government controls on prices

—predict the consequences of rent controls (a form of price ceiling)

—be aware of the historical problems that have confronted Canadian agriculture as distinguished from other sectors of the economy

—show the importance of elasticity concepts in explaining the "farm problem"

—describe the objectives and economic implications of government intervention in agricultural markets

Multiple-Choice Questions

1. At a disequilibrium price,
   (a) profits of sellers are eliminated
   (b) changes in demand must be matched by changes in supply
   (c) there are always unsold goods
   (d) the quantity bought and sold is determined by the lesser of quantity demanded or quantity supplied

2. Price ceilings below the equilibrium price and price floors above the equilibrium price will both lead to
    (a) production controls
    (b) rationing
    (c) a drop in quality
    (d) a reduction in quantity exchanged

3. A black market may occur whenever
    (a) producers' prices cannot be controlled but retailers' prices can be controlled
    (b) there is an excess supply of a commodity at the controlled price
    (c) consumers are prepared to pay more than the ceiling price and exchange between retailer and consumer cannot be enforced at the ceiling price
    (d) a floor price is maintained at too low a level

4. In a free market economy, the rationing of scarce goods is done primarily by
    (a) the price mechanism
    (b) the government
    (c) business firms
    (d) consumers

5. Allocation by sellers' preferences is feasible when
    (a) there is a disequilibrium price
    (b) quantity supplied is less than quantity demanded
    (c) there is a binding price floor
    (d) there is excess supply

6. A price control that leads to the formation of a black market may nonetheless be consistent with government policy if the government's objective is to
    (a) keep the price low
    (b) encourage output in this industry
    (c) help producers obtain a more reasonable price for their output
    (d) restrict output for conservation reasons

Questions 7 to 10 refer to the following graph.

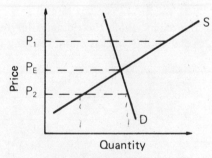

7. A price ceiling equal to P_1
    (a) results in excess supply
    (b) results in excess demand
    (c) results in neither excess demand nor excess supply
    (d) can lead to a black market

8. A price control set at P_2
    (a) leads to a level of consumption that is greater than quantity supplied
    (b) results in a greater quantity produced than is actually sold
    (c) is often justified as a means of helping producers
    (d) results in a quantity demanded that is greater than quantity supplied

9. A price floor equal to P_E would result in excess supply if
    (a) demand decreases due to a change in tastes
    (b) supply falls due to an increase in labor costs
    (c) the demand curve shifts to the right
    (d) either curve shifts in a direction that causes upward pressure on price

10. Suppose that the government decides that P_E is too high and therefore imposes a price ceiling equal to P_2. Further suppose that a black market develops that is able to sell all output at the highest attainable price. The black market price is
    (a) equal to P_E (c) greater than P_2 but less than P_E
    (b) greater than P_E (d) equal to P_2

11. Line-ups (or queues) are one possible allocative mechanism when there is
    (a) excess supply
    (b) a binding price floor
    (c) government intervention in the market that controls price above equilibrium level
    (d) an effective price ceiling

12. Rent controls are likely to produce all but which one of the following effects?
    (a) rental housing shortage in the long run
    (b) development of a black market
    (c) rental housing supply increases in the short run
    (d) resource allocation away from the rental housing industry

13. The rental housing market is characterized by
    (a) long- and short-run supply elasticities of equal magnitude
    (b) inelastic demand
    (c) short-run inelastic supply and long-run elastic supply
    (d) short-run elastic supply and long-run inelastic supply

Questions 14 and 15 refer to the following figure, in which the demand for rental housing increases from D_0 to D_1 (*SR* and *LR* refer to the short run and the long run).

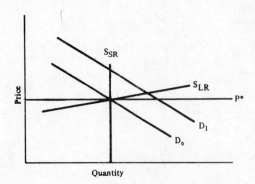

14. If demand increases from D_0 to D_1 and there are no rent controls,
    (a) there will be a greater quantity increase in the short run than in the long run
    (b) the short-run price overshoots its long-run equilibrium level
    (c) the amount of rental housing will not be affected in the long run
    (d) rents will rise more in the long run than in the short run

15. Assume that rents are controlled at price P^*. Which of the following *best* describes the likely events if demand increases from D_0 to D_1?
    (a) There will be no shortage of rental units in either the short run or the long run.
    (b) Landlords will have less opportunity to discriminate among prospective tenants.
    (c) Landlords will tend to spend more on maintenance of apartments.
    (d) The apartment shortage will tend to worsen in the long run.

16. One of the long-term trends in Canadian agriculture is
    (a) an increase in farm incomes relative to urban incomes
    (b) an increasing proportion of the Canadian labor force working in the agricultural sector
    (c) a relatively high income elasticity of demand for agricultural output by Canadians
    (d) growth in agricultural productivity that has been above the economy's average

17. The main reason for agricultural price supports is to
    (a) attempt to stabilize farm incomes
    (b) make certain that there are always extra stocks of goods on hand
    (c) give the government control over agriculture
    (d) reduce competition

18. Unplanned changes in output lead to greater fluctuations in price
    (a) the more inelastic is demand
    (b) the flatter is the demand curve
    (c) when demand is unit-elastic
    (d) the more inelastic is the planned supply curve

19. Most farm receipts vary inversely with output levels
    (a) whenever buyers' preferences change
    (b) because most farm products have inelastic demands
    (c) because lower outputs mean higher total costs
    (d) as long as supply is elastic

20. A low-yield crop would not alter total farm receipts if demand were
    (a) elastic
    (b) perfectly elastic
    (c) perfectly inelastic
    (d) of unit elasticity

21. A price completely stabilized at the equilibrium level by a government buying surpluses and selling its stocks when there are shortages means that
    (a) poor farmers will benefit the most
    (b) government has imposed a perfectly inelastic demand curve on farms
    (c) farmers' revenues will be proportional to output
    (d) all farms will have satisfactory incomes and farm receipts will be stabilized

22. When domestic farmers sell on world markets at a price that is unaffected by domestic output, they in effect face
    (a) perfectly elastic demand
    (b) perfectly inelastic demand
    (c) inelastic demand
    (d) unit-elastic demand

23. If domestic output is sold at a given world price, the incomes of domestic producers
    (a) are independent of domestic output
    (b) vary in the direction opposite that of domestic output
    (c) fluctuate in the same direction as fluctuations in domestic output
    (d) increase during domestic crop failures and decrease during domestic bumper crops

24. When domestic output is sold at a given world price, the most desirable means of stabilizing total farm receipts due to fluctuations in annual output is
    (a) for the government to introduce a price support at the world price
    (b) for farmers to stabilize the annual quantity sold by adding to storage in years with above average crops and depleting stocks in years with below average outputs
    (c) to sell each year's output and save the above average revenue from the good years until it is needed in a bad year and in the meantime earn interest
    (d) for the government to establish quotas at the average annual output

25. Suppose that annual domestic output is constant but is sold at a world price that fluctuates from year to year. Suppose further that the current year's price is unusually low and is expected to rise. The most desirable policy for maximizing average annual receipts is to
    (a) sell all output at an average world price
    (b) store output in order to sell at a higher future price
    (c) sell output and invest the revenue to earn interest
    (d) store or sell the output, depending on storage costs, the future price, and the interest rate

26. When there are fluctuations in output in a market with inelastic demand, quotas equal to the average annual output have the effect of
    (a) stabilizing annual output   (c) increasing average annual receipts
    (b) stabilizing annual receipts   (d) increasing average annual output

27. An unplanned increase in output
    (a) will allow producers to sell more and thereby increase their income
    (b) will always result in lower total receipts for producers
    (c) may increase or decrease total income, depending on whether the output is sold on domestic or world markets
    (d) may increase or decrease total income, depending on whether demand is inelastic or elastic

28. Quotas that lead to higher profits in some industry will in the long run
    (a) result in more producers in the industry
    (b) make it more costly to enter this industry
    (c) result in a larger output for each producer
    (d) help individuals who are just entering this industry

29. The Canadian Wheat Board is a good example of a marketing board that
    (a) acts as a selling agency for Canadian wheat in the international market
    (b) actively engages in supply management schemes in order to influence price
    (c) supports a market price that is well above the equilibrium price
    (d) administers an effective price ceiling

30. If markets are highly regulated and controlled,
    (a) costs can be lowered below those in unregulated markets
    (b) the signals required for the allocation of resources will not operate
    (c) relative prices will still change to reallocate resources
    (d) the distribution of income will be unchanged from that observed in an unregulated market

31. One of the central effects of imposing effective price controls in a market is to
    (a) shift the costs among consumers, producers, and taxpayers
    (b) lower the cost of providing a given quantity of a good
    (c) allow price to serve as the primary allocative mechanism
    (d) increase the actual quantity exchanged

Exercises

1. Given the two market situations described in the graphs, answer the following questions.

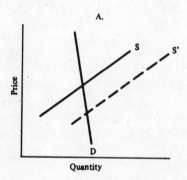 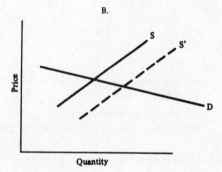

(a) If *S* and *D* denote the original supply and demand curves, indicate, by vertical hatching ‖‖‖, the total receipts (i.e., revenue) in both markets.

(b) If the supply curve shifts to *S'* in both markets, indicate the new receipts by horizontal hatching ≡.

(c) Which market shows the largest loss in total receipts? What is the nature of the demand curve in that market?

(d) Suppose that there was a price floor equal to the original equilibrium price (before the shift in supply) and the government was committed to purchasing unsold stocks at this price. Given the shift in supply in both markets, would there be any difference in the quantity the government would have to purchase in the two cases? Explain.

2. The graph depicts the domestic supply and demand curves, S_c and D_c, respectively, for a commodity in a market for which Canada is assumed to face a fixed world price.

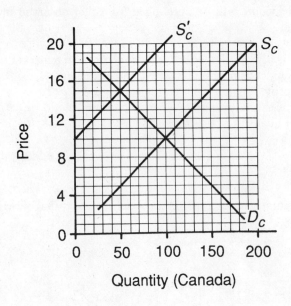

Quantity (Canada)

(a) At a world price of $5, Canadian producers sell _____ units, while Canadian consumers purchase _____ units. Canada therefore (imports, exports) _____ units of this commodity.

(b) If the world price increases to $12 per unit, Canadians would now consume _____ units but produce _____ units. Thus Canada now (imports, exports) _____ units.

(c) Should domestic supply shift to S'_c while the world price remains at $12, domestic production would now be _____ units and domestic consumption _____ units. Canada would therefore be an (importer, exporter) of _____ units.

3. The graph illustrates two situations in the rental housing market: (a) a short-run situation with the supply relatively inelastic, and (b) a long-run situation with a more elastic supply. The subscripts for the demand curves indicate demand for subsequent periods of time within either the short run or the long run.

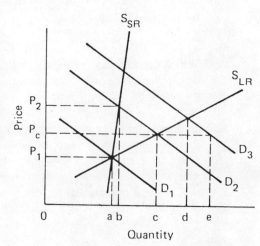

(a) Suppose that demand for rental housing shifts from D_1 to D_2. In the short run, price would be expected to increase from _____ to _____, and the equilibrium quantity from _____ to _____.

(b) (i) Assume that the predicted sharp increase in price alarms the public, so the government controls the price at P_c. Is this rent control an effective price ceiling? Explain.

(ii) In the long run, quantity supplied will increase to _____, and P_c will be the _____ price. The main effects of the price control will be a short-run shift of income from (landlords, tenants) to (landlords, tenants). The long-run allocation of resources will have been (efficient, inefficient), given P_c, because of short-run (overshooting, undershooting) of price.

(c) If P_c is maintained in the face of a further shift of the demand curve to D_3, P_c becomes a price (floor, ceiling), and the excess quantity demanded in the long run will be _____.

4. A small town in Saskatchewan has the following monthly demand and supply schedules for kumquats:

Price	Quantity demanded	Quantity supplied
$0.40	3,800	800
0.50	3,600	1,200
0.60	3,400	1,600
0.70	3,200	2,000
0.80	3,000	2,400
0.90	2,800	2,800
1.00	2,600	3,200
1.10	2,400	3,600
1.20	2,200	4,000
1.30	2,000	4,400
1.40	1,800	4,800

62

Chapter 6

(a) Plot the demand and supply curves for kumquats and label them D_1 and S_1, respectively.

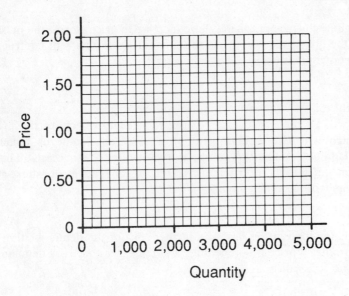

(b) What are the equilibrium price and quantity in this market?

The local government plans to assist kumquat producers by increasing the price of kumquats. It is studying the following two alternative schemes as a means of increasing price.

(c) In this first scheme, the government offers to purchase, at a price of $1.10 each, any amount of kumquats that are produced but not sold to consumers (it then intends simply to destroy its purchases). Producers therefore face a new demand that is the sum of consumer and government demand.
   (i) Draw this new demand curve, label it D_2, and determine the new equilibrium price and quantity in this market.
   (ii) How many kumquats are consumers purchasing, and how many is the government destroying?

   (iii) How much does this scheme cost the government? Shade in the area on your graph that represents the cost to the government. (*Note:* Ignore all administrative and disposal costs.)

(d) As an alternative scheme, suppose that the government decides to purchase, at a price of $1.10, all of the kumquats produced. It then puts all of its purchases on the market for resale to consumers at whatever price consumers are willing to pay for that quantity.

    (i)   Draw the demand curve facing producers under this scheme, label it D_3, and determine the equilibrium price and quantity.

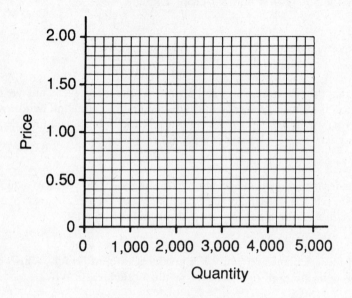

    (ii) What price will the government receive when it resells all of its purchases?

    (iii) What is the cost to the government of this scheme? Shade in with hatched lines the appropriate area on your graph to illustrate this cost (again, ignore administrative costs).

(e) What do you think are the relative merits of these two alternative policies?

5. The following diagram illustrates the demand and supply curves for an agricultural product whose output varies due to erratic weather conditions.

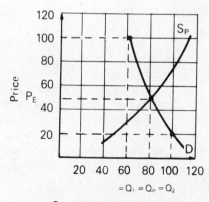

All output is sold in a domestic market where the demand curve is denoted D in the graph. S_P represents planned supply, so the expected equilibrium price is P_E, or \$50, and the planned quantity supplied is Q_P, or 80 million bushels. Suppose that actual output is either Q_1 (a crop failure) or Q_2 (a bumper crop) and that each is equally likely. (For convenience, you should assume that good and bad crop years always occur consecutively.)

(a) Are producers in this market better off as a group in the year with a crop failure or the one with a bumper crop? Explain.

(b) What is average annual farm income in this market?

(c) Suppose that producers organize and operate a scheme whereby any year's output exceeding average annual output is added to storage and wihdrawn in those years with below average outputs. Thus Q_P is offered for sale in each and every year. What are annual farm receipts?

(d) Now consider government intervention in this market in the form of a quota equal to Q_P. That is to say, any output in excess of Q_P must be destroyed. What would average annual receipts of producers be now?

(e) Which of these schemes do you think producers would prefer? Which do you think consumers of this product would prefer least? Why?

*6. This question addresses the problem of stabilizing domestic annual farm receipts in the presence of a fluctuating output that is sold entirely in export markets at some given world price.

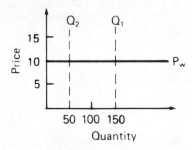

As illustrated in the graph, the world price is \$10 and is expected to remain constant. Annual output, however, varies between 150 and 50 units, with each being equally likely, so that average output is 100 units. Assume that the cost of storing a unit of output is \$5 and that any excess revenue can be deposited in a savings account that pays a rate of return equal to 10 percent.

Suppose that current output is 150 units and it is certain that next period's output will be 50 units. Should the producers' association stabilize annual receipts by ensuring that exactly 100 units are offered for sale each year, or should it sell all 150 units now?

*7. As in Exercise 6, all output is again sold entirely in export markets at the current world price. However, domestic output is constant from year to year, and it is the world price that fluctuates. As the following graph illustrates, the constant level of annual output is 100 units. However, the world price is currently low at $5 per unit but is expected to be $15 next period.

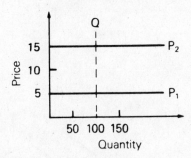

Suppose that the producers' association is committed to paying producers $1,000 each year even if it has to borrow in the first year to meet this obligation. Assume that storage costs are $5 per unit and that the association can borrow money at a 10 percent interest rate. Should the association attempt to stabilize annual receipts at $1,000 by putting all 100 units into storage in order to sell next year when price is high, or should it sell everything now and thereby avoid storage and large borrowing costs?

The following itemized statement of receipts and payments under each scheme will help you do this exercise.

	Receipts	Payments
If first year's output is stored		
Proceeds from loan	$	$
Payment to producers in year 1		
Borrowing costs		
Storage costs		
Crop revenue in year 2		
Loan repayment		
Payment to producers in year 2		
Total	$	$
If first year's output is sold		
Crop revenue in year 1	$	$
Proceeds from loan		
Payment to producers in year 1		
Borrowing costs		
Crop revenue in year 2		
Loan repayment		
Payment to producers in year 2		
Total	$	$

Answers

Multiple-Choice Questions

1. (d) 2. (d) 3. (c) 4. (a) 5. (b) 6. (d) 7. (c) 8. (d) 9. (a) 10. (b) 11. (d) 12. (c)
13. (c) 14. (b) 15. (d) 16. (d) 17. (a) 18. (a) 19. (b) 20. (d) 21. (c) 22. (a) 23. (c)
24. (c) 25. (d) 26. (c) 27. (d) 28. (b) 29. (a) 30. (b) 31. (a)

Exercises

1. (a) and (b)

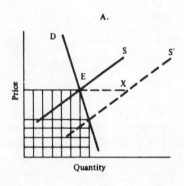 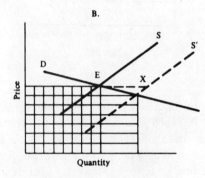

(c) Market A. The demand is inelastic compared to market B.

(d) No. The shift in supply is identical, and at a price equal to original equilibrium price, the quantity of unsold goods (EX in both markets) is the same.

2. (a) 50; 150; imports; 100
   (b) 80; 120; exports; 40
   (c) 20; 80; importer; 60

3. (a) $0P_1$ to $0P_2$; $0a$ to $0b$

   (b) (i) Yes, in the short run, since it is below the equilibrium price. [It would not be effective in the long run since it equals the equilibrium price as the quantity supplied expands (along S_{LR}) to meet the demand, $0c$, on D_2.]

       (ii) $0c$; equilibrium; landlords to tenants; efficient; overshooting

   (c) ceiling; ce

4. (a)

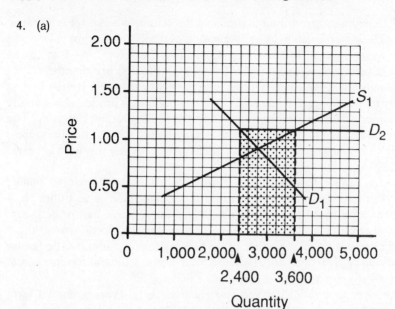

(b) At the intersection of D_1 and S_1 in the graph, the equilibrium price is 90 cents and the equilibrium quantity is 2,800 units per month.

(c) (i)   As shown in the graph, the new demand curve is perfectly elastic at a price of $1.10. For prices greater than $1.10, the demand curve is D_1. The equilibrium now obtains at the intersection of D_2 and S_1, where $P = \$1.10$ and $Q = 3,600$ per month.

(ii) At a price of $1.10, quantity demanded by consumers is 2,400, so the remaining 1,200 units are purchased and destroyed by the government.

(iii) The government is purchasing 1,200 units at $1.10 each, so total cost (to taxpayers) is $1,320 per month.

(d) (i)   In effect, producers face a perfectly elastic demand at a price of $1.10. As shown in the following graph, the new equilibrium occurs at the intersection of D_3 and S_1 with the same equilibrium price of $1.10 and equilibrium quantity of 3,600 per month.

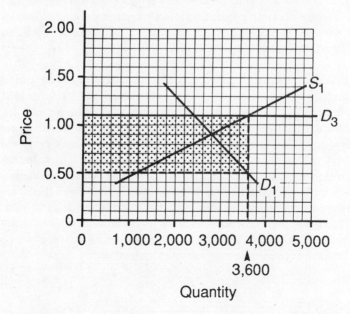

(ii) Consumers are willing to purchase 3,600 units when price is 50 cents.

(iii) The government pays $1.10 for each of its 3,600 units purchased and receives only 50 cents for each resale. Therefore, the cost to the government is 3,600 × ($1.10 −$0.50) = $2,160 per month.

(e) Although the second scheme costs the government more, it may be less costly for society as a whole in that everything that is produced is actually consumed, thereby yielding some benefits for consumers as well. The destroyed output in the first scheme is a net cost to society, since resources (which have an alternative use) are used up without any resulting benefits.

5. (a) In a crop failure year, output is 60 million bushels and price per bushel is $100; therefore, total receipts are $100 × 60 million = $6 billion. In a bumper crop year, total harvest is 100 million bushels, and price is $20, so total revenue is $2 billion. Therefore, in terms of total income, these producers as a group are better off in years with crop failures. The reason for the negative relationship between total output and total receipts is that demand for this product is inelastic.

(b) Since large and small harvests are equally likely, average annual farm receipts for this crop are $4 billion: ($6 billion + $2 billion)/2.

(c) When 100 million bushels are actually produced, 20 million are stored and only 80 million are offered for sale. In a year with a production level of only 60 million bushels, 80 million bushels are again put on the market for sale by withdrawing 20 million from stocks. Therefore, 80 million bushels are sold each year, and the equilibrium price each year is $50. Thus total receipts each year are $4 billion: $50 × 80 million.

(d) When output is 60 million bushels, it is sold for $6 billion. When output is 100 million, only the quota of 80 million bushels is sold, and the remaining 20 million bushels are destroyed. The 80 million bushels sell at a price of $50 so that total revenue is $4 billion. Average annual receipts are therefore $5 billion: ($6 billion + $4 billion)/2.

(e) Average annual revenue of producers is greatest with the quota. Therefore, in terms of income, producers as a group are better off with the quota. Since total revenue of producers is equal to total expenditure by consumers, consumers spend the most for this product under the quota scheme. Further, average annual consumption is lowest under the quota than under any other scheme: 70 million bushels as opposed to 80 million. Therefore, consumers would prefer the quota scheme the least.

*6. With a constant world price, it is always best to stabilize producers' annual income by selling the entire crop. Revenue from the 150 units is $1,500. Of this, $1,000 must be paid to producers, leaving $500 to invest at a 10 percent rate of return, which yields another $50 revenue. Next period, when output is below average, the $500 savings is added to the second year's crop revenue of $500 ($10 × 50) to keep total farm receipts at $1,000. Thus the association has stabilized incomes at the annual average of $1,000 and has a surplus revenue of $50 for further distribution. Had the association stored the 50 units exceeding average annual output in the first year, it would have incurred a storage cost of $250 ($5 × 50) and would not have the additional interest revenue from the investment. It would therefore be $250 short in its attempt to stabilize income at $1,000.

*7. Regardless of whether the association stores or sells the first year's output, it must under these circumstances borrow in order to meet its obligation of paying producers $1,000 in the first year. If it stores the crop, it has no crop revenue and must therefore borrow all $1,000. If it sells at the current price, it receives revenue of $500, implying that an additional $500 must be borrowed. The following is an itemized account of the receipts and payments associated with each scheme:

	Receipts	Payments
If first year's output is stored		
Proceeds from loan	$1,000	$
Payment to producers in year 1		1,000
Borrowing costs: (0.10 × $1,000)		100
Storage costs: ($5 × 100)		500
Crop revenue in year 2: ($15 × 200)	3,000	
Loan repayment		1,000
Payment to producers in year 2		1,000
Total	$4,000	$3,600
If first year's output is sold		
Crop revenue in year 1: ($5 × 100)	$ 500	$
Proceeds from loan	500	
Payment to producers in year 1		1,000
Borrowing costs: (0.10 × $500)		50
Crop revenue in year 2: ($15 × 100)	1,500	
Loan repayment		500
Payment to producers in year 2		1,000
Total	$2,500	$2,550

Therefore, storing year 1's output in order to sell next period when the price is high yields a net revenue (i.e., receipts less payments) of $400. Conversely, selling immediately so as to avoid storage costs yields a net revenue of −$50. Thus, in this particular numerical example, the association maximizes net revenues for producers by storing output. Unlike Exercise 6, there is no single best strategy when world price fluctuates. Rather, the decision whether to store or sell depends on prices in each period, storage costs, and the interest rate.

PART THREE

Consumption, Production, and Cost

Household Consumption Behavior

Learning Objectives

After studying this chapter, you should be able to:

—use price and income data to construct a budget line

—show how changes in relative prices and income affect the budget line

—illustrate how a demand curve for a commodity can be derived

—distinguish among normal goods, inferior goods, and Giffen goods

—explain what gives rise to consumers' surplus and the importance of the concept

Multiple-Choice Questions

1. A budget line
   (a) describes the demand for two goods
   (b) describes the quantity demanded at each and every price
   (c) ranks bundles of goods according to a household's preferences
   (d) separates bundles of goods that a household can afford to purchase at current income and prices from those that it cannot afford

2. An increase in income
   (a) makes the budget line steeper
   (b) shifts the budget line uniformly outward
   (c) does not affect relative prices and therefore does not affect the budget line
   (d) rotates the budget line outward on the axis with the more expensive good

3. An increase in income by 10 percent and an increase in all prices by 10 percent will
   (a) not affect the budget line
   (b) shift the budget line uniformly outward by 20 percent
   (c) shift the budget line uniformly inward by 20 percent
   (d) shift the budget line uniformly outward by 1 percent

4. An increase in the absolute price of one good increases
   (a) money income
   (b) real income
   (c) purchasing power
   (d) the opportunity cost of buying that good

5. A change in relative prices *always* implies
   (a) a change in real income
   (b) a change in purchasing power
   (c) a change in the opportunity cost of buying goods
   (d) that only one absolute price has changed

6. If the budget line shifts outward in parallel fashion,
   (a) prices increase by the same amount
   (b) relative prices have increased
   (c) prices and income increase in the same proportion
   (d) relative prices remain constant

Questions 7 to 11 refer to the following graphs, which depict an initial budget line labeled *ab* and a new budget line *a'b'*, which is caused by some change in income, prices, or both.

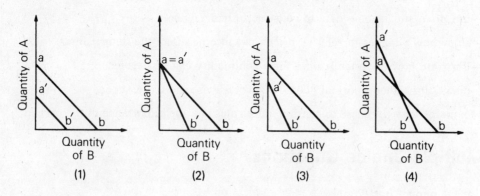

7. Which graph depicts the shift in a budget line that results from a decrease in income?
   (a) 1   (c) 3
   (b) 2   (d) 4

8. Which shift in the budget line could be explained by an increase in the price of good *B*?
   (a) 1   (c) 3
   (b) 2   (d) 4

9. Which shift (or shifts) could be explained by increases in the prices of both goods?
   (a) 1   (c) 1 and 3   •
   (b) 3   (d) 3 and 4

10. Which shift (or shifts) are consistent with a decrease in the price of good *A* and an increase in the price of good *B*?
    (a) 2   (c) 4
    (b) 3   (d) 3 and 4

11. Which graphs describe the shift in a budget line that results from decreases in both the price of good A and income?
    (a) 2
    (b) 2 and 4
    (c) 2 and 3
    (d) 2, 3, and 4

12. In response to a price change, the substitution effect is isolated from the income effect when
    (a) relative prices are held constant
    (b) real income is held constant
    (c) money income is held constant
    (d) the quantities demanded are held constant

Questions 13 to 16 refer to the following graph, which depicts several budget lines for food and clothing. The individual is initially on budget line *ab* and consuming at point *e*. The price of food then increases.

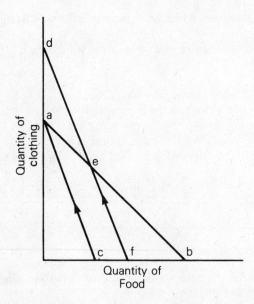

13. After the price increase, the individual selects a new consumption bundle somewhere on the line segment
    (a) *eb*
    (b) *ac*
    (c) *de*
    (d) *ef*

14. The substitution effect of this price increase induces the individual to choose a consumption bundle somewhere on line segment
    (a) *de*
    (b) *ac*
    (c) *ae*
    (d) *ef*

15. The income effect of this price increase is represented by a change in the consumption bundle somewhere on *de* to a point on
    (a) *ac*
    (b) *eb*
    (c) *ae*
    (d) *ef*

16. If an individual chooses bundle *e* when confronted with budget line *ab* and
    selects a bundle between *e* and *f* when confronted with budget line *df*, then
    (a) food is a normal good
    (b) clothing is an inferior good
    (c) real income has decreased
    (d) this individual would not be behaving in a consistent manner

17. The price change and its associated substitution effect on quantity purchased are
    (a) in the same direction for inferior goods
    (b) in the same direction for Giffen goods
    (c) always in opposite directions
    (d) in opposite directions for only downward-sloping demand curves

18. A positively sloped demand curve (i.e., a Giffen good)
    (a) is typical of all inferior goods
    (b) describes all goods for which the income and substitution effects are in
        opposite directions
    (c) implies an inferior good for which the income effect outweighs the
        substitution effect
    (d) implies a good for which the price change and the substitution effect are
        in the same direction

19. Demand curves for normal goods slope downward because
    (a) the substitution effect of a price change is greater than the income effect
    (b) substitution and income effects work in the same direction
    (c) the income effect is greater than the substitution effect
    (d) none of the above; demand curves for normal goods slope upward

20. The slope of the budget line with product *Y* on the vertical axis and product
    X on the horizontal axis is
    (a) $-(P_y/P_x)$ (c) $-(X/Y)$
    (b) -1 (d) $-(P_x/P_y)$

21. Consumers' surplus derived from the consumption of a commodity
    (a) is the difference between the total value placed on a certain amount of
        consumption and the total payment made for it
    (b) will always be less than the total amount paid for the commodity
    (c) will always be more than the total amount paid for the commodity
    (d) equals the total value of that commodity to consumers

22. If an individual is prepared to pay $3 for the first unit of a commodity, $2 for
    the second, and $1 for the third unit, and the market price is $1,
    (a) consumers' surplus is $3
    (b) the individual will purchase three units of the commodity
    (c) the individual's demand curve for this commodity is downward-sloping
    (d) all of the above

23. If I am willing to pay $50 for a particular pair of blue jeans, but when I arrive
    at the store they are on sale for $30,
    (a) I should buy all the blue jeans in the store
    (b) the value I place on the consumption of these blue jeans is lowered by $20
    (c) I receive consumer surplus of $20 if I purchase the pair of blue jeans
    (d) my valuation of consuming these blue jeans is now $70

24. The total value Mr. Wimpy places on his consumption of hamburgers equals
    (a) the amount he pays for them
    (b) price times marginal value
    (c) marginal value multiplied by quantity demanded
    (d) his total expenditure on hamburgers plus his consumers' surplus

25. Consumers' surplus can be measured by the area between the demand curve and the
    (a) quantity axis
    (b) supply curve
    (c) horizontal line at the market price
    (d) vertical line at the quantity demanded

Appendix Questions

The following questions are based on material in the two appendixes to this chapter. Read them before answering these questions.

Appendix A

26. An indifference curve indicates
    (a) constant quantities of one good with varying quantities of another
    (b) the prices and quantities of two goods that can be purchased for a given sum of money
    (c) all combinations of two goods that will give the same level of satisfaction to the household
    (d) combinations of goods whose marginal utilities are always equal

27. The relative prices of two goods can be shown by
    (a) the slope of the budget line
    (b) the slope of an indifference curve
    (c) the marginal rate of substitution
    (d) the price-consumption line

28. At the point where the budget line is tangent to an indifference curve,
    (a) equal amounts of goods give equal satisfaction
    (b) the ratio of prices of the goods must equal the marginal rate of substitution
    (c) the prices of the goods are equal
    (d) a household cannot be maximizing its satisfaction

29. A household's demand curve can be derived from
    (a) a single indifference curve
    (b) a single budget line
    (c) a price-consumption line
    (d) an income-consumption line

Appendix B

30. The hypothesis of diminishing marginal utility states that
    (a) the less of a commodity one is consuming, the less the additional utility obtained by an increase in its consumption
    (b) the more of a commodity one is consuming, the more the additional utility obtained by an increase in its consumption
    (c) the more of a commodity one is consuming, the less the additional utility obtained by an increase in its consumption
    (d) marginal utility cannot be measured, but total utility can

31. According to utility theory, a consumer will maximize total satisfaction when A and B are consumed in quantities such that MU_A/MU_B
    (a) equals the ratio of the price of A to the price of B
    (b) equals the ratio of total utility of A to that of B
    (c) equals the ratio of the price of B to the price of A
    (d) always equals unity

32. If a household's marginal utility decreases as more of a commodity is consumed, its total utility
    (a) is increasing
    (b) is also decreasing
    (c) is constant
    (d) may be increasing, decreasing, or constant

Exercises

1. A certain household has allocated a monthly budget of $500 for food. Assume for convenience that there are only two types of food consumed by this household: meat and vegetables. The price of meat consumed by this household is $20 per kilogram, and the price of the vegetables is $10 per kilogram.
   (a) Plot the household's monthly budget line for meat and vegetables.

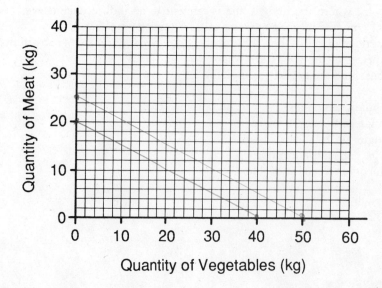

(b) If this household consumes 10 kilograms of meat a month, how many vegetables could it afford to purchase?

(c) (i)   What is the slope of the budget line?

(ii)   What is the relative price of vegetables to meat?

(iii) What is the opportunity cost of vegetables in terms of meat?

(d) Could this household afford to purchase:
(i)   14 kilograms of meat and 18 kilograms of vegetables?

(ii)   18 kilograms of meat and 14 kilograms of vegetables?

(iii) 18 kilograms of each?

(e) Suppose that the household decreases its expenditure on food to $400 per month. Plot the new budget line (assuming that the prices of meat and vegetables have not changed).

2. This exercise involves the same household and budget allocation problem as Exercise 1. However, although monthly expenditure on food is still $500, the price of meat falls to $12.50 per kilogram and the price of vegetables rises to $25 per kilogram.
(a) Plot the new budget line.

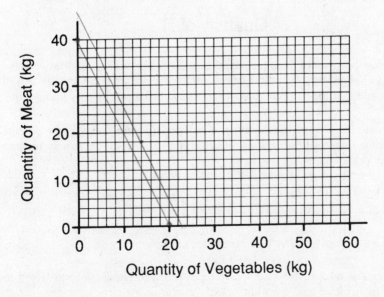

(b) Draw the budget line for which this household would just be able to afford 18 kilograms of meat and 14 kilograms of vegetables at the new prices and a money income of $500.

(c) Suppose that this bundle was in fact the one chosen by the household at the initial prices in Exercise 1. What change in income is required to restore the household's purchasing power (i.e., to make this bundle affordable)?

3. The text discusses two types of changes in income: a change in money income and a change in real income. This exercise illustrates the difference between these two concepts.
    A household has a weekly money income of $300 to spend on two goods, A and B. The price of good A is $10 a unit, and the price of good B is $20.
    (a) Plot the budget line.

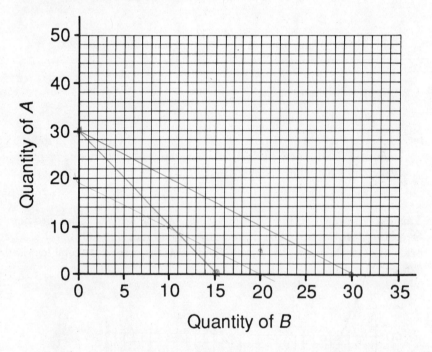

(b) Assume that money income remains at $300 per week but that relative prices change. Specifically, assume that the price of good B falls to $10 a unit and that the price of good A remains at $10. Plot the new budget line.

(c) Calculate the change in real income induced by the relative price change when the household's original consumption bundle, at the money income and prices in (a), is
    (i)   10 units of good A and 10 units of good B

    (ii)   20 units of good A and 5 units of good B

    (iii) 30 units of good A and none of good B

(*Hint:* Draw the budget line that would just permit the household to afford to purchase its original consumption bundle at the new prices.)

4. The following table provides budget data for an individual under three different combinations of income and prices. The table also gives quantities demanded of goods A and B by this individual for each budget constraint.

Budget	Money income	Price of good A	Price of good B	Quantity demanded of good A	Quantity demanded of good B
1	$100	$ 5	$10	10	5
2	150	10	10	8	7
3	100	10	10	4	6

(a) Plot each budget line, and identify the corresponding consumption bundle as E_1, E_2, and E_3 for budgets 1, 2, and 3, respectively.

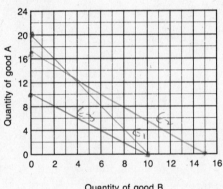

(b) Suppose that the individual initially faces budget 1, and then the price of good A increases. Assuming that the demand curve is linear, use the data in the table to plot the demand curve.

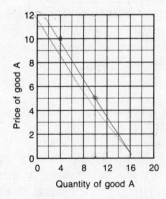

(c) What is the new ratio of relative prices?

(d) What is the substitution effect from the increase in the price of good *A*?

(e) What is the income effect induced by the price change?

(f) Are goods *A* and *B* normal or inferior?

5. The following graph depicts a household's demand for widgets, which have a current price of $2 per unit.

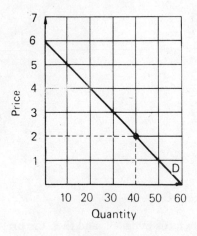

The total value this household places on its consumption of widgets is _____. However, the household's total expenditure on widgets is _____, so it receives consumers' surplus of _____. If the market price drops to $1, this household's total valuation of widgets would (increase, decrease) by _____ and its consumers' surplus would (increase, decrease) by _____. The value this household places on consumption of the twentieth widget is _____, and it is willing to pay _____ for 20 widgets.

*6. A certain chief executive officer with a large corporation instructs her personal secretary (a recent graduate of a prestigious M.B.A. program) to purchase tickets to the Stanley Cup playoffs. Specifically, she tells him, "If the tickets are $150 each, buy one ticket for me; at $100 each, buy two; and, if the price is $50 each, buy me three." The young secretary (eager to make an impression) responds, "Madame, your instructions appear to be inconsistent. You are saying that you are *willing to pay* more in total for two tickets than for three!" Is the secretary correct? Explain.
(*Hint:* Sketch the CEO's demand curve for tickets.)

Appendix Exercises

The following exercises are based on material in the two appendixes to this chapter. Read them before attempting these exercises.

Appendix A

7. (a) The following table shows information on the units of food and clothing that are on indifference curves I, II, and III.

Units of food			Units of clothing		
I	II	III	I	II	III
45	50	55	0	10	20
30	35	40	5	15	25
20	25	30	10	20	30
15	20	25	15	25	35
10	15	20	25	35	45

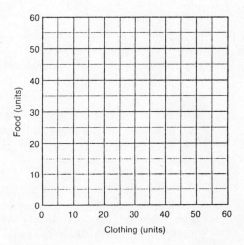

(i) Graph indifference curves I, II, and III.
(ii) Draw a budget line on the graph that represents a budget constraint of $350 and food and clothing prices of $10 and $15, respectively.
(iii) Given (i) and (ii), what combination of food and clothing will maximize consumer satisfaction? Explain.

(b) Extend the analysis and use the same graph to show the derivation of a demand curve for clothing by proceeding as follows (assume that "clothing" stands for "everything consumed except food").
   (i) Change the price of clothing so that a budget line with the same food intercept (35) is tangent to each of the indifference curves I, II, and III. Extend the X axis as necessary.

   The X intercepts for budget lines tangent to indifference curves I, II, and III are approximately _____ , _____ , and _____ , respectively.

   The prices of clothing represented by the budget lines are approximately _____ , _____ , and _____ , respectively.
   (ii) Draw the price-consumption line on the graph.
   (iii) Describe how the information on the price-consumption line can be used to derive a demand curve for clothing.

8. On the following graph, a household moves from one equilibrium E_0 to a new equilibrium E_1 after a decline in the price of commodity X.

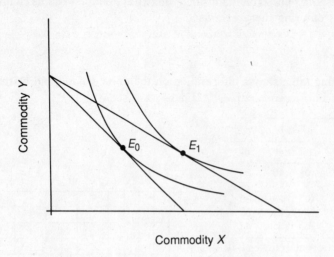

(a) Illustrate on the graph the size of the substitution effect.
(b) Illustrate on the graph the size of the income effect.
(c) Is commodity X an inferior good? Explain.

Appendix B

9. The table relates total utility and the number of milkshakes consumed per weekend.

Number of milkshakes per weekend	Total utility
0	0
1	50
2	90
3	120
4	130
5	130
6	120

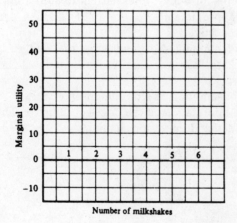

(a) On the grid, plot the marginal utility schedule.

(b) At what point does the consumer experience disutility (i.e., after how many milkshakes per weekend)?

10. Suppose that a consumer spends recreation time and income on two leisure activities: tennis and fishing. The consumer has the basic equipment to pursue both activities. The costs associated with these activities are court fees for tennis and the expense of boat rental for fishing.

The marginal utility schedules for hours spent on these activities are shown in the table.

Hours per week	Marginal utility schedule	
	Fishing	Tennis
1	20	20
2	18	19
3	16	18
4	14	17
5	12	16
6	10	15
7	8	14
8	6	13

(a) If the cost per hour of each activity is $1 and the consumer spends five hours per week on recreation activity, how many hours would be spent on each activity in order to maximize total utility?

(b) Suppose that the cost of tennis increased 19 percent. What change in the "mix" of tennis and fishing would be required to maximize utility? Explain, using marginal utility to price ratios, why this is the case. (Consider the initial cost of both activities in (a) to be $1 per hour.)

Answers

Multiple-Choice Questions

1. (d) 2. (b) 3. (a) 4. (d) 5. (c) 6. (d) 7. (a) 8. (b) 9. (c) 10. (c) 11. (d) 12. (b) 13. (b)
14. (a) 15. (a) 16. (d) 17. (c) 18. (c) 19. (b) 20. (d) 21. (a) 22. (d) 23. (c) 24. (d)
25. (c) 26. (c) 27. (a) 28. (b) 29. (c) 30. (c) 31. (a) 32. (a)

Exercises

1. (a) The budget line is labeled *ab* on the following graph.

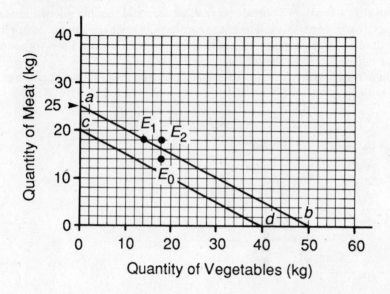

(b) By inspection of budget line *ab*, consumption of 10 kilograms of meat permits consumption of 30 kilograms of vegetables.

(c) (i) Slope is measured by rise over run. The rise of the budget line is 25 (ignoring the negative sign), and the run is 50; therefore, the slope is rise/run = 25/50 = 1/2.

(ii) The absolute price of vegetables is $10 per kilogram, while that of meat is $20; thus the relative price of vegetables to meat is $10/$20 = 1/2.

(iii) It takes $10 to purchase another kilogram of vegetables; to do so, $10 less must be spent on meat. Thus the opportunity cost of vegetables in terms of meat is 1/2 (i.e., for every additional kilogram of vegetables, 1/2 kilogram of meat must be forfeited).

(d) (i) Combination E_0 represents 14 kilograms of meat and 18 kilograms of vegetables. It lies inside budget line *ab* and is therefore affordable with income left over.

(ii) Bundle E_1 contains 18 kilograms of meat and 14 kilograms of vegetables; it lies on the budget line and is therefore affordable with all income spent.

(iii) E_2 contains 18 kilograms of each good; it lies outside the budget line and is therefore not affordable.

(e) The new budget line is labeled *cd* on the graph.

2. (a) The resulting budget line is labeled *ef* on the following graph.

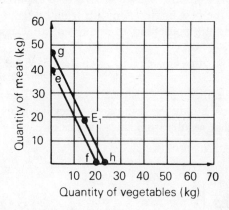

(b) This budget line would go through bundle E_1 with the same slope as budget line *ef*. It is labeled *gh* on the graph.

(c) To purchase 18 kilograms of meat at $12.50 each and 14 kilograms of vegetables at $25 each would cost $575. Therefore, this household requires another $75 to be able to purchase its initial commodity basket ($575 − $500 = $75).

3. (a) budget line *ab*

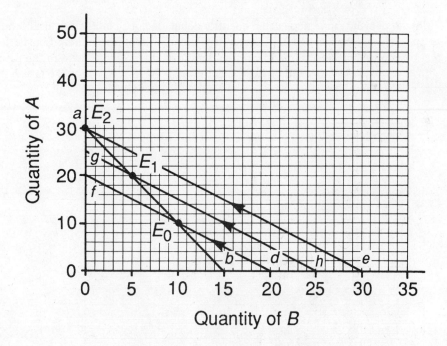

(b) budget line *ae*

(c) (i) $100. Budget line *fd* just enables the household to afford to purchase
           its original bundle E_0 at the new prices. The shift from budget *fd* to
           ae is equivalent to giving the household an additional $100 money
           income.

     (ii) $50. Budget line *gh* allows the household to repurchase E_1 at the
           new prices.

     (iii) There is no change in real income in this case. The budget line that
           can repurchase the original bundle E_2 at the new prices is simply *ae*,
           the actual budget line that results from the new prices.

4. (a)

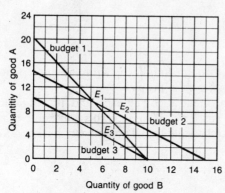

(b) A demand curve depicts the quantity demanded of a commodity at different
     prices, other things held constant. Thus points on the demand curve for
     good A can be obtained from the data in budgets 1 and 3 where the price
     of good A varies but where income and the price of good B are held
     constant. The demand curve is shown in the following graph.

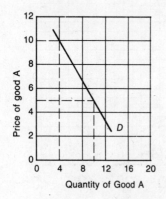

(c) $1 = \$10/\$10$

(d) The substitution effect refers to the impact of a change in relative prices
     on quantity demanded. Budgets 1 and 2 have the same *real* income so that
     each passes through the original consumption bundle E_1. Thus the change
     in consumption between these two budgets is due strictly to the change
     in relative prices. The substitution effect of this relative price change on
     the demand for good A is -2 since consumption falls from 10 to 8.

(e)   The income effect refers to the change in demand resulting from a change in income, holding new relative prices constant. This corresponds to a shift from budget 2 to budget 3. The income effect on the demand for good A is -4 since consumption falls from 8 to 4. The total reduction in quantity demanded of good A is 6.

(f)   In the shift from budget 2 to budget 3, income decreases and the quantity demanded of each good also decreases. Therefore, each is normal.

5. $160; $80; $80; increase; $15; increase; $45; $4; $100

*6.   No, the secretary is not correct. The CEO's demand curve is sketched in the following diagram. The CEO is willing to pay $150 for the first ticket, $100 for the second, and $50 for the third. Thus for two tickets she is willing to pay $250: ($150 + $100), and for three she is willing to pay $300: ($150 + $100 + $50). If the price is $100 per ticket, she has only to pay $200 for two, and if the price is $50, she has only to pay $150 for three. What she is willing to pay is determined by the value she places on the consumption of these goods, not on the cost of purchasing them.

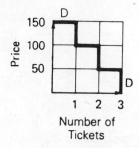

7.   (a)   (i) and (ii) The indifference curves and budget line are shown on the following graph.

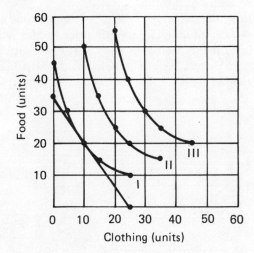

(iii) $F = 20$; $C = 10$. Given the budget constraint, curve I is the highest indifference curve attainable.

(b) (i)   Prices: \$15; \$5.65; \$3.33 Quantities: 23.3; 62; 105

(ii)   Connect points of tangency

(iii) Plot the corresponding price-quantity combinations on a graph with price on the Y axis and quantity demanded on the X axis.

8. (a) The substitution effect is AB in the graph.

(b) The income effect is BC in the graph.

(c) No. If X were an inferior good, there would have to be a negative income effect.

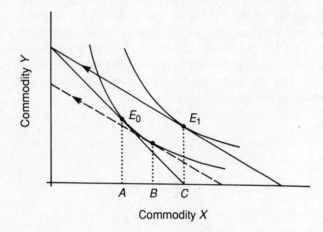

9. (a) The graph should show the following points (marginal utility is given in parentheses next to number of milkshakes consumed): 1(50), 2(40), 3(30), 4(10), 5(0), 6(−10).

(b) After the fifth milkshake.

10. (a) Three hours on tennis, two hours on fishing.

(b) Utility maximization requires that $MU_T/P_T = MU_F/P_F$. When tennis and fishing are priced the same (e.g., \$1.00 each), the condition is met when $18/1 = 18/1$. With the price of tennis increased to \$1.19 (19 percent), the condition is met when $19/1.19 = 16/1$ (approximately). Thus three hours are spent on fishing and two on tennis.

Chapter 8

Using Demand Theory

Learning Objectives

After studying this chapter, you should be able to:

—explain the derivation and meaning of market demand curves

—resolve the paradox of value

—distinguish between free goods and scarce goods

—differentiate among risk-neutral, risk-averse, and risk-loving behavior

—explain why there is a market for insurance and what the effects of moral hazard and adverse selection are

—understand the roles of risk pooling and risk sharing in the development of insurance markets

Multiple-Choice Questions

1. The market demand curve for a commodity is derived by
   (a) the vertical summation of individual household demand curves
   (b) taking each quantity demanded, determining the marginal value each household places on this quantity, and adding these to get total value
   (c) determining the quantity demanded by each household at each price and summing to get total quantity demanded
   (d) adding each household's total willingness to pay for a given quantity of the good

2. The "paradox of value" arises from the fact that
   (a) people are irrational in consumption choices
   (b) free goods are essential for life
   (c) there is no necessary positive relationship between households' marginal and total valuations of consumption
   (d) the higher the price of a good, the greater a household's valuation of the good

3. Diamonds have a higher price than water because
   (a) household total valuation of diamonds is greater than that of water
   (b) household total valuation of water is greater than that of diamonds
   (c) marginal valuation of diamonds by households is greater than that of water
   (d) households are willing to pay more in total for diamonds than for water

4. Good *A* is more of a luxury commodity than good *B* if
   (a) the price of *A* is greater than *B*
   (b) the price elasticity of demand for *A* is greater than that for *B*
   (c) the area under *A*'s demand curve is less than that under *B*'s
   (d) the quantity demanded of *A* is more responsive to price changes than the quantity demanded of *B*

5. The price elasticity of demand for a good depends on
   (a) only whether the good is a necessity or a luxury
   (b) the valuation households place on the consumption of one unit more or less
   (c) the total value placed on consumption
   (d) the market value of a good

6. A good with a market price of zero is indicative of
   (a) a good that nobody wants at any price
   (b) a good for which quantity supplied exceeds quantity demanded (at a price of zero)
   (c) a scarce good
   (d) an inferior good

7. A law setting the price of a scarce good at zero
   (a) ensures that only those households with the highest marginal values will consume this good
   (b) ensures that all households consume equal quantities of this good
   (c) is likely to result in some households with a low marginal value of consumption getting the good while others with a high marginal value do without
   (d) ensures that consumption continues until each household's marginal valuation is reduced to zero

8. That voters in a town could believe that an excellent school system is an important public asset but then vote down a school tax levy
   (a) is clearly irrational behavior because of the high value placed on education
   (b) suggests bias in the poll that led to an overassessment of the importance given to public education
   (c) indicates a low voter turnout except for antitaxers
   (d) could be quite consistent since high total valuations do not rule out low marginal valuations, especially in ranges of high total expenditure

9. A law requiring that water be provided free to everyone
   (a) ensures that only households with the highest marginal values will consume water
   (b) ensures that all households will consume equal quantities of water
   (c) is likely to result in some households with a low marginal value of water getting water while others with a higher marginal value do without
   (d) ensures that households can consume water until the marginal value of water is zero

10. The total market value of a commodity
    (a) is the same amount as the value consumers place on a given quantity of the commodity
    (b) is measured by the area under the demand curve at the quantity purchased
    (c) is the amount everyone spends to purchase it
    (d) varies negatively with its market price

11. The degree of risk attached to a given choice
    (a) refers to the dispersion in the possible results from that choice
    (b) is always negatively related to the expected value
    (c) is always positively related to the expected value
    (d) varies among risk-averse, risk-neutral, and risk-loving individuals

Questions 12 and 13 assume the following information. Consider a game involving repeated tosses of a fair coin. If the result is a head, $1 is won; if the result is a tail, $1 is lost.

12. The expected value of this game is
    (a) $1 (0.5) + $1 (0.5) = $1
    (b) $1 (1.0) + $1 (1.0) = $2
    (c) $1 (1.0) − $1 (1.0) = $0
    (d) $1 (0.5) − $1 (0.5) = $0

13. Risk-averse individuals
    (a) would play the game without a risk premium
    (b) should be indifferent about playing the game
    (c) would choose to play the game only if the number of tosses were sufficiently large
    (d) would not play the game

14. The main explanation of why insurance companies can afford to absorb their customers' risks is their ability to engage in
    (a) insuring against events such as war where a common cause acts on all insured units
    (b) risk pooling and risk sharing
    (c) adverse selection
    (d) moral hazard

15. A fair game is one in which
    (a) the expected value of the outcome is zero
    (b) the expected winnings equal the expected losses
    (c) the average gain or loss per play will tend to approach zero as the number of repetitive plays increases
    (d) all of the above

16. A risk-neutral individual
    (a) should never participate in a fair game
    (b) should be indifferent about participating in a fair game
    (c) should not buy a $1,000 insurance policy to protect against a 1/100 chance of losing $100,000
    (d) should avoid all risky situations

17. One reason insurance firms offer policies with only partial coverage is
    (a) moral hazard
    (b) risk-loving customers
    (c) that it permits the insurer to pool its risks
    (d) all of the above

Exercises

1. The table that follows provides data on the total valuation a household places upon the consumption of different quantities of pizza per week.

Pizzas per week	Total valuation	Marginal valuation
1	$14	_____
2	24	_____
3	31	_____
4	36	_____
5	40	_____

(a) Calculate the household's marginal valuation of each successive pizza consumed.

(b) If the price of a pizza is $5, how many will this household purchase per week?

(c) Calculate the associated consumers' surplus at a market price of $5 by subtracting total expenditure from total valuation.

(d) Calculate consumers' surplus by summing the incremental consumers' surplus derived from each successive unit purchased.

2. The table presents the amount a consumer is willing to pay for successive units of yogurt and movies during a weekly time period.

Unit consumed per week	Willingness to pay for each container of yogurt	Willingness to pay for each movie
1st	$8.00	$4.00
2nd	4.00	3.75
3rd	3.10	3.50
4th	2.40	3.25
5th	1.80	3.00
6th	1.40	2.75
7th	1.10	2.50
8th	0.90	2.25
9th	0.80	2.00
10th	0.75	1.75

Suppose that the price of yogurt is 90 cents and the price of a movie is $3.00.

(a) How many of each of these goods does this individual consume on a weekly basis?

(b) What are the market values of each of these consumption levels?

(c) What total value does this consumer place on the consumption of these goods at the current market prices?

(d) What consumers' surplus does he derive from each good?

3. The following is an individual's demand curve for playing squash each week:

$$Q^D = 10 - 2P$$

where Q^D is hours of squash time demanded per week and P is the price per hour (for each player) of court time (assume that this person can always find a partner).

(a) Plot this individual's demand curve for squash.

(b) The only squash courts available are at The Racquet Club, Inc., where each player is charged $2 per hour. How much squash does this person play per week?

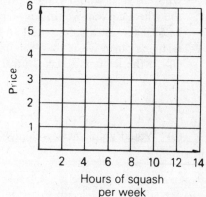

(c) What is this individual's total valuation of the games consumed per week?

(d) How much does this person actually spend on squash each week?

(e) What is this individual's consumer surplus?

(f) The Racquet Club, Inc., is considering a pricing scheme whereby individuals still pay $2 per hour of court time, but in addition they must also pay a mandatory membership fee. What is the largest fee The Racquet Club, Inc., could charge for a weekly membership without losing this individual as a customer?

(g) As an alternative pricing scheme, suppose that The Racquet Club, Inc., introduces a membership fee but does not charge members for court time (i.e., members are entitled to unlimited use of the facility). What is the maximum amount this individual is willing to pay for a weekly membership under these circumstances?

4. Suppose that there is one chance in a 100 that your $100,000 house will be damaged by flooding. You are considering the purchase of an insurance policy to cover the possible loss. You can either purchase the policy at a price of $1,000 and eliminate the risk or not buy it and risk the damage.

   (a) Calculate the expected value of both courses of action.

   (b) If you were risk-averse, would you buy the policy? Explain.

   (c) If you were risk-neutral, would you buy the policy? Explain.

   (d) Assume that the cost of the policy rises to $1,200. Would a risk-neutral person purchase it? A risk-averse person? Explain.

*5. Consider a farmer who can plant wheat or corn (but not both) on a given piece of land. If the weather is good, the wheat harvest will yield a profit of $4,000, whereas corn would yield a profit of $1,800. However, if the weather is bad, the wheat harvest would have a profit of only $1,000, but the corn profit would be $3,000. Assume that good and bad weather are equally likely and that the farmer's objective is to get as large a profit as possible.
   (a) If the farmer is risk-neutral, what will she plant on this piece of land?

   (b) Would your answer change if she were risk-averse?

Answers

Multiple-Choice Questions

1. (c) 2. (c) 3. (c) 4. (c) 5. (b) 6. (b) 7. (c) 8. (d) 9. (c) 10. (c) 11. (a) 12. (d) 13. (d) 14. (b) 15. (d) 16. (b) 17. (a)

Exercises

1. (a)

Pizzas per week	Total valuation	Marginal valuation
1	$14	$14
2	24	10
3	31	7
4	36	5
5	40	4

(b) 4

(c) consumers' surplus = total valuation − total expenditure

$$= \$36 - (\$5 \times 4) = \$16$$

(d) Consumers' surplus from each unit consumed equals the marginal valuation minus market price. Thus consumers' surplus on the first unit is $9, on the second $5, on the third $2, and zero on the last unit consumed. Summing these yields $16.

2. (a) Quantity demanded for yogurt is 8 and for movies 5.

(b) The market value of consumed yogurt is $7.20 (i.e., 8 × $0.90), and for movies the market value is $15 (i.e., $3 × 5).

(c) Consumer total valuation of yogurt consumption is $22.70: ($8 + $4 + ⋯ + $0.90), while for movie consumption it is $17.50: ($4 + $3.75 + ⋯ + $3).

(d) Consumers' surplus for yogurt is $15.50 and for movies $2.50.

3. (a)

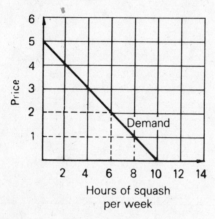

(b) Six hours per week

(c) $21 (obtained by calculating the area under the demand curve up to a quantity of 6)

(d) $12 (i.e., $2 × 6)

(e) $9 (obtained by calculating the area below the demand curve and above the price line)

(f) For consumption of six hours, this person is willing to pay the total valuation of $21. At a price of $2, current payment is $12 for six hours. Therefore, this individual is willing to pay an additional $9 to play six hours of squash, which may be collected as a membership fee.

(g) By joining the club, the price per hour is zero, so as a member this person would now play 10 hours of squash each week. The value this individual places on 10 hours of squash is $25. Thus $25 could now be charged for a membership in The Racquet Club, Inc., without losing this person as a member.

4. (a) expected value of buying: −$1,000; expected value of not buying: −$100,000 (0.01) + $0 (0.99) = − $1,000.

(b) Yes, because the expected value of the two choices (buy/not buy) are the same (−$1,000), but not buying the insurance is much riskier than buying it.

(c) A risk-neutral person would be indifferent between buying the insurance policy and not buying it since both courses of action have the same expected value (assuming that there are no other considerations).

(d) At $1,200 the expected net gain of buying the policy is negative. A
     risk-neutral person would not buy it. A risk-averse person would still buy
     the policy if the value of reducing the risk was worth more than the
     additional $200 cost.

5. (a) The risk-neutral farmer plants wheat, which has the higher expected profit:
         expected profit from wheat = 1/2 ($4,000) + 1/2 ($1,000) = $2,500; expected
         profit from corn = 1/2 ($1,800) + 1/2 ($3,000) = $2,400.

    (b) Uncertain. Although corn yields a lower expected profit, the dispersion
         of profit for corn due to weather is less than that for wheat. For a risk-averse
         individual, the lower expected profit of $100 may be more than offset by
         the lower risk associated with planting corn.

Chapter 9

The Role
of the Firm

Learning Objectives

After studying this chapter, you should be able to:

—identify the major differences among single proprietorships, partnerships, and corporations

—list the advantages of the corporate form of organization

—distinguish between debt and equity financing

—explain the meaning of opportunity cost, particularly in the context of decision making by the firm

—distinguish economic profits from other definitions of profits

—explain how profits provide important signals for the allocation of resources

Multiple-Choice Questions

1. One of the major differences between a partnership and a corporation is that
   (a) the owners of a corporation always outnumber the owners of a partnership
   (b) a corporation always has more assets
   (c) the owners of a corporation have limited liability, whereas partners have unlimited liability
   (d) corporations are always more profitable

2. One of the significant disadvantages of a corporation is
   (a) the double taxation of income
   (b) the limited liability
   (c) that the only way it can raise capital is by borrowing
   (d) that it must issue annual dividends

3. Which of the following groups of claimants would be the last to have their claims honored in a corporate bankruptcy?
   (a) bondholders
   (b) stockholders
   (c) commercial creditors
   (d) employees owed back wages

4. Corporations can finance their operations by
   (a) reinvesting profits
   (b) issuing bonds
   (c) issuing new equity
   (d) all of the above

5. The assumption that firms maximize profit
   (a) has yielded predictions of firms' behavior that have been substantially correct
   (b) is irrefutable
   (c) has been observed to be always true
   (d) implies that profits are the only factor that influence business decisions

6. Debt financing by firms involves
   (a) issuance of common stock only
   (b) selling bonds to the public or borrowing from financial institutions
   (c) issuance of common and preferred stock
   (d) obtaining financial capital by any of the above methods

7. A major assumption in the economic theory of the firm is that
   (a) decisions within the firm are made by consensus between labor and management
   (b) regardless of their size, firms are assumed to act as a single consistent decision-making unit
   (c) every firm behaves in a fundamentally different and unpredictable way
   (d) objectives of firms depend primarily on firm size

8. Which of the following firms are examples of public enterprises in Canada?
   (a) CBC or VIA Rail
   (b) Bell Canada or Canadian Pacific
   (c) any privately owned firm that serves the public, such as Harvey's Hamburgers or Famous Players' Theatres
   (d) any firm listed on the stock exchange, such as the Ford Motor Company of Canada

9. Suppose that you own a dairy store that makes and sells homemade ice cream, using an ice cream maker that has no alternative use and no resale value. It cost $1,500 when it was purchased 15 years ago. The opportunity cost of its use is
   (a) $100, representing the annual depreciation
   (b) zero
   (c) some number greater than zero (but not $100), representing the annual depreciation
   (d) the amount of imputed interest on the cost of a replacement machine

10. Economic profits are defined as the difference between
    (a) accounting profits and normal profits
    (b) total revenues and all opportunity costs
    (c) total revenues and the monetary costs of hiring resources for current use
    (d) net income before and after taxes

11. Opportunity cost refers to
    (a) what must be given up to secure the next best alternative
    (b) unexpected profits for the firm
    (c) the best rate of return possible on an investment
    (d) the return to using something in the most profitable way

12. Applying the concept of opportunity cost to the firm is difficult
    (a) because it requires imputing certain costs when a resource is not directly hired or purchased
    (b) because most of a firm's costs are monetary costs
    (c) to the extent that the modern corporation borrows from the bank
    (d) all of the above

13. Which of the following is most likely to represent an imputed cost to the firm?
    (a) wages paid to current employees
    (b) rent for use of a leased plant
    (c) interest paid on borrowed funds
    (d) interest that could have been received on money currently invested in inventory

14. When a firm uses its own funds to finance a project,
    (a) the cost of these funds is zero
    (b) profits are greater because the firm does not have to borrow
    (c) the forgone interest that could have been earned by these funds is an imputed cost of the project
    (d) all of the above

15. Depreciation, defined as the loss of value of an asset associated with its use in production,
    (a) is clearly a monetary cost
    (b) is a function only of wear and tear in use
    (c) is not an economic cost if the asset has no market value or alternative use
    (d) does not apply to used equipment

16. Accounting profits are
    (a) always positive
    (b) usually greater than economic profits
    (c) the same as normal profits
    (d) the result of technologically inefficient production

17. Normal profits refer to
    (a) what all firms, on average, obtain as a return on investment
    (b) the base used by Revenue Canada to levy business taxes
    (c) the imputed return to capital and risk taking required to keep firms in the industry
    (d) the level of profits necessary to ensure that the firm covers its day-to-day operating expenses

18. Sunk costs are
    (a) the costs to a firm of using its own capital
    (b) costs incurred in the past that involve no current opportunity cost
    (c) costs that must be accounted for only if the firm is producing current output
    (d) all of the above

19. If economic profits are zero for all firms in an industry, then
   (a) firms earning less than normal profits will shift resources toward alternative investments
   (b) revenues equal the monetary costs of operation
   (c) resources are earning a return in this industry at least equal to that available elsewhere
   (d) firms will cease production immediately

20. The major role of economic profits, as seen in this chapter, is to
   (a) provide income for shareholders
   (b) provide income for entrepreneurs
   (c) act as a signal to firms concerning the desirability of devoting additional resources to a particular activity
   (d) encourage labor to reform the system

Exercises

1. After five years of working, Mary Kaufman left a $25,000 job to start her own business with the use of $20,000 she had saved. She charged the business $15,000 a year for her services but made no allowance for the 10 percent she might have earned on her savings in an investment of equal risk. In 1990 her accounting profits were $10,000. Had the business been economically profitable to that point? What needs to be known to decide whether it is economically profitable to continue the business?

2. The table presents an annual income statement for Harry's Hardware Store. Harry worked full-time at the store. He had used $25,000 of his savings to furnish and stock the store (included in costs). He had recently been offered a $20,000 annual salary to work in another hardware store.

Annual Income Statement

Revenues		Costs	
Sales of merchandise	$90,000	Wholesale purchases	$60,000
Service revenues	5,000	Store supplies	2,000
		Labor costs (hired)	10,000
		Utilities	1,000
		Rent	5,000
		Depreciation on fixtures	2,000
Total revenues	$95,000	Total costs	$80,000

   (a) Calculate the accounting profits for Harry's Hardware Store.

   (b) What are some imputed costs that Harry should include in estimating the total costs of owning his business?

(c) Assume an interest rate of 10 percent. What are the total costs of Harry's owning this business?

(d) Calculate his economic profits.

3. (a) For $10,000 a firm purchases a machine with an estimated 10 years of economic life and zero salvage value. What is the straight-line depreciation per year?

(b) At the end of five years, this firm finds that the machine has a market value of only $1,000, which is expected to decline to zero after the five remaining years. What is the economically relevant depreciation per year now?

4. Arrange the following items and use the information presented here to obtain (a) net profit before taxes, (b) economic profit before taxes, and (c) economic profit after taxes. (*Hint:* See Table 9-1 in the text.)

- Revenue from sale of goods: $5 million
- Tax rate: 50 percent of net profit before tax
- Depreciation: $500,000
- Salaries: $1 million
- Imputed charges for use of own capital and risk taking: $500,000
- Cost of raw materials: $2 million

(a) Net profit before taxes = _____
(b) Economic profit before taxes = _____
(c) Economic profit after taxes = _____

5. Jean-Marc, a third-year honors economics student at Laurentian University, is considering the possibility of setting up his own business for the summer. Specifically, Jean-Marc plans to provide door-to-door delivery of the *Financial Post*, the *Wall Street Journal*, and the *New York Times* to cottagers in the Muskoka and Haliburtan resort regions of Ontario. Because he will be graduating and seeking permanent employment next year, this enterprise is for one summer only and is an alternative to earning $3,000 after-tax income as a lifeguard. The following list itemizes the particulars:

- Jean-Marc expects total revenues of $24,000 for the season.
- To deliver the papers, he must purchase a van for $6,000, which he is certain to sell at season's end for $4,000.
- The license for distributing newspapers in these regions costs $3,000 and lasts for three years. However, it is nontransferable (i.e., it cannot be sold or used by anyone else).
- To finance the purchase of the van and the license, Jean-Marc will withdraw $9,000 from his savings account for a period of six months. This account pays an annual interest rate of 10 percent.

- It will cost $8,000 to purchase the newspapers in bulk. To get this special price, Jean-Marc agrees to pay the $8,000 up front (i.e., at the beginning of the season). He borrows this amount from a bank for six months at an annual interest rate of 15 percent.
- Costs of promotion, gas, and other incidentals come to $2,500.
- Although Jean-Marc expects $24,000 in revenues, it may actually be less. Thus there is some risk involved. He feels that $1,000 would compensate him for taking the risk.
- The tax rate on his business is 50 percent of net income.

(a) What are Jean-Marc's direct and indirect costs for hired and purchased factors? (*Note:* Include any depreciation of assets.)

(b) What are Jean-Marc's imputed costs?

(c) What is Jean-Marc's net profit before taxes and after taxes?

(d) What are his economic profits after taxes?

(e) If the business tax rate were applied to economic profits rather than to net income, would Jean-Marc be more or less likely to undertake this enterprise?

Answers

Multiple-Choice Questions

1. (c) 2. (a) 3. (b) 4. (d) 5. (a) 6. (b) 7. (b) 8. (a) 9. (b) 10. (b) 11. (a) 12. (a)
13. (d) 14. (c) 15. (c) 16. (b) 17. (c) 18. (b) 19. (c) 20. (c)

Exercises

1. No, she would have been $2,000 better off to this point by working and investing separately. This is past history and could be expected in starting a business. Prospective profits must be estimated; current alternatives are what count—can she get $25,000 in the old job (or another)? Can she sell business assets for $20,000 and reasonably expect a $2,000 return? Will sales increase next year and tend toward greater future profits?

2. (a) $15,000
   (b) He should include imputed costs for annual interest on $25,000 investment (assuming that he could recover it) and $20,000 opportunity cost for his own salary.
   (c) Total costs would be accounting costs of $80,000 plus interest of $2,500 and $20,000 salary.
   (d) A *loss* of $7,500 is indicated for the past year (but it is the firm's prospective profitability that should determine his decision to work for someone else).

3. (a) $1,000
   (b) $200, the amount of market value given up by using machine one more year.

4. Revenue | $5.0 million

Revenue	$5.0 million
Less direct cost (salaries and materials)	−3.0 million
Less indirect cost (depreciation)	−0.5 million
(a) Net profit before taxes	$1.5 million
Less imputed cost of capital and risk taking	−0.5 million
(b) Economic profit before taxes	$1.0 million
Less taxes (0.5 × $1.5 million)	−0.75 million
(c) Economic profit after taxes	$0.25 million

5. (a) Direct costs:

License	$ 3,000
Interest payments on loan	600
Bulk purchase	8,000
Promotion, gas, etc.	2,500
Indirect costs:	
Depreciation of van	2,000
Total direct and indirect costs	$16,100

(b) Imputed costs:

Interest forgone on savings	$ 450
Risk compensation	1,000
Forgone lifeguard earnings	3,000
Total imputed costs	$ 4,450

(c) Net profit before taxes = revenue − (direct costs + indirect costs)
   = $24,000 − $16,100 = $7,900
   Net profit after taxes = $7,900 × 0.50 = $3,950

(d) Economic profit after taxes = net income after taxes − imputed costs
   = $3,950 − $4,450 = −$500

(e) Eonomic profit before taxes = revenue − imputed costs − (direct costs + indirect costs)
   = $24,000 − $4,450 − $16,100
   = $3,450
   Economic profit after taxes = $3,450 × 0.50 = $1,725

Jean-Marc is more likely to undertake this enterprise if the business tax is applied to economic profits instead of net profit. By taxing net income, Revenue Canada does not allow Jean-Marc to deduct real (albeit imputed) costs and thereby forces his economic profit into a loss of $500.

Chapter 10

Production and Cost in the Short Run

Learning Objectives

After studying this chapter, you should be able to:

—explain how the different time horizons (the short, long, and very long runs) affect decision making by firms

—explain the hypothesis of diminishing marginal returns

—show how total, average, and marginal product curves summarize production information in alternative ways

—relate the family of production curves to the family of cost curves

—explain the economic definition of capacity

Multiple-Choice Questions

1. The short run is defined as a period
   (a) of less than a month
   (b) during which there is insufficient time to change the quantity employed of any factor
   (c) during which some factors are fixed and others are variable
   (d) during which new firms can enter an industry and old firms can exit

2. The long-run time horizon
   (a) is the same for all firms
   (b) allows the impact of new inventions to be felt
   (c) is defined as the minimum length of time it takes to vary output
   (d) is a length of time that is sufficient for all factors to be variable

3. Which of the following is an example of a short-run production decision?
   (a) A contractor buys two additional trucks and hires two new drivers for them.
   (b) A contractor decides to work his crew overtime to finish a job.
   (c) A railway decides to eliminate all passenger service.
   (d) A paper company installs antipollution equipment.

4. The production function relates
   (a) outputs to inputs
   (b) outputs to labor inputs
   (c) outputs to costs
   (d) an economy's attainable combinations of output to alternative resource allocations

5. Assuming that capital is a fixed input and that labor is variable, the total product curve relates
   (a) output to various levels of capital and labor employment
   (b) output to various levels of labor employment with capital held constant
   (c) labor cost to the level of output
   (d) total cost to various levels of labor employment

6. An increase in the fixed input
   (a) shifts the total product curve upward
   (b) does not affect the total product curve
   (c) lengthens the firm's long-run time horizon
   (d) necessarily implies an increase in output

7. When a firm increases the quantity of variable input employed, it
   (a) shifts the production possibility curve
   (b) shifts its total product curve upward
   (c) moves along its total product curve
   (d) is making a long-run decision

8. If labor is the variable factor, average product is defined as
   (a) total product divided by total output
   (b) the quantity of labor divided by total product
   (c) the additional output produced by the last unit of labor
   (d) output per unit of labor

9. The change in output that results when another unit of the variable factor is employed is referred to as
   (a) marginal product   (c) average fixed product
   (b) average product   (d) total product

10. If average product is falling,
    (a) marginal product is less than average product
    (b) marginal product is equal to average product
    (c) marginal product is greater than average product
    (d) marginal product can be greater than, equal to, or less than average product

11. If marginal product is falling,
    (a) marginal product is always less than average product
    (b) marginal product is always equal to average product
    (c) marginal product is always greater than average product
    (d) marginal product can be greater than, equal to, or less than average product

12. The hypothesis of diminishing returns states that
    (a) as output increases, the rate of increase in costs will eventually decrease
    (b) as output increases, profits will eventually decline
    (c) the incremental output achieved by increases in a variable factor will eventually decrease
    (d) as more labor is employed, the wage rate will increase and thereby increase costs

13. A firm's wage bill in the short run equals its
    (a) short-run total costs   (c) total fixed costs
    (b) total variable costs   (d) marginal costs

14. "Spreading one's overhead" is equivalent to
    (a) increasing capital to spread total costs
    (b) decreasing average fixed costs
    (c) increasing output to decrease average total costs
    (d) any decrease in total costs

15. Using the notation in the text, AFC equals
    (a) $ATC - AVC$ (c) ATC at its minimum point
    (b) $AVC + MC$ (d) $TC - TVC$

16. AVC equals
    (a) $MC + AFC$ (c) $ATC + AFC$
    (b) TVC per unit of labor   (d) MC at the minimum point of AVC

Questions 17 to 20 refer to the following graph, which illustrates a firm's average total cost (ATC) and average variable cost (AVC) curves.

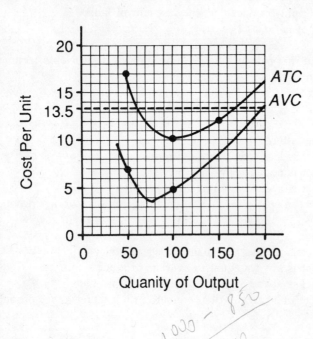

$ATC = AFC + AVC$

17. When the firm is producing 200 units of output, total costs in the short run are
    (a) $3,200
    (b) $2,700
    (c) $16
    (d) $13.50

18. When output equals 100 units, marginal cost is
    (a) $5
    (b) $15
    (c) $10
    (d) cannot be determined

19. At a total product of 200 units, AFC is
    (a) $2.50
    (b) $13.50
    (c) $16
    (d) cannot be determined

20. If the level of production is 50 units, TFC is
    (a) $350
    (b) $7
    (c) $500
    (d) cannot be determined

21. Total cost is $30 at 10 units of output and $32 at 11 units of output. In this range of output, marginal cost is
    (a) equal to average total cost
    (b) greater than average total cost
    (c) less than average total cost
    (d) cannot be determined from the information provided

22. If the difference between average total cost (ATC) and average variable cost (AVC) at 100 units of output is $1, at 200 units of output the difference between ATC and AVC must be
    (a) $2
    (b) $1
    (c) 50 cents
    (d) cannot be determined

23. A firm's capacity
    (a) continuously declines as output increases
    (b) is the output level corresponding to minimum average total cost
    (c) is the size of its plant
    (d) is the maximum output that can physically be produced with a given amount of capital

24. The hypothesis of diminishing marginal returns implies
    (a) decreasing average variable costs
    (b) increasing marginal costs
    (c) decreasing marginal revenue
    (d) increasing average fixed costs

25. A change in the wage rate paid to the variable factor labor will shift
    (a) the ATC curve
    (b) the AVC curve
    (c) the MC curve
    (d) all three curves

Exercises

1. The data in the following table relate employment levels of a variable factor to the resulting output.

Variable factor	Total product	Average product	Marginal product
1	10	_____	
			_____
2	160	_____	
			_____
3	330	_____	
			_____
4	480	_____	
			_____
5	600	_____	
			_____
6	670	_____	
			_____
7	680	_____	

(a) Fill in the blanks.
(b) Graph the total product curve in panel (i) and the average product and marginal product curves in panel (ii). (Remember that marginal product is plotted at the midpoint on the horizontal axis—see Table 10-1 in the text.)

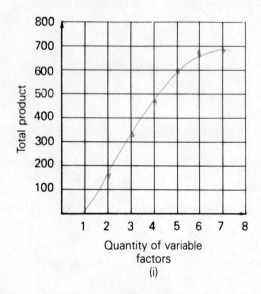

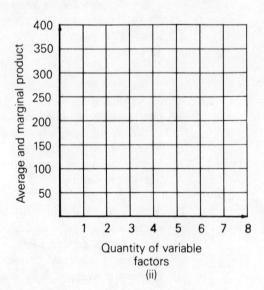

(c) At what output do diminishing returns begin?

2. This exercise is designed to illustrate the relationship between productivity and cost with very few figures. Take $30 as the cost associated with the fixed factors and $10 as the cost of each variable unit. Consider, for example, an agricultural situation in which the variable factors are seed, labor, fertilizer, and equipment and the fixed factor is land.

(a) Complete the following table.

Units of variable factor	Total product	Marginal product	Average product	Total cost	Marginal cost	Average total cost
0	0		0	$30		∞
		2			$5	
1	2		2	40		$20
		3			3,3	
2	5		2.5	50		10
		2			5	
3	7		2,3	60		8.57
		1			10	
4	8		2	70		8.75
		0			∞	
5	8		1,6	80		10

(b) Graph the total, average, and marginal product curves in panel (a) and the three cost curves in panel (b). To emphasize the negative relationship between product and cost, number each point plotted with the number of variable factor units used. Remember that these "marginal" points are plotted at the midpoints of the intervals on the horizontal axis.

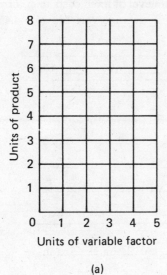

(a)

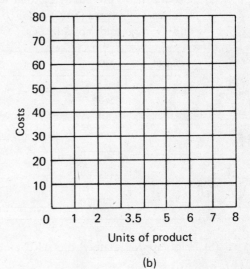

(b)

3. The following graph presents the marginal cost curve for a particular firm. Because marginal cost is plotted at the midpoint, the marginal cost of producing (for example) the first unit of output is $50. In addition, suppose that the firm's fixed costs are $100.

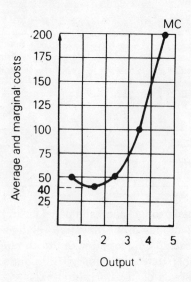

(a) Use the firm's *MC* curve together with the level of fixed costs to determine total variable costs (*TVC*), total costs (*TC*), average variable costs (*AVC*), and average total costs (*ATC*).

Output	MC	TVC	TC	AVC	ATC
0		0	100	0	∞
1	$50	50	150	50	150
2	40	90	190	45	95
3	50	140	240	47	80
4	100	240	340	160	85
5	200	440	540	88	108

(b) Plot (approximately) the *AVC* and *ATC* curves on the graph.

4. Given the cost curves of the hypothetical firm shown here, answer the following questions.
(a) The capacity of this firm occurs at an output of ___6.5___.
(b) The effect of diminishing marginal returns occurs after an output level of ___5___.
(c) The effect of diminishing average returns occurs after an output level of ___8___.

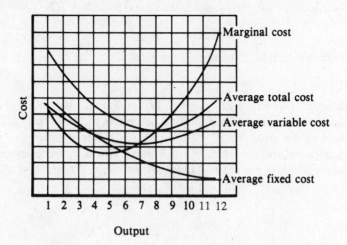

Output

*5. Assume that you are in the business of producing a commodity for which short-run total cost is represented by the following equation:

$$TC = 30 + 3Q + Q^2$$

where Q is output of the commodity and TC is total costs.

(a) What are total fixed costs equal to?

(b) What is the equation that represents total variable costs?

(c) Derive the equation for average total costs (ATC).

(d) Fill in the blanks in the following table.

Q	TVC	TFC	TC	ATC	MC
0	____	____	____	____	
1	____	____	____	____	____
2	____	____	____	____	____
3	____	____	____	____	____
4	____	____	____	____	____
5	____	____	____	____	____
6	____	____	____	____	____
7	____	____	____	____	____
8	____	____	____	____	____
9	____	____	____	____	____
10	____	____	____	____	____

(e) What is the capacity of this firm?

(f) What is marginal cost at this capacity output?

(g) The equation for this firm's MC curve is $MC = 3 + 2Q$ (if familiar with calculus, you will note that this is the first derivative of the TC curve). To understand why marginal cost is plotted at the midpoints, use the equation for MC to calculate MC at outputs of 5, 5.5, and 6. Compare these answers with the marginal cost you derived in (d), which was calculated by taking the difference in TC between outputs of 5 and 6.

Answers

Multiple-Choice Questions

1. (c) 2. (d) 3. (b) 4. (a) 5. (b) 6. (a) 7. (c) 8. (d) 9. (a) 10. (a) 11. (d) 12. (c)
13. (b) 14. (b) 15. (a) 16. (d) 17. (a) 18. (c) 19. (a) 20. (c) 21. (c) 22. (c) 23. (b)
24. (b) 25. (d)

Exercises

1. (a)

Variable factor	Total product	Average product	Marginal product
1	10	10	
			150
2	160	80	
			170
3	330	110	
			150
4	480	120	
			120
5	600	120	
			70
6	670	112	
			10
7	680	97	

(b)

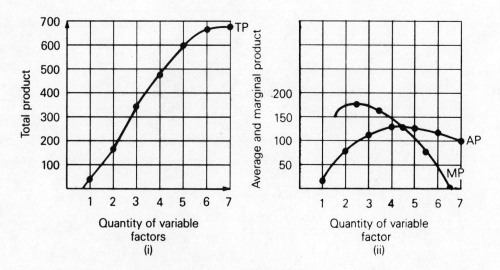

(c) Maximum *MP* is 170, which obtains for the third unit of the variable factor (plotted at 2.5 units). Thus diminishing returns begin after employment of the third variable factor.

2. (a) Blanks should be filled as follows:

Marginal product	Average product	Total cost	Marginal cost	Average total cost
3	2.5	50	3.33	10.00
2	2.3	60	5.00	8.57
1	2.0	70	10.00	8.75
0	1.6	80	∞	10.00

(b)

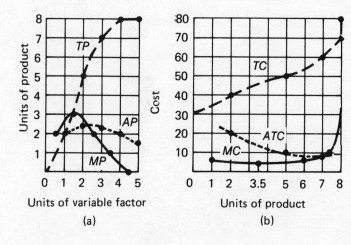

3. (a)

Output	MC	TVC	TC	AVC	ATC
0		$ 0	$100	—	—
	$ 50				
1		50	150	$50.00	$150
	40				
2		90	190	45.00	95
	50				
3		140	240	46.67	80
	100				
4		240	340	60.00	85
	200				
5		440	540	88.00	108

(b)

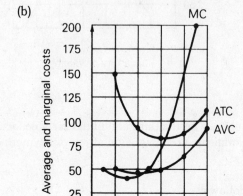

4. (a) 8 (b) 5 (c) 7

*5. (a) 30
   (b) $TVC = 3Q + Q^2$
   (c) $ATC = TC/Q = (30 + 3Q + Q^2)/Q = 30/Q + 3 + Q$
   (d)

Q	TVC	TFC	TC	ATC	MC
0	$ 0	$ 30	$ 30	—	
					$ 4
1	4	30	34	$34	
					6
2	10	30	40	20	
					8
3	18	30	48	16	
					10
4	28	30	58	14.5	
					12
5	40	30	70	14	
					14
6	54	30	84	14	
					16
7	70	30	100	14.3	
					18
8	88	30	118	14.8	
					20
9	108	30	138	15.3	
					22
10	130	30	160	16	

(e) Somewhere between output levels 5 and 6.

(f) 14

(g) The marginal costs of outputs 5, 5.5, and 6 are 13, 14, and 15, respectively. The difference in TC between outputs 5 and 6 is 14, which is precisely the MC at the midpoint of 5.5 units of output.

Chapter 11

Production and Cost in the Long Run and the Very Long Run

Learning Objectives

After studying this chapter, you should be able to:

—apply the principle of substitution in explaining a firm's input use

—distinguish the long run and the very long run from the short run

—explain the relationship between long-run average cost and economies of scale

—understand how long-run and short-run cost curves are related

—interpret the economic basis for a saucer-shaped long-run average total cost curve

—distinguish between invention and innovation

—understand how productivity is measured

—relate energy use to industrialization and growth in productivity

—recognize the role of research and development in determining future productivity

Multiple-Choice Questions

1. In addition to choosing the level of output, a firm in the long run must also select
   (a) the appropriate technology
   (b) the amount of overtime for its labor force
   (c) the cost-minimizing combination of inputs
   (d) the profit-maximizing quantity of labor to employ with its fixed plant

2. The cost-minimizing factor mix obtains when
   (a) the marginal products of all factors are equalized
   (b) the marginal product per dollar expended on each factor is equalized
   (c) the marginal product of each factor divided by total expenditure on that factor is equalized across all factors
   (d) the cost of employing an additional unit of each factor is equalized across all factors

3. The profit-maximizing combination of capital (K) and labor (L) occurs when these factors are employed such that
   (a) $MP_K/P_K = MP_L/P_L$
   (b) $MP_K/K = MP_L/L$
   (c) $MP_K/P_L = MP_L/P_K$
   (d) $P_K \times K = P_L \times L$

4. Suppose that the marginal product of capital in a particular firm is 5 and that of labor is 10, and the price of capital is $2 and that of labor is $1. To minimize costs, this firm will
   (a) substitute more capital and less labor
   (b) substitute more labor and less capital
   (c) not alter its factor mix
   (d) hire more capital and keep labor constant

   $\frac{5}{10}$ $\frac{MP_K}{MP_L} = \frac{P_K}{P_L}$ $\frac{2}{1}$

Questions 5 and 6 refer to the following table, which presents four possible combinations of capital (K) and labor (L) and their associated marginal products. Each combination produces exactly 100 units of output. Assume that the firm wishes to minimize production costs.

Combination	K	MP_K	L	MP_L
A	14	12	1	10
B	12	14	3	7
C	8	16	4	4
D	6	20	7	2

5. If the ratio of the price of capital to the price of labor is 2, a firm will employ combination
   (a) A
   (b) B
   (c) C
   (d) D

6. If the relative price of capital to labor falls, the firm *may* (depending on the magnitude of the fall) wish to use combination
   (a) A
   (b) B
   (c) C
   (d) D

7. A firm's long-run average cost curve depicts
   (a) what costs will be attainable with technological improvement
   (b) the lowest attainable unit costs when all factors are variable
   (c) a firm's profit-maximizing output choices
   (d) the lowest attainable average cost when all factor prices vary

8. The long-run average cost curve is determined by
   (a) technology and tastes
   (b) long-run supply
   (c) population growth
   (d) technology and input prices

9. If the long-run average cost curve is sloping upward, the firm is experiencing
   (a) long-run decreasing returns
   (b) diseconomies of scale
   (c) increasing costs
   (d) all of the above

10. Constant long-run average costs for a firm means that
    (a) there are greater advantages to small than to large plants
    (b) an unlimited amount of output will be produced
    (c) any scale of production costs the same per unit as any other
    (d) total cost is independent of the level of output

11. Suppose that a firm doubles employment of all of its factors and, as a result, output increases from 100 units to 300 units. This firm is operating under
    (a) diseconomies of scale   (c) decreasing costs
    (b) long-run decreasing returns (d) decreasing total cost

12. A firm experiencing long-run increasing returns that decides to increase output should do so by
    (a) substituting more labor and less capital
    (b) employing a new technology
    (c) building smaller plants
    (d) building larger plants

13. One possible explanation for economies of scale is
    (a) invention and innovation
    (b) the introduction of new, improved inputs
    (c) a decrease in a factor price
    (d) increased specialization of production tasks

14. A downward shift in the family of short-run cost curves as well as the long-run average cost curve could be explained by
    (a) economies of scale
    (b) an increase in the fixed factor such as plant size
    (c) a decrease in a factor price
    (d) a larger capital-labor ratio

15. Which of the following is the best measure of productivity?
    (a) total output
    (b) total output per hour
    (c) total output per unit of resource input
    (d) total output per dollar of cost

16. The historical growth in the productivity of Canadian workers over the past century can be attributed to all but which of the following?
    (a) an increasing capital-labor ratio   (c) improved quality of labor
    (b) invention and innovation   (d) decreasing average fixed costs

17. The very long run
    (a) is necessarily longer than the long run
    (b) always involves a greater range of output than the short run or the long run
    (c) applies to a period in which new production methods can be introduced
    (d) extends long-run analysis to higher production levels

18. An *economically efficient* method of production is one that
    (a) uses the smallest number of resource inputs
    (b) necessarily involves the use of roundabout methods of production
    (c) costs the least
    (d) cannot also be technologically efficient

Appendix Questions

The following questions are based on material in the appendix to this chapter. Read the appendix before answering these questions.

19. If the marginal rate of substitution is -2 at a point on an isoquant involving two factors,
     (a) the ratio of factor prices is $+1:2$
     (b) the ratio of marginal products is $-1:2$
     (c) the ratio of marginal products is -2
     (d) one factor of production has negative marginal product

20. An isocost line for two factors C and L (their respective prices are P_C and P_L) could have which of the following equations?
     (a) $LC = \$100$ (c) $\$100 = P_L L + P_C C$
     (b) $\$100 = P_C + P_L$ (d) $\$100 = P_L P_C$

21. If two factors C and L are graphed in the same unit scale with C on the vertical axis, and an isocost line has a slope $= -2$, then
     (a) $P_L = 2P_C$ (c) $C = 2L$
     (b) $P_C/P_L = 2$ (d) $L = 2C$

22. At the point of tangency of the isocost line in question 21 with an isoquant,
     (a) the desired factor combination has $2C$ for each L
     (b) the marginal product of labor is twice that of capital
     (c) the desired factor combination has $2L$ for each C
     (d) the marginal product of capital is twice that of labor

Exercises

1. In the table that follows, three different firms are able to combine capital (K) and labor (L) in various ways, resulting in pairs of marginal products as shown. (Note that higher number combinations substitute more capital for less labor, which decreases MP_K and increases MP_L.) For all firms, the price of a unit of capital is $10, and the price of labor is $5.

Combination number	Firm A		Firm B		Firm C	
	MP_K	MP_L	MP_K	MP_L	MP_K	MP_L
1	10	1	6	3	25	2
2	8	2	5	4	20	4
3	6	3	4	6	14	7
4	4	4	3	8	10	8
5	2	5	2	10	5	10

(a) Firm A is currently using combination 3, Firm B is using combination 2, and Firm C is using combination 4. Which firm is minimizing its costs? Explain.

(b) How would the firms that are not minimizing their costs have to alter their use of capital and labor to do so?

2. At the beginning of some time period, it is observed that a firm producing 1,000 bottles of wine per month uses the following inputs of capital (K) and labor (L) per month: $K = 5$ units and $L = 100$ units. The price of capital is $20, and the price of labor is $4 per unit.

As the firm increases its output over a period of time, the following changes in the use of capital and labor are observed:

Output per month	K	L
2,000	10	180
4,000	18	300
6,000	25	400
8,000	34	650
10,000	60	1,000

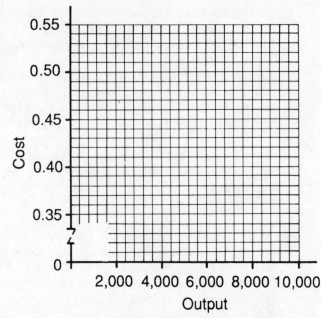

(a) Calculate and graph the long-run average cost curve.

(b) At what output level do long-run increasing returns cease?

*3. A firm is operating in an industry in which it is technologically possible to construct only two classes of plant. The first, Class A, is highly automated and requires an initial investment of $1,000,000; production in this plant takes place at a marginal cost of $3 per unit of output. The Class B plant employs a more labor-intensive production process and therefore requires a relatively smaller fixed cost of $500,000. However, this class of plant has a relatively higher marginal cost of $4 a unit. Thus the total cost curve for each class of plant can be represented by the following equations:

Class A plant: $TC_A = \$1{,}000{,}000 + 3Q$
Class B plant: $TC_B = \$500{,}000 + 4Q$

(a) Plot the firm's long-run average cost curve (i.e., the lowest attainable average cost for each output with plant size variable).

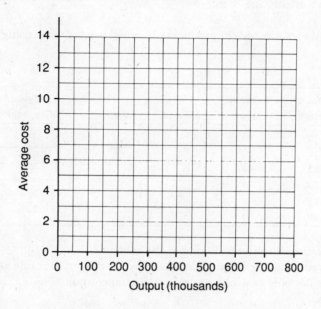

(b) If this firm plans to produce 400,000 units of output, which plant should it employ? Explain.

(c) Over what range of output do economies of scale occur for each class of plant? Why?

4. A firm has four alternative methods of producing 100 gizmos. Each method represents different combinations of three factors: labor, lathe time, and raw materials. The inputs required by each method are given in the following table.

	Method			
	A	B	C	D
Labor hours	100	90	60	80
Lathe hours	25	75	80	70
Raw materials (pounds)	160	150	120	100

(a) Suppose that the price per unit of each factor is $1. Determine the cost of each production method and indicate which is economically efficient.

(b) Suppose that the price of an hour of lathe time increases to $2 (other prices remaining constant). What method(s) would a profit-maximizing firm now use?

(c) Which of these methods is technically inefficient? Explain.

Appendix Exercises

The following exercises are based on material in the appendix to this chapter. Read the appendix before attempting them.

*5. The table shows six methods of producing 10 widgets per month using capital and labor.

Method	Units of capital	Units of labor	ΔCapital	ΔLabor	Estimated MRS of capital for labor
A	10	80			
B	15	58	____	____	____
C	25	40	____	____	____
D	40	24	____	____	____
E	58	15	____	____	____
F	80	9	____	____	____

(a) Complete the last three columns in the table.
(b) On the graph, plot the isoquant indicated by the data in the table. (Assume these are the only feasible methods, and connect points by straight line segments.)

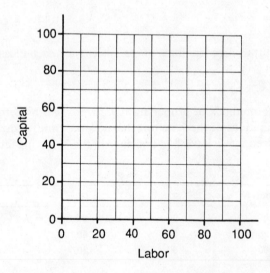

(c) For each of the following price combinations, calculate the slope of the isocost line P_L/P_K and determine the economically efficient method of production by drawing in the minimum isocost line.

	Price of labor	Price of capital	P_L/P_K	Method
(1)	$1,000	$ 500	_____	_____
(2)	1,000	1,000	_____	_____
(3)	1,000	2,000	_____	_____

6. The graph illustrates how several levels of output could be produced with different combinations of capital and labor.

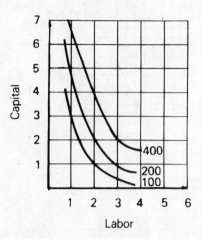

(a) If the relative price of labor to capital were 1, how many units of capital and labor would this firm employ to produce 100 units of output (at minimum cost)?

(b) If the price of capital were to become one-half its original level, and the firm wanted to produce 200 units of output at minimum cost, how much capital and labor would it now employ? Explain.

(c) By examining these three isoquants what, if anything, can be said about returns to scale?

Answers

Multiple-Choice Questions

1. (c)   2. (b)   3. (a)   4. (b)   5. (b)   6. (a)   7. (b)   8. (d)   9. (d)   10. (c)   11. (c)   12. (d)
13. (d)   14. (c)   15. (c)   16. (d)   17. (c)   18. (c)   19. (c)   20. (c)   21. (a)   22. (b)

Exercises

1. (a) Firm A is minimizing costs since, with combination 3, the ratio of the marginal products of capital and labor are equal to the ratio of their cost per unit of the factor employed (6/3 = 10/5).
   (b) Firm B would have to move to combination 1 by using less capital, and thereby raise the MP_K, and more labor, thereby reducing the MP_L. Firm C would have to move to combination 3, increasing MP_K (reducing capital use) and decreasing MP_L (increasing labor use).

2. (a)

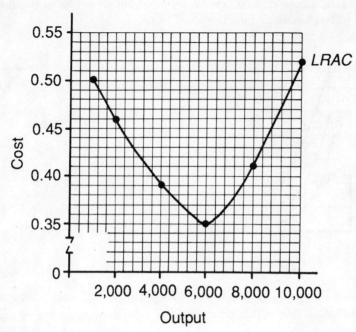

(b) 6,000

*3. (a)

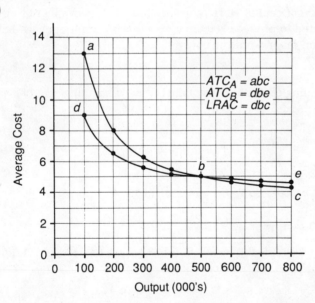

(b) Class B. With a Class A plant, it would cost $2.2 million to produce 400,000 units but only $2.1 million with a Class B plant.

(c) Economies of scale occur over the entire range of output from 1 to infinity. Each total cost curve is characterized by a fixed cost and constant marginal cost. It is easy to determine that average variable cost is also constant (and equal to marginal cost). Under these conditions, average total cost will continuously decrease as output increases because average variable cost is not rising to offset the impact of a declining average fixed cost.

4. (a) Method D is economically efficient. Method A costs $285, B costs $315, C costs $260, and D costs $250.

   (b) Method A, which costs $310. (Method B now costs $390, C costs $340, and D costs $320.)

   (c) Method B is technically inefficient since method D uses fewer units of *each* factor. Thus method B would not be economically efficient under any set of factor prices.

*5. (a)

Method	ΔCapital	ΔLabor	Estimated *MRS* of capital for labor
A	—	—	—
B	+ 5	−22	−0.23
C	+10	−18	−0.56
D	+15	−16	−0.94
E	+18	− 9	−2.00
F	+22	− 6	−3.67

(b)

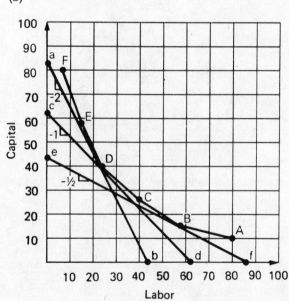

(c) For price combination 1, the relative price of labor to capital is 2, and the minimum isocost line for producing 100 widgets is *ab* in the graph. The tangency of the isocost line and the straight line segment joining *E* and *D* implies that either method E or D could be employed. Combination 2 has a price ratio of 1, and a minimum isocost line *cd*, which implies method D. Combination 3 has a price ratio of 0.5, a minimum isocost line *ef*, and implies that method B is employed.

6. (a) one unit of capital and two units of labor

   (b) The slope of an isocost line is now -2, which yields a tangency with the isoquant representing 200 units of output at approximately two units of capital and two units of labor.

   (c) Yes, these isoquants indicate economies of scale. Take any factor mix such as two units each of capital and labor. Double these to four units of each. Since factor prices are constant, doubling all factors serves to double total cost exactly. However, the combination of four units of each factor lies above the isoquant representing 400 units of output. Therefore, doubling all factors results in more than double the output. A doubling of costs and a more than doubling of output implies that long-run average cost is decreasing.

PART FOUR

Markets and Pricing

Chapter 12

Competitive Markets

Learning Objectives

After studying this chapter, you should be able to:

—understand the distinction between competitive behavior and competitive structure

—explain the behavioral rules for a profit-maximizing firm

—understand why individual competitive firms are price takers and face a horizontal demand curve

—define average revenue, marginal revenue, and price under perfect competition

—explain how the short-run industry supply curve can be derived

—describe the role of entry and exit of firms in achieving long-run market equilibrium

—distinguish short-run and long-run equilibrium of competitive firms and industries

—understand why an industry's response to changing technology depends on whether it is growing or declining

Multiple-Choice Questions

1. A perfectly competitive market structure is best described by firms that
   (a) allocate a substantial share of their budget to advertising
   (b) engage in cutthroat competition by denigrating each others' products
   (c) are subjected to government controls ensuring fair competition
   (d) do not engage in active competitive behavior

2. Which of the following characteristics is *not* an important determinant of the type of market structure?
   (a) the number of sellers and the number of buyers
   (b) whether the firms are foreign-owned transnational corporations
   (c) the firm's ability to influence demand by advertising
   (d) the ease of entry and exit in the industry

3. If output occurs where marginal cost equals marginal revenue, then
   (a) the last unit produced adds the same amount to costs as it does to revenue
   (b) the firm is maximizing profits
   (c) there is no reason to reduce or expand output, as long as TR is greater than or equal to TVC
   (d) all of the above

4. A firm, regardless of market structure, should shut down and suffer a loss equal to its fixed cost if
   (a) average revenue is less than average variable cost
   (b) average revenue is less than average total cost but greater than average variable cost
   (c) total revenue is less than total cost but greater than total variable cost
   (d) its economic profits are negative and smaller in absolute value than total fixed cost

5. Should it decide to produce a positive output, any profit-maximizing firm should produce the output level for which
   (a) the incremental change in revenue equals the incremental change in costs
   (b) total revenue exceeds total costs
   (c) average revenue equals average total costs
   (d) average costs are minimized

6. The assumption that each firm in a perfectly competitive market is a price taker basically means that
   (a) regardless of how much an individual firm produces, it will never have any impact on market price
   (b) the market price is independent of the level of industry output
   (c) each firm's supply curve is perfectly elastic
   (d) for reasonable variations in a single firm's output, the impact on market price is negligible

7. Which one of the following characteristics of a market would you expect to be inconsistent with price-taking behavior?
   (a) There are a large number of firms in the industry.
   (b) Each firm produces a product that is somehow distinguishable from that of its competitors (e.g., in terms of quality or brand name).
   (c) Each firm's share of total industry output is insignificant.
   (d) Each firm behaves as though it faces a perfectly elastic demand curve.

8. A firm that faces a perfectly elastic demand curve has a
   (a) linear total revenue curve with a slope equal to the market price
   (b) horizontal total revenue curve
   (c) constant total revenue regardless of the level of output
   (d) total revenue curve shaped like an inverted U

9. In a perfectly competitive market, each firm's demand curve is coincident with the
   (a) average revenue curve
   (b) marginal revenue curve
   (c) horizontal line drawn at the market price
   (d) all of the above

10. A perfectly competitive firm does not try to sell more of its product by lowering its price below the market price because
    (a) this would be considered unethical price chiseling
    (b) its competitors would not permit it
    (c) its demand is inelastic, so total revenue would decline
    (d) it can sell whatever it produces at the market price

11. Assuming that Rule 1 for profit maximization is satisfied, a perfectly competitive firm is in short-run equilibrium when it produces the output where
    (a) price equals average total cost
    (b) price equals short-run marginal cost
    (c) short-run marginal cost equals average total cost
    (d) all of the above

12. A firm producing a positive output level, covering variable costs but making a loss in the short run,
    (a) is not maximizing profits
    (b) should definitely shut down
    (c) should exit the industry
    (d) may nonetheless be doing the best that it can with respect to profits

Questions 13 to 20 refer to the following graph, which depicts the short-run cost curves of a perfectly competitive firm that currently faces a market price of $9.

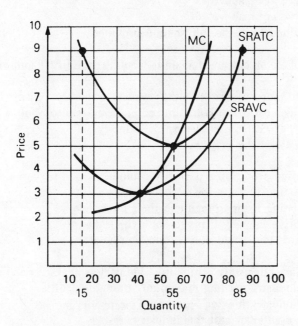

13. The profit-maximizing output of this firm is
    (a) 15   (c) 55
    (b) 70   (d) 85

14. At this output, total costs are equal to
    (a) $135   (c) $630
    (b) $765   (d) $420

15. The firm's total profit is equal to
    (a) $210   (c) $280
    (b) $220   (d) cannot be determined

16. Should the market price fall to $4, this firm will
    (a) shut down and make zero profit
    (b) shut down and suffer a loss equal to fixed cost
    (c) continue operating in the short run and suffer a loss that is less than its fixed cost
    (d) produce 50 units and make a loss equal to total variable cost

17. This firm's maximum attainable profit level would equal zero if
    (a) it were in short-run equilibrium
    (b) it produces any output where marginal cost equals marginal revenue
    (c) the market price were $5
    (d) the market price were $3

18. This firm would shut down production if the market price were below
    (a) $5   (c) marginal cost
    (b) $3   (d) average total cost

19. The short-run supply curve for this firm is its
    (a) marginal cost curve
    (b) marginal cost curve at or above $3
    (c) marginal cost curve at or above $5
    (d) cannot be determined from the information provided

20. With a market price of $5, an output of 55 units would be the firm's long-run equilibrium output if
    (a) it were not possible for this firm to either expand or contract plant size
    (b) its long-run average cost curve is minimized at 55 units of output
    (c) other firms were barred from entering this industry
    (d) this firm could not exit the industry

21. The existence of positive profits in a perfectly competitive industry
    (a) is a signal for existing firms to lower their price
    (b) is a signal for existing firms to maintain their plant size
    (c) provides an incentive for new firms to enter the industry
    (d) encourages all firms to expand their production levels

22. Long-run equilibrium in a perfectly competitive industry is characterized by
    (a) each firm in the industry earning maximum attainable profits
    (b) each firm in the industry making zero economic profits
    (c) no firm desiring to enter or exit this industry
    (d) all of the above

23. The conditions for long-run competitive equilibrium include all but which of the following?
    (a) $P = AVC$ (c) $P = MR$
    (b) $P = MC$ (d) $P = LRAC$

24. When all firms in a perfectly competitive industry are producing at minimum efficient scale and just covering costs,
    (a) it is physically impossible for existing firms to increase output
    (b) new firms could enter, produce at minimum efficient scale, and also cover their costs
    (c) profits could be made only with larger plants
    (d) the industry is in long-run equilibrium

25. Which of the following characteristics is true of a perfectly competitive industry that is subject to continuous technological change?
    (a) Only plants of recent vintage and thus greater efficiency will operate.
    (b) The market price equals the minimum average total cost of the most efficient plants.
    (c) The market price equals the minimum average total cost of the least efficient plant still in use.
    (d) Plants with a greater than average level of efficiency will make positive profits.

Exercises

1. The graph shows the short-run cost situation of a hypothetical perfectly competitive, profit-maximizing firm.
   (a) Fill in the blanks in the table.

If market price is	$10.00	$7.50	$5.50
(i) equilibrium output will be			
At this output,			
(ii) total revenue is			
(iii) total cost is			
(iv) total profit is (+ or −)			
(v) marginal revenue is			
(vi) marginal cost is			
(vii) average total cost is			
(viii) profit per unit is			

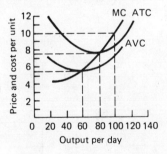

(b) Why is neither $10.00 nor $5.50 the long-run market price?

2. Consider the following information regarding output levels, costs, and market price for two perfectly competitive firms operating in different industries. Each firm has an upward-sloping marginal cost curve.

Firm A: output = 5,000   total variable cost = $2,500
           price = $1.00   total fixed cost   = $2,000
                       marginal cost   = $1.20

Firm B: output = 5,000   average total
                       costs   = $1.00
           price = $1.20   (at their
                       minimum
                       level)

	Firm A	Firm B
(a) Are these firms making profits?	_____	_____
(b) If so, how much?	_____	_____
(c) Are these firms making maximum profits?	_____	_____
(d) Should these firms produce more, less, or the same output? Explain.	_____	_____

3. Output of peanuts in the United States, it is assumed, is 2 million tons in a given year. One of the many producers, Mr. Shell, has experienced a doubling of his output over his previous year's output of 40 tons. All other producers report no change in their output. The market elasticity of demand is estimated to be 0.20.

(a) Calculate the effect on the world price of peanuts from Mr. Shell's increase in output (in percentage terms).

(b) Calculate the elasticity of demand Mr. Shell's firm faces.

(c) Does your answer for (b) indicate that the firm is likely to act as a price taker? Explain.

4. The following graphs present the marginal cost curves of three firms, which, for simplicity, are assumed to be the only firms in a perfectly competitive industry. Minimum average variable costs for the three firms are as follows: Firm A, $3; Firm B, $5; Firm C, $7. Further, minimum average total costs are as follows: Firm A, $5; Firm B, $7; Firm C, $8.

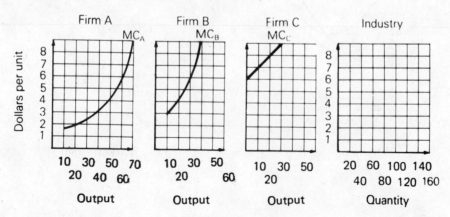

(a) Derive the industry short-run supply curve, and plot it in the industry grid.

(b) If the market price is $6.50, what is the quantity supplied by this industry, and what is the output of each of the three firms? (approximate answers)

(c) For each of the three firms, indicate if it is making a profit or a loss.

5. This exercise traces some of the long-run adjustments that take place in a perfectly competitive market in response to a change in demand (we ignore adjustments that current firms may make to plant size). Assume that each firm currently in this industry, as well as each potential entrant, has the cost structure depicted in panel (i) of the following graph (where the notation is identical to that in the text). Panel (ii) shows the industry's short-run supply curve S and the current market demand curve D.

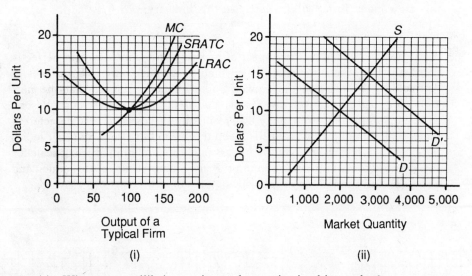

Output of a Typical Firm	Market Quantity
(i)	(ii)

(a) What are equilibrium price and quantity in this market?

(b) What is the output of each firm in this industry, and what is the resulting level of profit?

(c) How many firms are operating in this industry?

(d) Is the industry in long-run equilibrium? Explain.

(e) Now suppose that the demand for this good shifts to D'. What are the new equilibrium market price and quantity in the short run?

(f) What is the short-run quantity response of each firm in the industry?

(g) What is each firm's profit in this short-run equilibrium?

(h) Explain what will happen to the industry short-run supply curve once sufficient time has elapsed for entry and exit to occur.

(i) Once the new long-run equilibrium is established, what are the market price and quantity?

(j) What are the level of output and associated profit of each firm in the new long-run equilibrium?

(k) How many firms will be active in this industry?

*6. This exercise addresses the impact of a change in technology in a perfectly competitive market. For simplicity we shall consider only two vintages of technology, the old and the new. For the moment, assume that the new technology has not yet been invented, so that all firms employ the current (soon to be old) production technology that results in the cost structure depicted in panel (i) of the following graph. To keep the graph tidy, the *LRAC* curve has not been drawn; however, you should assume that minimum efficient scale for these firms occurs at 10 units of output. Panel (ii) provides the market demand curve (*D*) and the industry short-run supply curve (*S*).

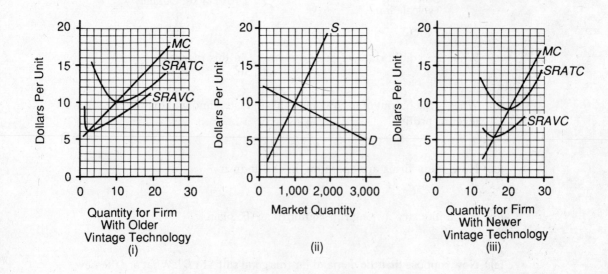

(a) What are the long-run equilibrium market price and quantity?

(b) What is each firm's output and profit level in the long-run equilibrium? How many firms are in the industry?

(c) Now suppose that a new technology is invented so that any firm now entering this industry can do so with the cost structure depicted in panel (iii). Assume that the minimum efficient scale for these firms occurs at 20 units of output. Will new firms enter the industry? Explain.

(d) When will entry into this industry cease?

(e) In the new long-run equilibrium,
  (i) what are market price and quantity?

  (ii) what are the output level and profit of firms using the newer-vintage technology?

  (iii) what are the output level and profit of firms employing the older-vintage technology?

  (iv) how many firms in the industry use the newer technology and how many use the older, less efficient technology?

(f) Should all of the plants using the less efficient technology be replaced by those with the newer production technology?

Answers

Multiple-Choice Questions

1. (d) 2. (b) 3. (d) 4. (a) 5. (a) 6. (d) 7. (b) 8. (a) 9. (d) 10. (d) 11. (b) 12. (d)
13. (b) 14. (d) 15. (a) 16. (c) 17. (c) 18. (b) 19. (b) 20. (b) 21. (c) 22. (d) 23. (a)
24. (d) 25. (b)

Exercises

1. (a)
   (i)   100; 80; 60   (v) $10.00; $7.50; $5.50
   (ii) $1,000; $600; $330   (vi) $10.00; $7.50; $5.50
   (iii) $800; $600; $480   (vii) $8.00; $7.50; $8.00
   (iv) $200; 0; −$150   (viii) $2.00; 0; −$2.50

   (b) At $10.00, profits will induce entry; at $5.50, losses will induce exit of firms, so the industry supply curve shifts.

2. (a) Yes, for both firms
    (b) Firm A: $500; Firm B: $1,000
    (c) No, for both firms. Neither firm is producing where $P = MC$ (note that for Firm B, $MC = \$1$ because at minimum ATC, $ATC = MC$).
    (d) Firm A should produce less output. At current output $P < MC$; since P is constant for a perfectly competitive firm and MC is positively sloped, a decrease in output changes MC toward P. For Firm B, $P > MC$; this firm will therefore maximize profits by producing more output.

3. (a) The market elasticity of demand (η) is given by the formula

$$\eta = \frac{\text{percentage change in output}}{\text{percentage change in price}}$$

Here,

$$0.20 = \frac{40/2,000,000}{\text{percentage change in price}}$$

Thus, the percentage change in price = 0.0001.

    (b) The firm's elasticity of demand is the percentage change in the output of the firm divided by the percentage change in the price [calculated in (a)]. This is equal to

$$\frac{40/60}{0.0001} = 6,667$$

    (c) Yes. For practical purposes the elasticity is (negative) infinity (perfectly elastic), and the firm has no effect on price.

4. (a)

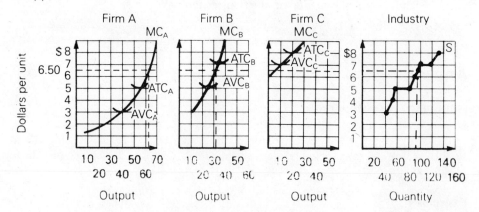

Each firm's short-run supply curve corresponds to the portion of its MC curve that is greater than or equal to AVC. Thus no firm produces at a price less than $3. Between $3 and just slightly below $5, only Firm A produces output. When the price hits $5, Firm B abruptly raises output from zero to approximately 25 units—this explains the horizontal segment of the industry supply curve at $5. Similarly, the discrete jump in output by Firm C when price reaches $7 explains the other horizontal segment of the industry supply curve. As the number of firms in the industry increases, these discrete jumps in output by additional firms coming on line would become small relative to total industry output, so the industry supply curve would be much smoother.

(b) At a market price of $6.50, Firm A produces approximately 62.5 units and Firm B, approximately 32.5 units. Since the market price is less than Firm C's AVC (at every level of output), it shuts down and produces no output in the short run. Thus the quantity supplied by the industry at this price is approximately 95 units.

(c) Firm C is making a loss equal to its fixed cost. Firm A is making a profit, but we do not have enough information to determine how much. At 62.5 units of output, we do not know the level of Firm A's ATC. However, we do know that the ATC curve is rising at this output because it is to the right of minimum ATC. Since ATC is rising, $MC(=P)$ is greater than ATC, and profit is therefore positive. For Firm B, price is greater than AVC (same reason as before) but less than ATC. Firm B is therefore making a loss that is less than its fixed cost. Again, we cannot determine the magnitude of the loss because the information provided does not indicate the level of AVC at 32.5 units of output.

5.

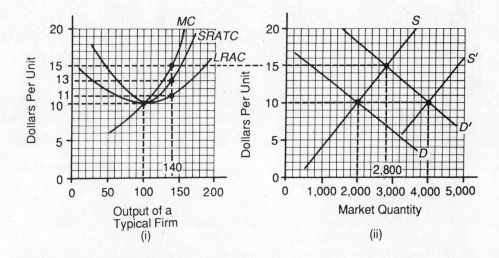

(a) $10 and 2,000 units, respectively

(b) Each firm produces 100 units of output (i.e., where $MC = MR = P = \$10$). Since at an output of 100 units average revenue (P) equals $SRATC$, profits are therefore equal to zero.

(c) 20 (= 2,000/100)

(d) Yes. The typical firm is producing where $MC = MR$ and is on its $LRAC$ curve; thus it is producing the profit-maximizing output at the lowest attainable cost. Further, since the level of economic profit is zero, there is no incentive for new firms to enter or old firms to exit.

(e) $15 and 3,000 units, respectively

(f) At a market price of $15, each existing firm increases output to 140 units where $P = MC$.

(g) Each firm's total revenue is $2,100 (i.e., 15×140). The average total cost of producing 140 units (given that the firm cannot adjust plant size) is $13.

Thus total cost is $1,820 ($13 × 140). Therefore, short-run profit for each firm is $2,100 − $1,820 = $280.

(h) Since industry profits are positive, new firms will enter. This entry is captured in the graph by the industry short-run supply curve shifting to the right and thereby lowering price.

(i) Long-run equilibrium obtains when each firm is doing the best that it can and there is no incentive for further entry. Both conditions are satisfied when price is again equal to $10 at the intersection of the new demand curve D' and a new industry short-run supply curve (e.g., S' in the graph). The associated equilibrium market quantity is 4,000 units.

(j) Each firm produces 100 units and earns an economic profit equal to zero, which is the same as the initial long-run equilibrium position of each firm in (b).

(k) The difference with the initial long-run equilibrium is that there will be more firms in the industry; specifically, there will be 40 firms (4,000/100).

6.

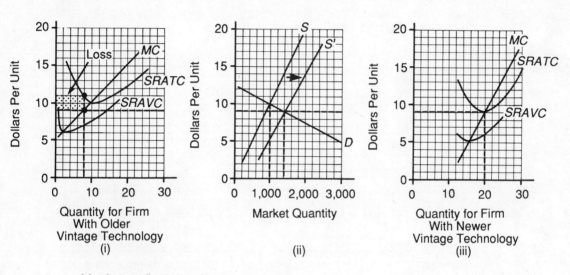

Quantity for Firm With Older Vintage Technology (i)

Market Quantity (ii)

Quantity for Firm With Newer Vintage Technology (iii)

(a) $10 and 1,000 units, respectively

(b) Each firm produces 10 units of output and makes zero profits. There are 100 firms in the industry (i.e., 1,000/10).

(c) Yes. A firm entering with the new technology faces the same price as the existing firms, and by producing 20.5 units (where $MR = MC$ for the newer plants), it can make a positive profit; at this output, average revenue is greater than average total cost.

(d) Entry will cease when profits of a potential entrant are driven to zero. This occurs when the market price is $9, implying that plants of recent vintage would operate at minimum efficient scale.

(e) (i) $9 and 1,400 units, respectively
     (ii) 20 units of output and zero profit
     (iii) 8 units of output and a loss of $16
     (iv) Since total revenue exceeds total variable cost for plants employing
           the older technology, all 100 of these firms remain in the industry.
           Total output by these firms is therefore 800 units (100 × 8), which
           leaves 600 units that are produced by the newer-vintage plants (1,400
           − 800). Each of these produces 20 units, so there are 30 plants with
           the new technology.

(f) No. The market value of the output of each of these firms is $72 ($9 × 8),
     greater than the value of resources that are currently used to produce this
     output (i.e., total variable cost), which is $63.

Chapter 13

Monopoly

Learning Objectives

After studying this chapter, you should be able to:

—explain the relationship between price and marginal revenue for a monopolist

—relate marginal revenue, total revenue, and elasticity

—illustrate potential monopoly profits in any competitive equilibrium

—distinguish between natural and created barriers to entry

—explain why cartels tend to develop and the reasons for their instability

—define price discrimination and identify conditions that make price discrimination both possible and profitable

Multiple-Choice Questions

1. A fundamental feature of a monopolistic market is that the firm
   (a) can sell any quantity it desires
   (b) can obtain any price for any quantity of output
   (c) faces a perfectly inelastic demand curve
   (d) faces the price and quantity trade-off depicted by market demand

2. For the single-price monopolist, the average revenue curve
   (a) is a horizontal line drawn at the market price
   (b) is the same as the market demand curve
   (c) is the same as the marginal revenue curve
   (d) does not exist

3. If average revenue declines as output increases, marginal revenue
   (a) must increase
   (b) must also decline and be less than average revenue
   (c) must also decline because it is equal to average revenue
   (d) must also decline and be greater than average revenue

4. Since the profit-maximizing monopolist produces the output where marginal cost equals marginal revenue, we can conclude that
   (a) $P = MC$ (c) $P > MC$
   (b) $P = MR$ (d) $P < MR$

5. As long as marginal cost is positive, a monopolist will be operating
   (a) on the elastic portion of the demand curve
   (b) where demand is unit-elastic and total revenue for the market is therefore at a maximum
   (c) on the inelastic portion of the demand curve
   (d) on any portion of the demand curve, depending on the supply curve

6. A linear downward-sloping demand curve has a marginal revenue curve that is
   (a) itself linear, with the same price intercept as the demand curve and half the quantity intercept
   (b) coincident with the average revenue curve
   (c) horizontal
   (d) itself linear, with half the slope of the demand curve

7. A single-price monopoly is able to make positive profits only if the average total cost curve
   (a) intersects the demand curve
   (b) is tangent to the demand curve
   (c) declines over a substantial portion of market demand
   (d) lies above the marginal revenue curve

8. In perfect competition, the industry short-run supply curve is the horizontal summation of the marginal cost curves (above AVC) of all of the firms in the industry. In monopoly, the short-run supply curve
   (a) is the single firm's marginal cost curve
   (b) is the portion of the single firm's marginal cost curve that lies above average variable cost
   (c) the downward-sloping segment of the average total cost curve
   (d) does not exist

Questions 9 to 12 refer to the following graph, which depicts the marginal cost curve of a monopoly and the market demand it faces.

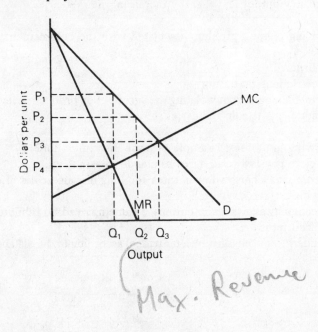

Max. Revenue

9. The monopolist's profit-maximizing output is
   (a) Q_1 (c) Q_3
   (b) Q_2 (d) cannot be determined

10. The price set by the monopolist for the profit-maximizing output is
    (a) P_1 (c) P_3
    (b) P_2 (d) P_4

11. The level of output that corresponds to maximum revenue is
    (a) Q_1 (c) Q_3
    (b) Q_2 (d) cannot be determined

12. A monopolist that is able to practice perfect price discrimination will produce output
    (a) Q_1 (c) Q_3
    (b) Q_2 (d) cannot be determined

13. If a firm's minimum efficient scale occurs at an average cost of $4 and an output of 4 million units, the quantity demanded at a price of $4 is 3 million units, and the demand curve is downward-sloping, then
    (a) the firm is a natural monopoly
    (b) the firm's profits can be sustained only if it creates barriers to entry
    (c) it is always impossible for the firm to make positive profits regardless of the output level
    (d) the firm always breaks even

14. Barriers to entry, which sustain a monopoly, may be due to all but which of the following?
    (a) economies of scale   (c) long-run increasing average costs
    (b) patent laws   (d) large set-up costs

15. A cartel increases the industry's profits by
    (a) fully capturing all economies of scale
    (b) ceasing all active competitive behavior with respect to price
    (c) agreeing to sell all current output at an agreed-upon fixed price
    (d) decreasing industry output and thereby increasing market price

16. Which of the following is *not* a problem associated with the enforcement of a successful cartel?
    (a) entry of new firms
    (b) government restrictions on output
    (c) preventing cartel members from violating the agreed-upon production level
    (d) convincing other firms to join the cartel

17. Which of the following is the best example of price discrimination?
    (a) Some air travelers pay lower air fares as standby passengers.
    (b) A telephone company charges lower rates for long-distance calls after midnight than during the day.
    (c) A local transit company allows senior citizens, the unemployed, and children to ride at reduced fares.
    (d) The London underground charges each individual according to the distance traveled.

18. Price discrimination is possible because
    (a) different individuals are willing to pay different amounts for the same commodity
    (b) different individuals have different incomes
    (c) each individual is willing to pay a different amount for each successive unit of the same commodity
    (d) both (a) and (c)

19. Price discrimination increases a monopoly's profits because it
    (a) increases the willingness of households to pay for a good
    (b) allows the firm to capture some consumers' surplus
    (c) allows the firm to exploit economies of scale more fully
    (d) shifts the demand curve the firm faces

20. Which of the following is *not* true of price discrimination?
    (a) Output is generally larger than under a single-price monopoly.
    (b) Any given level of output yields a larger revenue.
    (c) To be successful, resale must be impossible or prevented.
    (d) Lower-income individuals must be charged lower prices.

21. Perfect price discrimination implies that
    (a) demand is perfectly elastic
    (b) the firm is perfectly able to prevent resale among customers
    (c) the firm sells each unit at a different price and captures all consumers' surplus
    (d) all of the above

Exercises

1. The graph shows the demand and unit cost situation of a monopolist.

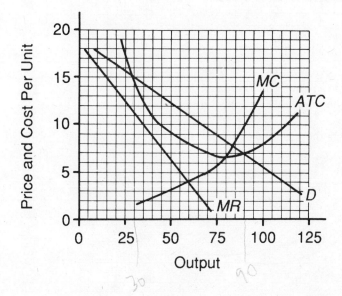

(a) What is the output where the firm's profits are at a maximum? _____
(b) What is the price at this output? _____
(c) What is the total revenue at this output? _____
(d) What are the total costs? _____
(e) What are the economic profits? _____
(f) Within what range of output is there at least *some* economic profit? _____

2. The following data relate to a monopolistic firm and its product.
   (a) Calculate marginal cost (*MC*), marginal revenue (*MR*), total revenue (*TR*), and profit to complete the table.

Output	Total cost	Price	Quantity demanded	MC	MR	TR	Profit
0	$20	$20	0				
1	24	18	1	____	____	____	____
2	27	16	2	____	____	____	____
3	32	14	3	____	____	____	____
4	39	12	4	____	____	____	____
5	48	10	5	____	____	____	____
6	59	8	6	____	____	____	____

   (b) Plot average revenue (*AR*), *MR*, and *MC* in panel (i), *TC* and *TR* in panel (ii).

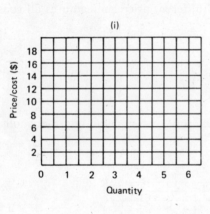
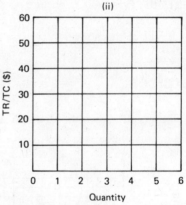

   (c) What is the profit-maximizing output (whole units)? _____
   (d) At what price will the monopolist sell the product (whole units)? _____
   (e) What are the monopolist's economic profits? _____

3. The graph shows the cost and revenue curves for a monopolist.

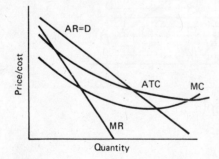

(a) Illustrate on the graph the price the profit-maximizing monopolist will set and the quantity that will be sold. (Label the P_M and Q_M.)

(b) Indicate monopoly profits by vertical hatching, ⅏⅏⅏ .

(c) Suppose that the monopolist, to be allocatively efficient, sets price (AR) equal to marginal cost. Label the price P_E and the output Q_E. Would this output be sustainable in the long run? Explain with reference to the costs the monopolist faces in the graph.

*4. Some of the basic cost data for a monopolist are given in the following table.

Output	Total cost
0	$ 40
5	50
10	65
15	90
20	130
25	190
30	275

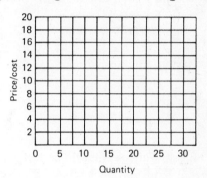

The demand schedule is given by $Q^D = 20 - 1.0P$, where Q^D is quantity demanded and P is average revenue or price.

(a) Compute and graph the average total cost, marginal cost, and average revenue curves. (Noting that the MR curve intersects the horizontal axis at half the output of the demand curve intersection, draw the MR curve.)

(b) Show the profit-maximizing monopolist's profits by shading in the appropriate area.

5. This exercise focuses on price discrimination. A local amusement park has estimated the following demand curves for its new roller coaster ride, the Double-Loop Monster:

$$Q_a = 1,000,000 - 125,000P_a$$

$$Q_c = 8,000,000 - 500,000P_c$$

where Q_a and Q_c are the annual quantity demanded of rides by adults and children, respectively, and P_a and P_c are the prices charged to each of these groups. The marginal cost of every additional rider on the Double-Loop Monster is calculated to be $1, regardless of the age of the rider. Use the grids to determine the profit-maximizing prices for the amusement park. Indicate (approximately) the number of rides taken by each group.

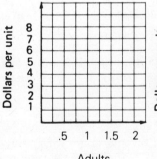

Adults
quantity (millions)

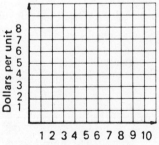

Children
quantity (millions)

*6. This exercise focuses on the cartelization of a perfectly competitive industry.
     The graph on the left presents the cost structure for one of many identical firms
     in a perfectly competitive industry. On the right you are given the market
     demand curve and the industry supply curve, which (you should recall) is the
     horizontal summation of the marginal cost curves of all firms in the industry.

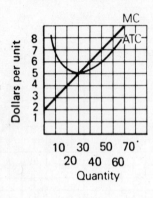
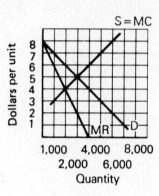

(a) Suppose that the industry is in long-run competitive equilibrium.
     (i)   What are market price and quantity?

     (ii)   What is the output of each firm?

     (iii) What is the profit of each firm?

(b) Now suppose that all firms in the industry collude by forming a cartel to
     maximize joint profits. What market price and quantity maximize profits
     for the cartel?

(c) What output would the cartel instruct each firm to produce?

(d) What is the level of profits for each firm in the cartel?

(e) Given the market price established by the cartel, what output would an
     individual firm like to produce? What are the associated profits? Explain.

7.   The following graph applies to a monopoly. *AL* is the market demand curve
     and *AK* the marginal revenue curve. *EH* is the long-run supply curve for the
     industry, and the *LRAC* = *LRMC* for the monopolist. (There are no significant
     economies of scale or scope. It is a constant cost industry, and to change output
     the monopolist would simply shut down or open plants that had each previously
     been competitive firms.)

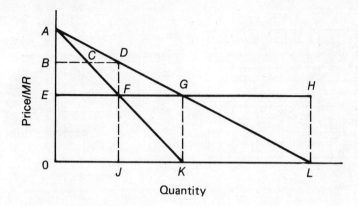

(a) Assume that the monopolist sets a single price and maximizes profits.
Predict the following:
(i) the monopolistic price _____ and output _____
(ii) the amount of consumer surplus at that price _____
(iii) the amount of economic profits at that price _____

(b) Assume that a discriminating monopolist is able to obtain the maximum
price for each unit. Predict the following:
(i) the price range, from _____ to _____
(ii) the output _____
(iii) the amount of consumers' surplus _____
(iv) the amount of economic profits _____

Answers

Multiple-Choice Questions

1. (d) 2. (b) 3. (b) 4. (c) 5. (a) 6. (a) 7. (a) 8. (d) 9. (a) 10. (a) 11. (b) 12. (c)
13. (a) 14. (c) 15. (d) 16. (b) 17. (c) 18. (d) 19. (b) 20. (d) 21. (c)

Exercises

1. (a) 60   (d) $480
   (b) $11   (e) $180
   (c) $660   (f) output: 30 to 90 units;
                                           price is $15 to $7

2. (a)

Output	MC	MR	TR	Profit
0			$ 0	$ -20
	$ 4	$18		
1			18	-6
	3	14		
2			32	5
	5	10		
3			42	10
	7	6		
4			48	9
	9	2		
5			50	2
	11	-2		
6			48	-11

(b)

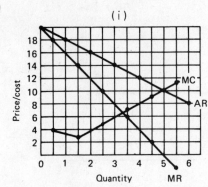

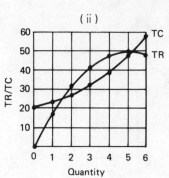

(c) 3 units
(d) $14 (price to sell output where $MR = MC$)
(e) At 3 units of output, TR is $42, TC is $32, and profits are $10.

3. (a) and (b)

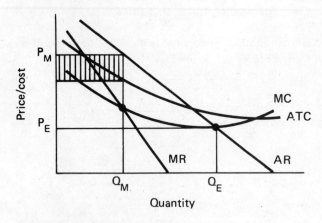

(c) No, it would not, because the ATC exceeds the price, so business could not be sustained for long.

*4. (a) and (b)

Output	ATC	MC	P = AR
0	—		$20
		$ 2	
5	$10.0		15
		3	
10	6.5		10
		5	
15	6.0		5
		8	
20	6.5		0
		12	
25	7.6		—
		17	
30	9.2		—

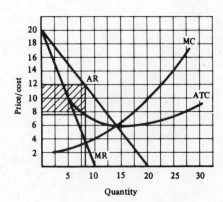

5.

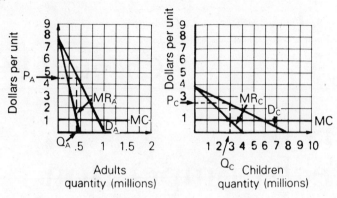

Adults
quantity (millions)

Children
quantity (millions)

*6. (a) (i) $5 and 3,000 units, respectively
        (ii) 30 units
        (iii) zero profits
    (b) $6 and 2,000 units, respectively
    (c) 20 units; where *MC* of each firm equals market *MR* of $4.
    (d) $10. At 20 units of output, average revenue is $6 and average total cost
        is $5.50.
    (e) The output of any individual firm constitutes an insignificant share of total
        output (in this example, one-hundredth), so market price is negligibly
        affected by changes in any single firm's output. Therefore, each firm
        behaves as a price taker and would like to produce 40 units where marginal
        cost is equal to marginal revenue for the firm. The resulting profit level
        would be $20 =($6 − $5.50) × 40.

7. (a) (i) *OB, OJ* (ii) *ABD* (iii) *BDEF*
    (b) (i) *OA* to *OE* (ii) *OK* (iii) zero (iv) *AEG*

Chapter 14

Patterns of Imperfect Competition

Learning Objectives

After studying this chapter, you should be able to:

—explain how imperfectly competitive market structures differ from the perfectly competitive and monopoly models

—explain the importance of product differentiation in monopolistically competitive markets

—distinguish the different types of collusion and their behavioral implications

—understand why oligopolistic prices tend to be sticky, not changing continually as free market prices do

—understand that profits in oligopolistic industries can persist in the long run only if there are significant barriers to entry

Multiple-Choice Questions

1. A concentration ratio is intended to measure
   (a) how much of an industry is concentrated in central Canada
   (b) the number of firms in an industry
   (c) how much production in a given market is controlled by a few firms
   (d) how much of a given industry is concentrated in the hands of foreign-owned transnational corporations

2. Neither the model of perfect competition nor that of monopoly provides a completely satisfactory description of the Canadian economy because there are significant sectors of the economy with
   (a) many small firms that still have some price-setting ability
   (b) only a few small firms
   (c) many firms, but with a disproportionate amount of production concentrated in the hands of a few
   (d) all of the above

3. Firms that sell a differentiated product (such as Burger King and Harvey's Hamburgers) each
   (a) face a downward-sloping demand curve
   (b) have some ability to administer price
   (c) receive information on market conditions through changes in quantity sold at the set price
   (d) all of the above

4. Which of the following is *not* a characteristic of a market that features monopolistic competition?
   (a) There is a large number of firms.
   (b) Each firm faces a downward-sloping demand curve.
   (c) The firms sell an identical product.
   (d) There is freedom of entry and exit.

5. The excess capacity theorem in monopolistic competition
   (a) means that these firms will not be producing at minimum average total cost in the long-run equilibrium.
   (b) implies that the trade-off for product variety is a higher unit production cost
   (c) arises because of the assumptions of freedom of entry and downward-sloping demand curves
   (d) all of the above

6. In the sense used in this chapter, administered prices are
   (a) prices determined by international forces
   (b) prices controlled by the government
   (c) prices determined by market forces
   (d) set by individual firms rather than in response to market forces

7. An important feature that distinguishes monopolistic competition from perfect competition is that
   (a) monopolistic competitors sell a differentiated product rather than a homogeneous one
   (b) the monopolistic competitor's demand curve is the same as the market demand curve
   (c) in long-run equilibrium, monopolistic competitors earn economic profits, whereas perfectly competitive firms do not
   (d) there are important barriers to entry in monopolistic competition

8. An important prediction of monopolistic competition is that the long-run equilibrium output of the firm is
   (a) where price exceeds average total cost
   (b) less than the point at which average total cost is at a minimum
   (c) less than the point at which average total cost equals average revenue
   (d) less than the point at which marginal cost equals marginal revenue

Questions 9 and 10 refer to the following graph.

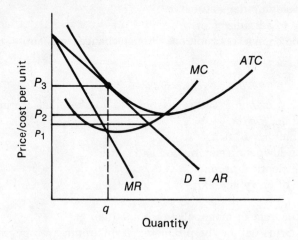

9. The firm in monopolistic competition will set its price equal to
    (a) P_1 (c) P_3
    (b) P_2 (d) minimum MC

10. The situation described by price P_3 and output q is
    (a) a long-run equilibrium in perfect competition since there are no economic
         profits
    (b) a long-run equilibrium in monopolistic competition
    (c) unstable; new firms will enter the industry to eliminate economic profits
    (d) not the profit-maximizing output for a monopolistic competitor

11. The feature that distinguishes perfect competition from all other market
    structures is that competitive firms
    (a) face negatively sloped demand curves
    (b) sell an identical product and are price takers
    (c) actively compete through various forms of nonprice competition such as
         advertising
    (d) administer their prices

12. In some markets, there may be room for only a few firms because
    (a) of economies of scale and scope
    (b) the industry produces a homogeneous good
    (c) individual firms face perfectly elastic demand curves
    (d) all of the above

13. A noncooperative equilibrium among oligopolistic firms
    (a) tends to be unstable because each firm has an incentive to cut price and
         increase output
    (b) is the same outcome that a single monopoly firm would reach if it owned
         all the firms in the industry
    (c) results in each firm producing more, but earning less, than it would in a
         cooperative equilibrium
    (d) maximizes joint profits for the firms in the industry

14. Other things being equal, oligopolistic industries are likely to come closer to the joint profit-maximizing output level
    (a) the greater the number of firms in the industry
    (b) when the industry's market is growing rather than contracting
    (c) when other firms can easily enter the industry
    (d) if the product can be easily differentiated

15. Which of the following contributed to OPEC's collapse as an output-restricting cartel in the late 1980s?
    (a) new productive capacity by non-OPEC countries
    (b) individual OPEC members producing in excess of their quotas
    (c) development of substitute products and new technologies more efficient in their use of oil
    (d) all of the above

16. "Stickiness" in oligopoly theory refers to the fact that
    (a) oligopolists tend to stick together
    (b) profit levels of competing oligopolists tend to rise and fall together
    (c) oligopolistic firms tend to keep price constant and vary quantity in response to cyclical demand shifts
    (d) for oligopolistic firms, demand and supply tend to shift together

17. Oligopolistic prices ordinarily change
    (a) whenever there are changes in production costs
    (b) with seasonal fluctuations in demand
    (c) in response to large, unexpected shifts in demand
    (d) all of the above

18. One explanation of the observed "saucer-shaped" cost curves is
    (a) decreasing costs
    (b) indivisibility of the fixed factor
    (c) variations in output below full capacity accomplished by reducing both labor and capital
    (d) sticky prices

19. One implication of saucer-shaped cost curves is that oligopolistic firms tend to receive their signals on market conditions from
    (a) prices   (c) volume of sales
    (b) profit levels   (d) Statistics Canada

20. Holding price constant in the face of short-term fluctuations in demand
    (a) can never be profitable
    (b) is a frequent occurrence in competitive markets
    (c) can be profitable only if the cost of announcing new prices (e.g., through catalog changes) is prohibitive
    (d) can be profitable if average costs are stable over the range of output fluctuations

21. As long as output remains over the range of the cost curve that is flat, an increase in an oligopolistic firm's demand will be followed by
    (a) an increase in price only
    (b) an increase in both price and quantity
    (c) an increase in quantity only
    (d) no change in either sticky price or quantity

22. Which of the following qualify as possible barriers to entry that oligopolistic firms may erect?
    (a) production of many competing brands of a good by a single firm
    (b) large advertising budgets
    (c) a credible threat to engage in predatory pricing
    (d) all of the above

23. Economic profits can exist in an oligopolistic industry in the long run because of
    (a) natural barriers to entry
    (b) barriers created by existing firms
    (c) barriers created by government policy
    (d) all of the above

24. According to the theory of contestable markets,
    (a) the mere threat of potential entry encourages oligopolists to hold profits near the competitive level
    (b) firms must actually enter an industry if prices and outputs are to be held near the competitive level
    (c) many firms in an industry make it contestable
    (d) high costs of entry make markets more contestable

Appendix Questions

The following questions are based on material in the appendix to this chapter. Read the appendix before answering these questions.

25. Which of the following is *not* a reason for oligopolistic price stickiness?
    (a) tacit collusion
    (b) economies of scope
    (c) the kinked demand curve
    (d) the costs of changing quoted prices

26. The kinked demand curve is based on the assumption that each oligopolist conjectures that its rivals will match
    (a) its price increases but not price decreases
    (b) its price decreases but not price increases
    (c) all of its price changes
    (d) all of its changes in output

Exercises

1. The graph describes a firm in a monopolistically competitive industry characterized by easy entry, product differentiation, and a large number of firms.

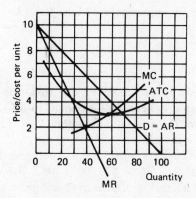

    (a) What price will a profit-maximizing firm set? _____
    (b) What total economic profit will this firm receive? _____
    (c) Given that entry is relatively easy, is this a long-run equilibrium situation? Explain.

    (d) Which curves will be affected and in which direction if the firm now increases its advertising expenditures by a fixed amount, causing increased sales?

    (e) If new firms were attracted to this industry, what curves in the graph would be affected the most? Why? What would be the *main* consequence for this firm?

    (f) Explain how the result in (e) illustrates the excess capacity theorem.

2. A firm has the choice of constructing a plant with either of the average variable cost curves shown in the accompanying graph.

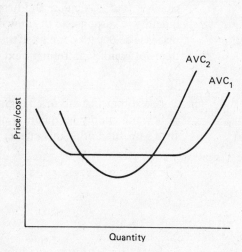

(a) If there were considerable uncertainty about demand for the product, which plant would the firm choose to build? Why?

(b) What does the shape of AVC_1 suggest about the nature of the fixed factors in this plant?

*3. The saucer-shaped (flat) average cost curve discussed in the text can be represented in the relevant range of output (where AVC is equal to MC) by a total cost function that takes the form $TC = a + bQ$, where $a = TFC$, $b = MC = AVC$, and $Q =$ output per month.

  (a) Assume the firm's "normal" demand curve is $Q = 5,000 - 100P$ and that its total cost curve in the relevant range is $TC = \$20,000 + 10Q$. Use the following grid to derive the firm's normal profit-maximizing price and quantity and the resulting level of monthly profits.

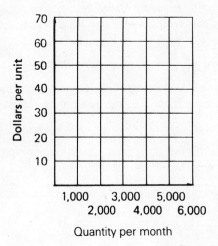

  (b) Now suppose that there is a temporary shift in monthly demand to $Q = 6,000 - 100P$. Calculate the firm's profit when it changes both price and quantity in response to the new demand. Assume that the cost of changing prices is $3,000 (this includes the cost of readjusting price when "normal" demand conditions return next month).

  (c) Suppose that instead of changing price, the firm adopted a sticky price policy and simply let quantity adjust to clear the market. Determine the firm's profits under this strategy.

4. Use economic analysis to discuss each of the following events described in newspaper headlines. Use supply and demand diagrams to the extent possible.
   (a) "Prices of Petroleum Products Rise As OPEC Restricts Oil Supplies" (1974)
   "OPEC Plans Further Restrictions on Oil Supplies to Maintain Prices" (1983)
   "Oil Prices Plummet with OPEC Price War" (1986)

   (b) "Coffee Growers Agree on Marketing Program That Could Lift Prices" (1980)
   "Cracks in World Coffee Pact Appear As Demand Declines and Production Increases" (1983)
   "Brazil Drought Buoys Coffee Market" (1986)

   (c) "Spurred by Rise in Postal Rates, Publishers Expand Use of Private Delivery Systems" (1980s)

   (d) " 'Rent-a-Wreck' Used-Car Rental Agency Competes with Hertz and Avis for Car Rentals" (1978)

Appendix Exercise

The following exercise is based on material in the appendix to this chapter. Read the appendix before attempting the exercise.

*5. Suppose that D is the demand curve for an oligopoly firm if all the firms in the industry act together, and that d is the demand curve for the firm when it alone in the industry varies its price. Assume that the price is now $2.

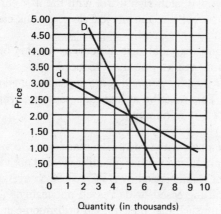

(a) If the firm lowers its price from $2.00 to $1.50 and no other firm does, its sales will go from _____ to _____, and total revenue will go from _____ to _____ .

(b) If the firm lowers its price from $2.00 to $1.50 and every other firm does too, its sales will go from _____ to _____, and total revenue will go from _____ to _____ .

(c) If the firm raises its price from $2.00 to $2.50 and no other firm does, its sales will go from _____ to _____ , and its total revenue will go from _____ to _____ .

(d) If the firm raises its price from $2.00 to $2.50 and every other firm does too, its revenue will go from _____ to _____ .

(e) Assuming that this firm has a fairly level variable cost of about 75 cents in the relevant range of output, under what circumstances, if any, would the manager consider raising the price? Lowering it?

(f) Does this situation encourage collusive action by the firms in the industry to raise prices together? _____ To lower prices together? _____ .

Answers

Multiple-Choice Questions

1. (c) 2. (d) 3. (d) 4. (c) 5. (d) 6. (d) 7. (a) 8. (b) 9. (c) 10. (b) 11. (b) 12. (a) 13. (c) 14. (b) 15. (d) 16. (c) 17. (c) 18. (c) 19. (c) 20. (d) 21. (c) 22. (d) 23. (d) 24. (a) 25. (b) 26. (b)

Exercises

1. (a) $6.00
   (b) ($6.00 − $3.50) × 40 = $100.00
   (c) No. The entry of new firms will reduce economic profits.
   (d) The ATC curve rises; the D curve will shift rightward, with the MR curve shifting accordingly. The MC curve will be unchanged since, in this case, advertising is a fixed amount.
   (e) The average revenue (demand) and marginal revenue curves for this firm would shift leftward, and economic profits would be reduced.
   (f) The leftward shift of the downward-sloping demand curve produces tangency with the declining part of ATC. This must be at less than capacity, which is defined as output at which ATC is minimum.

2. (a) The firm would likely choose the plant with AVC_1. If demand were to vary considerably, the average cost of producing various quantities would not vary considerably, whereas with a plant characterized by AVC_2, costs, on average, could rise considerably if demand increased or decreased noticeably.
   (b) It suggests that the fixed factors are such that their rate of utilization can be varied so as to keep the variable-to-fixed factor ratio constant or close to constant.

*3. (a)

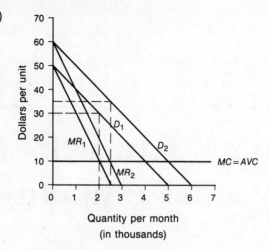

Quantity per month
(in thousands)

This demand curve is labeled D_1 in the graph, and has an associated marginal revenue curve labeled MR_1, which is equal to the marginal cost of $10 at an output of 2,000 units and a price of $30. Therefore, $TR = \$30 \times 2,000 = \$60,000$, and $TC = \$20,000 + (10 \times 2,000) = \$40,000$, so profit $= TR - TC = \$20,000$.

(b) See D_2 and MR_2 in the graph. The adjusted price and quantity are 2,500 units and $35, respectively. $TR = \$35 \times 2,500 = \$87,500$, and $TC = \$20,000 + (10 \times 2,500) + \$3,000 = \$48,000$. Therefore, profits are $39,500.

(c) Holding the price at $30 in the presence of the new demand implies a quantity demanded of 3,000 units. $TR = \$30 \times 3,000 = \$90,000$, and $TC = \$20,000 + (10 \times 3,000) = \$50,000$. Profits are therefore $40,000 with a strategy of sticky prices, or $500 greater than those obtained by adjusting both price and quantity.

4. (a) leftward shifts of the supply curve in 1974 and 1983; rightward shift in 1986

(b) restriction of supply in 1980 (cartel); demand shift leftward and supply rightward in 1983; supply curve shift leftward in 1986

(c) movement up demand curve for postal services; demand for private delivery systems shifts rightward

(d) provision of low-priced service finds niche in differentiated market; modest shift of demand to left for standard rental companies

*5. These answers are approximate, depending on how you read the values on the horizontal axis.

(a) from 5,000 to 7,000; from $10,000 to $10,500

(b) from 5,000 to 5,500; from $10,000 to $8,250

(c) from 5,000 to 3,000; from $10,000 to $7,500

(d) from $10,000 to $11,250

(e) It would raise price only if everyone else did; it would not lower it even without retaliation because additional revenue would be less than additional costs. For instance, at 6,000 units MC would equal 75 cents but MR would be only 50 cents.

(f) Yes, the answers to (d) and (e) show that some form of tacit collusion, such as price leadership, would increase profits; no, the answers to (a) and (e) indicate that lower prices are unprofitable even when firm has a price advantage over competitors. In this example, the decision to raise price or not depends on the assumption made about the response of other firms.

Chapter **15**

Public Policy Toward Monopoly and Competition

Learning Objectives

After studying this chapter, you should be able to:

—distinguish between productive efficiency and allocative efficiency

—identify the inefficiency of monopoly compared to perfect competition

—understand the purposes of government competition policies

—discuss the difficulties of regulating natural monopolies

—understand that although the main thrust of anticombines and regulatory policies has been the protection of competitive forces, regulation has also been used to protect firms from competition

—discuss the purposes and progress of the deregulation movement

Multiple-Choice Questions

1. Resources are allocated efficiently when
   (a) there are no unemployed resources
   (b) all firms are producing at the lowest attainable cost
   (c) prices are as low as possible
   (d) no alternative allocation of resources makes at least one household better off without making at least one other household worse off

2. If two firms are producing the same product with different marginal costs, then
   (a) a reallocation of output between the firms can lower the industry's total cost
   (b) neither firm is producing its output at the lowest attainable cost
   (c) some resources must be unemployed
   (d) each firm is being wasteful

164

3. Allocative efficiency holds when for all goods
    (a) price equals marginal cost
    (b) the consumer valuation of the last unit produced equals the value of resources used to produce this unit
    (c) the sum of consumers' and producers' surplus is maximized
    (d) all of the above

4. Productive efficiency holds
    (a) when $P = MC$ for perfect competition
    (b) for perfect competition and monopolistic competition where long-run profits are zero
    (c) for natural monopolies where economies of scale are fully exploited
    (d) throughout the market economy where the objective of firms is to maximize profits

5. Producers' surplus is defined as
    (a) profits
    (b) retained earnings
    (c) total revenue less total costs
    (d) total revenue less total variable costs

6. A major difference between equilibrium in a competitive industry and monopoly is that
    (a) the monopoly produces where $MR = MC$, but the perfect competitor does not
    (b) perfect competitors achieve productive efficiency, but monopolies do not
    (c) the perfect competitor produces where $P = MC$, but the monopoly does not
    (d) all of the above

7. The deadweight loss of monopoly is
    (a) its fixed cost
    (b) any negative profit due to cyclical decreases in demand
    (c) the forgone surplus due to the allocatively inefficient monopoly output level
    (d) the cost of maintaining effective barriers to entry

Questions 8 to 11 refer to the following graph, in which the supply curve relates to a perfectly competitive industry and the marginal cost curve relates to a monopoly.

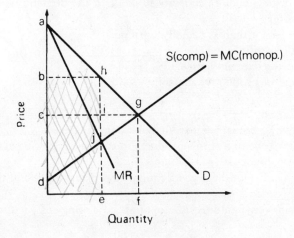

8. The allocatively efficient levels of output and price are
    (a) e and b, respectively   (c) f and c, respectively
    (b) e and c, respectively   (d) f and a, respectively

9. If this industry switches to monopoly from perfect competiton, the changes in
    price and quantity are
    (a) + cb and −fe, respectively   (c) +db and +ef, respectively
    (b) − bc and − fe, respectively   (d) +dc and +ef, respectively

10. Under monopoly, producers' surplus is area
    (a) bdjh   (c) cdg
    (b) bdgh   (d) adj

11. If price increases from c to b, and therefore quantity demanded is reduced from
    f to e, consumers' surplus is reduced by area
    (a) hig   (c) hjg
    (b) bcih   (d) bcgh

12. The condition of allocative efficiency is satisfied only under perfect competition
    because only this market structure guarantees that
    (a) long-run profits equal zero
    (b) firms are price takers, thereby implying that $P = MR$
    (c) there is complete freedom of entry and exit
    (d) firms truly maximize profits through cutthroat competition

13. Average cost pricing for a falling-cost natural monopoly results in
    (a) zero profits
    (b) allocative efficiency
    (c) production at the optimal output
    (d) all of the above

14. The larger the minimum efficient scale of firms, *ceteris paribus,*
    (a) the more likely a concentrated market will improve productive efficiency
    (b) the greater the tendency toward natural monopoly
    (c) the greater the advantages of large-scale production
    (d) all of the above

15. A rising-cost firm that installs enough capacity to meet all the demand when
    price is set equal to average cost
    (a) will create more capacity than is socially optimal
    (b) will ultimately make profits
    (c) must be subsidized to cover its losses
    (d) will optimally invest in productive capacity

16. Cross-subsidization refers to
    (a) the taxation of growing industries to subsidize declining ones
    (b) the use of profits from one of a firm's products to subsidize another of its
         products at a price below cost
    (c) transfers of profits between crown corporations and private firms in the
         same industry
    (d) transfers from rising-cost natural monopolies to falling-cost natural
         monopolies

17. If a natural monopoly is regulated to charge a price that is equal to marginal cost where the marginal cost curve intersects the demand curve and is less than average cost, the resulting level of output is
    (a) allocatively efficient, and a positive profit is earned
    (b) allocatively efficient, but the firm must be paid a subsidy or it will go out of business
    (c) less than the allocatively efficient level, and profits are zero
    (d) less than the allocatively efficient level, but negative profits are earned

18. The original philosophy behind the regulation of natural monopolies such as public utilities
    (a) was to guarantee consumers a low price
    (b) involved government ownership in key economic sectors
    (c) was to achieve the advantages of large-scale production but prevent the monopoly from restricting output and raising price
    (d) was to erect dependable and effective barriers to entry

19. Which of the following is *not* one of the forces encouraging deregulation and privatization in advanced industrial nations?
    (a) the experience that many regulatory bodies serve to reduce competition rather than increase it
    (b) the growing evidence that nationalized industries do not enhance productivity growth or allocative efficiency
    (c) increased pressures from world competition
    (d) the conclusion that industrial performance improves when an oligopoly is replaced by a nationalized monopoly

20. There is a growing consensus that natural monopoly regulation by public utility regulatory commissions
    (a) has served effectively to protect consumers from natural monopolies
    (b) has led to allocative efficiency
    (c) is concerned more with protecting firms from competition than with protecting consumers from natural monopoly
    (d) all of the above

21. "Protectionist" policies by regulatory commissions
    (a) are aimed at protecting the consumer
    (b) reflect a concern for existing firms and limiting the entry of potential competitors
    (c) concern the trade-offs between domestic and foreign trade policy
    (d) deal with work safety and environmental issues

22. In the decision to privatize a crown corporation, government faces a trade-off between
    (a) deregulation and selling the crown corporation
    (b) the selling price and future competition in the industry
    (c) average cost pricing and rate of return regulation
    (d) productive and allocative efficiency

23. The lack of effective combines enforcement in Canada prior to 1976 was partly due to
    (a) the inability of courts to cope with complex economic issues
    (b) the passage of the Combines Investigation Act as criminal rather than civil legislation
    (c) the fact that the fines were rather small
    (d) all of the above

24. Since 1976 all but which of the following has been introduced into Canadian competition policy?
    (a) the power to prohibit suppliers from refusing to supply
    (b) prohibiting producers from advertising a bargain price without reasonable quantities
    (c) prohibition of resale price maintenance
    (d) extension of the act to include service industries

Exercises

1. In the graph, *DD* is the market demand curve, and *DM* is the marginal revenue curve. *AN* is the long-run supply curve for a competitive industry and also the marginal cost curve for a monopolist.

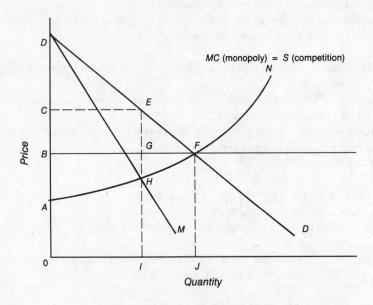

    (a) For perfect competition, predict the following:
        (i)   equilibrium price _____ and quantity _____
        (ii) consumers' surplus _____
        (iii) producers' surplus _____
        (iv) the sum of producers' and consumers' surplus _____

(b) For monopoly, predict the following:
    (i)   equilibrium price _____ and quantity _____
    (ii) consumers' surplus _____
    (iii) producers' surplus _____
    (iv) the sum of producers' and consumers' surplus _____
(c) The surplus transferred from consumers to producers with monopolization of a competitive industry _____
(d) The deadweight loss from monopoly _____

2. The graphs illustrate a perfectly competitive market and a monopolistic market under identical demand conditions.

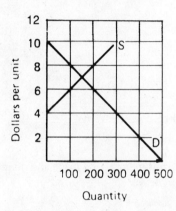 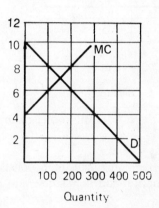

(a) What are the equilibrium levels of price and output in the perfectly competitive market? In the monopoly market?

(b) What shift in the monopolist's *MC* curve (relative to perfect competition) is required to have the levels of price and output the same in both market structures?

(c) Starting from the equilibrium situations depicted in (a), illustrate that both price and quantity would change by less in the monopolistic market than in perfect competition in response to an increase in marginal costs by $2 per unit of output.

3. The following graph depicts a market demand curve and a firm's cost structure characterized by constant marginal cost (MC) and a large set-up cost so that average cost (AC) is continuously declining over market demand. The firm is therefore a natural monopoly.

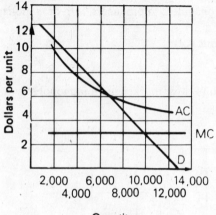

(a) What is the allocatively efficient level of output? Why?

(b) What are the unregulated monopolist's profit-maximizing price and quantity in this market and the associated profit level?

(c) What is the resulting deadweight loss?

(d) Suppose that a regulatory agency attempts to force this monopolist to produce the allocatively efficient output. Would the agency be successful? Why or why not?

(e) As an alternative, suppose that the agency imposes "average cost pricing" on the monopolist. What is the regulated price and the resulting quantity?

(f) Compare the level of profits and deadweight loss under "average cost pricing" with that under the scheme in (d).

4. The demand curve for a product is $Q_d = 90,000 - 1,000P$ with P (price) expressed in dollars. In a competitive market, the supply curve is $2,000P - 45,000$ (with the supply being zero at $P \leq \$22.50$). Remember, the competitive supply curve is the horizontal summation of the firm's marginal cost curves above the minimum average variable cost (here, 22.50).

(a) Determine the equilibrium price and quantity of the product necessary for allocative efficiency. Use the graph in (b) or solve algebraically.

(b) Graph consumers' and producers' surpluses (total net benefits, in dollars) under allocative efficiency.

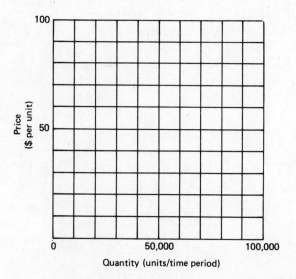

(c) Assume that the product was supplied instead by a monopoly. Determine the quantity that will be supplied and the market price, and graph the consumers' and producers' surpluses. The counterpart of the competitive supply curve is $MC = 22.5 + 0.0005Q$. [Note the graphic identity of MC in this graph to S in (b).]

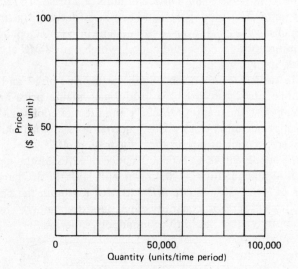

(d) Compare producers' surplus, consumers' surplus, and total net benefits in (c) with those in (b).

Answers

Multiple-Choice Questions

1. (d)   2. (a)   3. (d)   4. (d)   5. (d)   6. (c)   7. (c)   8. (c)   9. (a)   10. (a)   11. (d)   12. (b)
13. (a)   14. (d)   15. (a)   16. (b)   17. (b)   18. (c)   19. (d)   20. (c)   21. (b)   22. (b)   23. (d)
24. (c)

Exercises

1. (a) (i) B, J (ii) area BDF (iii) area ABF (iv) area ADF
   (b) (i) C, I (ii) area CDE (iii) area $ACEH$ (iv) area $ADEH$
   (c) area $CBEG$
   (d) area HEF

2. (a)

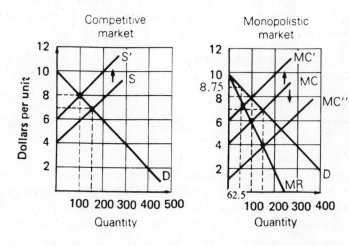

The initial equilibrium in perfect competition obtains at a price of $7 and
a quantity of 150 units. The monopoly equilibrium is derived by first
drawing the monopolist's marginal revenue curve (same price intercept and
half the quantity intercept as the demand curve), which equals MC at an
output of 100 units, implying a price of $8.

(b) The equilibrium in perfect competition obtains at a price of $7 and a
quantity of 150 units. For these to be the profit-maximizing price and
quantity of the monopolist, the market MR curve and the monopolist's MC
curve must intersect at a quantity of 150. This requires (for a uniform shift)
that MC be $3 lower per unit of output—for illustration, MC''.

(c) In panel (i), shift the supply curve a vertical distance of $2 to S'; the new
equilibrium price is $8 and quantity is 100. In panel (ii), shift the MC curve
a vertical distance of $2 to MC'; equate MR and MC' to obtain the new
profit-maximizing price of $8.75 and quantity of 62.5 (approximately). Thus
both price and quantity change less in the monopoly situation.

3.

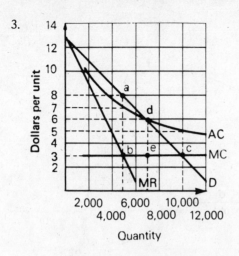

(a) 10,000. Because the value of the resources used to produce the 10,000th unit (i.e., *MC*) equals the value that households place on the consumption of this unit.

(b) $8, 5,000 units, and $5,000

(c) area *abc* = ($8 − $3) (10,000 − 5,000)/2 = $12,500

(d) If the firm produces 10,000 units, the market price would be $3, implying a *TR* of $30,000, but *AC* would be $5, which implies a *TC* of $50,000. Therefore, the firm would be making a loss of $20,000.

(e) Price could be regulated at $6, which would yield a market quantity of 7,000 units.

(f) Under average cost pricing in (e), profits are zero but the deadweight loss is area *dec* = ($6 − $3) (10,000 − 7,000)/2 = $4,500. The scheme in (d) does not yield any deadweight loss, but the firm is forced to incur an operating loss.

4. (a) Set demand equal to supply and solve for price (45) and output (45,000). (See panel (i) of the graph.)

(b) Consumers' surplus is (a) and producers' surplus is (b) in panel (i).

(c) Price is *h* and quantity is 27,000. In panel (ii), consumers' surplus is shown by the triangle *ehg*; producers' surplus is the quadrangle 22.5 *hgf*.

(d) Under competitive conditions, consumers' surplus (*CS*) is more and producers' surplus (*PS*) is less than under monopoly. For example, *CS* in (c) is the area *ehg* in panel (ii), which is less than triangle (a) in panel (i).

Net benefits (consumers' surplus plus producers' surplus) are less under monopoly. The amount of the reduction (the so-called deadweight allocative loss) is shown by the triangle *ifg* in panel (ii).

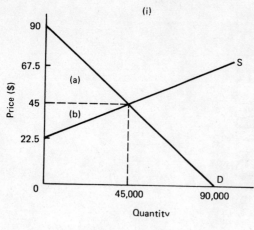

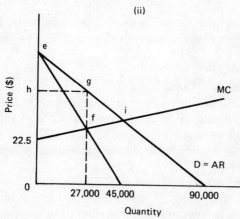

Chapter 16

Market for Corporate Control: Takeovers, Foreign Investment, and Profit Maximization

Learning Objectives

After studying this chapter, you should be able to:

—explain how the separation of ownership from control creates divergent interests in operating a firm

—apply principal-agent analysis to indicate why managers may not pursue stockholders' interests

—distinguish key predictions of firm behavior based on theories of profit maximization, sales maximization, full-cost pricing, and nonmaximization

—explain why firms may fail to make changes that would reduce costs

—understand why the organizational structure of a firm may affect the business decisions made

—understand that if a firm does not realize its profit potential, it is vulnerable to a takeover bid

—evaluate who primarily benefits from corporate takeover activity and to what extent any costs are imposed on the economy as a whole

—recognize the role of profits in all of the theories discussed

—discuss the costs and benefits of transnational corporations to the host country

Multiple-Choice Questions

1. A merger between a publisher and a printing company is an example of a
   (a) conglomerate merger
   (b) vertical merger
   (c) horizontal merger
   (d) leveraged buyout

2. New management in a takeover may make more efficient use of a target firm's assets by
   (a) operating the target firm more efficiently
   (b) providing funds that the target firm could not obtain
   (c) providing access to markets that the target firm could not obtain independently
   (d) all of the above

3. Most economists believe that the threat of a takeover
   (a) induces an inefficient resource allocation
   (b) will eventually drive the economy into another recession
   (c) restricts managers from pursuing objectives other than profit maximization
   (d) has no effect on the current managers of firms

4. Hostile takeovers have tended to benefit most the
   (a) workers of the acquired firms
   (b) stockholders of the acquired firms
   (c) managers of the acquired firms
   (d) stockholders of the acquiring firms

5. Junk bonds are
   (a) viewed as inferior investments that offer lower interest rates
   (b) sold to finance leveraged buyouts
   (c) any bonds with an interest yield below the market rate
   (d) a form of debt held by scrap dealers

6. Leveraged buyouts
   (a) are a means of dismantling unprofitable conglomerates
   (b) provide current management with a defense against hostile takeover bids
   (c) are takeovers financed with borrowed funds
   (d) all of the above

7. One economic rationale for a conglomerate merger is
   (a) economies of scale
   (b) the division of labor at the management level
   (c) the principal-agent problem
   (d) the spreading of risk across different industries

8. Which of the following is viewed in Canada as a potential benefit associated with transnational corporations?
   (a) extraterritoriality
   (b) arbitrage of country-specific economic policies
   (c) centralized relocation of research and development activities
   (d) a more rapid rise in capital per worker than could be provided by domestic savings

9. Government attempts to limit leveraged buyouts are most warranted on economic grounds if
   (a) risks to the economy exceed the risks borne by acquiring firms
   (b) managers of acquired firms lose their jobs
   (c) the acquiring firm goes bankrupt and bondholders lose money
   (d) the government is also able to reduce the severity of the business cycle

10. Principal-agent problems are more likely to arise when
    (a) managers are protected from hostile takeovers by poison pills
    (b) managers' performance can be easily evaluated relative to competitors'
    (c) owners manage the firm
    (d) a few stockholders own most of the shares outstanding

11. The hypothesis of minority control
    (a) refers to programs that have encouraged stock ownership by native peoples
    (b) recognizes that a group holding much less than 51 percent of total shares may effectively select directors and management
    (c) holds that a minority of employees, the top managers, control the firm
    (d) maintains that a minority of corporations, those in the military-industrial complex, control our economy

12. The fact that a well-organized minority may exercise control of a corporation does not in itself deny the predictions derived from the theory of the firm because
    (a) their control may require the proxy votes of a majority
    (b) management is generally unresponsive to shareholders, whether they are a minority or a majority
    (c) the overriding objective may still be profit maximization with disputes centering on the means of maximizing profits
    (d) all of the above

13. The theory of sales maximization subject to a minimum profit constraint is based on the premise that
    (a) a controlling management derives personal benefits from the size of a firm as well as its profit level
    (b) the firm's objectives are always decided at the annual shareholders' meeting
    (c) a minority of shareholders, who have goals different from those of the majority of shareholders, can form a majority of actual votes
    (d) firms only desire a normal return to their investments

14. A firm that practices full-cost pricing
    (a) sets price equal to marginal cost
    (b) sets price equal to average cost at the profit-maximizing output
    (c) equates marginal revenue with marginal cost
    (d) sets price equal to average cost at normal capacity output plus some markup

15. Full-cost pricing
    (a) can never be consistent with profit maximization, even if it is costly to change prices
    (b) is consistent with slow response, in terms of price, to any change in cost or demand
    (c) if followed by the firm, leads to more frequent price changing than profit maximization
    (d) implies that firms, when setting prices, seek merely to break even

16. Satisficing theory argues that
    (a) the majority of shareholders are satisfied with their management
    (b) the firm's objective is not profit maximization but simply to attain some minimally acceptable profit level
    (c) the firm will produce the output corresponding to maximum market share
    (d) the most successful firms are those that produce goods that best satisfy consumers

17. A basic difference between satisficing theory and the theories of profit maximization and sales maximization is that
    (a) satisficing is based on the goals of management, whereas the others are based on the goals of shareholders
    (b) satisficing predicts the largest level of output among the three theories
    (c) satisficing predicts that the firm will never produce the output level corresponding to either maximum profits or maximum sales
    (d) satisficing predicts a range of outputs; the others predict unique output levels

18. Recent evolutionary theories of firm behavior
    (a) stress tradition and routine in firms' decisions
    (b) incorporate profit-maximizing assumptions
    (c) emphasize dynamic and innovative elements
    (d) suggest that firms react quickly to changing economic conditions

19. The recommended approach for testing theories about firms' behavior is to
    (a) ask business management whether it maximizes profits, satisfices, or maximizes sales
    (b) judge which theory rests on the most realistic assumptions
    (c) try to find evidence to show what firms have done under different circumstances
    (d) watch a business manager make a decision to see how it is done

20. A difference between maximizing and nonmaximizing theories of firm behavior is
    (a) the speed and magnitude, but not the general direction, of the response to changes in demand or cost conditions
    (b) that firms are nonmaximizers because they have inadequate information to maximize profits
    (c) that maximizing and nonmaximizing firms respond entirely differently to changes in economic conditions
    (d) that maximizing firms display a great deal of inertia

21. The sales-maximizing hypothesis implies that a firm
    (a) sells as many units as it can at a fixed price
    (b) attempts to maximize its market share without regard to profits
    (c) cuts price in order to sell the level of output where $MR = MC$
    (d) seeks to maximize sales revenue, subject to a profit constraint

Exercises

1. The following graph represents demand and cost conditions for a firm.

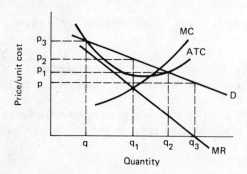

(a) What would be the choice of price and output for a profit maximizer? _____

(b) What would be the range of price and output for a profit satisficer who is content to cover opportunity costs as a minimum? _____

(c) What could be the price and output of a sales maximizer who is willing to accept losses for short periods (assume sufficient economies of scale so that $LRAC$ will be less than p at q_3)? _____

2. Assume that a firm is capable of making a reasonable projection of its profits (π) as it expands output (Q) and that this relationship is

$$\pi = 7Q - Q^2 - 6$$

(a) For values of $Q = 1, 2, 3, 3.5, 4, 5,$ and 6, plot the profit function on the graph.

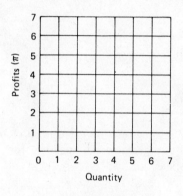

(b) If a satisficing firm has a profit target of 4, what ranges of output will that firm accept?

(c) What output is consistent with profit maximization?

(d) If the firm is a sales maximizer and the only constraint was to have profits of a least 2, approximately what output will it choose?

*3. To suggest why economists tend to be dissatisfied with nonmaximizing models for price-output decisions, this problem extends the analysis of Exercise 2. In doing that exercise, you should already have noted that the satisficing firm has a rather wide range of outputs to choose from.

Note that the profit function can be assumed to be the difference between $TR = 17Q - Q^2$ and $TC = 10Q + 6$. The MR is $17 - 2Q$, and the demand curve is $P = 17 - Q$.

(a) Confirm that the profit-maximizing output is 3.5, at which the price is 13.5.

(b) Now allow fixed costs to increase by 1 so that $TC = 10Q + 7$. How are the decisions for satisficer, profit maximizer, and sales maximizer altered? You may use the graph to help derive your answers.

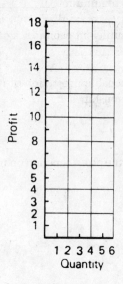

(c) Now change the cost function to $11Q + 6$ to test the effect of a change in marginal costs. You should get straightforward answers for the maximizers, but what about the satisficer?

(d) Now assume the original cost conditions but with a favorable demand shift to $P = 17 - 0.5Q$ (which also increases the demand elasticity at every price). Work out the decisions for the maximizers. How might the profit satisficer deal with the wide range of choices that meet the criterion that profits be at least 4?

Answers

Multiple-Choice Questions

1. (b)   2. (d)   3. (c)   4. (b)   5. (b)   6. (d)   7. (d)   8. (d)   9. (c)   10. (a)   11. (b)   12. (c)
13. (a)   14. (d)   15. (b)   16. (b)   17. (d)   18. (a)   19. (c)   20. (a)   21. (d)

Exercises

1. (a) p_2 and q_1 (b) from p_3 and q to p_1 and q_2 (c) p and q_3
2. (a)

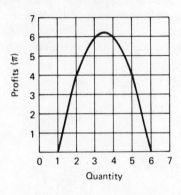

    (b) from $Q = 2$ to $Q = 5$
    (c) $Q = 3.5$
    (d) $Q = 5.5$ (approximately)

*3. (a) In this case, marginal cost is constant at 10. Setting $MC = MR$ yields 10
         $= 17 - 2Q$, which solves for $Q = 3.5$; $P = 17 - Q$, or 13.5.
    (b) This has the effect of shifting the profit curve down a vertical distance of
         $1 at each level of output. The resulting profit curve is labeled b in the
         following graph.

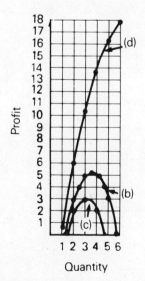

The output of the profit maximizer is unaffected. The output of the satisficer with a profit target of $4 now ranges from 2.5 to 4.5, approximately. The sales maximizer who has a profit target of $2 reduces output to approximately 5.25.

(c) The resulting profit curve is labeled *c* in the graph. The profit maximizer produces three units, and the sales maximizer produces four units. The satisficer can no longer attain the minimum profit level of $4. The closest it can come is $3, which is achieved when the profit-maximizing output of three units is produced.

(d) The resulting profit curve is labeled *d* in the graph. As requested in Exercise 2, the profit curve is plotted only up to an output level of six units, which is the output of both the profit maximizer and the sales maximizer (actually, each would like to increase output beyond six units). The satisficer produces anywhere between (approximately) 1.25 and 6 units, despite the substantial difference in profits over this range.

PART FIVE

The Distribution
of Income

Chapter 17

Factor Mobility
and Factor Pricing

Learning Objectives

After studying this chapter, you should be able to:

—comprehend how Canadian income is distributed by factors (functional distribution of income) and across households (size distribution of income)

—understand that the price of a factor of production and the total income received by it are determined by the forces of demand and supply for that factor in all activities in which it is used and among all uses to which it can possibly be put

—appreciate the key role of factor mobility, across firms and across industries, in determining (1) how a market system allocates resources, (2) the proportions of a factor's total pay, which are transfer earnings and rents, and (3) how disequilibrium differentials in earnings are eliminated

—be aware of special conditions in the supply of various factors, particularly the importance of nonmonetary considerations in the choice of labor

—understand the forces that create disequilibrium and equilibrium differentials in compensation

—grasp the concept of economic rent and understand how the proportion of a factor's earnings that is rent depends on the alternatives that are open to the factor of production

—be aware of the determinants of the pricing and rate of extraction of an exhaustible resource

Multiple-Choice Questions

1. In which of the following percentage ranges is the share of functional income paid as employee compensation in Canada?
   (a) 1 to 7
   (b) 65 to 75
   (c) 80 to 100
   (d) 35 to 50

2. The "size distribution of income" provides a profile of income distribution
   (a) by size of household
   (b) for each social class within a country
   (c) without reference to the source of income of the household
   (d) by the relative magnitudes of wages, rents, and profits

3. Complete equality of income distribution would appear on a Lorenz curve as a
   (a) diagonal line   (c) concave curve
   (b) convex curve   (d) single point

4. The total demand for an input is the
   (a) mirror image of the supply of an input
   (b) sum of the derived demands for it in all its various uses
   (c) sum of the demands for all of the goods the input produces
   (d) sole determinant of the price of the input

Questions 5 to 7 refer to the following graph. The demand and supply curves pertain
to a competitive market for a factor of production. Point A is the initial market
equilibrium situation; other points represent alternative equilibria caused by parallel
shifts in either the demand curve or the supply curve, but *not* both.

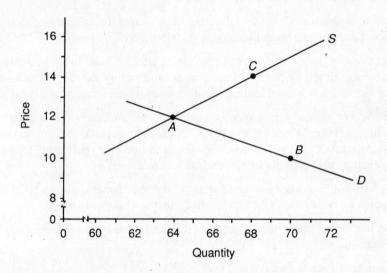

5. At the initial equilibrium situation at point A,
   (a) total income paid to the factor is $12
   (b) total factor earnings are $768
   (c) the economic rent of the sixty-fourth unit is zero
   (d) both (b) and (c)

6. If the equilibrium in this factor market changed from point A to point B, then
   (a) the supply curve for the factor has shifted to the right
   (b) total factor earnings are $700
   (c) the economic rent of the sixty-fourth unit is now positive
   (d) all of the above

7. If the equilibrium in this factor market changed from point *A* to point *C*, then
   (a) the new equilibrium unit price of the factor is $14
   (b) total factor earnings are lower at *C* than those associated with point *A*
   (c) the total demand for the factor decreased
   (d) both (a) and (b)

8. A highly mobile factor of production
   (a) is one that shifts easily between uses in response to small changes in incentives
   (b) displays supply inelasticity in most uses
   (c) is a particularly applicable concept for the short run
   (d) will tend to have a large proportion of its earnings made up of economic rents

9. Equilibrium differentials in factor prices may reflect
   (a) intrinsic differences in factor characteristics
   (b) acquired differences in factor characteristics
   (c) nonmonetary advantages in uses of the factor
   (d) all of the above

10. Which of the following is *not* an example of an equilibrium differential in a factor price?
    (a) Land in downtown Toronto is more expensive than land in the suburbs.
    (b) Wages in the Quebec construction trades are higher than elsewhere in the country because of a booming Quebec economy.
    (c) Individuals working in isolated communities tend to be paid more than their counterparts in the more accessible cities.
    (d) A dentist is paid more than a dental hygienist.

11. One would expect which of the following to view most of the payment to Jimmy Key of the Toronto Blue Jays as transfer earnings?
    (a) the Toronto Blue Jays
    (b) the professional baseball industry
    (c) university professors
    (d) national transfer payment recipients

12. In a free market economy, teachers would get paid more than truck drivers
    (a) only if teachers' wages reflected compensation for the relatively higher training and educational requirements compared with those of truckers
    (b) only if teachers were smarter
    (c) because of the nonmonetary advantages of teaching
    (d) both (a) and (c)

13. Economic rent
    (a) refers exclusively to the income of landowners
    (b) is taxable under the income tax law, whereas transfer earnings are not
    (c) is earned only by completely immobile factors
    (d) is the excess of income over transfer earnings

14. A disequilibrium differential in factor earnings
    (a) will be more quickly eliminated if factor supply is inelastic rather than elastic
    (b) will tend to cause reallocation (or mobility) of factors
    (c) is greater the greater the mobility of the factor
    (d) none of the above

15. In the short run, the net income received from a machine with only one use is generally considered to be
    (a) a transfer earning
    (b) economic rent
    (c) equal to the interest rate because a machine represents an exhaustible factor
    (d) both (b) and (c)

16. Assume that a disequilibrium differential exists such that the wages in occupation A are higher than those in occupation B. According to the hypothesis of equal net advantage, we would expect
    (a) the disequilibrium differential to be eliminated eventually by the movement of labor from occupation B to occupation A
    (b) the supply curve of labor in occupation B to shift to the right as workers moved to occupation A
    (c) nonmonetary advantages to be equalized between the two occupations
    (d) all of the above

17. With perfect competition, the real price of an exhaustible resource with a known stock and whose extraction and transportation costs are negligible should rise by
    (a) a constant percentage amount from year to year until the stock is depleted
    (b) 10 percent if the real rate of interest is also 10 percent
    (c) the same rate as the extraction rate
    (d) the rate of growth of national output

18. The actual rate at which an exhaustible resource is extracted will be more even through time when
    (a) the demand curve for the resource is perfectly elastic
    (b) there are many substitutes for this resource
    (c) the demand curve for the resource is relatively steep
    (d) both (a) and (b)

19. Which of the following would *not* be a likely consequence of an expected increase in the price of a nonrenewable resource like oil?
    (a) Substitute products (such as solar energy) would be developed.
    (b) Current rates of extraction by owners would be moderated.
    (c) Recycling and discovery of new sources of supply would be encouraged.
    (d) Quantity demanded will increase as the stocks are depleted.

Exercises

1. This exercise focuses on the Lorenz curve and changes in the distribution of income. The following table provides data on the distribution of family income in Canada for 1981.

Family income rank	Percentage share of aggregate income, 1981
Lowest fifth	6.6
Second fifth	15.6
Middle fifth	23.7
Fourth fifth	21.2
Highest fifth	32.9

Source: Statistics Canada, 13-208.

(a) Calculate the cumulative income-population distribution for Canada in 1981.

(b) Plot the 1981 Lorenz curve for Canada on the following grid.

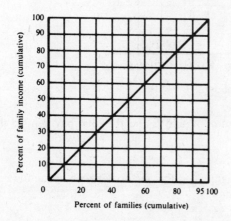

(c) By visual inspection of your Lorenz curve, can you conclude that income in Canada was equally distributed?

2. Given that DD is the demand for a factor of production and P is equilibrium monthly earnings, draw in supply curves consistent with
   (a) all earnings being transfer earnings
   (b) all earnings being economic rents
   (c) half of earnings being transfer earnings and half being economic rent

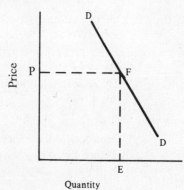

3. Consider a labor market for a specific type of worker for which the demand is given by the equation $L^D = 95 - 0.25W$, where L^D is the quantity demanded of labor and W is the wage. There are two possible supply curves: case A, $L^S = 0.5W - 10$, and case B, $L^S = 60$, where L^S is the quantity of labor supplied.

(a) Draw the demand curve and two supply curves on the following grid.

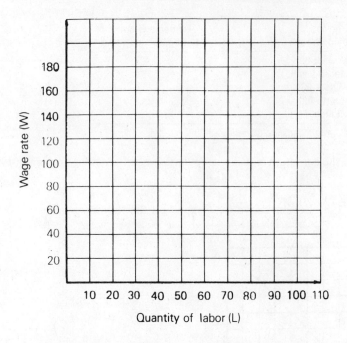

Quantity of labor (L)

(b) What are the equilibrium values of W and L and the total payment to this factor in each case?

(c) What is the division of total payment to this factor between economic rent and transfer earnings in each case?

(d) For case A, what is the division between transfer earnings and economic rent for the sixtieth unit of labor? The fortieth?

(e) Assuming that case A holds, now suppose that the government attempts to increase employment in this industry by increasing the demand for labor to $L^D = 110 - 0.25W$. What are the new equilibrium wage and quantity of labor?

(f) By how much does the government policy increase economic rents in this market?

(g) How much of the increase in economic rents goes to labor that was employed before the policy was introduced?

*4. There are two competitive labor markets in a particular economy. The labor force, which is always fully employed, is equal to the value OK in the graph. A downward-sloping demand curve for labor in market A (D_A) is drawn such that the quantity of employment increases from left to right on the horizontal axis as the wage rate in that market falls. Moreover, a downward-sloping labor demand curve for market B (D_B) is drawn such that a decrease in the wage in that market causes an increase in the quantity demanded, which in this case means a movement from right to left along the horizontal axis. Labor is assumed to be perfectly mobile between the two markets, and no nonmonetary advantages exist in either market.

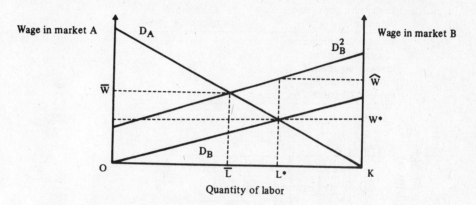

(a) What will be the equilibrium values of wages and employment in each market given demand curves D_A and D_B? Explain.

(b) Suppose that the demand for labor in market B increased such that the labor demand curve shifts from D_B to D_B^2. What adjustments will occur in the two markets and what will happen to the equilibrium levels of wages and employment in the two markets?

5. A mythical nonrenewable natural resource, zube oil, is produced and sold in a perfectly competitive market. The reserves of zube oil are known with certainty, and demand is constant. The entire stock is of identical quality and can be extracted and delivered to market with negligible extraction and transportation costs. Its price in 1991 is $100 per barrel. The rate of interest is 10 percent.

(a) Explain why, under these assumptions, the price of zube oil in 1992 will be $110 per barrel.

(b) Predict the consequences of the following for the price of zube oil:
    (i)   Demand for zube oil increases as the economy grows and population and per capita incomes increase.

    (ii) Additional reserves of zube oil are unexpectedly discovered.

(c) Predict the consequences on the exhaustion rate of zube oil if the government set the price of oil below the competitive equilibrium price.

Answers

Multiple-Choice Questions

1. (b)   2. (c)   3. (a)   4. (b)   5. (d)   6. (d)   7. (a)   8. (a)   9. (d)   10. (b)   11. (a)   12. (a)
13. (d)   14. (b)   15. (b)   16. (a)   17. (b)   18. (c)   19. (d)

Exercises

1. (a)

Cumulative population (families)	Cumulative percent of income
Lowest 20 percent	6.6
Lowest 40 percent	22.2
Lowest 60 percent	45.9
Lowest 80 percent	67.1
Lowest 100 percent	100.0

(b)

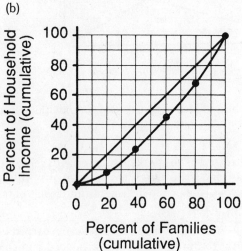

(c)   No; the Lorenz curve for 1981 lies below the diagonal line.

2. (a)   horizontal supply curve at P
   (b)   vertical supply curve at E
   (c)   Any positively sloped supply curve passing through F and dividing rectangle $OPEF$ into two equal areas; a straight line from the origin is one possibility.

3. (a)

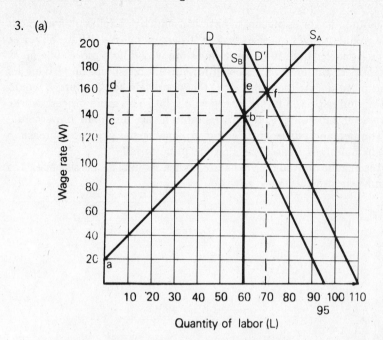

(b) In each case, $W = \$140$ and $L = 60$, so total factor payment is \$8,400.

(c) In case A, economic rent is the area below the wage line and above the supply curve (area *abc* in the graph), which equals \$3,600 ($=(120 \times 60) \div 2$). Transfer earnings equal total factor payments minus economic rent or, in this case, \$4,800. In case B, there is a perfectly inelastic supply curve, so all \$8,400 of factor payments are economic rent.

(d) For the sixtieth unit of labor, transfer earnings equal the wage rate of \$140. The fortieth unit is willing to work for \$100 but is paid \$140. Therefore, for this unit transfer earnings equal \$100 and economic rent is \$40.

(e) The new equilibrium wage and quantity are \$160 and 70 units, respectively.

(f) Economic rents now equal area *adf* in the graph. Thus the increase in economic rent is area *bcdf*, which equals \$1,300.

(g) The 60 units of labor employed prior to the policy change receive area *bcde* in additional rents; this equals \$1,200.

*4. (a) Since labor is mobile, there will be no net advantage to being in one particular market. Hence the wage rate in market A will be equal to that in market B or, in this case, W^*. Employment in market A is OL^*, and employment in market B is KL^*.

(b) The wage in market B will rise. For example, at KL^* employment in market B, the wage is now $\hat{W}$. A disequilibrium differential between the two markets has been created, and thus labor will leave market A and migrate to market B. As this process occurs, the supply of labor in market A will decrease, causing wages in this market to rise, and the supply of labor in market B will increase, causing the wage increase to be less than $\hat{W}$. That is, labor mobility will eliminate the disequilibrium differential. The final equilibrium will be a wage rate of $\overline{W}$ in both markets. Employment in market B will have increased from KL^* to a level of $K\overline{L}$, and employment in market A will have fallen from OL^* to a level of $O\overline{L}$.

5. (a) Firms with inventories must earn exactly as much per dollar of investment
        as they would by investing elsewhere at 10 percent interest. If zube oil prices
        were rising faster than 10 percent, investors would hold more zube oil as
        an investment rather than release it for current consumption, driving its
        current price up. At the same time, the stock held for the future would
        increase, and expected future prices would fall. The same process works
        in reverse if zube oil prices were rising at a rate less than 10 percent.
    (b) (i)   The demand curve shifts outward, causing the price to increase.
        (ii) The supply increases, causing the price to fall.
    (c) Reserves of zube oil would be exhausted much faster since persistent excess
        demand exists in the market.

Chapter 18

More on Factor Markets

Learning Objectives

After studying this chapter, you should be able to:

—understand why the demand for factors of production is regarded as a derived demand

—demonstrate why firms will continue to hire a variable factor only as long as the added revenue produced by the factor is greater than or equal to the added cost

—explain what conditions result in more elastic factor demand

—recognize the influence of market conditions on factor earnings, even in the labor market, where nonmonetary and noncompetitive conditions are often important

—appreciate the role of pricing in accordance with scarcity to ensure an efficient allocation of resources

—understand the concepts of the present value of future returns and the marginal efficiency of capital

—explain the way the maximum purchase price of capital services is related to the rental price of a capital good and to the interest rate

—recognize that investment in capital goods is profitable as long as the marginal efficiency of capital is less than the interest rate or as long as the purchase price of capital is less than the present value of the capital's income stream

Multiple-Choice Questions

1. Which of the following statements is *not* true about the demand for a factor of production?
   (a) It is more elastic the more elastic the demand for the final product.
   (b) It is more elastic in cases where technology does not permit substitution with other factors.
   (c) It is less elastic the smaller its contribution to the total cost of the product.
   (d) It is more elastic the longer the time period considered.

2. The marginal revenue product of a factor is the
   (a) cost of employing additional units of a factor
   (b) additional output produced by the last unit of a factor
   (c) change in revenue as sales are increased by one unit of output
   (d) change in revenue resulting from the sale of the additional output produced by the last unit of a factor employed

3. A profit-maximizing firm that is a price taker in factor markets hires a factor up to the point at which
   (a) the factor's price equals its marginal revenue product
   (b) the marginal cost of hiring the factor equals the additional revenue obtained from that factor's marginal contribution to output
   (c) the factor's price equals its marginal product times the product's price
   (d) all of the above

4. Which of the following explains why a price-taking, profit-maximizing firm's demand curve for labor slopes downward? As the quantity of labor employed rises,
   (a) the marginal product of labor eventually falls
   (b) the firm's marginal revenue declines as output increases
   (c) the marginal cost of hiring another unit of labor increases
   (d) all of the above

5. Profit-maximizing firms that employ factors until marginal revenue product equals the factor's price will hire
   (a) additional units of the factor if its price falls, *ceteris paribus*
   (b) less of the factor if the price of the product it produces falls, *ceteris paribus*
   (c) more of the factor if technology changes such that the factor's marginal product increases at every employment level, *ceteris paribus*
   (d) all of the above

6. Which of the following is likely to shift the demand curve for carpenters to the right?
   (a) a decrease in carpenters' wages
   (b) an increase in unemployed workers' benefits
   (c) an increase in the demand for residential construction
   (d) a decrease in carpenters' productivity

7. Which of the following conditions is required for a market economy to yield an allocation of factors that maximizes the monetary value of total output?
   (a) Factors migrate to maximize their net advantage.
   (b) Firms hire factors to maximize profits.
   (c) Nonmonetary benefits of employment are not present.
   (d) All of the above.

8. If the quantity demanded for a factor of production decreases by 10 percent when its price increases by 8 percent, the elasticity of demand for the factor is
   (a) −1.25   (c) −0.8
   (b) 1.25 percent   (d) −2.0

9. The rental price of capital for a given period
   (a) is always equal to its purchase price
   (b) will be equated with the capital's marginal revenue product in that period as a result of profit maximization
   (c) is zero if the firm owns its capital
   (d) is the rate of return on capital for each dollar invested in that capital

10. If the interest rate is i, the present value of x dollars a year from now is
    (a) xi
    (b) $x/(1 + i)$
    (c) x/i
    (d) $i/(1 + x)$

11. If the interest rate is 5 percent, the present value of an annual return of $500 that lasts forever is
    (a) $10,000
    (b) $476.19
    (c) $525
    (d) infinity

12. If the rate of interest changes from 4 percent to 5 percent, the present value of $200 paid annually and forever
    (a) declines by $500
    (b) declines by $1,000
    (c) increases by $2,000
    (d) increases by $1,000

13. Suppose that a machine whose purchase price is $10,000 produces a perpetual stream of net revenues per period of $700. It follows that
    (a) the capital's marginal efficiency of capital is 7 percent
    (b) a firm will invest in this machine as long as the interest rate that it would receive for other assets is less than or equal to 7 percent
    (c) the present value of the stream of net revenues is greater than $10,000 if the interest rate were 6 percent
    (d) all of the above

14. A firm will *not* invest in a piece of capital equipment if
    (a) the interest rate is less than the capital's marginal efficiency
    (b) the capital's purchase price is less than the present value of expected net revenues
    (c) the present value of the stream of the capital's marginal revenue product is less than the purchase price
    (d) the rental price is less than the marginal revenue product of the capital

15. The purchase price of a capital good that indefinitely generates a steady stream of revenue equals
    (a) the present value of the stream of income produced by the capital good
    (b) the rental price of the capital good divided by the interest rate
    (c) MRP/i, where i represents the interest rate
    (d) all of the above

16. The marginal efficiency of capital measures the
    (a) additional output produced by another dollar's worth of capital
    (b) cost of employing another dollar's worth of capital
    (c) increase in revenue from hiring one more unit of a capital good
    (d) return on capital per dollar invested in that capital

17. The marginal efficiency of capital schedule is negatively sloped because
    (a) of the "law" of diminishing returns
    (b) the capital stock eventually wears out
    (c) the price of additional output must fall for more to be sold
    (d) all of the above

18. If a machine yields an annual stream of $100 income indefinitely, the price of the machine is P, and the interest rate is i percent, a firm should buy the machine if
    (a) $\$100 \times (1 + i) = P$ (c) $\$100/P < i$
    (b) $\$100/i > P$ (d) $\$100/(1 + i) < P$

19. The higher the interest rate, *ceteris paribus*,
    (a) the more profitable a given capital good investment will be
    (b) the lower a firm's equilibrium capital stock will be
    (c) the higher the present value of the income stream produced by a capital good
    (d) all of the above

20. The *MEC* curve shifts to the right as
    (a) capital is accumulated
    (b) the interest rate falls
    (c) technology improves capital productivity
    (d) diminishing returns occur

Answer questions 21 through 25 using the following data concerning a machine. You will find it useful to refer to Table 18-1 in the text.

A business can buy a machine that yields net revenue of $1,000 at the end of the first year and $2,000 at the end of the second year, after which the machine falls apart and thus has no scrap value.

21. If the rate of interest is 10 percent, the present value of the $1,000 received one year hence is equal to
    (a) $900   (c) $10,000
    (b) $909   (d) $100

22. If the rate of interest in both years is 10 percent, the *total* present value of the machine over the two-year period is
    (a) $2,561   (c) $3,000
    (b) $2,727   (d) $3,520

23. Assuming an interest rate of 10 percent, the firm will buy this machine if its purchase price is
    (a) less than or equal to $2,561
    (b) greater than $2,561 but less than $2,727
    (c) equal to $2,727
    (d) somewhere in the range $3,000 to $3,520

24. The interest rate that generates a total present value of net revenue flows for this machine of $2,487 is
    (a) 15 percent   (c) 12 percent
    (b) 8 percent   (d) between 13 and 14 percent

25. If the interest rate were 12 percent and the purchase price were $3,000, what would be the minimum value of the first year's net revenue to warrant purchasing this machine? Continue to assume that the net returns after two years remain at $2,000.
    (a) $893
    (b) $1,406
    (c) $1,255
    (d) $1,574

Appendix Questions

The following questions are based on the material in the appendix to this chapter. Read the appendix before answering these questions.

26. The demand curve for a variable factor is the
    (a) upward- and downward-sloping portions of the marginal revenue product curve
    (b) downward-sloping portion of the marginal revenue curve
    (c) downward-sloping portion of the marginal revenue product curve where it is above the average revenue product curve
    (d) downward-sloping portion of the marginal revenue product curve where it is below the average revenue product curve

27. *Ceteris paribus*, a monopolist's demand curve for a variable factor will
    (a) be steeper than that for a competitive firm
    (b) have a higher elasticity of demand for the factor than a competitive firm will
    (c) be flatter than that for a competitive firm
    (d) not be equal to the downward-sloping portion of the marginal revenue product curve

Exercises

1. This exercise demonstrates that the "law" of diminishing returns yields a downward-sloping factor demand curve for a profit-maximizing firm that sells its product in a perfectly competitive market. It also shows what causes shifts in the demand curve for the factor. The following table is partly completed to assist you. Three cases are illustrated: Case B reflects a lower product price than for case A. Case C assumes that labor productivity is different from that in cases A and B.

Total labor employed	Units of output per week	Marginal product (MP)	Case A		Case B		Case C		
			MR	MRP	MR	MRP	MP	MR	MRP
1	50	50	$30	$1,500	$27	$1,350	60	$30	$1,800
2	63	13	30	390	27	351	15	30	450
3	75	12	30	360	27	324	14	30	420
4	85	10	30	300	27	270	12	30	360
5	94	_____	30	_____	27	_____	11	30	_____
6	99	_____	30	_____	27	_____	7	30	_____

(a) Complete the table and plot all three *MRP* curves.

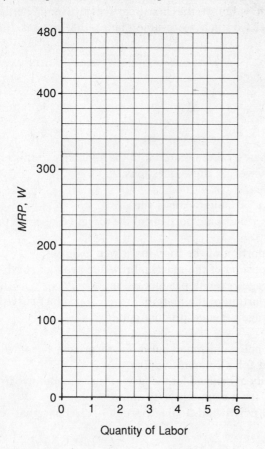

(b) Explain why the *MRP* curve slopes downward in all three cases.

(c) For case A, what is the firm's demand for workers per week if the weekly wage is $360? Explain your answer.

(d) For case A, explain why the firm's hiring would increase if the weekly wage fell from $360 to $270. What is the new profit-maximizing amount of labor?

(e) For case B, what is the firm's demand for workers per week if the weekly wage is $270? How does this value compare with that for case A in part (d)?

(f) For every wage rate, explain why the firm's demand for labor is less in case B than in case A.

(g) For case C, what is the firm's demand for labor when the weekly wage is $360? How does this value compare with that of case A, in part (c)?

(h) Explain why the firm's demand for labor at every wage is greater for case C than for case A.

2. The demand and supply conditions in a competitive factor market are portrayed in the accompanying graph. Two possible demand scenarios are labeled D_1 and D_2. The current equilibrium values of price and employment are 8 and 40, respectively.

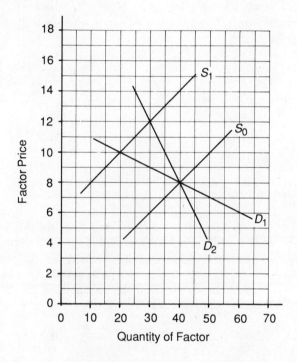

(a) If S_0 holds, what are current total factor earnings? What is the value of economic rents for the thirtieth unit?

(b) Suppose that the supply curve for the factor shifts up to the line labeled S_1. What are the new equilibrium values of price and employment for the two demand scenarios?

(c) Using midpoints between the new and old equilibrium values, calculate the elasticity of demand for both demand curves. Which demand curve has the higher elasticity?

(d) In terms of the elasticity values you have calculated, which demand curve implies, *ceteris paribus*,

  (i)   a lower elasticity of demand for the product that this factor produces?
  (ii) a higher degree of substitutability of other factors for this factor when its price increases?
  (iii) larger increases in the factor's marginal productivity as less of the factor is used?
  (iv) lower total factor earnings at the new equilibrium situation compared with those at the initial equilibrium?

3. (a) A firm's demand for a factor of production is given by its marginal revenue product, and if the price of the factor is given, the quantity demanded can be determined as in Exercises 1 and 2. Using the *MRP* schedules for Firms A and B given here, determine the quantity of machines they will each rent if the rental price is $8.

Quantity of machines	MRP_A	MRP_B
10	10	8
20	9	6
30	8	4
40	7	2
50	6	0
60	5	0

Quantity of machines rented: Firm A _____ ; Firm B _____

(b) A single firm may be able to take the rental price as given, but if A and B represent the *MRP* in two different industries and if the total number of machines available to these two industries is fixed, industry A can acquire more machines only by bidding them away from industry B. Assuming that the stock of machines available is 70, how should they be most efficiently allocated between the two industries?

Quantity of machines rented: Industry A _____ ; Industry B _____

(c) You can show the result from (b) graphically by plotting the two *MRP* curves in the machine market represented by the graph. The horizontal axis represents the total number of machines available. The *MRP* of machines in A is measured from the left-hand origin, and the *MRP* of machines in B is measured from the right-hand origin. The *MRP* for B is plotted for you. Plot the *MRP* for A, and determine the rental price where these two curves intersect. What is this price, and how are the machines allocated between the two industries?

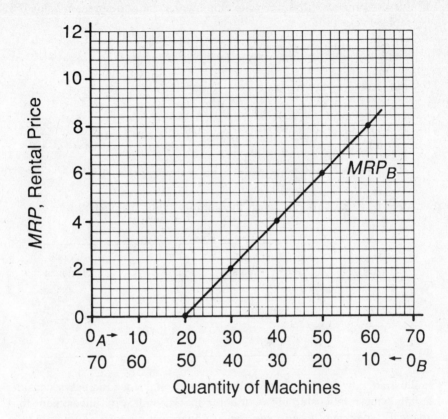

(d) Suppose that the productivity of machines in industry B rises because of technological improvements, and the new *MRP* schedule in B is as shown here. Plot this curve, and determine the new equilibrium rental price and allocation of machines between the two industries.

Quantity	MRP_B
10	11
20	9
30	7
40	5
50	3

(e) By how many machines did the *MRP* curve shift horizontally to the left, and how many additional machines did industry B end up renting? Explain why the number of machines B rents does not rise by as much as the *MRP* curve shifts to the left.

4. (a) Just for practice, fill in the following blanks using the present value (*PV*) table, Table 18-1.

This many dollars	In *n* years	Has this *PV*	At *i* rate of interest
10	5	_____	6%
100	50	$60.80	_____
1,000	—	3.00	12
_____	6	4.56	14

(b) More practice, this time with the annuity table, Table 18-2.

This many dollars	Received each year for *n* years	Has this *PV*	At *i* rate of interest
10	5	_____	6%
100	50	$3,919.60	_____
1,000	—	8,304.00	12
_____	6	38.89	14

5. To illustrate how the *MEC* can decline as the capital stock increases, consider the following relationship between home insulation (capital investment that, practically speaking, lasts forever) and annual heating costs. The amount of insulation in a home is measured by its R factor; assume that the cost of each increment of four units in the R factor for a particular home is constant at $5,000. The annual savings in heating costs that result from improved insulation can be interpreted as the additional revenue generated from the additional capital (i.e., the marginal revenue product). The following table provides the particulars.

1 Capital stock	2 Incremental insulation cost	3 Annual heating cost	4 Annual savings in costs	5 Estimated *MEC* (4) ÷ (2)
0	$ 0	$4,000	$ _____	_____ %
R4	5,000	2,500	_____	_____
R8	5,000	1,600	_____	_____
R12	5,000	1,200	_____	_____
R16	5,000	1,000	_____	_____

(a) Fill in the blanks, and plot the *MEC* curve on the grid.

(b) What is this homeowner's optimal stock of
insulation when the interest rate is 8 percent?
When it is 4 percent? Explain.

(c) Suppose that the price of insulation increases
to $10,000 for every four units of R value. Plot
the new *MEC* curve. What is the optimal
insulation level when the interest rate is 4
percent?

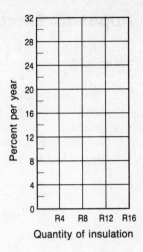

*6. There are two regional labor markets within a country, X and Y. Workers are
equally qualified to perform the same type of job in either region, and they
have no nonmonetary preferences with respect to the region in which they work
and live. The initial situation in each labor market is portrayed in the graph,
point *a* for market X and point *h* for market Y.

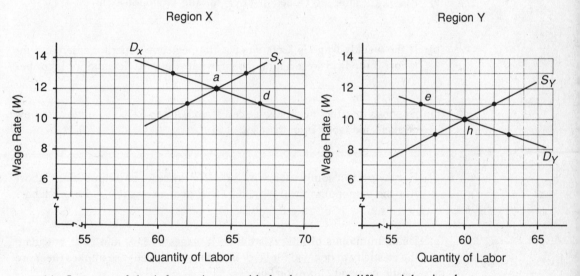

(a) In terms of the information provided, what type of differential exists between the two markets?

(b) In terms of the principle of net advantage, explain why labor flows will
cause shifts in the labor supply curves such that new equilibria might occur
at points *d* and *e*.

(c) Prove that the labor flows have increased economic efficiency by increasing
the country's value of total output. (*Hint:* The change in the value of output
for either market is the area under its labor demand curve evaluated from
the initial equilibrium wage to the new one, $W = \$11$.)

Appendix Exercise

The following exercise is based on material in the appendix to this chapter. Read the appendix before attempting this exercise.

7. This exercise illustrates how demand curves for labor differ by the firm's market structure (i.e., perfect competition versus a monopoly). A firm with a given production function sells its product for $30 regardless of the level of output (it is a perfect competitor). If it were a monopolist, its marginal revenue would depend on the level of its output. This information is given in the table below.

Total labor employed	Units of output per week	Marginal product (MP)	Perfect competitor MRP	Monopolist MR	Monopolist MRP
1	50	50	$1,500	$40	$2,000
2	63	13	390	34	_____
3	75	12	360	30	_____
4	85	10	300	27	_____
5	94	9	270	21	_____
6	99	5	150	20	_____

(a) Fill in the missing values of MRP for the monopolist case.

(b) If the weekly wage is $360, what is the perfect competitor's demand for labor? If the firm were a monopolist, what would its demand for labor be?

(c) Suppose that the weekly wage fell from $360 to $270. Compute the new demand for labor in both cases.

(d) For the perfect competitor, why did MRP decrease as it hired more labor? For the monopolist firm, why did MRP decrease as it hired more labor?

(e) Using midpoints of intervals between wages of $360 and $270, calculate the elasticity of demand for labor in each case. Which case implies the more elastic demand curve for labor?

Answers

Multiple-Choice Questions

1. (b) 2. (d) 3. (d) 4. (a) 5. (d) 6. (c) 7. (d) 8. (a) 9. (b) 10. (b) 11. (a) 12. (b)
13. (d) 14. (c) 15. (d) 16. (d) 17. (a) 18. (b) 19. (b) 20. (c) 21. (b) 22. (a) 23. (a)
24. (c) 25. (d) 26. (d) 27. (a)

Exercises

1. (a)   Marginal product: 9, 5; case A, MRP = 270, 150; case B, MRP = 243, 135; case C, MRP = 330, 210

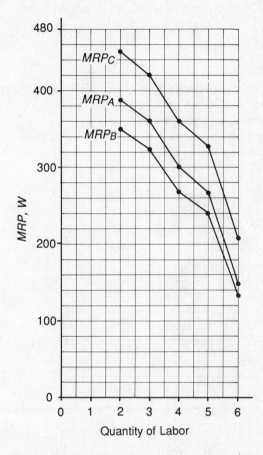

(b)   As more labor is employed, marginal productivity falls; this is the "law" of diminishing returns.

(c)   The firm demands three units of labor. The firm's profits will be maximized if it equates the marginal cost of obtaining labor ($360) to the marginal revenue product.

(d)   Three units of labor no longer represents a profit-maximizing situation since the MRP of the third unit of labor is $360 while the wage rate is $270. The firm will hire two more units of labor (a total of five), at which point MRP = $270.

(e)   For case B, the firm will hire four units of labor, at which point MRP = $270. This is one less unit of labor than in case A.

(f)   The price (marginal revenue) per unit is less; compare $27 with $30.

(g)   For case C, the firm will hire four units of labor, which is one more than in case A, part (c).

(h)   The demand for labor in case C will be greater than for case A since the marginal productivity of each unit of labor has increased.

208

Chapter 18

2. (a) Total factor earnings are $320. The thirtieth unit is prepared to supply services for $6 but receives $8. Hence, economic rent is $2 for the thirtieth unit.

(b) For D_1, quantity is 20 and price per unit is $10. For D_2, quantity is 30 and price per unit is $12.

(c) Elasticity for D_1 = 20/30 × 9/2 = 3.00; elasticity for D_2 = 10/35 × 10/4 = 0.71. Clearly, D_1 has the higher elasticity.

(d) (i) D_2 (ii) D_1 (iii) D_2 (iv) D_1

3. (a) Firm A, 30; Firm B, 10

(b) The 70 machines must have the same *MRP* regardless of the industry where they are used. Hence if 50 machines are allocated to industry A and 20 to industry B, *MRP* will be equalized at 6.

(c) The two curves intersect at a rental price of $6, where industry A rents 50 machines and industry B rents 20.

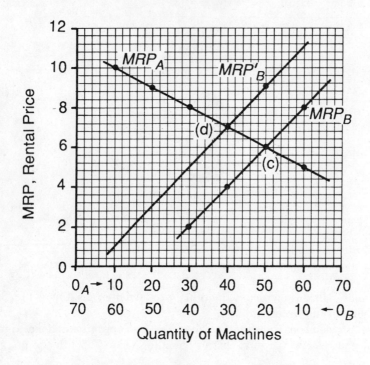

(d) Industry A rents 40 machines, and industry B rents 30. The equilibrium rental price increases from $6 to about $7.

(e) The *MRP* curve shifts to the left by about 15 machines, and industry B rents 10 more machines than initially. B does not rent 15 more machines because A is willing to pay a higher rental price to avoid losing that many machines ($7 rather than $6). If B is to match that higher rental price, it would rent only 10 more machines.

4. (a) $7.47, 1 percent, 50, $10

(b) $42.12, 1 percent, 50, $10

5. (a) Savings: $1,500, $900, $400, $200

   *MEC*s: 1,500/5,000 × 100% = 30%; 900/5,000 × 100% = 18%; 400/5,000 × 100% = 8%; 200/5,000 × 100% = 4%.

   (b) R12, R16. With the lower interest rate, the discounted present value of savings is greater, justifying more insulation.

   (c) The new *MEC*s are 15 percent, 9 percent, 4 percent, and 2 percent; this implies a leftward shift in the *MEC* curve. When the interest rate is 4 percent, the optimal insulation level is R12.

*6. (a) There is a disequilibrium differential of $2 per unit of labor since there are no nonmonetary considerations, no differences in labor productivity, and no difference in the types of jobs.

   (b) There are net advantages between the two regions; workers by moving from Y to X will increase their wage rate. As this flow occurs, the supply curve for labor in region Y will shift to the left and the supply curve in region X will shift to the right. Wages will rise in Y and fall in X. Migration from Y to X will continue until the wage differential is eliminated (wage = $11 in both regions).

   (c) The decrease in the value of output in region Y is the area under the demand curve between wage rates of $10 and $11. This value is given by $(-3 \times 10) + 0.5(3 \times 1) = -\$31.50$. The increase in the value of output in region X is given by $(3 \times 11) + 0.5(3 \times 1) = +\$34.50$. Hence the total value of output has increased by this reallocation of labor.

7. (a) *MRP* = $442, $360, $270, $189, $100

   (b) The perfect competitor would hire three units of labor since *MRP* = $360. The monopolist would also hire three units.

   (c) The monopolist would now hire four units while the competitive firm would hire five units.

   (d) *MRP* decreased as more labor units were employed because of diminishing marginal productivity. This is also true for a monopolist firm. However, the monopolist's *MRP* also decreased as output increased because its marginal revenue fell.

   (e) Elasticity for the perfect competitor is 1.75 (2/4 × 315/90). The monopoly firm has an elasticity of 1.00 (1/3.5 × 315/90). Thus, the perfect competitor has the more elastic demand curve for labor.

Table 18-1   Present Value of $1

$$PV = \left(\frac{1}{1+i}\right)^n$$

Years hence (n)	1%	2%	4%	5%	6%	8%	10%	12%	14%	15%	16%	18%	20%	22%	24%	25%	26%	28%	30%	35%	40%	45%	50%
1	0.990	0.980	0.962	0.952	0.943	0.926	0.909	0.893	0.877	0.870	0.862	0.847	0.833	0.820	0.806	0.800	0.794	0.781	0.769	0.741	0.714	0.690	0.667
2	0.980	0.961	0.925	0.907	0.890	0.857	0.826	0.797	0.769	0.756	0.743	0.718	0.694	0.672	0.650	0.640	0.630	0.610	0.592	0.549	0.510	0.476	0.444
3	0.971	0.942	0.889	0.864	0.840	0.794	0.751	0.712	0.675	0.658	0.641	0.609	0.579	0.551	0.524	0.512	0.500	0.477	0.455	0.406	0.364	0.328	0.296
4	0.961	0.924	0.855	0.823	0.792	0.735	0.683	0.636	0.592	0.572	0.552	0.516	0.482	0.451	0.423	0.410	0.397	0.373	0.350	0.301	0.260	0.226	0.198
5	0.951	0.906	0.822	0.784	0.747	0.681	0.621	0.567	0.519	0.497	0.476	0.437	0.402	0.370	0.341	0.328	0.315	0.291	0.269	0.223	0.186	0.156	0.132
6	0.942	0.888	0.790	0.746	0.705	0.630	0.564	0.507	0.456	0.432	0.410	0.370	0.335	0.303	0.275	0.262	0.250	0.227	0.207	0.165	0.133	0.108	0.088
7	0.933	0.871	0.760	0.711	0.665	0.583	0.513	0.452	0.400	0.376	0.354	0.314	0.279	0.249	0.222	0.210	0.198	0.178	0.159	0.122	0.095	0.074	0.059
8	0.293	0.853	0.731	0.677	0.627	0.540	0.467	0.404	0.351	0.327	0.305	0.266	0.233	0.204	0.179	0.168	0.157	0.139	0.123	0.091	0.068	0.051	0.039
9	0.914	0.837	0.703	0.645	0.592	0.500	0.424	0.361	0.308	0.284	0.263	0.225	0.194	0.167	0.144	0.134	0.125	0.108	0.094	0.067	0.048	0.035	0.026
10	0.905	0.820	0.676	0.614	0.558	0.463	0.386	0.322	0.270	0.247	0.227	0.191	0.162	0.137	0.116	0.107	0.099	0.085	0.073	0.050	0.035	0.024	0.017
11	0.896	0.804	0.650	0.585	0.527	0.429	0.350	0.287	0.237	0.215	0.195	0.162	0.135	0.112	0.094	0.086	0.079	0.066	0.056	0.037	0.025	0.017	0.012
12	0.887	0.788	0.625	0.557	0.497	0.397	0.319	0.257	0.208	0.187	0.168	0.137	0.112	0.092	0.076	0.069	0.062	0.052	0.043	0.027	0.018	0.012	0.008
13	0.879	0.773	0.601	0.530	0.469	0.368	0.290	0.229	0.182	0.163	0.145	0.116	0.093	0.075	0.061	0.055	0.050	0.040	0.033	0.020	0.013	0.008	0.005
14	0.870	0.758	0.577	0.505	0.442	0.340	0.263	0.205	0.160	0.141	0.125	0.099	0.078	0.062	0.049	0.044	0.039	0.032	0.025	0.015	0.009	0.004	0.002
15	0.861	0.743	0.555	0.481	0.417	0.315	0.239	0.183	0.140	0.123	0.108	0.084	0.065	0.051	0.040	0.035	0.031	0.025	0.020	0.011	0.006	0.004	0.002
16	0.853	0.728	0.534	0.458	0.394	0.292	0.218	0.163	0.123	0.107	0.093	0.071	0.054	0.042	0.032	0.028	0.025	0.019	0.015	0.008	0.005	0.003	0.002
17	0.844	0.714	0.513	0.436	0.371	0.270	0.198	0.146	0.108	0.093	0.080	0.060	0.045	0.034	0.026	0.023	0.020	0.015	0.012	0.006	0.003	0.002	0.001
18	0.836	0.700	0.494	0.416	0.350	0.250	0.180	0.130	0.095	0.081	0.069	0.051	0.038	0.028	0.021	0.018	0.016	0.012	0.009	0.005	0.002	0.001	0.001
19	0.828	0.686	0.475	0.396	0.331	0.232	0.164	0.116	0.083	0.070	0.060	0.043	0.031	0.023	0.017	0.014	0.016	0.009	0.007	0.003	0.002	0.001	
20	0.820	0.673	0.456	0.377	0.312	0.215	0.149	0.104	0.073	0.061	0.051	0.037	0.026	0.019	0.014	0.012	0.010	0.007	0.005	0.002	0.001	0.001	
21	0.811	0.660	0.439	0.359	0.294	0.199	0.135	0.093	0.064	0.053	0.044	0.031	0.022	0.015	0.011	0.009	0.008	0.006	0.004	0.002	0.001		
22	0.803	0.647	0.422	0.342	0.278	0.184	0.123	0.083	0.056	0.046	0.038	0.026	0.018	0.013	0.009	0.007	0.006	0.004	0.003	0.001	0.001		
23	0.795	0.634	0.406	0.326	0.262	0.170	0.112	0.074	0.049	0.040	0.033	0.022	0.015	0.010	0.007	0.006	0.005	0.003	0.002	0.001			
24	0.788	0.622	0.390	0.310	0.247	0.158	0.102	0.066	0.043	0.035	0.028	0.019	0.013	0.008	0.006	0.005	0.004	0.003	0.002	0.001			
25	0.780	0.610	0.375	0.295	0.233	0.146	0.092	0.059	0.038	0.030	0.024	0.016	0.010	0.007	0.005	0.004	0.003	0.002	0.001	0.001			
26	0.772	0.598	0.361	0.281	0.220	0.135	0.084	0.053	0.033	0.026	0.021	0.014	0.009	0.006	0.004	0.003	0.002	0.002	0.001				
27	0.764	0.586	0.347	0.268	0.207	0.125	0.076	0.047	0.029	0.023	0.018	0.011	0.007	0.005	0.003	0.002	0.002	0.001	0.001				
28	0.757	0.574	0.333	0.255	0.196	0.116	0.069	0.042	0.026	0.020	0.016	0.010	0.006	0.004	0.002	0.002	0.002	0.001	0.001				
29	0.749	0.563	0.321	0.243	0.185	0.107	0.063	0.037	0.022	0.017	0.014	0.008	0.005	0.003	0.002	0.002	0.001	0.001	0.001				
30	0.742	0.552	0.308	0.231	0.174	0.099	0.057	0.033	0.020	0.015	0.012	0.007	0.004	0.003	0.002	0.001	0.001	0.001					
40	0.652	0.453	0.208	0.142	0.097	0.046	0.022	0.011	0.005	0.004	0.003	0.001	0.001										
50	0.608	0.372	0.141	0.087	0.054	0.021	0.009	0.003	0.001	0.001	0.001												

Table 18-2 Present Value of $1 Received Annually for n Years

$$PV = \left(\frac{1}{1+i}\right)^1 + \left(\frac{1}{1+i}\right)^2 + \cdots + \left(\frac{1}{1+i}\right)^n$$

Years (n)	1%	2%	4%	5%	6%	8%	10%	12%	14%	15%	16%	18%	20%	22%	24%	25%	26%	28%	30%	35%	40%	45%	50%
1	0.990	0.980	0.962	0.952	0.943	0.926	0.909	0.893	0.877	0.870	0.862	0.847	0.833	0.820	0.806	0.800	0.794	0.781	0.769	0.741	0.714	0.690	0.667
2	1.970	1.942	1.886	1.859	1.833	1.783	1.736	1.690	1.647	1.626	1.605	1.566	1.528	1.492	1.457	1.440	1.424	1.392	1.361	1.289	1.224	1.165	1.111
3	2.941	2.884	2.775	2.723	2.673	2.577	2.487	2.402	2.322	2.283	2.246	2.174	2.106	2.042	1.981	1.952	1.923	1.868	1.816	1.696	1.589	1.493	1.407
4	3.902	3.808	3.630	3.546	3.465	3.312	3.170	3.037	2.914	2.855	2.798	2.690	2.589	2.494	2.404	2.362	2.320	2.241	2.166	1.997	1.849	1.720	1.605
5	4.853	4.713	4.452	4.329	4.212	3.993	3.791	3.605	3.433	3.352	3.274	3.127	2.991	2.864	2.745	2.689	2.635	2.532	2.436	2.220	2.035	1.876	1.737
6	5.795	5.601	5.242	5.076	4.917	4.623	4.355	4.111	3.889	3.784	3.685	3.498	3.326	3.167	3.020	2.951	2.885	2.759	2.643	2.385	2.168	1.983	1.824
7	6.728	6.472	6.002	5.786	5.582	5.206	4.868	4.564	4.288	4.160	4.039	3.812	3.605	3.416	3.242	3.161	3.083	2.937	2.802	2.508	2.263	2.057	1.883
8	7.652	7.325	6.733	6.463	6.210	5.747	5.335	4.968	4.639	4.487	4.344	4.078	3.837	3.619	3.421	3.329	3.241	3.076	2.925	2.598	2.331	2.108	1.922
9	8.566	8.162	7.435	7.108	6.802	6.247	5.759	5.328	4.946	4.772	4.607	4.303	4.031	3.786	3.566	3.463	3.366	3.184	3.019	2.665	2.379	2.144	1.948
10	9.471	8.983	8.111	7.722	7.360	6.710	6.145	5.650	5.216	5.019	4.833	4.494	4.192	3.923	3.682	3.571	3.465	3.269	3.092	2.715	2.414	2.168	1.965
11	10.368	9.787	8.760	8.306	7.887	7.139	6.495	5.938	5.453	5.234	5.029	4.656	4.327	4.035	3.776	3.656	3.544	3.335	3.147	2.752	2.438	2.185	1.977
12	11.255	10.575	9.385	8.863	8.384	7.536	6.814	6.194	5.660	5.421	5.197	4.793	4.439	4.127	3.851	3.725	3.606	3.387	3.190	2.779	2.456	2.196	1.985
13	12.134	11.348	9.986	9.394	8.853	7.904	7.103	6.424	5.842	5.583	5.342	4.910	4.533	4.203	3.912	3.780	3.656	3.427	3.223	2.799	2.469	2.204	1.990
14	13.004	12.106	10.563	9.899	9.295	8.244	7.367	6.628	6.002	5.724	5.468	5.008	4.611	4.265	3.962	3.824	3.695	3.459	3.249	2.814	2.477	2.210	1.993
15	13.865	12.849	11.118	10.380	9.712	8.559	7.606	6.811	6.142	5.847	5.575	5.092	4.675	4.315	4.001	3.859	3.726	3.483	3.268	2.825	2.484	2.214	1.995
16	14.718	13.578	11.652	10.838	10.106	8.851	7.824	6.974	6.265	5.954	5.669	5.162	4.730	4.357	4.033	3.887	3.751	3.503	3.283	2.834	2.489	2.216	1.997
17	15.562	14.292	12.166	11.274	10.477	9.122	8.022	7.120	6.373	6.047	5.749	5.222	4.775	4.391	4.059	3.910	3.771	3.518	3.295	2.840	2.492	2.218	1.998
18	16.398	14.992	12.659	11.690	10.828	9.372	8.201	7.250	6.467	6.128	5.818	5.273	4.812	4.419	4.080	3.928	3.786	3.529	3.304	2.844	2.494	2.219	1.999
19	17.226	15.678	13.134	12.085	11.158	9.604	8.365	7.366	6.550	6.198	5.877	5.316	4.843	4.442	4.097	3.942	3.799	3.539	3.311	2.848	2.496	2.220	1.999
20	18.046	16.351	13.590	12.462	11.470	9.818	8.514	7.469	6.623	6.259	5.929	5.353	4.870	4.460	4.110	3.954	3.808	3.546	3.316	2.850	2.497	2.221	1.999
21	18.857	17.011	14.029	12.821	11.764	10.017	8.649	7.562	6.687	6.312	5.973	5.384	4.891	4.476	4.121	3.963	3.816	3.551	3.320	2.852	2.498	2.221	2.000
22	19.660	17.658	14.451	13.163	12.042	10.201	8.772	7.645	6.743	6.359	6.011	5.410	4.909	4.488	4.130	3.970	3.822	3.556	3.323	2.853	2.498	2.222	2.000
23	20.456	18.292	14.857	13.489	12.303	10.371	8.883	7.718	6.792	6.399	6.044	5.432	4.925	4.499	4.137	3.976	3.827	3.559	3.325	2.854	2.499	2.222	2.000
24	21.243	18.914	15.247	13.799	12.550	10.529	8.985	7.784	6.835	6.434	6.073	5.451	4.937	4.507	4.143	3.981	3.831	3.562	3.327	2.855	2.499	2.222	2.000
25	22.023	19.523	15.622	14.094	12.783	10.675	9.077	7.843	6.873	6.464	6.097	5.467	4.948	4.514	4.147	3.985	3.834	3.564	3.329	2.856	2.499	2.222	2.000
26	22.795	20.121	15.983	14.375	13.003	10.810	9.161	7.896	6.906	6.491	6.118	5.480	4.956	4.520	4.151	3.988	3.837	3.566	3.330	2.856	2.500	2.222	2.000
27	23.560	20.707	16.330	14.643	13.211	10.935	9.237	7.943	6.935	6.514	6.136	5.492	4.964	4.524	4.154	3.990	3.839	3.567	3.331	2.856	2.500	2.222	2.000
28	24.316	21.281	16.663	14.898	13.406	11.051	9.307	7.984	6.961	6.534	6.152	5.502	4.970	4.528	4.157	3.992	3.840	3.568	3.331	2.857	2.500	2.222	2.000
29	25.066	21.844	16.984	15.141	13.591	11.158	9.370	8.022	6.983	6.551	6.166	5.510	4.975	4.531	4.159	3.994	3.842	3.569	3.332	2.857	2.500	2.222	2.000
30	25.808	22.396	17.292	15.372	13.765	11.258	9.427	8.055	7.003	6.566	6.177	5.517	4.979	4.534	4.160	3.995	3.842	3.569	3.332	2.857	2.500	2.222	2.000
40	32.835	27.355	19.793	17.159	15.046	11.925	9.779	8.244	7.105	6.642	6.233	5.548	4.997	4.544	4.166	3.999	3.846	3.571	3.333	2.857	2.500	2.222	2.000
50	39.196	31.424	21.482	18.256	15.762	12.233	9.915	8.304	7.133	6.661	6.246	5.554	4.999	4.545	4.167	4.000	3.846	3.571	3.333	2.857	2.500	2.222	2.000

Chapter 19

Labor Markets
and Discrimination

Learning Objectives

After studying this chapter, you should be able to:

—see the effects of labor market structure (competitive, seller's monopoly, and buyer's monopsony) on wages and employment levels

—recognize the pros and cons of legislated minimum wages

—understand the conflict that unions face between the goals of raising wages and preserving employment opportunities

—develop a historical perspective on unionism and labor legislation

—see how simple models can help you understand aspects of race and gender discrimination and the remedies proposed, including the idea of comparable worth

Multiple-Choice Questions

1. If a union negotiates a wage above the competitive level in a competitive industry, all but which of the following will occur?
   (a) Employment in the industry will fall.
   (b) The people employed will earn a higher wage rate than before.
   (c) A pool of unemployed workers will be created.
   (d) The supply curve of labor shifts to the right.

2. Where the supply curve of labor slopes upward, the marginal cost curve of labor to the monopsonist
   (a) is the same as the supply curve of labor
   (b) lies above the supply curve of labor
   (c) lies below and parallel to the supply curve
   (d) intersects the supply curve at the equilibrium wage

3. A labor union entering a competitive labor market can achieve higher wages for some workers by
   (a) restricting entry into the occupation
   (b) negotiating a higher wage through collective bargaining
   (c) increasing the supply of labor into the occupation
   (d) both (a) and (b)

4. A monopsonist in a nonunion labor market
   (a) lowers both the wage rate and employment below their competitive levels
   (b) lowers the wage rate but not employment below their competitive levels
   (c) has no effect on either the wage rate or employment
   (d) raises the wage rate but decreases employment with respect to their competitive levels

5. A union negotiating a higher wage in a monopsonistic labor market
   (a) will cause increased unemployment in the industry
   (b) can raise the wage rate but not employment over the monopsonistic level
   (c) can raise both the wage rate and employment over the monopsonistic level
   (d) has the same effect on employment as a minimum wage set above the competitive level

6. A minimum wage is said to be *binding* or *effective* if
   (a) it has been set by a union
   (b) the minimum is above the market wage that would otherwise prevail
   (c) it is the lowest wage that affords individuals a subsistence life-style
   (d) all workers who desire employment at that wage are in fact employed

7. There is extensive evidence that much of the incidence of unemployment caused by minimum wage legislation is borne by
   (a) young and inexperienced workers
   (b) workers in the automobile industry
   (c) members of craft unions
   (d) college graduates

8. Which of the following statements concerning the likely consequences of a comprehensive minimum wage is correct?
   (a) In competitive labor markets, a binding minimum wage has no adverse employment effects.
   (b) In monopsonistic labor markets, a minimum wage set equal to the competitive wage will increase wages but not employment.
   (c) The employment effects of minimum wages in competitive labor markets will be the same as in monopsonistic labor markets.
   (d) In monopsonistic labor markets, a binding minimum wage may increase both wages and employment.

9. Suppose that there are two occupations, A and B. All things being equal, which of the following would create a higher wage in A than in B?
   (a) Occupation B requires more postsecondary education.
   (b) Occupation A involves more health risks.
   (c) Workers in occupation B are relatively more scarce than those in occupation A, but the demand for both occupations is the same.
   (d) Workers in occupation A enjoy more nonmonetary benefits than workers in occupation B.

10. Which of the following are likely reasons for the appeal of employer-supplied fringe benefits?
    (a) They appeal to employees because they are often not subject to income taxes.
    (b) Fringe benefits are often supplied to employees at lower cost than they could purchase them privately.
    (c) Certain fringe benefits tend to bind workers more closely to their employers, thereby decreasing turnover rates.
    (d) All of the above.

11. The objective of "two-tier" wage structures is to
    (a) pay different wages to men and women
    (b) recognize differences in the intrinsic value of different jobs
    (c) lower labor costs while preserving the higher wages for existing employees
    (d) pay unproductive workers lower wages

Questions 12 to 18 refer to the following graph, which depicts a labor market for unskilled workers.

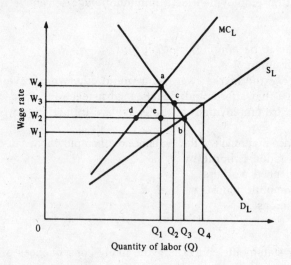

Quantity of labor (Q)

12. If perfect competition existed in this market, the wage and quantity of employment would be
    (a) W_4 and Q_1 (c) W_3 and Q_2
    (b) W_1 and Q_1 (d) W_2 and Q_3

13. If this market were monopsonistic, the firm would hire
    (a) Q_1 workers   (c) Q_3 workers
    (b) Q_2 workers   (d) Q_4 workers

14. A profit-maximizing monopsony would pay a wage of
    (a) W_1 (c) W_3
    (b) W_2 (d) W_4

15. If a minimum wage of W_2 is imposed on the monopsony, the supply curve of labor becomes
    (a) $MC_L - S_L$ (c) acb
    (b) W_2bS_L (d) W_2daMC_L

16. In this case, the minimum wage of W_2 would generate employment of
    (a) Q_1 (c) Q_3
    (b) Q_2 (d) Q_4

17. If a minimum wage of W_3 were imposed on the market, the monopsonist
    would hire
    (a) Q_2 workers
    (b) more than Q_3 workers since the marginal cost of labor would fall
    (c) Q_4 workers because the demand for labor shifts to the right
    (d) Q_1 workers

18. With a minimum wage of W_3, total unemployment in this market would be
    (a) $Q_3 - Q_2$ (c) $Q_4 - Q_3$
    (b) $Q_4 - Q_2$ (d) $Q_4 - Q_1$

19. If discrimination prevented a certain group of people from entering labor market
    E but not labor market O,
    (a) the wage rate would be lower than the competitive level in both markets
    (b) the labor supply curve is farther to the left than it would otherwise be in
        both markets
    (c) wage rates will tend to be higher in market E and lower in market O than
        they would be with no discrimination
    (d) individuals in labor market E would benefit only if the demand curve for
        labor is elastic

20. Which of the following is *not* a cause of the female-male "salary gap"?
    (a) Women are underrepresented in high-paying occupations.
    (b) Proportionately fewer women than men reach higher-paying jobs in the
        occupations in which they both work.
    (c) Because women have greater labor force attachment than men, they are
        paid less for comparable work.
    (d) Women who do reach higher-paying jobs do so more slowly than men.

21. The doctrine of comparable worth holds that
    (a) occupations with the same intrinsic value should receive the same rate of
        pay
    (b) supply and demand should determine relative wages
    (c) returns to labor and capital should be comparable across the economy
    (d) it is not possible to determine objectively whether discrimination has
        occurred in a given occupation

Exercises

1. Suppose that there is a competitive market for workers in a particular industry. The equilibrium level of employment is 200, and the wage rate is $50. The labor demand and supply curves are given by $Q_D = 300 - 2W$ and $Q_S = 4W$, respectively.

   (a) A union now successfully organizes workers and obtains a wage rate of $60. Assuming that unionization does not affect the industry's demand curve, calculate the number of unionized members who are employed in this industry. How many workers lost their jobs? How many workers would like to work in this industry?

   (b) A union could have achieved the same levels of the wage rate and employment by restricting the supply of workers using required apprenticeship programs and/or reduced openings for trainees. Show that a new, restricted labor supply curve of $Q_S = -60 + 4W$ would yield the same wage and employment levels as in (a).

   (c) The reduction in employment caused by a union wage that is above the competitive level depends on the elasticity of labor demand. If the industry's demand curve for labor had been given by $Q_D = 200$, what is the implied elasticity of labor demand? How many workers would have lost their jobs due to unionization? (Assume that the labor supply curve is $Q_S = 4W$.)

2. Columns 1 and 2 represent the supply-of-labor relationship for a monopsonistic employer. Fill in the values for total cost in column 3 and then calculate the marginal cost values in column 4. This exercise should demonstrate to you that the marginal cost of labor lies above the supply curve of labor in a nonparallel fashion.

(1) Quantity of labor	(2) Wage rate	(3) Total cost	(4) Marginal cost
8	$10.00	$80.00	
9	10.50	_____	_____
10	11.00	_____	_____
11	11.50	_____	_____
12	12.00	_____	_____
13	12.50	_____	_____
14	13.00	_____	_____

3. Referring to the graph, which represents the labor market in an industry, answer the following questions.

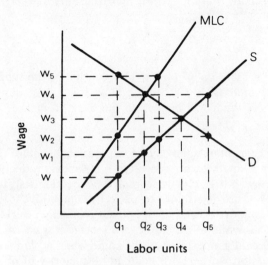

(a) If a competitive market prevailed, the equilibrium wage would be _____ , and the amount of employment would be _____ .

(b) If a wage-setting union enters this (competitive) market and tries to establish a higher wage at, for example, w_4, the amount of employment would be _____ , and the amount of surplus labor unemployed would be _____ . How would the labor supply curve look?

(c) Assume that this market consists of a single large firm hiring labor in a local market. If the firm hired q_1 workers, it would have to pay all workers the wage _____ , but the marginal labor cost of the last person hired would be _____ . Because the marginal revenue product of the last person (q_1) hired is equal to the amount _____ , there is an incentive for the firm to continue hiring up to the amount _____ , at which the wage will be _____ , the marginal labor cost will be _____ , and the marginal revenue product will be _____ . Compare this with the result in (a).

(d) Suppose that a union now organizes in the monopsonist market and sets a wage at w_3. The amount of employment will be _____ .

(e) Draw a new labor supply curve showing what happens when a union organizes this labor market but instead of setting a high wage excludes workers by stiff apprenticeship rules. Predict the effects.

4. There are two competitive labor markets in the economy of Saskatchewan. Market X has a labor demand function given by $W = 360 - 3Q$ and a labor supply function $W = 40 + 2Q$. The wage rate is denoted as W, and the quantity of labor is Q. Market Z has the same labor demand function as X but a labor supply function $W = 20 + 2Q$.

(a) Calculate the competitive equilibrium levels of W and Q in each labor market.

(b) Suppose that a minimum wage of 162 had been imposed in market Z. At the minimum wage, what is the quantity of labor demanded? The quantity of labor supplied? How many workers are displaced in this market?

(c) If all of the unemployed persons in (b) entered labor market X, the supply curve of labor in X becomes $W = 30 + 2Q$. How many will obtain employment in market X? What will happen to the wage in market X?

5. This exercise focuses on the concept of equal pay for work of equal value. The graphs depict the markets in a small town for two types of labor: production line workers and office employees (e.g., clerks, secretaries, receptionists). The initial equilibria in these markets are determined by perfectly competitive forces and are characterized by 500 employees in each market, but production workers are paid an hourly wage of $8, while office employees receive a wage of $4. Although everyone (regardless of gender) is paid the same wage *within* each market, a majority of production workers are male and a majority of office employees are female; therefore, the *average* female wage is lower than the *average* male wage. These average statistics suggest that indirect discrimination due to historical occupational restrictions on women *may* be present. Assume that the government sends its experts (the "pay police") to investigate. After the experts rate these occupations with respect to required skills and education, working conditions, accountability, and mental demands, they conclude that these occupations are indeed of comparable worth or equal value and should be paid the same hourly wage. The firms in this town are therefore in violation of the pay equity legislation and must rectify the situation immediately.

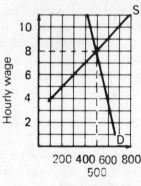

Quantity of
production line workers

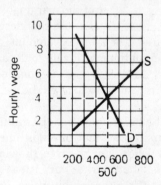

Quantity of
office employees

(a) Suppose that firms comply with the legislation by paying the average wage of $6 in each market. Discuss the implications for employment and unemployment in each market (be sure to indicate how many people lose their jobs and how many join the labor force).

(b) Suppose that the firms comply instead by paying everyone in each market $8 an hour. Discuss the implications for employment and unemployment in each market.

(c) Who decides the "worth" of the "experts"?

(d) Indicate on the graph what happens to the competitive wage structure over time as more women move across occupations.

Answers

Multiple-Choice Questions

1. (d) 2. (b) 3. (d) 4. (a) 5. (c) 6. (b) 7. (a) 8. (d) 9. (b) 10. (d) 11. (c) 12. (d)
13. (a) 14. (a) 15. (b) 16. (c) 17. (a) 18. (b) 19. (c) 20. (c) 21. (a)

Exercises

1. (a) Substituting $W = 60$ into the demand equation, we obtain an employment level of 180. Twenty workers lost their jobs. At $W = 60$, 240 individuals wish to work in this industry.

    (b) Equating the new supply equation with the demand equation, we obtain $W = 60$ and employment of 180, which is the same result as in (a).

    (c) The new demand curve is perfectly inelastic; changes in the wage rate have no effect on the quantity of labor demanded. As a result, the union could increase the wage by any amount without loss of jobs.

2.   Total cost: $80,00; 94.50; 110.00; 126.50; 144.00; 162.50; 182.00
        Marginal cost: $14.50; 15.50; 16.50; 17.50; 18.50; 19.50

3. (a) w_3; q_4

    (b) q_2; $q_5 - q_2$; horizontal at w_4 to q_5 on supply curve and thereafter the supply curve for wages greater than w_4.

    (c) w; w_2; w_5; q_2; w_1; w_4; w_4; employment is less and the amount of wages is lower than in (a).

    (d) q_4

    (e) The supply curve shifts leftward. All wage predictions are raised, and employment levels are lowered.

4. (a) For market X, equilibrium Q is found by equating $360 - 3Q$ to $40 + 2Q$. Hence $Q = 64$ and $W = 168$. For market Z, $Q = 68$ and $W = 156$.

    (b) At the minimum wage, the quantity of labor demanded is 66 while the quantity of labor supplied is 71. Unemployment is therefore 5, and employment in market Z would be 2 fewer than under competitive conditions.

    (c) The supply curve in X now becomes $W = 30 + 2Q$ (or $Q = 0.5W - 15$ instead of $Q = 0.5W - 10$). Setting $D = S$ and solving, $Q = 66$ and $W = 162$. Thus, two of the unemployed workers from Z are now employed in X, and the wage in X falls to 162 from 168.

5. (a) At \$6 per hour, the quantity supplied of production line workers is 300, and the quantity demanded is 550. Hence there are 250 vacant jobs in this market (50 new jobs and 200 vacated jobs). At the same wage, the quantity demanded for office employees is 400 but the quantity supplied is 700. Therefore, there are 300 unemployed in this market. Of these, 100 had jobs before the wage increase and 200 entered the labor force because of the more attractive wage.

   (b) At the \$8 wage rate, the market for production line workers is in equilibrium. However, in the market for office employees, there are now only 300 employed and 600 unemployed—200 of whom had jobs prior to the wage increase.

   (c) Your guess is as good as ours.

   (d) Over time, as women acquire new skills and change occupations, or as new female workers make different unrestricted career choices, the supply of production workers shifts to the right as women enter this occupation, and the supply of office employees shifts to the left as women exit. The wage gap therefore decreases. As it is impossible to account for and calibrate all of the differences in nonmonetary advantages and disadvantages between these occupations (to both women and men), it is impossible to say if the wage gap will close completely. However, we can say that the net advantage of either occupation to gender will be eliminated by market forces.

PART SIX

International Trade

Chapter 20

The Gains from Trade

Learning Objectives

After studying this chapter, you should be able to:

—recognize that international trade among countries involves basically the same principles of exchange that apply to trade among individuals

—realize that although gains from trade occur even when production is fixed, further gains arise when nations increase output of goods in which they have a comparative advantage

—understand that comparative advantage arises from differences in the opportunity costs of producing particular goods

—acknowledge that comparative advantage may be determined by natural resource endowments and climate but may also be determined dynamically by changing human skills and experience in production

—explain that the terms of trade, defined as the ratio of export prices to import prices, indicate how the gains from trade are divided between buyers and sellers

Multiple-Choice Questions

1. Country X has an absolute advantage over country Y in the production of widgets if
    (a) fewer resources are required in X to produce a given quantity of widgets than in Y
    (b) a given amount of resources in X produces more widgets than the same amount of resources in Y
    (c) relative to Y, more widgets can be produced in X with fewer resources
    (d) all of the above

2. If two countries share a reciprocal absolute advantage in the production of two goods, total output of the two countries can be increased if each country
   (a) consumes all of its own production
   (b) specializes in producing the good in which it has an absolute advantage
   (c) specializes in the product in which it has an absolute disadvantage
   (d) allocates its resources between the two commodities in proportion to the domestic marginal products of the resources

3. Comparative advantage is said to exist whenever
   (a) one country can produce a given level of output with fewer resources compared to another country
   (b) a given amount of resources produces more output in one country compared to another
   (c) one country has an absolute advantage over another country in the production of all goods
   (d) different countries have different opportunity costs in production

4. If there are two countries A and B, and two goods X and Y, and if A has a comparative advantage in the production of X, it necessarily follows that
   (a) A has an absolute advantage in the production of X
   (b) B has an absolute advantage in the production of X
   (c) A has a comparative disadvantage in the production of Y
   (d) B has an absolute advantage in the production of Y

5. In a two-country and two-good model, gains from trade would not exist if
   (a) one country had an absolute advantage in the production of both goods
   (b) a given amount of resources produced more of both goods in one country
   (c) one country was endowed with far more resources than the other
   (d) the countries had the same opportunity costs in the production of both goods

6. Which of the following statements is *not* true about opportunity cost?
   (a) Equal opportunity costs for pairs of commodities between two countries lead to gains from trade.
   (b) Opportunity costs depend on relative production costs.
   (c) Differences in opportunity costs across countries can enhance total output of both goods through trade and specialization.
   (d) Comparative advantage can be expressed in terms of opportunity costs.

7. If production of each unit of wool in country A implies that beef production must be decreased by four units, while in country B each additional unit of beef decreases wool output by four units, the gains from trade
   (a) are maximized if country A specializes in wool production and country B in beef
   (b) are maximized if country A specializes in beef production and country B in wool
   (c) are maximized if country A allocates 80 percent of its resources to wool and the remainder to beef, while country B does the opposite
   (d) cannot be realized because opportunity costs in the two countries are the same

8. Gains from specialization can arise when
   (a) countries have different opportunity costs in production
   (b) there are economies of scale in production
   (c) experience gained via specialization lowers cost through learning by doing
   (d) all of the above

9. Free trade within the European Community led to
   (a) each member country specializing in specific products (e.g., furniture, cars, clothing)
   (b) a large increase in product differentiation, with countries tending to specialize in subproduct lines
   (c) no perceptible alteration in production patterns
   (d) less trade among EC members

10. Economies of scale and learning by doing are different because
    (a) one refers to an increase in variable costs and the other to a decrease
    (b) economies of scale refer to a movement along the average cost curve, whereas learning by doing shifts the average cost curve
    (c) economies of scale affect variable costs, but learning by doing affects only fixed costs
    (d) learning by doing affects profits but not costs

11. The gains from specialization and trade depend on the pattern of _____ advantage, not _____ advantage.
    (a) absolute, comparative
    (b) monetary, nonmonetary
    (c) absolute, reciprocal
    (d) comparative, absolute

12. The terms of trade
    (a) refer to the quantity of imported goods that can be obtained for each unit of an exported good
    (b) are measured by the ratio of the price of exports to the price of imports
    (c) determine the division of the gains from trade
    (d) all of the above

13. A rise in export prices as compared to import prices is considered a favorable change in the terms of trade since
    (a) one can export more per unit of imported goods
    (b) employment in export industries will increase
    (c) one can acquire more imports per unit of exports
    (d) all of the above

14. By trading in international markets, countries
    (a) can consume beyond their production possibility boundary
    (b) will not alter their previous production patterns
    (c) can produce outside of their production possibility boundary
    (d) must choose one of the intercepts on the production possibility boundary, indicating complete specialization

Questions 15 to 18 refer to the data in the following table.

| Country | One unit of resources can produce | |
	Lumber (bd m)	Aluminum (kg)
Australia	4	9
Canada	9	3
Brazil	3	2

15. Considering just Australia and Canada,
    (a) Australia has an absolute advantage in lumber
    (b) Australia has an absolute advantage in aluminum
    (c) there are no possible gains from trade
    (d) Canada should specialize in aluminum production

16. Considering just Canada and Brazil,
    (a) Brazil has an absolute advantage in lumber
    (b) Brazil has a comparative advantage in aluminum
    (c) Canada has an absolute advantage in only one commodity
    (d) there are no possible gains from trade

17. In Australia, the opportunity cost of 1 board meter of lumber is
    (a) 2.25 kg of aluminum   (c) 0.36 kg of aluminum
    (b) 0.44 kg of aluminum   (d) 3.60 kg of aluminum

18. In Canada, the opportunity cost of 1 kilogram of aluminum is
    (a) 0.33 bd m of lumber   (c) 3.0 bd m of lumber
    (b) 2.70 bd m of lumber   (d) 3.33 bd m of lumber

Exercises

1. For each of the situations described, determine which commodity each country should specialize in and trade.

   (a) One unit of resources can produce: The opportunity costs are:

	Radios	Cameras		1 Radio	1 Camera
Japan	2	4	Japan	_____	_____
Korea	3	1	Korea	_____	_____

   Japan should specialize in the production of _____ .
   Korea should specialize in the production of _____ .

   (b) One unit of resources can produce: The opportunity costs are:

	Radios	Cameras		1 Radio	1 Camera
Japan	2	4	Japan	_____	_____
Korea	1	3	Korea	_____	_____

   Japan should specialize in the production of _____ .
   Korea should specialize in the production of _____ .

(c)   One unit of resources can produce: The opportunity costs are:

	Radios	Cameras		1 Radio	1 Camera
Japan	2	4	Japan	_____	_____
Korea	1	2	Korea	_____	_____

Japan should specialize in the production of _____ .
Korea should specialize in the production of _____ .

(d)   Which case represents reciprocal absolute advantage?

(e)   Which case demonstrates that absolute advantage is not a sufficient condition for trade to occur? Explain.

(f)   Which case suggests why a nation as technologically advanced as Japan can gain from trading with other countries with lower wages? Explain.

2.   Countries A and B are both currently producing both watches and dairy products. Assume that country A gives up the opportunity to produce 100 pounds of dairy products for each watch it makes, and B could produce one watch at a cost of 200 pounds of dairy products.
   (a)   The opportunity cost of making watches (in terms of dairy products) is lower in country _____ .
   (b)   The opportunity cost of making dairy products (in terms of watches) is lower in country _____ .
   (c)   Country B should specialize in _____ and let country A produce
         _____ .
   (d)   The terms of trade (the price of one product in terms of the other) would be somewhere between _____ and _____ pounds of dairy products for one watch.

3.   The following table provides data on the index of merchandise export prices and the index of merchandise import prices during the 1970s in Canada.

Year	Index of export prices	Index of import prices	Terms of trade
1970	100.6	98.6	_____
1972	103.3	102.3	_____
1974	157.1	135.6	_____
1976	176.6	157.9	_____
1978	205.4	200.7	_____

(a)   Using the definition of the terms of trade that involves indexes, complete the table by calculating the terms of trade to one decimal place.

(b)   What does an increase in the terms of trade signify?

(c)   Would you classify the change in the terms of trade during the period 1972 to 1974 as favorable to Canada? Explain.

4.   The following table provides data on the productivity of a single unit of a resource in producing wheat and microchips in both Canada and Japan.

	One unit of resource produces	
	Wheat (t)	Microchips
Canada	50	20
Japan	2	12

(a)   Which country has an absolute advantage in the production of wheat? Of microchips?

(b)   What is the opportunity cost of producing a ton of wheat in Canada? In Japan?

(c)   Which country has a comparative advantage in the production of wheat? Of microchips?

(d)   Suppose that Canada is endowed with 2 units of this all-purpose resource while Japan is endowed with 10 units. Draw each country's production possibility boundary.

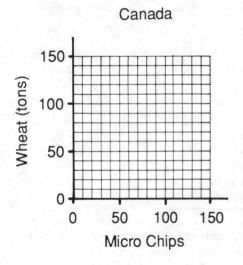

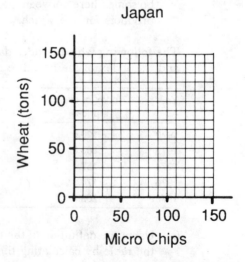

(e) Suppose that prior to trade, each country allocated half of its resource endowment to production of each good. Indicate the production and consumption points of each country in the graphs (for simplicity, assume that these are the only two countries in the world).

(f) What is world output of each good?

(g) Indicate the production points of each country after trade, and determine world production levels.

(h) Suppose that the terms of trade are one microchip for one ton of wheat and that Canada consumes as much wheat after trade as it did before trade. Indicate the posttrade consumption points of each country and each country's imports and exports.

(i) If the terms of trade changed to two microchips for one ton of wheat, which country would benefit? Explain.

*5. The following graph depicts a country's production possibility curve between wool and lumber. Prior to trade, the country is producing and consuming at point R, which involves 10 units of wool and 10 units of lumber. Due to large increases in construction activity in this economy, the country now decides that it wishes to consume 14 units of lumber.

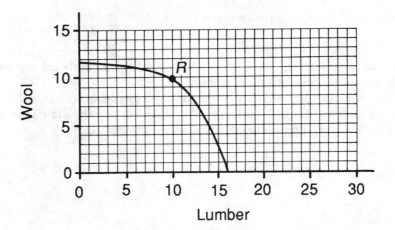

(a) How much wool must this country give up to obtain the additional four units of lumber in a no-trade environment. Explain.

(b) Suppose that the terms of trade in international markets are one unit of wool for two units of lumber. Assuming that production remains at R, how much wool would the country have to give up to obtain the additional four units of lumber if it engages in international trade? Explain.

Answers

Multiple-Choice Questions

1. (d) 2. (b) 3. (d) 4. (c) 5. (d) 6. (a) 7. (b) 8. (d) 9. (b) 10. (b) 11. (d) 12. (d)
13. (c) 14. (a) 15. (b) 16. (b) 17. (a) 18. (c)

Exercises

1. (a) Japan: 1 radio costs 2 cameras; 1 camera costs ½ radio.
        Korea: 1 radio costs ⅓ camera; 1 camera costs 3 radios.
        Japan should produce cameras. Korea should produce radios.

   (b) Japan: 1 radio costs 2 cameras; 1 camera costs ½ radio.
        Korea: 1 radio costs 3 cameras; 1 camera costs ⅓ radio.
        Japan should produce radios. Korea should produce cameras.

   (c) Japan: 1 radio costs 2 cameras; 1 camera costs ½ radio.
        Korea: 1 radio costs 2 cameras; 1 camera costs ½ radio.
        Japan should produce both and Korea should produce both. There would
        be no gains from trade.

   (d) Case (a) represents reciprocal absolute advantage; Japan has an absolute
        advantage in cameras, and Korea has an absolute advantage in radios.

   (e) Case (c) shows that even though Japan has an absolute advantage in
        producing both goods, no trade will occur because relative prices (or
        opportunity costs of production) are identical to those in Korea.

   (f) Case (b) shows that even though Japanese workers are more productive
        in both industries (and therefore can expect to earn more than Korean
        workers), mutually beneficial trade can still occur if each country exports
        the good for which it has a comparative advantage.

2. (a) A (b) B (c) dairy products, watches (d) 100, 200

3. (a) 102.0, 101.0, 115.9, 111.8, 102.3

   (b) An increase in the terms of trade means that fewer exports are required
        to pay for a given amount of imports.

   (c) The terms of trade changed from 101.0 to 115.6; this was a favorable change
        in our terms of trade. It cost us fewer exports to buy the same imports,
        or for the same exports we received more imports.

4. (a) Canada has an absolute advantage in both goods.
    (b) 0.4, 6.0
    (c) Canada, Japan
    (d)

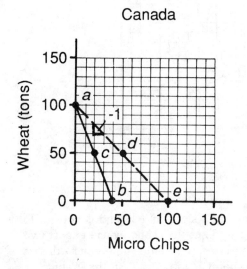

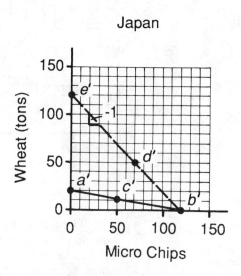

Canada's production possibility boundary is denoted *ab*, and Japan's is *a'b'*.

(e) Canada would be producing and consuming 50 tons of wheat and 20 microchips (point *c* in the diagram), and Japan would be producing and consuming 10 tons of wheat and 50 microchips (point *c'*).

(f) Assuming that these are the only countries making up the world, total output of wheat is 60 tons and world production of microchips is 70 units.

(g) Each country specializes in the commodity in which it has a comparative advantage. Thus Canada specializes completely in wheat production (see point *a*), and Japan specializes completely in microchip production (see point *b'*). World ouput is now 100 tons of wheat and 120 microchips

(h) Terms of trade equal to one ton of wheat for one microchip mean that Canada can trade from its production point *a* to any point on its consumption possibility curve *ae*—which has a slope of −1, representing the terms of trade. Similarly, Japan can trade from point *b'* to any point on its consumption possibility curve *b'e'*. Since it was assumed that Canada consumes the same amount of wheat both before and after trade, its consumption bundle is represented by point *d*, which contains 50 units of each good. Therefore, Canada is exporting 50 tons of wheat in return for imports of 50 microchips. Japan, having exported 50 microchips to Canada, has 70 remaining for its own consumption. When this is combined with its 50 tons of wheat imports, Japan consumes at point *d'*.

(i) The terms of trade lines in the graphs would become flatter with a slope of −½. Thus Canada's consumption possibilities would increase (the dashed line rotates outward on point *a*), while Japan's decrease (the dashed line rotates inward on point *b'*). Thus Canada would get a larger share of the gains from trade.

*5. Five units. This requires a movement along the production possibility boundary from point R to point A on the following graph.

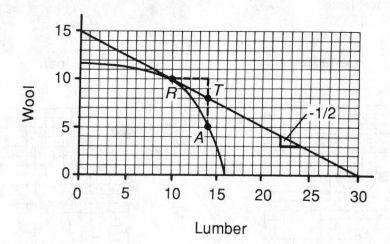

(b) Two units. The terms of trade line has a slope of $-\frac{1}{2}$ and is tangent to the production possibility curve at R. Thus the economy can export two units of wool in return for imports of four units of lumber—this is represented by a movement from point R to point T on the graph.

Chapter **21**

Barriers to Free Trade

Learning Objectives

After studying this chapter, you should be able to:

—cite the benefits and costs of expanding international trade

—understand how tariffs and quotas influence patterns of output and trade and affect a nation's standard of living

—recognize fallacious arguments for free trade and for protectionism

—understand trade policy remedies and procedures available in major trading countries

—grasp issues under consideration in multilateral, regional, and bilateral trade negotiations

—follow the debate in Canada on the Free Trade Agreement with the United States

—recount the important highlights of the Free Trade Agreement and the early evidence of its impact on the Canadian economy

Multiple-Choice Questions

1. Which of the following statements is *not* true of free trade?
   (a) Free trade leads to a maximization of world output.
   (b) Free trade maximizes world living standards.
   (c) Free trade always makes each individual better off.
   (d) Free trade can increase the average income in a country.

2. Which of the following trade practices is *not* specifically designed as a device to promote protectionism?
   (a) ad valorem tariffs
   (b) voluntary export restrictions
   (c) countervailing duties
   (d) import quotas

3. A central difference in the effects of a tariff and a voluntary export restriction (VER)—equal to the same quantity as under the tariff—is that
   (a) the VER yields a higher price for consumers than the tariff
   (b) the tariff pushes the consumer price beyond the price associated with the VER
   (c) government tariff revenue becomes suppliers' revenue with a VER
   (d) the revenue of producers decreases with the VER as the quantity sold decreases

4. Suppose that the nominal tariff rate applied to finished imported widgets is 20 percent and that widgets cost $100 to produce in Canada, but this includes $40 of raw materials that were imported duty-free. The effective rate of tariff protection on widgets is
   (a) 33.3 percent   (c) 50 percent
   (b) 20 percent   (d) 10 percent

5. Which of the following national objectives is a valid argument for some degree of protectionism?
   (a) concentration of national resources in a few specialized products
   (b) increases in average incomes
   (c) diversification of a small economy in order to reduce the risk associated with cyclical fluctuations in price
   (d) ability of domestic firms to operate at minimum efficient scale

6. Protection against low-wage foreign labor is a fallacious protectionist argument because
   (a) free trade benefits everyone
   (b) the gains from trade depend on comparative, not absolute, advantage
   (c) when the foreign country increases its exports to us, their wages will rise
   (d) the terms of trade will equalize for low- and high-wage countries

7. A large country that accounts for a significant share of world demand for a product can increase its national income by
   (a) encouraging domestic production
   (b) restricting domestic demand for the product, thereby decreasing its price and improving the terms of trade
   (c) imposing import quotas on the product
   (d) subsidizing imports of the good and thereby monopolize world consumption

8. If the objective of a government is to maximize national income, which of the following is the *least* justifiable reason for using tariff protection?
   (a) to protect against unfair subsidization of foreign firms by their governments
   (b) to protect against unfair low wages paid to foreign labor
   (c) to protect newly developing industries
   (d) to protect against "dumping" of foreign-produced goods

9. Countervailing duties are attempts to maintain "a level playing ground" by
   (a) retaliating against foreign tariffs
   (b) raising or lowering tariffs multilaterally
   (c) establishing a common tariff wall around a customs union
   (d) assessing tariffs that will offset foreign government subsidies

10. Strategic trade policy
    (a) involves government assistance for key growth industries by protecting domestic markets and/or providing subsidies
    (b) involves erecting higher tariff and nontariff barriers across the board to protect domestic industry
    (c) means that the government negotiates special trade agreements with its important defense partners
    (d) is designed to encourage the migration of certain industries to other countries so as better to exploit domestic comparative advantage

11. Which of the following is *not* a fallacious protectionist argument?
    (a) Buy Canadian, and both the money and the goods stay at home.
    (b) Trade cannot be mutually advantageous if one of the trading partners is much larger than the other.
    (c) Too many imports lower Canadian living standards as our money is shipped abroad.
    (d) A foreign firm, temporarily selling in Canada at a much lower price than in its own country, threatens the Canadian industry's existence.

12. The problem with restricting imports as a means of reducing domestic unemployment is that
    (a) it merely redistributes unemployment from import-competing industries to our export industries when trading partners retaliate
    (b) Canadians would rather do without than have to buy Canadian-produced goods
    (c) our import-competing industries are not labor-intensive
    (d) our import-competing industries are always fully employed

13. Which of the following statements about nontariff barriers to trade (NTBs) is incorrect?
    (a) The use of NTBs has declined worldwide since the mid 1930s.
    (b) The misuse of antidumping and countervailing duties unilaterally constitutes an increasingly important NTB.
    (c) Voluntary export restraints, negotiated agreements, and quotas are examples of NTBs.
    (d) Most NTBs are ostensibly levied for trade relief purposes but end up being protectionist.

14. Which of the following motivations for dumping can be of permanent benefit to the buying country?
    (a) predatory pricing
    (b) cyclical stabilization of sales
    (c) enabling foreign producers to achieve lower average costs and therefore price
    (d) all of the above

15. Although the Kennedy and Tokyo rounds of GATT each reduced tariffs by about a third, it gives a misleading picture of the change in the freedom of trade because
    (a) countries trade less than they used to
    (b) the use of nontariff barriers to trade has grown
    (c) most countries simply replaced their tariffs with import taxes
    (d) many countries simply imposed countervailing duties

16. The "staples thesis" of Professor Innis states that
    (a) the goods that Canada imports and exports are complementary or, in his words, "stapled together"
    (b) it is small, inexpensive items such as staples and toothpicks that spur the Canadian export sector
    (c) Canadian economic growth has been tied to a sequence of exports of primary products
    (d) Canadian economic growth has been tied to a sequence of exports of manufactured products

17. The central trade feature of Sir John A. MacDonald's National Policy in 1878 was
    (a) bilateral tariff reductions with the United States
    (b) a treaty with the United States that permitted all primary products to cross the border free of any tariff burden
    (c) Canada's entry as a full partner in GATT
    (d) increased tariff protection for Canadian manufacturing

18. The primary effect on Canadian industry from the GATT trade liberalization in the 1970s and 1980s has been
    (a) the total elimination of certain industries
    (b) an increase in intra-industry trade, with firms reducing the number of product lines
    (c) the forcing of Canadian industry to specialize in certain products
    (d) large increases in imports and substantial reductions in exports

19. The countries in a free trade area
    (a) impose no tariffs on each other's goods
    (b) each have an independent tariff structure with the rest of the world
    (c) do not permit the free movement of labor across their borders
    (d) all of the above

20. Which of the following is *not* one of the features of the Canada–United States Free Trade Agreement (FTA)?
    (a) elimination of all tariffs within 10 years
    (b) elimination of countervailing duties between the two countries
    (c) exemption of cultural industries
    (d) continuance of quotas to support provincial supply management schemes

21. The principle of national treatment that is embedded in the FTA means that Canada could, for example, introduce any product standards it likes, so long as
    (a) they apply only to Canadian-produced goods
    (b) the standards are no more stringent than those existing in the United States
    (c) they apply equally to Canadian- and American-produced goods sold in Canada
    (d) they apply only to Canadian exports

22. Which of the following is *not* an argument that was put forward by Canadian supporters of the FTA?
   (a) The FTA will help Canadian firms fully to capture economies of scale.
   (b) The FTA will provide Canadian firms with a more secured access to American markets.
   (c) The FTA will force a harmonization of Canadian social policies with those of the United States.
   (d) The FTA is simply a continuation of Canadian trade liberalization trend that began in 1935.

Exercises

1. (a) The three graphs illustrate the demand and supply of an imported commodity Z in a free trade environment. Revise these graphs according to the protectionist policy outlined below each, and indicate the new price as P^* and the new quantity as Q^*.

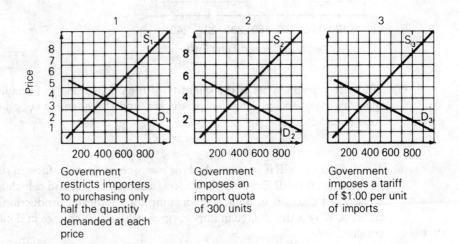

| Government restricts importers to purchasing only half the quantity demanded at each price | Government imposes an import quota of 300 units | Government imposes a tariff of $1.00 per unit of imports |

(b) If the demand for Z were highly inelastic, which policy would the government likely *not* choose if it wanted to maximize its restriction on the amount of the import purchased? Why?

(c) Which policy would the government likely choose if it were concerned that protectionist policies might be inflationary? Why?

2. For goods that are homogenous (domestic and foreign products are identical), imports, domestic production, and domestic consumption can be represented on the same graph. For this exercise, consider the market for canned tuna. The foreign supply curve (S_f) is horizontal, which implies that Canada accounts for a relatively small share of the world market and any change in Canadian purchases does not affect world prices.

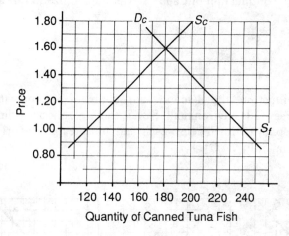

(a) Under free trade, what is the quantity of tuna consumed in Canada, the quantity supplied by Canadian producers, and the quantity supplied by foreign producers?

(b) If a 20 percent tariff is imposed, by how many cents does the foreign supply curve shift upward? Draw the new foreign supply curve, and calculate the consequent changes in domestic consumption, domestic production, and imports. Why is the change in imports greater than the change in domestic production?

(c) If the government wants to ensure that domestic production rises to 160, how large a quota for imported tuna should it allow? Explain.

3. The following graph depicts the demand and supply curves for an imported good. D_C represents demand in Canada, and S_f represents foreign supply.

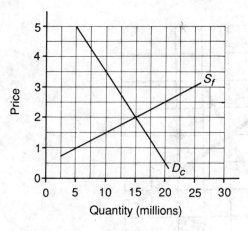

(a) What are equilibrium price and quantity and the total revenue of foreign firms?

(b) Suppose that the government imposes a specific tariff on this commodity equal to $2 per unit. What are the resulting equilibrium price Canadian consumers pay and the quantity they import? Illustrate this on the graph.

(c) What are the revenues of foreign firms and the Canadian government?

(d) Instead of the tariff, suppose that the Canadian government imposed an import quota on this good equal to 10 million units. What is the new supply curve that Canadian consumers effectively face?

(e) What would be the resulting market price and revenue of both foreign firms and the government under the quota scheme?

*4. The following graph illustrates the domestic supply of steel (S_D), the foreign supply of steel (S_F), and the domestic demand (D).

(a) Draw the total supply curve for steel and establish the overall price (P_0).

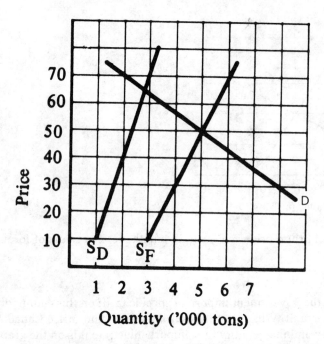

(b) What is the level of Canadian consumption, and how much of this is due to imports and how much to domestic production?

(c) The domestic government now levies a tariff of $20 per ton on steel from foreign suppliers. Using a broken line, draw the after-tariff supply curve for foreigners and the new total supply curve. Label the new price and quantity P_1 and Q_1, respectively.

(d) What effect has the tariff had on imports and domestic production?

*5. This exercise on the efficiency gain from free trade examines the impact on consumers' and producers' surplus in moving from a no-trade situation to free trade for an imported good and then an exported good (the same analysis can be applied to the removal or reduction of tariffs). In what follows, assume that Canadian demand is a small part of world demand so that the world price P_W is independent of both Canadian demand D_C and supply S_C. Thus foreign supply is perfectly elastic at P_W. In the no-trade situation, the equilibrium price and quantity are P_E and Q_E.

(a) In the following graph, P_W is less than P_E, so trade will result in imports of this good.

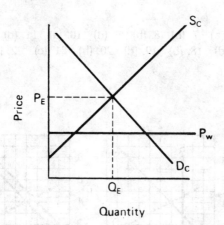

Once trade is permitted,
(i)   label domestic consumption D_D
(ii)   label domestic production S_D
(iii) What is the change in consumers' surplus in Canada?
(iv)   What is the change in producers' surplus of Canadian firms?
(v)   Is the net change in total surplus for Canada positive or negative?

(b) In this graph, P_W is greater than P_E, so trade will result in exports of this commodity.

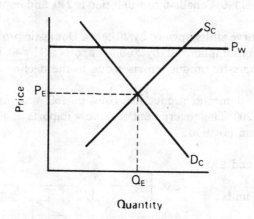

Once trade is permitted,
(i)   label domestic consumption D_D
(ii)   label domestic production S_D
(iii) What is the change in consumers' surplus in Canada?
(iv)   What is the change in producers' surplus of Canadian firms?
(v)   Is the net change in total surplus for Canada positive or negative?

Answers

Multiple-Choice Questions

1. (c)   2. (c)   3. (c)   4. (a)   5. (c)   6. (b)   7. (b)   8. (b)   9. (d)   10. (a)   11. (d)   12. (a)
13. (a)   14. (c)   15. (b)   16. (c)   17. (d)   18. (b)   19. (d)   20. (b)   21. (c)   22. (c)

Exercises

1. (a)

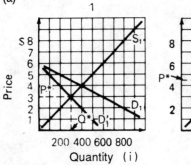
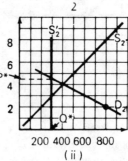
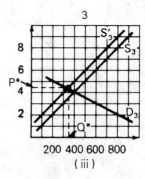

(b)   It would not choose the tariff policy. Price would rise by almost the full amount of the tariff, and there would be little change in equilibrium quantity.

(c)   Policy (i): A restriction on demand not only reduces imports but also lowers the price.

2. (a)   Canadian production is 120, Canadian consumption is 240, and imports are 120.

(b)   The foreign supply curve shifts upward by 20 cents. Domestic production rises by 20, domestic consumption falls by 20, and imports fall by 40. Imports fall by more than domestic production rises due to the decline in total quantity demanded.

(c)   At a price of $1.40, domestic production rises to 160, and domestic consumption falls to 200. The government can allow imports of 40 if this is to be an equilibrium position.

3. (a) $2, 15 million units, and $30 million, respectively

(b) $3.50 and 10 million units, respectively

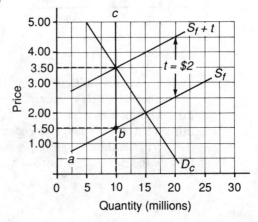

(c) Canadian consumers pay $3.50 per unit, of which $2 goes to the government. Therefore, government tariff revenue is $20 million and that of foreign firms is $15 million.

(d) The new effective supply curve is labeled *abc* in the graph.

(e) The price per unit is $3.50, revenue of foreign firms equals $35 million, and, since there is no tariff, government revenue is zero.

*4. (a) and (c)

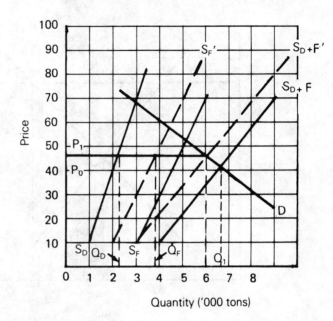

(b) Approximately 6,000 tons are consumed, of which 4,500 are imported and 2,000 are produced domestically.

(d) The tariff forces a reduction in the quantity supplied by foreign producers (i.e., imports) to Q_F and an increase in the quantity supplied by domestic producers to Q_D.

*5. (a) (i) and (ii)

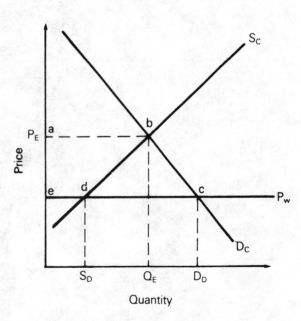

(iii) Canadian consumers' surplus increases by area *abce*.
(iv) Canadian producers' surplus decreases by area *abde*.
(v)   Positive. The increase in consumers' surplus outweighs the loss in producers' surplus—Canada receives a net gain in efficiency equal to area *bcd*.

(b) (i) and (ii)

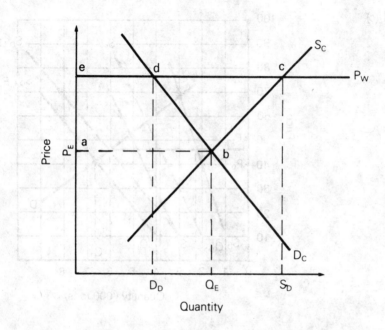

(iii) Canadian consumers' surplus decreases by area *abde*.
(iv) Canadian producers' surplus increases by area *abce*.
(v)   Positive. The increase in producers' surplus outweighs the loss in consumers' surplus—Canada receives a net gain in efficiency equal to area *bcd*.

PART SEVEN

The Market Economy: Problems and Policies

Chapter 22

Benefits and Costs of Government Intervention

Learning Objectives

After studying this chapter, you should be able to:

—explain how the market system coordinates the allocation of resources

—explain the role of windfall profits and losses

—distinguish between private valuations and social valuations of benefits and costs

—identify the major causes of market failure and of government failure

—define *externalities* and identify methods for internalizing them

—understand that society's goals for government involvement include activities beyond those concerned with economic efficiency

—explain why it is neither possible nor efficient to correct all market failures, nor is it always efficient to do nothing

Multiple-Choice Questions

1. The likely result in a market economy if the government taxed away all windfall profits would be
   (a) a more rapid shift of resources to expanding industries
   (b) the removal of the most important incentive for resource allocation
   (c) improved market signals and responses
   (d) increased information about temporary shortages and surpluses

2. Which of the following is *not* an argument for increased reliance on markets for allocating resources?
   (a) The market system coordinates millions of independent economic decisions automatically.
   (b) With competitive markets, price will tend to equal minimum average total cost of production.
   (c) Markets function best when external benefits are associated with consumption or production.
   (d) Market forces tend to correct disequilibrium situations.

3. The appearance of windfall profits in one industry in a market economy indicates
   (a) unexpected changes in supply and/or demand in the industry
   (b) a disequilibrium phenomenon
   (c) an unanticipated benefit to producers in that industry
   (d) all of the above

4. One of the most important features of the price system is
   (a) long-term stability of prices and output
   (b) its ability to respond quickly and automatically to changing demand and supply conditions
   (c) the assurance that consumers will pay for collective consumption goods
   (d) that it solves the problem of scarcity and provides abundance for all

5. If a ton of newspaper costs $350 to produce and in the process causes $10 worth of pollution damage to the environment,
   (a) the private cost is $360 per ton
   (b) the social cost is $10 per ton and the private cost is $350 per ton
   (c) the private cost is $350 per ton and the social cost is $340 per ton
   (d) the social cost is $360 per ton and the private cost is $350 per ton

6. Which of the following is the best example of a collective consumption good in a classroom?
   (a) a pencil   (c) a copy of the textbook
   (b) a student's notes   (d) the temperature in the room

7. Adverse selection refers to a situation where
   (a) the managers of corporations pursue goals other than profits
   (b) the values of consumers and producers differ
   (c) one party to a transaction has more information about, say, the quality of the product than the other party
   (d) the government selects the wrong form of intervention for correcting a market failure

8. If there are costly externalities associated with an economic activity and that activity is carried out until the private marginal benefit equals the private marginal cost,
   (a) this activity should be subsidized
   (b) the social marginal net benefit is positive
   (c) private costs exceed social costs
   (d) too many resources are being allocated to this activity

9. The presence of external benefits associated with production implies that
   (a) private output exceeds the socially optimal output
   (b) private output is less than the socially optimal output
   (c) private output corresponds to the socially optimal output
   (d) any of the above, depending on the relative magnitude of social and private costs

10. A positive externality would probably result from
    (a) a discharge of a toxic waste into the St. Lawrence River
    (b) a newly painted house
    (c) the dumping of wastes in an outgoing tide
    (d) cigarette smoking

11. A market economy is unlikely to provide a sufficient amount of a collective consumption good like national defense because
    (a) national defense does not benefit everyone to the same degree
    (b) private firms produce national defense less efficiently than does the government
    (c) consumers are poorly informed about the benefits of national defense
    (d) it is impossible to withhold national defense from people who don't pay for it

12. Which one of the following would *not* be a source of inefficient market outcomes?
    (a) externalities
    (b) collective consumption goods
    (c) windfall profits and losses
    (d) information asymmetries

13. A Toronto resident who drives a car to work rather than take public transportation
    (a) is maximizing private utility
    (b) is likely to be creating a negative externality
    (c) creates a situation in which social cost is likely to exceed private cost
    (d) all of the above

14. Efficient government intervention requires that
    (a) the costs of government enforcement be zero
    (b) the marginal benefits of intervention be just equal to the marginal costs of intervention
    (c) intervention should continue until all negative externalities have been eliminated
    (d) there be no productivity losses in the private sector as a result of government intervention

15. Which of the following can the government use to correct market failure?
    (a) taxes and/or subsidies
    (b) rules and regulations restricting market activity
    (c) public provision of goods and services
    (d) all of the above

16. Principal-agent problems that government agencies confront are similar to those that private firms face, but they
    (a) are less serious because stockholders of a firm almost never agree on the objectives of the firm
    (b) are more serious because managers of firms can be more easily replaced than government bureaucrats
    (c) should not be considered a form of government "imperfection"
    (d) should be considered a benefit rather than a cost of government intervention

17. Arrow's impossibility theorem
    (a) shows that in some cases the majority-rule voting procedure results in inconsistent social decisions
    (b) proves that efficient government intervention is impossible
    (c) concerns the inability of governments to make sound social decisions without logrolling
    (d) suggests that it is impossible for markets to achieve efficient outcomes because of various market imperfections

18. The economically efficient quantity of a public good is the level of output at which
    (a) the sum of everyone's individual valuations of the good is just equal to its marginal cost
    (b) the marginal cost of additional output of the public good is zero
    (c) the sum of the individual marginal valuations is maximized
    (d) the marginal valuations of all individuals are equal

Exercises

1. The graph illustrates the situation for a firm that is producing a good that imposes external costs on neighboring residences. Marginal revenues to the firm are shown by the line AB; PMC represents the private marginal costs to the firm; MD represents the external costs or marginal damage resulting from production. Label the graph as needed to answer the questions.

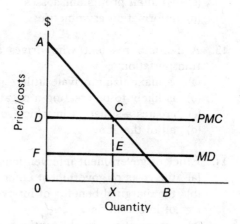

    (a) Explain why output X is the private optimum (profit-maximizing) output for the firm.

    (b) Draw the social marginal cost curve on the graph.
    (c) The total external cost of producing quantity X is indicated by area _____ .
    (d) Indicate on the graph the socially optimal output level as Z.
    (e) The additional external costs from producing X instead of Z is equal to the area _____ .
    (f) The additional private costs from producing X instead of Z is equal to the area _____ .
    (g) Explain why there will be a net gain in welfare (that is, net social benefits will be positive) in reducing output from X to Z.

2. Assume that Mr. Maple has access to his wooded retreat by way of a 2-kilometer road that he and another individual, Mr. Oak, must maintain. The demand for quality on the part of Mr. Oak and Mr. Maple is shown in the graphs, where the quality of the road can be measured as the number of times the road is graded or tons of gravel added. The cost of increasing the quality is shown as $S = MC$. (We assume that "zero" quality implies that the road is barely passable.)

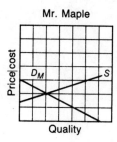
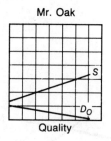
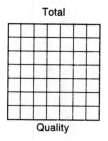

(a) What quality level will Mr. Maple maintain without considering Mr. Oak?

(b) How would you illustrate the social demand for road quality? Use the graph. (*Hint:* Recall the discussions in the text on external benefits and collective consumption goods.)

(c) Given the costs of quality improvements as shown, would the socially desirable quality result in an improvement in the quality of the road compared to the quality maintained by Mr. Maple alone?

(d) If the level of road quality given by (c) was produced and the costs were shared, would Mr. Maple pay more or less than in (a)?

3. For each of the government programs or regulations cited, identify what types of market failure might be used as a rationale.
(a) national defense

(b) pollution control regulations

(c) public health insurance programs

(d) Environment Canada Weather Service

(e) student loan programs

(f) government support for scientific research

(g) truth-in-lending laws, requiring lenders to disclose to borrowers the true rate of interest

(h) minimum wage legislation

(i) quotas limiting the number of fish that can be caught

(j) zoning regulations

4. In the accompanying graph, the marginal social damage (*MSD*) schedule refers to incremental pollution costs associated with a unit increase in production activity. The marginal net private benefit (*MNPB*) schedule is the net private gain ($MR - MC$) to the producer as output is increased.

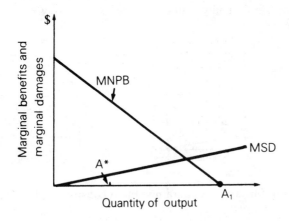

(a) With no government intervention, what level of output would the producer choose? Why?

(b) From society's point of view, what is the optimal output level? Explain.

(c) Suppose that the government, unaware of the precise shape of the *MSD* schedule, limits the producer to A^* of output. At A^*, is society better off or worse off than in a no-intervention situation? Explain.

5. A small community is in the process of repainting city hall. The citizens have narrowed the potential colors down to a choice of either red, white, or blue and have also agreed that combinations of the three are undesirable. To choose one color from among the three, a committee of three individuals has been selected. Each of the committee members has a personal preference ranking of the alternatives as indicated in the following schedule (1 is most preferred, 3 is least preferred).

Individual Preference Rankings

| | Committee member | | |
Color	A	B	C
Red	1	3	2
White	2	1	3
Blue	3	2	1

Since a vote over the entire field of three colors results in a three-way tie (each committee member has a different most preferred color), the committee has agreed to select the winning color by elimination through majority voting in pairwise matches (i.e., the color with the most votes in the first contest between any two colors proceeds to a second contest with the remaining color).

(a) If the agenda calls for red versus white in the first contest, what will ultimately be the color of city hall?

(b) If the first round had pitted white against blue, what color would have been chosen from the three?

(c) Alternatively, if the first round had matched red against blue, what color would city hall have been painted?

Answers

Multiple-Choice Questions

1. (b)   2. (c)   3. (d)   4. (b)   5. (d)   6. (d)   7. (c)   8. (d)   9. (b)   10. (b)   11. (d)   12. (c)
13. (d)   14. (b)   15. (d)   16. (b)   17. (a)   18. (a)

Exercises

1.

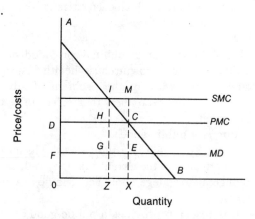

(a) output X maximizes net private benefit ($MR = PMC$)
(b) graph: $SMC = PMC + MD$
(c) $OFEX$
(d) on graph
(e) $ZGEX$
(f) $ZXCH$
(g) Reducing output from X to Z will decrease social costs by $ZIMX$ ($ZHCH + ZGEX$) but will decrease revenues to the firm by a lesser amount, $ZICX$. The triangle IMC represents the net social gain.

2. (a) The point where the demand and $S(= MC)$ curves intersect for Mr. Maple.
   (b) Add the demand schedules vertically; that is, find the total willingness to pay for each level of quality from 0 to Q^*.

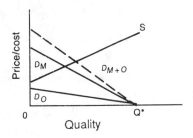

   (c) Yes. The line $S = MC$ would intersect D_{M+0} to the right of the D_M intersection with S, indicating an improvement in road quality.
   (d) It depends on how the costs are shared. If both Mr. Oak and Mr. Maple pay one-half, Mr. Maple would pay less. The new cost would be only slightly above what Mr. Maple paid before, but half the cost would be borne by Mr. Oak. Other cost-sharing arrangements are certainly possible.

3. (a) National defense is a collective consumption good. Adding to the population of a country does not diminish the extent to which each citizen is defended by a given size and quality of the armed forces.
   (b) Pollution is an external cost.
   (c) Asymmetric information. Until the advent of publicly provided health insurance, it was difficult for the elderly to purchase health insurance because insurance companies were aware of the problem of adverse selection (i.e., they feared that only those who knew themselves to be bad risks would buy health insurance).
   (d) Providing weather information is a public good.
   (e) Student loan programs are designed to increase the general educational level in the society (a public good) and, to the extent that they reduce the immediate financial burden of going to college, should contribute to a more equitable distribution of income.
   (f) It can be argued that scientific research provides a public good.
   (g) Information asymmetry. Financial institutions are far more likely than the average borrower to know the true rate of interest.
   (h) Minimum wage legislation is a form of price floor. Proponents usually argue that it will achieve a more equitable distribution of income.
   (i) External cost. Fish are a common-property resource. An individual taking more fish reduces the catch of others but does not count this as a cost, though it is to society.
   (j) Zoning laws regulating such things as lot size and signage and prohibiting certain types of activities (such as fraternities in a residential area) are meant to reduce external costs.

4. (a) The producer would choose output A_1 since this output corresponds to $MNPB = 0$, which implies that net private benefits are at a maximum. Each unit less than A_1 adds to net private benefits because $MNPB > 0$; similarly, each unit greater than A_1 deceases net private benefits.

  (b) Where the $MNPB$ and MSD curves intersect at output A_0. Beyond this, the additional costs to society exceed the additional benefits.

  (c) Worse off. By restricting output to A^*, the net benefit forgone by society (compared to the optimal output A_0) is area ZTQ (that is, the loss in net benefits to the producer, A^*TQA_0, minus the reduction in marginal social damages, A^*ZQA_0).

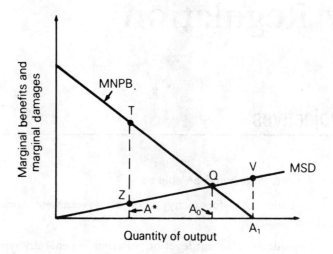

5. (a) Blue. Both A and C prefer red to white, so red proceeds to the second contest against blue. Both B and C prefer blue to red, so blue is the ultimate winner.

  (b) Red. White wins the first round, and red wins over white in the second round.

  (c) White.

Chapter 23

Environmental and Safety Regulation

Learning Objectives

After studying this chapter, you should be able to:

—understand the economic basis for many types of government social and environmental regulation

—explain why the economically efficient level of pollution is generally not zero

—compare the different policy instruments that can be used to control pollution

—understand the economic basis for health and safety regulation

—distinguish cost-effectiveness and benefit-cost analysis and their role in evaluating government regulations

Multiple-Choice Questions

1. A profit-maximizing competitive firm
    (a) always produces in excess of the output that is allocatively efficient
    (b) always generates pollution as a by-product of production
    (c) produces more than the allocatively efficient output when it ignores external costs associated with its production
    (d) automatically considers external costs in making production decisions

2. The socially optimal level of output of a good is the quantity at which
    (a) all marginal costs, private plus external, equal the marginal benefits, private plus external
    (b) external costs are minimized
    (c) the social benefit of the last unit of output is just equal to its external cost
    (d) all of the above

3. If the incremental costs of pollution abatement increase with increasing levels of abatement,
   (a) the optimal level of pollution is the minimum attainable
   (b) the optimal level of pollution reduction is the amount where the marginal benefits of prevention equal the marginal costs
   (c) optimal pollution is necessarily zero
   (d) the optimal amount of abatement is zero

4. A firm currently emitting harmful pollutants would have an incentive to reduce emissions if
   (a) an emissions tax per unit of discharge were imposed
   (b) private citizens were able to sue for pollution damages
   (c) it were forced to hold a tradable emissions permit
   (d) any of the above actions were taken

5. A common problem with the successful use of emissions taxes is that
   (a) information on external costs is not always available for setting tax rates
   (b) the economy is already overtaxed
   (c) firms will generally not reduce emissions to zero
   (d) the government must also specify the means by which firms are to abate pollution

6. Tradable emissions permits
   (a) are, in effect, equivalent to creating a market for "bads"
   (b) can achieve the same resource allocation as emissions taxes
   (c) are cost-effective in that for a given amount of pollution, the total cost of abatement is minimized
   (d) all of the above

Questions 7 to 10 refer to the following graph.

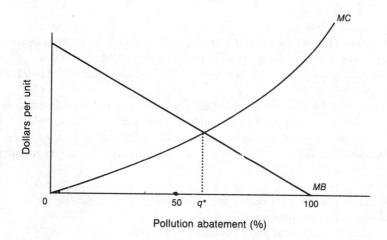

7. The marginal benefits of pollution abatement
   (a) are the value of reducing pollution damages, representing a "demand curve" for pollution control
   (b) increase as *MB* shifts rightward
   (c) decline as the level of abatement increases
   (d) all of the above

8. The economically efficient amount of pollution control is
   (a) the output at which marginal benefits equal marginal costs
   (b) 100 percent, since that maximizes the gains from pollution control
   (c) zero
   (d) impossible to determine without additional information about the type of pollution

9. New findings of adverse health effects or other damages from this pollutant will
   (a) shift the marginal cost curve rightward
   (b) shift the marginal benefit curve rightward
   (c) shift both the marginal benefit curve and the marginal cost curve rightward
   (d) have no effect on either the marginal benefit curve or the marginal cost curve

10. Other things being equal, an improvement in pollution control technology
    (a) shifts *MC* rightward, increasing the optimal level of pollution control
    (b) shifts *MC* leftward, decreasing the optimal level of pollution control
    (c) shifts both the *MC* and *MB* curves rightward
    (d) shifts *MB* rightward, increasing the optimal level of pollution control

11. With multiple emitters, economic efficiency in pollution control requires that
    (a) all emitters reduce pollution by the same percentage
    (b) marginal costs of abatement be equal for all emitters
    (c) all emitters reduce pollution by the same absolute amount
    (d) there be zero emissions

12. Requiring that all sources adopt a specific pollution control technique when there are many methods for controlling a certain type of pollution
    (a) is likely to be the most efficient way to achieve a certain amount of pollution abatement
    (b) is likely to be less efficient than either emissions taxes or tradable emissions permits in achieving a given amount of abatement
    (c) is more efficient the more divergent the abatement costs of different firms
    (d) eliminates the need for monitoring and enforcement by the regulatory agency

13. The federal Department of Consumer and Corporate Affairs
    (a) sets standards for product safety
    (b) can remove dangerous products from the marketplace
    (c) regulates "truth in advertising"
    (d) all of the above

14. Government regulations covering health and safety issues are necessary because
    (a) health and safety information is a public good
    (b) information about product safety may be impossible to obtain or to evaluate
    (c) when information is costly, health and safety standards can enhance efficiency
    (d) all of the above

15. Comparing different life-saving options by computing the cost per life saved by each is an example of
    (a) cost-effectiveness analysis
    (b) benefit-cost analysis
    (c) the engineering approach to public decision making
    (d) paternalism as the basis of regulatory policy

16. If the plastics industry has been disposing of its wastes free of charge, government regulation to ensure a more efficient use of resources would affect the industry's output and product price in which of the following ways?
    (a) Both output and price would decrease.
    (b) Output would decrease, but there would be no change in price.
    (c) Output would be unchanged, but price would increase.
    (d) Price would increase and output would decrease.

Exercises

1. Suppose that installing an antipollution device adds $10 to the cost of making each unit of a product at every level of output. Other things being equal and assuming a downward-sloping demand curve,
    (a) marginal cost will _____ .
    (b) average cost will _____ .
    (c) the supply curve will _____ .
    (d) short-run equilibrium price will _____ ,
        but by less than _____ .
    (e) short-run equilibrium output will _____ .

2. The following schedule shows (a) how the cost of production increases as a pulp and paper firm expands output and (b) the effect of pollution from the firm on commercial fishing in the area.

Output (tons per week)	Total private cost	Value of fishing loss due to pollution
0	$ 0	$ 0
1	500	100
2	550	225
3	620	365
4	710	515
5	820	675
6	1,050	845
7	1,350	1,025

(a) Complete the following table, and graph your results.

Output (tons per week)	Average private cost (APC)	Marginal private cost (MPC)	Average social cost (ASC)	Marginal social cost (MSC)
1	_____		_____	
2	_____	_____	_____	_____
3	_____	_____	_____	_____
4	_____	_____	_____	_____
5	_____	_____	_____	_____
6	_____	_____	_____	_____
7	_____	_____	_____	_____

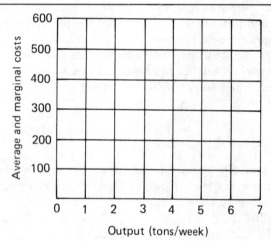

(b) If the firm were producing 4 tons of output per week, how much revenue would be required to cover its private costs? How much revenue would be required to cover the social costs?

(c) Assume that the market for this firm's product (paper) is perfectly competitive and that the firm's private costs of production are typical for the industry. Predict the long-run equilibrium price and the output for this firm in the absence of pollution controls.

(d) Assume now that firms in this industry are required either to pay compensation for the negative externalities or incur abatement costs. The industry price would be (higher, the same, lower) and the output (less, the same, greater). This firm's ability to survive would depend on the long-run equilibrium price for paper being at least _____ or on its being able to keep the total of negative externalities and costs of abatement at levels as (low, high) as those of its competitors.

3. A policy analyst in a government agency has been told to choose among the following programs designed to save lives. Assume that all of the programs produce the same outcome over the same time period except in the expected number of lives saved.

Program	Total number of lives saved	Program costs (billions)	Cost per life saved (millions)
A	10	$1.2	_____
B	20	3.1	_____
C	20	2.8	_____
D	40	6.8	_____

(a) Complete the table to compute the program that is most cost-effective in saving lives.

(b) If you had to choose among these four programs, what additional information would you need to make the choice using benefit-cost analysis?

*4. The graphs present the marginal cost curves for pollution abatement for two firms in a given industry (for simplicity, assume that there is no fixed cost associated with abatement). The regulatory agency has determined that the level of pollution emissions must decrease by a total of eight units. Assume that the type of pollution in this industry is readily measurable.

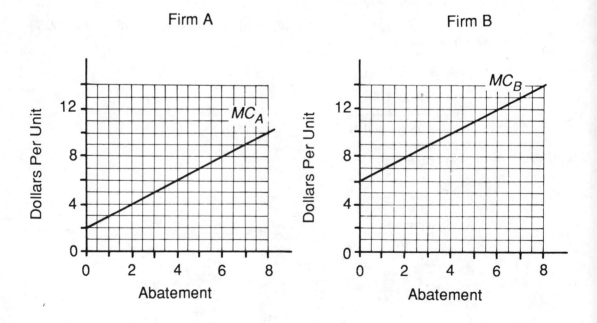

(a) Suppose that the regulatory agency directly controls these firms by ruling that each firm must decrease emissions by four units. What is the total industry cost of abating the eight units of pollution?

(b) Instead of direct controls, suppose that the regulatory agency imposes a tax on emissions of $8 per unit. What is the level of abatement by each firm?

(c) What is the total cost of abatement for the industry when the emissions tax is imposed?

(d) Now consider the effect of the regulatory agency's introducing a system of tradable emissions permits. Specifically, suppose that the agency rules that each firm must abate emissions by four units but that either firm can reduce this by any amount so long as it can induce the other firm to increase its abatement by an offsetting amount. What would be the resulting levels of abatement by these firms? Explain.

(e) What is the total abatement cost to the industry under the system of tradable emissions permits?

Answers

Multiple-Choice Questions

1. (c)   2. (a)   3. (b)   4. (d)   5. (a)   6. (d)   7. (d)   8. (a)   9. (b)   10. (a)   11. (b)   12. (b)
13. (d)   14. (d)   15. (a)   16. (d)

Exercises

1. (a) rise by $10
   (b) rise by $10
   (c) shift to the left
   (d) rise; less than $10
   (e) decline

2. (a)

Output (tons/week)	APC	MPC	ASC	MSC
0	$ 0		$ 0	
		$500		$600
1	500		600	
		50		175
2	275		387.50	
		70		210
3	206.67		328.33	
		90		240
4	177.50		306.25	
		110		270
5	164		299	
		230		400
6	175		315.83	
		300		480
7	192.86		339.29	

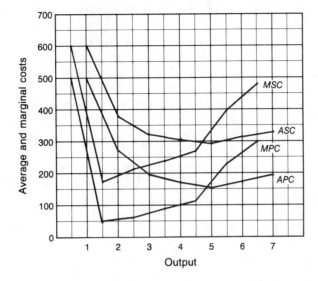

(b) $710 (per ton price of $177.50); $1,225 (per ton price of $306.25)
(c) $164; 5 tons per week (this is the output where average costs are at a minimum)
(d) higher; less; $299 (the lowest average social cost); low

3. (a) $120; $155; $140; $170. Program A is the most cost-effective program.
    (b) You would need information regarding the value of the additional lives saved. For example, only programs B and C produce an identical outcome (20 lives saved). The others produce different outcomes. A related ethical issue is whether the value of a life varies across individuals; court decisions awarding compensation to victims of accidents, negligence, and other torts indicate that our society does make such distinctions.

*4. (a) Each firm abates four units, so the marginal abatement costs for Firms A and B are $6 and $10, respectively. Since there are no fixed costs to abatement, total abatement cost for each firm is given by the area under its abatement marginal cost curve measured up to its level of abatement. Thus for Firm A, total abatement cost is $16 = ($2 × 4) + [($6 − $2) × 4]/2; for Firm B, it is $32 = ($6 × 4) + [($10 − $6) × 4]/2. Therefore, industry abatement cost is $48 = $16 + $32.
     (b) A tax of $8 imposed on each unit of emissions represents a savings of $8 for each unit of abatement. Thus each firm abates until the savings from an additional unit of abatement equals the marginal cost of abatement. For Firm A this occurs at a level of abatement equal to six units, while for Firm B it occurs at two units of abatement.
     (c) Given the levels of abatement determined in (b), abatement cost for Firm A is $30 = ($2 × 6) + [($8 − $2) × 6]/2, while for Firm B it is $14 = ($6 × 2) + [($8 − $6) × 2]/2. Thus industry abatement cost is $44.

(d)   Abatement of the fourth unit costs Firm A $6 but costs Firm B $10; thus
      the potential for gains from trade exists. For example, Firm B would pay
      up to $10 to avoid having to abate the fourth unit of emission, and Firm
      A would accept anything over $6 to induce it to increase slightly its level
      of abatement ($7 for the fifth unit). Thus these firms will negotiate to buy
      and sell emissions permits until no further gains from trade are achievable.
      This occurs when the firms face equal marginal abatement costs; Firm B
      will have reduced its level of abatement by two units to a total of two,
      and Firm A will have increased its level by an offsetting two units to a
      total of six.

(e)   Since the level of abatement for each firm is the same as that under the
      emissions tax discussed earlier, the total abatement cost for the industry
      is the same at $44.

Chapter 24

Taxation and Public Expenditure

Learning Objectives

After studying this chapter, you should be able to:

—understand the role of the tax system in raising revenue, redistributing income, and affecting resource allocation

—explain progressive and regressive taxes

—understand that the incidence of a tax does not depend on who writes the cheque to pay the tax bill

—explain the economic logic for the distribution of government responsibilities in fiscal federalism

—recognize the key issues in debates about the relative merit of public and private expenditures and about the desirable size of government

—understand the operation and economic implications of the Goods and Services Tax (GST)

Multiple-Choice Questions

1. Horizontal equity refers to
   (a) the East-West distribution of income
   (b) the treatment of individuals with identical incomes but different circumstancss
   (c) the treatment of households of similar composition but with different incomes
   (d) the flat-rate tax scheme

2. If the amount of tax paid increases as income rises,
   (a) the tax is proportional
   (b) the tax is progressive
   (c) the tax is regressive
   (d) cannot be determined from the information provided

3. If rich people and poor people smoke the same amount, a sales tax on cigarettes is regressive because
   (a) everyone spends the same proportion of income on cigarettes
   (b) the demand for cigarettes is inelastic
   (c) the tax paid per person represents a larger proportion of a poor person's income
   (d) the rich are better informed about the health hazards of smoking

4. If a tax takes the same amount of money from everyone regardless of income, the tax is
   (a) a flat-rate tax
   (b) proportional
   (c) regressive
   (d) horizontally inequitable

5. If the income tax is progressive, the marginal tax rate must be
   (a) less than the average tax rate
   (b) the same as the average tax rate
   (c) greater than the average tax rate
   (d) continuously increasing with income

6. If an individual's average tax rate is 30 percent and marginal tax rate is 50 percent, an additional $100 income would imply additional tax payments of
   (a) $50
   (b) $30
   (c) $80
   (d) $20

7. Tax expenditures refer to
   (a) how the government spends its tax revenues
   (b) an individual's annual tax payments
   (c) tax concessions that are made to influence the behavior of taxpaying units
   (d) intergovernmental transfers

8. The central idea behind the Laffer curve is that as tax rates increase,
   (a) the tax base will increase
   (b) a tax revolt by taxpayers will be ignited
   (c) more economic activity will go unreported so as to evade income taxation
   (d) tax revenue will reach a maximum and then decline as tax rates continue to increase

9. Tax incidence indicates
   (a) who actually bears the final burden of the tax
   (b) who pays the tax to the government
   (c) the degree of progressivity in the tax
   (d) the degree of vertical equity in the tax

10. Which of the following is *not* a feature of the negative income tax (NIT) proposal?
    (a) Individuals and firms with annual negative incomes (i.e., net debts or losses) will still have to pay taxes.
    (b) NIT provides a guaranteed minimum income.
    (c) NIT provides more incentive for low-income individuals to seek work because the tax rate on earned income is less than 100 percent.
    (d) The administrative cost of providing relief can be reduced because NIT can replace many of the existing programs.

11. The incidence of a sales tax
    (a) is borne entirely by consumers, who must pay the tax in addition to the good's price
    (b) is borne entirely by producers, who lower prices by the amount of the tax in order to sell
    (c) is generally shared by consumers and producers, depending on the elasticities of demand and supply
    (d) none of the above

12. Which of the following is *not* an example of a government transfer payment to individuals?
    (a) salaries of government employees
    (b) family allowance payments
    (c) unemployment insurance benefits
    (d) child tax credits

13. Under the equalization payments program, the federal government
    (a) equalizes the tax revenue of each province
    (b) transfers money from its general revenue to provinces with below average tax capacity
    (c) transfers tax revenue to provinces to ensure a reasonably equal educational expenditure per student across the country
    (d) ensures that each province taxes income at the same rate—except Quebec, which collects its own income tax

14. According to the benefit principle of taxation,
    (a) the amount of taxes paid should be equal across income groups
    (b) taxes should be paid according to the benefits that taxpayers derive from public expenditure
    (c) there should be no user charges for government services
    (d) the greater one's income, the greater the benefit generally received from public expenditures

15. Decentralization of government economic activity can be justified by all *but* which of the following?
    (a) regional preferences
    (b) income redistribution efforts
    (c) particular local needs for public expenditure
    (d) internalizing the spillover of services across jurisdictions

16. Increasing amounts of tax revenue have been transferred to the provincial and municipal governments for all *but* which of the following reasons?
    (a) There is a high income elasticity of demand for municipal services.
    (b) Municipal services tend to use labor whose productivity growth has been below the national average, so relative costs of these services have risen.
    (c) Federal government sources of tax revenue have risen more rapidly with income than that of the other governments.
    (d) Provincial and municipal governments do not collect tax revenue themselves.

17. Which of the following is *not* a feature of the Goods and Services Tax (GST)?
    (a) The GST eliminates tax cascading.
    (b) It improves the international competitiveness of Canadian-produced goods.
    (c) It is a value added tax.
    (d) It applies to a narrower tax base than the federal (or manufacturers') sales tax.

18. The judgment concerning whether a tax is regressive, proportional, or progressive is based on a comparison of the amount of tax with the
    (a) tax base   (c) taxpayer's income
    (b) value of the item being taxed   (d) distribution of income

19. The more elastic the demand for a commodity on which a specific excise is levied, other things being equal,
    (a) the greater the after-tax price increase
    (b) the less the reduction in the quantity produced
    (c) the more elastic the associated supply curve
    (d) the less the after-tax price increase and the greater the reduction in quantity

20. Vertical equity in a tax system
    (a) concerns equity across income groups
    (b) focuses on comparisons of taxes paid by taxpayers with different incomes
    (c) is often used to support progressive taxation
    (d) all of the above

Exercises

1. (a) The table shows the amount of tax paid by individuals in four different income categories. For each of the three taxes, A, B, and C, indicate whether the tax is proportional, regressive, or progressive.

    Amount of Tax Paid by Income Level

		Income level		
Tax	$10,000	$20,000	$40,000	$60,000
A	$ 1,000	$ 2,000	$ 4,000	$ 6,000
B	800	1,400	2,600	3,600
C	400	1,200	3,000	5,600

    Tax A is _____ .
    Tax B is _____ .
    Tax C is _____ .

   (b) Taking all taxes together (A + B + C), is the tax system progressive, regressive, or proportional? _____

2. (a) Suppose that a negative income tax provides $5,000 guaranteed income for a family and a 50 percent marginal tax rate on earnings. Complete the table.

(A) Before-tax earnings	(B) Income tax ($-$5,000 + 0.5A$)	(C) After-tax income ($A - B$)
$ 0	−$5,000	$5,000
2,000	−$4,000	_____
5,000	_____	$7,500
7,000	_____	_____
10,000	_____	_____

(b) The following version of the negative income tax was part of a 1970 experiment.

A man with a family of five earns $96 a week in income and receives $10.75 a week in cash from the government; if his earnings fall to $50, he will receive $43 a week from the government, and if he earns nothing, he will receive $78 a week from the government.

Calculate the implicit marginal rate of taxation.

Earnings	Change in earnings	Cash transfer	Change in cash transfer	Marginal rate of taxation
$ 0	_____	$78.00	_____	_____
50	_____	43.00	_____	_____
90		15.00		

3. The three graphs represent three different market situations with respect to the supply and demand for rental accommodation in the short run. Assume that a property tax equal to a fixed amount per rental unit is imposed in all three situations.

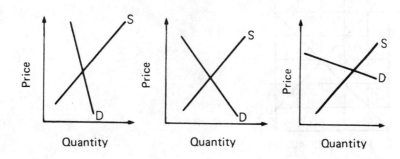

(a) In which market situation would the landlord bear most of the tax burden? Explain.

(b) The following graph reproduces the situation in the center graph. Draw a possible long-run supply curve, and compare the long-run shifting of the property tax burden with your answer to (a). (*Hint:* Draw the long-run supply curve through the initial short-run equilibrium.)

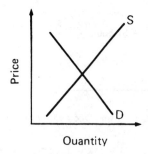

Quantity

(c) In which of these market situations is there the smallest change in the quantity of rental accommodation due to the tax? Why? (Restrict your answer to the short run.)

(d) Suppose that in situation (ii), rent controls had fixed the rent or price at the original equilibrium. Is the tax burden shouldered by landlords altered because of rent control?

4. The following graph depicts market demand and supply curves for a commodity prior to any government intervention; the equilibrium price and quantity are therefore $3 and $30 units, respectively. A tax of $2 per unit is now imposed on this commodity.

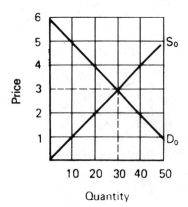

Quantity

   (a) Suppose that the tax is levied on (i.e., paid by) producers.
       (i)   Characterize the introduction of the tax by drawing the effective supply curve that consumers face. Label it S_1.
      (ii)   What price will consumers pay per unit?

     (iii) What is the after-tax "net price" paid to firms?

     (iv) Tax incidence per unit can be defined for firms as the difference between the initial price and the after-tax net price. What is the incidence per unit borne by firms?

      (v)   What is the incidence per unit borne by consumers?

     (vi) What is government tax revenue?

   (b) Suppose now that the tax is levied on consumers.
       (i)   Characterize the introduction of the tax by drawing the effective demand curve that producers face. Label it D_1.

      (ii)   What price will consumers pay per unit (inclusive of the tax)?

     (iii) What is the net-of-tax price that firms retain?

     (iv) What is the incidence per unit borne by firms?

      (v)   What is the incidence per unit borne by consumers?

     (vi) What is government tax revenue?

   (c) Does tax incidence depend on who pays the tax?

5. This exercise compares the Retail Sales Tax (RST), the Goods and Services Tax (GST), and the Manufacturers' Sales Tax (MST) when applied to a commodity that has four stages of production. The following schedule presents the purchases and sales at each stage.

Production stage	Purchases from other firms	Sales to other firms
Primary	$ 0	$ 1,000
Manufacturing	1,000	4,000
Wholesale	4,000	6,000
Retail	6,000	10,000

(a) Suppose that an RST of 7 percent is introduced. At which stage in the production process is it imposed, and what is total tax revenue?

(b) Instead, suppose that a GST of 7 percent is imposed such that at each stage a 7 percent tax is paid on sales, but all taxes paid on purchases from other firms are credited. What is the net tax paid at each stage, and what is total tax revenue?

(c) Suppose that a value added tax of 7 percent is imposed. What is the tax liability at each stage, and what is total tax revenue?

(d) What is the difference between the value added tax and the GST?

(e) An alternative scheme is the MST. Suppose that this program must guarantee the same total tax yield ($700) as those in parts (a), (b), and (c). What is the required tax rate for the MST?

Answers

Multiple-Choice Questions

1. (b)   2. (d)   3. (c)   4. (c)   5. (c)   6. (a)   7. (c)   8. (d)   9. (a)   10. (a)   11. (c)   12. (a)
13. (b)   14. (b)   15. (d)   16. (d)   17. (d)   18. (c)   19. (d)   20. (d)

Exercises

1. (a) Tax A is proportional; tax B is regressive; tax C is progressive.
   (b) The tax rates are 22 percent for $10,000, 23 percent for $20,000, 24 percent for $40,000, and 25.3 percent for $60,000. The tax system is slightly progressive.

2. (a) column B: – $5,000; – $4,000; – $2,500; – $1,500; 0
       column C: $5,000; $6,000; $7,500; $8,500; $10,000

   (b) Marginal tax rate $= \dfrac{\Delta T}{\Delta Y} = \dfrac{43 - 15}{40}$ or $\dfrac{35}{50} = 0.70$

3. (a) Situation (iii). Demand is very elastic, and the quantity demanded of accommodation would decline significantly with a small change in price.
   (b) The long-run supply curve is more elastic than the short-run supply curve. In the following graph, it is represented by the flatter curve S_L going through the initial equilibrium point. The tax shifts each supply curve uniformly upward by the same distance (e.g., t). The short-run equilibrium is E_S, and the long-run equilibrium is E_L. The price paid by consumers is therefore higher in the long run, and the quantity of accommodation is smaller. Thus in the long run when supply is more elastic, landlords can shift a greater share of the tax burden onto the shoulders of consumers.

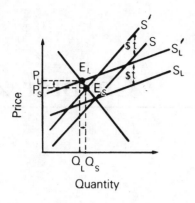

(c) Situation (i). Demand is inelastic and does not respond significantly to the higher price.

(d) In the short run, the landlord would shoulder all of the tax burden.

4. (a) (i) see graph (ii) $4 (iii) $2 (iv) $1 = $3 − $2 (v) $1 = $4 − $3 (vi) $40

   (b) (i) see graph (ii) $4 (iii) $2 (iv) $1 = $3 − $2 (v) $1 = $4 − $3 (vi) $40

   (c) No; in both cases firms and consumers share the burden of the tax equally.

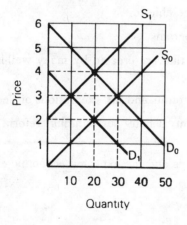

5. (a) It is imposed on sales of $10,000 at the retail level. Thus total tax revenue is $700.

   (b) Primary pays $70 = 0.07 × $1,000. Manufacturing pays $210 = (0.07 × $4,000) − $70. Wholesale pays $140 = (0.07 × $6,000) − $210 − $70. Finally, retail pays $280 = (0.07 × $10,000) − $140 − $210 − $70. Total tax revenue is $700 = $70 + $210 + $140 + $280.

   (c) Value added at the primary stage is $1,000, so tax payments are $70. At the manufacturing stage, value added is $3,000 (= $4,000 − $1,000), so taxes here are $210. The value added of wholesalers is $2,000, implying a tax liability of $140. Finally, the value added of retailers is $4,000, so tax payments at the retail level are $280. The total is $700.

   (d) There is no difference.

   (e) Sales of manufactured goods are $4,000, and the government must collect $700 in tax revenue. Thus the required MST rate is 17.5 percent [($700/$4,000) × 100 percent].

Chapter 25

Social Policy

Learning Objectives

After studying this chapter, you should be able to:

—understand Canada's various social programs

—appreciate the economic inefficiencies that are created by many well-intended policies

—understand the relative impacts of tax credits and tax exemptions or deductions

—be more conversant with the current debate surrounding reform of the unemployment insurance program

—understand the issues regarding pensions and the expected economic effects of an aging population

Multiple-Choice Questions

1. A demogrant is a social policy with
    (a) an income-related eligibility criterion
    (b) an age or residence eligibility requirement
    (c) a specified length of employment as a qualifying criterion
    (d) no eligibility requirement, in that it is given to all Canadians

2. A program such as the child tax exemption
    (a) is an income-tested benefit
    (b) is known as a tax expenditure
    (c) is most beneficial to people with no taxable income
    (d) provides the same benefit to all similarly structured households, regardless of income

3. Which of the following is *not* one of the major challenges that must be addressed by Canadian social policy in the upcoming decades?
   (a) an increasing burden of child-related tax concessions as the average age of the population decreases
   (b) the burden of the deficit and debt on government expenditures
   (c) the requisite adjustments that must be made in Canada to an ever-changing international market
   (d) the impact of an aging population on the health and pension systems

4. Any effective reform of Canada's social programs necessitates federal-provincial coordination for which for the following reasons?
   (a) Many social policies have different regional impacts.
   (b) Many federal and provincial programs overlap.
   (c) Much of federal expenditure on social programs is in the form of transfers to the provinces.
   (d) All of the above.

5. Among industrial nations, Canada allocates a below average share of its national income to social spending. One reason why this statistic may be misleading is that
   (a) Canada has a smaller than average population
   (b) Canada has a relatively larger proportion of retirees who do not contribute to national income
   (c) it does not include tax expenditures, which play an important role in Canadian social programs
   (d) Canada's national income is small relative to that of most industrial nations, so we are less able to afford social programs

6. The implicit tax-back rate refers to
   (a) the rate at which individuals must pay their taxes to the government
   (b) the reduction in earned income due to income taxation
   (c) the rate at which social benefits are reduced due to earned income
   (d) the speed with which the government processes refunds on individuals' annual income tax statements

7. Because of "stacking," a low-income individual who is currently receiving social benefits and is considering earning additional income through part-time employment may face an effective marginal tax rate on the earned income
   (a) no higher than the explicit income tax rate
   (b) no higher than the highest explicit marginal tax bracket in the country
   (c) no higher than 100 percent, or all of earned income
   (d) higher than 100 percent

8. Which of the following is *not* a feature of universality in social programs?
   (a) Benefits are provided without a means test.
   (b) Recipients are made to feel demeaned.
   (c) Because the benefits are taxable, the net benefits are not universal.
   (d) Because a large number of people benefit from these programs, they are politically more difficult to dismantle.

9. Which of the following statements is a reasonable economic argument for some subsidization of postsecondary education?
   (a) All of the benefits of a university education accrue to the student in the form of a higher lifetime income.
   (b) It is vertically equitable that all taxpayers pay to educate individuals who will earn above average incomes.
   (c) Charging the full cost of education would eliminate all the gifted students.
   (d) There are external benefits to the entire nation from a better-educated population.

10. Which of the following is likely to occur if the qualification period for unemployment insurance were shortened to 10 weeks in some regions?
    (a) The scheme would tend to become a subsidy for seasonal employment.
    (b) Provincial and municipal governments would create make-work schemes that provide employment for 10 weeks.
    (c) The rate of labor turnover would increase.
    (d) All of the above.

11. All *but* which of the following have been proposed as reforms to Canada's unemployment insurance program?
    (a) provide more extended benefits (i.e., shorter qualifying periods and longer weeks of benefits) in regions with above average unemployment rates
    (b) make the benefits dependent on income during the prior 52 weeks rather than the prior 10 or so weeks
    (c) increase the premiums in industries with larger risks of unemployment
    (d) increase the number of weeks of employment required to qualify for benefits

12. Which of the following is *not* true of the family allowance plan?
    (a) Mothers receive the cheques, but the spouse with the higher income reports it as taxable income.
    (b) It contributes to horizontal equity because benefits increase with the number of children.
    (c) It diminishes vertical equity because the after-tax benefits are independent of income.
    (d) It is a universal program.

13. An individual with a marginal tax rate of 25 percent would prefer a child tax credit of $200 to a child tax exemption up to
    (a) $200   (c) $1,000
    (b) $50   (d) $800

14. Many of the proposals for reform of the family benefits program recommend an increasing role for child tax credits. One of the central problems with an increased reliance on the child tax credit is that
    (a) everyone receives the same after-tax benefit, regardless of income
    (b) relative to other transfer mechanisms, it is very costly to administer
    (c) it is paid once a year and based on last year's income, not current needs
    (d) it does not contribute to horizontal equity

15. The next few decades promise to be a time of difficulty for retirement schemes in Canada because
    (a) private pension plans are being replaced by government plans
    (b) a greater proportion of the population will be retired, and a smaller proportion will be working
    (c) more people are refusing to accept mandatory retirement at age 65
    (d) the popularity of RRSPs has meant that there is less saving for retirement years

16. "Vestibility" in a pension scheme means that
    (a) the pension contributions made by the employer belong to the employee
    (b) the employee can change jobs without losing any benefits
    (c) there is a minimum qualifying period of employment before an employee can join a pension plan
    (d) the pension plan is fully indexed and protected from inflation

17. Which of the following is *not* a feasible proposal for reform of the system of elderly benefits?
    (a) index the guaranteed income supplement, and deindex old age security, which is not income-related
    (b) gradually raise the eligibility age for old age security
    (c) impose extensive expenditure-neutral reforms, redistributing the benefits among current recipients
    (d) tax back some old age security benefits with either a surtax or the elimination of the pension and old age tax deductions

18. The argument that medical doctors induce patient demand for their own services is based on
    (a) a system of per capitation payments
    (b) a fee-for-service system
    (c) the growing popularity of health maintenance organizations (HMOs)
    (d) intrinsic dishonesty on the part of many doctors

Exercises

1. (a) Classify each of the following Canadian social programs as a demogrant (D) or income-tested (I).

	Class
Family allowance	
Unemployment insurance	
Old age security	
Pension income exemption	
Child tax exemption	
Canada Assistance Plan	
Child tax credit	
Age exemption	

   (b) Identify three of these social programs that contribute to horizontal equity.

2. This exercise is designed to highlight the relative impacts on the distribution of income from child tax credits and child tax exemptions. Consider five families, each of which has two children of similar ages. The incomes of these families are listed in the following table, with the associated marginal tax rates.

Gross family income	Marginal tax rate (per $10,000 bracket)
$10,000	0.1
20,000	0.2
30,000	0.3
40,000	0.4
50,000	0.5

Assume that each marginal tax rate applies to income brackets of $10,000, so that the first $10,000 earned is subject to a 10 percent tax, the next $10,000 earned is subject to a 20 percent tax, and so on. Thus someone earning $20,000 must pay $3,000 in tax: $1,000 on the first $10,000 and $2,000 on the next $10,000.

(a) Determine the after-tax income of each household prior to the introduction of any benefit program for families with children.

(b) Suppose that the government introduces a child tax credit (CTC) equal to $1,000 per child. Suppose further that this credit is subject to a tax-back rate that depends on family income according to the following schedule:

Gross family income	Tax-back rate applied to CTC
up to $10,000	0.00
$10,001–$20,000	0.25
$20,001–$30,000	0.50
$30,001–$40,000	0.75
$40,001 and above	1.00

Determine the after-tax income of each of the five families.

(c) Instead of a child tax credit, suppose that the government introduces a child tax exemption equal to $1,667 per child. Determine the after-tax income of each family.

(d) Contrast the effect of these two benefit programs on the distribution of income. Which better satisfies the objective of vertical equity?

(e) Compare the costs of these programs to the government in terms of forgone tax revenue.

Answers

Multiple-Choice Questions

1. (b)   2. (b)   3. (a)   4. (d)   5. (c)   6. (c)   7. (d)   8. (b)   9. (d)   10. (d)   11. (a)   12. (c)
13. (d)   14. (c)   15. (b)   16. (a)   17. (c)   18. (b)

Exercises

1. (a)

	Class
Family allowance	D
Unemployment insurance	I
Old age security	D
Pension income exemption	D
Child tax exemption	D
Canada Assistance Plan	I
Child tax credit	D
Age exemption	D

(b) Family allowance, child tax exemption, and child tax credit

2. (a) $9,000, $17,000, $24,000, $30,000, and $35,000
    (b) Calculate: gross income − taxes + (2 × $1,000) (1 − tax-back rate), which
         yields $11,000, $18,500, $25,000, $30,500, and $35,000.
    (c) Each household's taxable income is now its gross income minus $3,334 (i.e.,
         the exemption for two children). The resulting taxes payable are calculated
         by applying the marginal tax rates to the tax brackets for taxable income.
         Stated otherwise, relative to (a), each household's after-tax income increases
         by its marginal tax rate multiplied by $3,334. This yields $9,333, $17,667,
         $25,000, $31,334, and $36,667.
    (d) In going from child tax credit in (b) to a child tax exemption in (c), the
         after-tax incomes of the two low-income households decrease, while those
         of the two higher-income households increase. Thus the child tax credit
         provides more vertical equity than the child tax exemption.
    (e) Each scheme costs $5,000 (ignoring the rounding error of $1).

PART EIGHT

National Income
and
Fiscal Policy

Chapter 26

An Introduction to Macroeconomics

Learning Objectives

After studying this overview chapter, you should be able to:

—understand how macroeconomics deals with the operation of the economy as a whole

—be able to define key macroeconomic concepts such as inflation, gross domestic product, unemployment, the interest rate, and the exchange rate

—recognize important issues that arise in measuring and interpreting these macroeconomic variables

—appreciate general trends in these macro variables over the past half century

Multiple-Choice Questions

1. Which of the following is not a macroeconomic issue?
    (a) changes in the unemployment rate
    (b) the change in the price of VCR machines relative to the price of movie theater tickets
    (c) a fall in the Consumer Price Index
    (d) fluctuations of national income around its long-run trend

2. The Consumer Price Index measures the level of prices in a given year relative to some base year and is calculated using a weighted average of prices for a typical bundle of goods. The weights are
    (a) the same for each good
    (b) equal to the share of income spent on each good in the base year
    (c) equal to the share of income spent on each good in the current year
    (d) different across goods but assigned randomly

3. If a particular index number in 1987 is 149 and the base year is 1980, then the index shows an increase of
   (a) 4.9 percent between 1980 and 1987
   (b) 149 percent between 1980 and 1987
   (c) 49 percent between 1980 and 1987
   (d) an indeterminable percent, since the value of the index in 1980 is unknown

4. Between February and March 1990, the CPI increased from 155.8 to 156.3. If this rate of increase continued throughout the year, the *annual* rate of inflation would approximately equal
   (a) 6.0 percent   (c) 3.9 percent
   (b) 5.0 percent   (d) 3.2 percent

5. Suppose that a price index was 160 last month and rose by 2 percent during the current month. The price index for the current month is
   (a) 162.0   (c) 163.2
   (b) 160.02   (d) 198.4

6. Suppose that the annual rate of inflation in 1990 was 4.7 percent. If a family's income grew from $20,000 in 1989 to $21,000 in 1990, the family experienced
   (a) an increase in both nominal and real income
   (b) an increase in nominal income but a decrease in real income
   (c) an increase in nominal income but no change in real income
   (d) no change in either real or nominal income

7. Assume that prices over the year increase by 4 percent. Who of the following will experience a decrease in purchasing power?
   (a) a creditor who negotiated an annual contract at a nominal rate of interest of 6 percent and who wanted a 2 percent real rate of return
   (b) a firm that is committed to increasing its wages by 5 percent over the year but whose prices are likely to increase only by the overall rate of inflation
   (c) a person whose pension is totally indexed for price inflation
   (d) a landlord who successfully negotiates a 7 percent increase in rent over the year

8. Changes in real national income (Y) reflect only changes in output, whereas changes in nominal national income reflect
   (a) only price changes
   (b) only output changes
   (c) changes in price and/or output
   (d) changes in neither output nor price

9. Completely unexpected inflation is likely to
   (a) benefit creditors
   (b) benefit pensioners whose monthly pension payments are fixed in nominal terms
   (c) benefit debtors
   (d) both (a) and (b)

10. If inflation is expected to be 5 percent in the coming year and the annual nominal interest rate is 8 percent, then the real rate of interest is
    (a) 13 percent   (c) 3 percent
    (b) $8/5 \times 100$ percent   (d) $5/8 \times 100$ percent

11. The output or GDP gap is defined as
    (a) potential real GDP minus real actual GDP
    (b) the change in real GDP over two time periods
    (c) the difference between nominal and real GDP
    (d) none of the above

12. Actual GDP may exceed potential GDP for a short period of time when
    (a) the unemployment rate is high
    (b) factors of production are employed at levels that are above normal utilization levels
    (c) nominal GDP is less than real GDP
    (d) all of the above

13. An example of frictional unemployment is when
    (a) carpenters are laid off because of a decline in housing starts
    (b) Montreal textile workers lose jobs due to a loss in Canadian export shares of textile products in world markets
    (c) unemployed textile workers are refused jobs since they do not have knowledge of computer software packages required by firms in another industry
    (d) a teenager quits a job at K mart in order to find a better-paying job at one of the three large department stores in the same city

14. The labor force in Canada is defined as the total of individuals 15 years and older who are
    (a) employed   (c) employed and unemployed
    (b) unemployed   (d) residents of Canada

15. An economy that has a labor force of 55 persons, 45 of whom are employed has an unemployment rate of
    (a) 8.18 percent   (c) 22.22 percent
    (b) 10 percent   (d) 18.18 percent

16. Full employment in Canada
    (a) implies that the measured unemployment rate is zero
    (b) occurs when the output gap is positive
    (c) occurs when the only existing unemployment is structural and frictional
    (d) has not been achieved in the past 50 years

17. Periods of high economic activity are generally characterized by
    (a) low unemployment
    (b) growth in real income per capita
    (c) a negative value of the output gap
    (d) all of the above

18. If real GDP in less developed countries grows 2 percent annually while the population grows 3 percent annually, per capita real GDP is changing at an approximate annual rate of
    (a) 5 percent   (c) 1 percent
    (b) −1 percent   (d) 6 percent

19. Productivity changes refer to changes in
    (a) the labor force
    (b) the production of a constant labor force
    (c) prices of all goods and services
    (d) the level of frictional and structural unemployment

20. The assumption that productivity and the labor force are constant in the short run means that any increase in real GDP will be accompanied by
    (a) an increase in employment and a decrease in the unemployment rate
    (b) an increase in both employment and the unemployment rate
    (c) a decrease in employment and the unemployment rate
    (d) a decrease in employment and an increase in the unemployment rate

21. Between 1988 and 1989, the British pound fell from C$2.19 to C$1.94. It follows that
    (a) the external value of the pound rose
    (b) Canadians could buy more pounds per dollar in 1989 than they could in 1988
    (c) the internal value of the Canadian dollar must have risen
    (d) the external value of the dollar fell

22. Between 1978 and 1988, the Japanese currency, the yen, increased from C$0.0055 to C$0.0096. It follows that the external value of
    (a) the Canadian dollar increased
    (b) the Japanese yen decreased
    (c) both the yen and the Canadian dollar increased
    (d) the yen increased but the external value of the Canadian dollar decreased

23. If the value of a country's imports exceeded the value of its exports by $50 million, it follows that
    (a) it has a $50 million deficit on its balance of trade
    (b) the country must also have a positive output gap of $50 million
    (c) its balance of payments must necessarily be in a deficit position of $50 million
    (d) both (a) and (c)

Exercises

1. This exercise features the construction of a Consumer Price Index. Suppose that the government's data collection agency has estimated the prices of six broad groups of consumer expenditure as well as the *average* proportions of consumers' income that is spent on these expenditure groups as follows:

	Prices (base year)	Prices (next year)	Proportion of income consumers spend (on average)
Shelter	$3,000	$3,300	30%
Food	2,500	2,500	25
Transportation	5,000	5,000	15
Clothing	100	110	10
Entertainment	60	60	10
Other	300	330	10

(a) Compute the average price level in the base year and in the next year. (Assume that the proportions do not change.)

(b) The price index for the base year, by definition, is 100. Compute the price index for the next year.

(c) You may have noticed that the price of shelter, clothing, and other goods increased by 10 percent each. Does your answer to (b) indicate a 10 percent increase in the price index from the base year? Why or why not?

(d) Suppose that a group of households in this country consumes the products listed in the table in the following proportions: shelter, 40 percent; food, 30 percent; transportation, 5 percent; clothing, 15 percent; entertainment, 0 percent; other, 10 percent. Does the increase in the overall price index in (b) underestimate or overestimate the cost of living increase for this particular group of households?

2. An economy produces four different goods and services within the current year. The level of production and the price per unit of each are listed here.

Item	Production level	Price per unit
Steel	500,000 tons	$100 per ton
Wheat	15,000 tons	8 per ton
Haircuts	6,000	9 each
Television sets	10,000 sets	500 per set

(a) Calculate the value of the economy's nominal national income in the current year.

(b) In the next year nominal national income is measured at $55,725,740. Express this value as an index of last year's value.

(c) What is the percentage increase in nominal national income (compared with the base year)? Do this calculation two ways.

3. Here are some data for Canadian national income measured in terms of gross domestic product (GDP). The first column refers to current dollar (nominal) GDP, the second displays constant dollar (real) GDP, and the third refers to real potential GDP.

Year	GDP in current dollars (billions)	GDP in constant dollars (1981 = base year) (billions)	Real potential GDP (billions)
1980	309.9	343.4	348.7
1981	356.0	356.0	362.7
1982	374.4	344.5	372.6
1983	405.7	355.5	376.0
1984	444.7	377.9	385.9
1985	478.0	395.9	398.6
1986	504.6	408.1	411.8
1987	550.3	426.4	426.6
1988	601.5	447.8	446.1
1989	648.5	460.6	464.1

(a) Express the 1985 constant dollar value of GDP as an index (to one decimal place) of the 1981 constant dollar value of GDP. Do the same for the 1980 constant dollar value of GDP as an index in terms of 1981.

(b) What is the value of the output gap in 1984? In 1988? Were resources fully employed in these two years?

(c) What phase of the business cycle is represented by the 1981–1982 period?

(d) What was the percentage increase in current dollar GDP between 1981 and 1985? What was the percentage increase in constant dollar (real) GDP in the same period? What does the difference in the two percentages represent (approximately)?

4. You are given the following price indexes for various years. The base year (year 1) has an index of 100.

Year	Price index	Annual inflation rate (percent)
7	118.1	—
8	121.9	_____
9	125.1	_____
10	_____	1.1

(a) Calculate the annual inflation rate (to one decimal place) for years 8 and 9, and fill in the blanks in the third column.

(b) What was the inflation rate over the period from the base year through year 9?

(c) Calculate (to one decimal place) the price index for year 10.

5. The following table provides information about the Canadian economy for a seven-year period.

Year	Real GDP in constant 1981 prices (billions)	Labor force (thousands)	Unemployed (thousands)	Employed (thousands)	Unemployment rate (percent)	Population (millions)
1976	$300.6	10,206	_____	9,479	7.123	23.0
1977	311.5	_____	850	_____	8.097	23.3
1978	325.8	10,882	_____	_____	8.362	23.5
1979	338.4	11,207	838	_____	_____	23.7
1980	343.4	11,522	867	10,655	7.525	23.9
1981	356.0	_____	898	10,933	7.590	24.2
1982	344.5	11,879	1,305	10,574	_____	24.5

(a) Fill in the missing values in the table.

(b) Calculate the percentage change in real GDP between 1978 and 1979. Compare this value with the percentage change in employment in this period. Do the same analysis for the two-year period 1981–1982.

(c) Does there appear to be a positive or negative relationship between real GDP and employment for these two periods?

(d) Between 1977 and 1978 the unemployment rate increased while employment increased. How is this possible?

(e) Calculate the value of real per capita GDP for 1979 and 1982.

6. The exchange rate is another important macroeconomic variable discussed in Chapter 26. The information here is intended to provide practice interpreting exchange rate changes. The values are actual figures for the Canadian dollar relative to the German mark (dollars per mark).

Year	Dollars per mark	Marks per dollar
1985	$0.4677	_____
1986	0.6425	_____
1987	0.7384	_____
1988	0.7028	_____
1989	0.6304	_____

(a) Fill in the entries for the value of the mark per dollar for each of the years shown.

(b) Over the period 1985–1986, the external value of the Canadian dollar (increased, decreased). Over the period 1986–1987, the external value of the German mark (increased, decreased).

(c) Suppose that you purchased a one-year asset worth 100 marks at the end of 1985 (at an exchange rate of $0.4677). How many dollars did you require to buy this asset?

(d) If the German asset had an annual nominal interest rate of 6 percent, how many marks would you have received at the end of 1986? How many Canadian dollars would you have received when you converted the marks into dollars at the end of 1986? What would be your rate of return over the year as a percentage of the dollar amount you invested?

7. The text stresses that the nominal interest rate is set on the basis of the expected real interest rate plus the expected future rate of inflation. For the present purpose, consider the nominal interest rate on five-year mortgages. Suppose that the lender, a financial institution, wishes to have a 3 percent real rate of return on an annual basis. Consider the following data.

Year	Nominal annual interest rate on new five-year mortgages	Annual average inflation rate		Period
		Expected	Actual	
1970	8.45	_____	6.76	1970–1975
1975	9.00	_____	8.90	1975–1980
1980	12.66	_____	5.48	1980–1985

(a) Calculate the institution's expected annual rate of inflation when it set the five-year mortgage rate in 1970. Do the same for the two other five-year periods, and complete the entries in the table.

(b) By comparing the actual annual inflation rate with the nominal interest rate, did the financial institution make its 3 percent real rate of interest on five-year mortgages in 1970? In 1975? In 1980?

Answers

Multiple-Choice Questions

1. (b) 2. (b) 3. (c) 4. (c) 5. (c) 6. (a) 7. (b) 8. (c) 9. (c) 10. (c) 11. (a) 12. (b)
13. (d) 14. (c) 15. (d) 16. (c) 17. (d) 18. (b) 19. (b) 20. (a) 21. (b) 22. (d) 23. (a)

Exercises

1. (a) Base year: $(3,000 \times 0.3) + (2,500 \times 0.25) + (5,000 \times 0.15) + (100 \times 0.1)$
   $+ (60 \times 0.1) + (300 \times 0.1) = 2,321$
   Next year: $(3,300 \times 0.3) + (2,500 \times 0.25) + (5,000 \times 0.15) + (110 \times 0.1)$
   $+ (60 \times 0.1) + (330 \times 0.1) = 2,415$
   (b) Index $= (2,415/2,321) \times 100 = 104.0$
   (c) No; prices increased by approximately 4 percent. This is because shelter, clothing, and other goods are only 50 percent of total expenditures.
   (d) The price increase from the base year for this group of households (using their fixed weights) is 5.5 percent. Hence the overall price increase reflected by the overall price index underestimates the cost of living increase of this group.

2. (a) $55,174,000 (Calculate price times quantity for each item and add the products of the four equations together)
   (b) 101 ($55,725,740 \div 55,174,000 \times 100$)
   (c) 1 percent. This can be obtained two ways. First, divide the change in income (551,740) by 55,174,000 and multiply by 100 percent. Alternatively, the index value for the next year indicates that the nominal value of output has increased by 1 percent.

3. (a) For 1985: 111.2 ($395.9 \div 356.0 \times 100$). For 1980: 96.5 ($343.4 \div 356.0 \times 100$).
   (b) The output gap is defined as potential real GDP minus real actual GDP. Hence there was a positive output gap of 8 ($385.9 - 377.9$) in 1984 and a negative output gap of -1.7 in 1988. There was unused productive capacity (less than full employment) in 1984, whereas resources in 1988 were fully employed, although their utilization rate was greater than the normal rate of utilization.
   (c) Between the two years, real GDP fell and the output gap increased (compare 6.7 with 28.1). This period represented a recessionary phase or a slump. The trough occurred sometime in 1982.
   (d) Current dollar GDP increased by 34.3 percent; constant dollar GDP increased by 11.2 percent. The difference between these represents approximately the percentage increase in prices of all final goods and services over this period.

4. (a) Year 8: 3.2 percent ($3.8 \div 118.1 \times 100$ percent)
   Year 9: 2.6 percent ($3.2 \div 121.9 \times 100$ percent)
   (b) 25.1 percent
   (c) 126.5 (125.1×1.011)

5. (a) Labor force: 1977: 10,498 (850 ÷ 0.08097); 1981: 11,831 (898 + 10,933)
        Unemployed: 1976: 727; 1978: 910 (10,882 × 0.08362)
        Employed: 1977: 9,648; 1978: 9,972; 1979; 10,369
        Unemployment rate: 1979: 7.477 percent; 1982: 10.986 percent
    (b) 1978–1979: Real GDP increased by 3.87 percent while employment increased by 3.98 percent.
        1981–1982: Real GDP decreased by 3.23 percent while employment decreased by 3.28 percent.
    (c) Positive relationship; they changed in the same direction.
    (d) The labor force increased more in percentage terms than did employment. That is, more of those who entered the labor force became unemployed than employed.
    (e) 1979: $14,278; 1982: $14,061

6. (a) 2.1381, 1.5564, 1.3543, 1.4229, 1.5863
    (b) decreased; increased
    (c) 100 marks cost $46.77.
    (d) At the end of 1986, you receive 106 marks (100 + 6). When you convert the 106 marks into dollars, you receive approximately $68.11. This represents a rate of return of 45.62 percent (21.34 ÷ 46.77 × 100 percent). This high rate of return resulted primarily from the large increase in the external value of the mark (37.4 percent) over the 1985–1986 period.

7. (a) 1970–1975: 5.45 percent; 1975–1980: 6.00 percent; 1980–1985: 9.66 percent
    (b) 1970: No; real return was 1.69 percent (8.45 − 6.76). 1975: No; real return was 0.10 percent. 1980: Yes; real return was 7.18 percent.

Chapter 27

Measuring Macroeconomic Variables

Learning Objectives

After studying this chapter, you should be able to:

—recognize how value added in various stages of production is related to the value of final goods and services sold

—comprehend that summing the value added of all producers represents the value of the economy's total output or its gross domestic product (GDP)

—understand that GDP can be measured in two other ways, either through expenditures for currently produced final goods or through income generated in their production

—distinguish the four broad categories of final expenditures (consumption, investment, government expenditure, and net exports) and the reasons for treating them separately

—understand the distinction between the value of total production in Canada (GDP) versus the total income received by Canadians (gross national product or gross national expenditure)

—calculate certain related income concepts such as personal income, disposable personal income, and per capita real income

—understand how to calculate real GDP using implicit deflators

—appreciate various qualifications in interpreting national income measures, particularly the importance of omitted items

Multiple-Choice Questions

1. Value added in production is equal to
   (a) purchases from other firms
   (b) profits of all firms
   (c) total value of output including intermediate goods
   (d) total value of output minus the value of intermediate goods

2. Estimating final output (GDP) by adding the sales of all firms
   (a) will overstate total output because it counts the output of intermediate goods more than once
   (b) will understate the total value of national output
   (c) is a measure of income accruing to Canadian residents
   (d) provides the same value as net national income

3. Suppose that a firm sells its output for $40,000, that it pays $22,000 in wages, $10,000 for materials purchased from other firms, and $3,000 to bankers, and that it declares profits of $5,000. The firm's value added is
   (a) $18,000   (c) $30,000
   (b) $40,000   (d) $35,000

4. Which of the following would *not* be included in measures of the consumption component of aggregate expenditure?
   (a) expenditures for new houses
   (b) expenditures for durable goods, such as new automobiles
   (c) expenditures for services
   (d) expenditures for nondurable goods

5. GDP at market prices is equal to
   (a) GDP at factor cost minus indirect taxes
   (b) GDP at factor cost plus the sum of indirect taxes and subsidies
   (c) GDP at factor cost plus depreciation (capital consumption allowances) minus subsidies
   (d) GDP at factor cost plus indirect taxes less subsidies

6. Which of the following would *not* be included in the measures of the investment component of aggregate expenditure?
   (a) Sally Smith buys Canadian Airlines International shares.
   (b) An accounting firm buys three personal computers.
   (c) General Motors (Canada) increases its inventory holdings of parts produced in Brantford, Ontario.
   (d) A construction company builds 20 new homes in Kelowna, British Columbia.

7. Which of the following would *not* be included in measures of the government expenditure component of aggregate expenditure?
   (a) salaries of civil servants whose responsibilities include the collection of the Goods and Service Tax (GST)
   (b) the city of Moncton's purchase of forms from a Mississauga, Ontario, printing company
   (c) Canada pension payments to residents of Sherbrooke, Quebec
   (d) expenditures for new naval minesweepers built in Nova Scotia

8. Gross domestic product at market prices
   (a) is equal to net national product minus depreciation
   (b) excludes indirect taxes but includes capital consumption allowances
   (c) must equal gross national product since both include capital consumption allowances
   (d) includes replacement investment, which is measured by the level of capital consumption allowances

9. The income approach to measuring GDP at market prices
    (a) usually results in a higher value for total national income than results from the output or expenditure approach
    (b) usually results in a lower value for total national income than the two other approaches since owner-occupier rents are excluded from the income approach
    (c) includes the value of indirect business taxes
    (d) includes only profits retained by firms

10. National income can be correctly measured in all but which of the following ways?
    (a) by the market value of final goods and services produced
    (b) by adding all money transactions in the economy, including purchases of financial assets
    (c) by the market value of expenditures made to purchase final output
    (d) by the value of payments made to factors of production that have been used to produce final goods and services

11. Disposable personal income is
    (a) always the same as personal income
    (b) income that is used only for consumption
    (c) personal income remaining after income taxes
    (d) exclusive of transfer payments such as unemployment insurance payments

12. Which of the following would *not* be included in the measurement of GDP by the income approach?
    (a) inventory expenditures
    (b) depreciation or capital consumption allowances
    (c) indirect business taxes net of subsidies
    (d) imputed rents of owner-occupied dwellings

13. In a particular year an economy's GDP at market prices is $401 billion, *net* payments to foreigners are $46 billion, and indirect taxes less subsidies are $5 billion. The value of the economy's GNP at market prices is
    (a) $447 billion   (c) $350 billion
    (b) $355 billion   (d) $360 billion

14. If nominal GDP is $150 and real GDP is $125, the value of the implicit deflator is
    (a) 120   (c) 0.83
    (b) 1.2   (d) 83

15. If an economy's annual nominal GDP increases by 11 percent and prices increase on an annual basis by 9 percent, then real GDP
    (a) increases by approximately 20 percent
    (b) increases by approximately 2 percent
    (c) decreases by approximately 2 percent
    (d) decreases by $2/9 \times 100$ percent

16. If nominal GDP rises from \$400 billion to \$408 billion and the implicit GDP deflator rises from 125 to 127,
    (a) real GDP has risen
    (b) real GDP has fallen
    (c) real GDP is unchanged
    (d) everyone is necessarily better off since nominal GDP has increased

17. If do-it-yourself homeowners stopped building their backyard decks and instead hired self-employed university students, then national income would
    (a) be reduced as now measured
    (b) be unaffected if the students reported their earnings
    (c) increase if the students reported their earnings
    (d) be unaffected since the students are not wage earners

18. The implicit deflator
    (a) can be used only for the expenditure approach
    (b) is a fixed-weight index
    (c) the index used to measure the prices of goods and services purchased by households
    (d) is a variable-weight index

19. GDP understates the total production of goods and services for all *but* which one of the following reasons?
    (a) No allowances are included for the imputed rents of owner-occupied homes.
    (b) Illegal activities are not included in the GDP estimate.
    (c) Legal production in the "underground economy" is not reported for income tax purposes.
    (d) Nonmarketed household services such as gardening and cleaning performed by family members are not included.

20. If the implicit deflator increased from 120 in year 7 to 126 in year 8, then prices of final goods and services
    (a) increased 20 percent on average from the base year to year 7
    (b) increased 5 percent on average between years 7 and 8
    (c) increased by 6 percent since the index increased by 6 points
    (d) both (a) and (b)

21. The implicit deflator is defined as
    (a) GDP at current prices ÷ GDP at base period prices × 100 percent
    (b) real GDP ÷ nominal GDP × 100 percent
    (c) the CPI minus the rate of inflation of indirect business taxes
    (d) both (a) and (c)

22. A widely used measure of the purchasing power of the average person in a country is
    (a) real GDP ÷ total population
    (b) nominal GDP ÷ price deflator × 100 percent
    (c) real disposable income ÷ total population
    (d) real disposable income ÷ total number of employed and self-employed individuals

Exercises

1. The value of a product in its final form is the sum of the value added by each of the various firms throughout the production process. Using the information provided here, calculate the value of one loaf of bread that is ultimately sold to a household. In doing so, calculate the value added at each stage of production. (This example demonstrates that the value added approach avoids multiple counting.)

State of production	Selling price to next stage	Value added
1. Farmer (production of wheat)	$0.30	$_____
2. Milling company (flour)	0.55	_____
3. Bakery (production of wholesale bread)	0.90	_____
4. Retailer (sale to household)	1.00	_____
Total	2.75	$_____

2. Identify the items in the statements according to the following code. Some statements have more than one answer.

C   Consumption
I   Investment
G   Government spending on goods and services

M   Imports
X   Exports
N   None of the above

_____ (1) The Bank of Nova Scotia expands its computer facilities in its head office.

_____ (2) Canadians travel to London, England, and stay at the Savoy Hotel.

_____ (3) China buys beef cattle from Alberta beef cattle breeders.

_____ (4) Canadians purchase $5 billion in new homes.

_____ (5) Montreal Stock Exchange sales in January are $5 billion.

_____ (6) Ontarians take holidays in Quebec parks.

_____ (7) The province of Saskatchewan builds a new highway.

_____ (8) Sue buys a used motorcycle from a friend.

_____ (9) General Motors (Canada) increases its inventory holdings of glass windshields.

_____ (10) The government of New Brunswick pays for the services of a New York consulting company.

3. This exercise focuses on nominal and real output and the implicit deflator. Assume that there are only two industries in an economy. Output and unit price for each industry are shown for three years. Year 1 is the base year.

Year	Quantity of Industry A (tons)	Quantity of Industry B (meters)	Price in Industry A (per ton)	Price in Industry B (per meter)
1	4,000	20,000	$20	$5
2	6,000	21,000	22	4
3	6,000	18,000	24	6

(a) Calculate the nominal value of output in Industry A in each of the three years. Do the same for Industry B. Find national output in nominal terms for each of the three years by adding the two output values for A and B.

(b) Recalling that year 1 is the base year, calculate the real value of output in Industry A for each of the three years. Do the same for Industry B. What is the value of real output in the economy for each of the three years? (Use base year prices.)

(c) Calculate the value of the implicit deflator for each of the three years.

4. You are given the following items and their magnitudes in millions of dollars.

GDP at market prices	$436.7
Investment income received from nonresidents	5.5
Indirect taxes less subsidies	44.3
Investment income paid to nonresidents	20.7

Calculate the following values.
(a) GNP at market prices _____
(b) GDP at factor cost _____

5. This chapter emphasizes the *output approach* to national income measurement, which yields the value of the gross domestic product. However, there are two other methods of measuring GDP—the income and expenditure approaches. This problem deals with the calculation of gross domestic product at market prices using these two approaches. Select only the *appropriate* items. (Figures are in billions of dollars.)

Government purchases of goods and services	$ 58.5
Indirect taxes less subsidies	29.0
Personal income taxes	41.5
Wages and employee compensation (including personal income taxes)	165.5
Interest on the public debt	15.5
Consumption expenditure	168.4
Exports	90.9
Capital consumption allowance	33.5
Imports	93.3
Gross investment	67.2
Net interest income	19.0
Statistical discrepancy (expenditure approach)	+ 0.2
Corporate profits before taxes	36.5

Rental income plus net farm income plus net income of
unincorporated business   8.6
Statistical discrepancy (income approach)   − 0.2

Calculate the following values.
(a) GDP at market prices (income approach) _____
(b) GDP at market prices (expenditure approach) _____
(c) GDP at factor cost (either approach) _____
(d) Assuming that *net* payments to foreigners had been $8 billion,
      calculate the value of GNP at market prices. _____

6. This exercise focuses on other measures of national income. You are given the
    following national income measures for an economy in a particular year. (Figures
    are in billions of dollars.)

Gross domestic product at market prices $285
Capital consumption allowances (depreciation)   32
Retained earnings   12
Government transfers to households   30
Personal income taxes   42
Indirect taxes less subsidies   30
Consumer expenditure   168
Business taxes   12
Net foreign investment income received   5

(a) Calculate net national income at factor cost.

(b) Calculate the value for personal income and personal disposable income.

(c) Define personal saving as personal disposable income minus consumption
      expenditure. What is its magnitude?

7. From 1950 to 1970, personal disposable income in Canada rose from $12.69
    billion to $53.60 billion. Population increased from 13.71 million to 21.41 million
    in the same period. The price index increased from approximately 100.0 to 142.2.
    What was the total percentage increase in the per capita standard of living as
    measured by per capita real personal disposable income from 1950 to 1970?
    (*Hint:* Do this in parts. First, calculate the levels of *real* personal disposable
    income. Second, calculate the levels of real personal disposable income per
    capita. Then calculate the percentage change over the period 1950–1970.)

8. Which of the following transactions (or events) will be recorded in the GDP accounts in that year? Explain.

   (a) Jim, who normally earns $20 per hour, volunteers 100 hours of his time to assist a local politician.

   (b) The federal government sends three Canadian warships to the Persian Gulf area during the Iraq-Kuwait crisis in August 1990.

   (c) Drug smugglers, using funds from the drug trade, purchase a new hotel in Vancouver.

   (d) A self-employed carpenter buys $1,000 worth of nails and lumber to build a fence for one of his customers. He charges the customer $1,800 but doesn't report the $800 of wages or profits to the tax authorities.

   (e) Pollution of the Toronto beachfront forces the city of Toronto to lay off three lifeguards.

   (f) All welfare recipients are hired as municipal workers.

   (g) Publicly supported abortion clinics are closed when the Supreme Court rules that abortions are illegal under the Criminal Code.

Answers

Multiple-Choice Questions

1. (d) 2. (a) 3. (c) 4. (a) 5. (d) 6. (a) 7. (c) 8. (d) 9. (c) 10. (b) 11. (c) 12. (a)
13. (b) 14. (a) 15. (b) 16. (a) 17. (c) 18. (d) 19. (a) 20. (d) 21. (a) 22. (c)

Exercises

1. The market value of one loaf of bread is $1.00. This is found by the sum of the value added (0.30 from the first stage plus 0.25 from the second stage plus 0.35 from the third stage plus 0.10 from the fourth stage). Thus the sum of the value added at each stage equals the value of the final product.

2. (1) I (2) C, M (3) X (4) I (5) N; this represents an exchange of assets (6) C (7) G (8) N (9) I (10) G, M

3. (a)

	Nominal value of output		
Year	In A	In B	In economy
1	80,000	100,000	180,000
2	132,000	84,000	216,000
3	144,000	108,000	252,000

(b) *Industry A*:
real value in year 1 = 4,000 × 20 =   80,000
in year 2 = 6,000 × 20 = 120,000
in year 3 = 6,000 × 20 = 120,000

Industry B:
in year 1 = 20,000 × 5 = 100,000
in year 2 = 21,000 × 5 = 105,000
in year 3 = 18,000 × 5 =   90,000

Real output in economy:
in year 1 =   80,000 + 100,000 = 180,000
in year 2 = 120,000 + 105,000 = 225,000
in year 3 = 120,000 + 90,000 = 210,000

(c) year 1: 180,000 ÷ 180,000 × 100 = 100.0
year 2: 216,000 ÷ 225,000 × 100 =   96.0
year 3: 252,000 ÷ 210,000 × 100 = 120.0

4. (a) $436.7 + $5.5 − $20.7 = $421.5
(b) $436.7 − $44.3 = $392.4

5. (a) 29.0 + 165.5 + 33.5 + 19.0 + 36.5 + 8.6 − 0.2 = 291.9
(b) 58.5 + 168.4 + 67.2 + 90.9 − 93.3 + 0.2 = 291.9
(c) 291.9 − 29.0 = 262.9
(d) 291.9 − 8.0 = 283.9

6. (a) NNI at factor cost = GDP + net foreign investment income − capital consumption allowance − indirect taxes less subsidies; in this case, NNI = 285 + 5 − 32 − 30 = 228.
(b) Personal income = NNI − retained earnings − business taxes + government transfers; 228 − 12 − 12 + 30 = 234.
Personal disposable income = 234 − 42 = 192.
(c) Personal saving = personal disposable income − consumption expenditure; in this case, S = 192 − 168 = 24.

7. Real disposable income was $12.69 billion in 1950 and $37.69 billion in 1970. Thus per capita disposable income was $926.60 in 1950 and $1,760.39 in 1970. The percentage increase was 89.98 percent.

8. (a) This is an example of a nonmarketed activity and therefore would not be included in GDP accounts. If the politician had paid Jim $2,000 for his 100 hours of work, then Jim's income would have been included in the GDP accounts.
(b) This is a straightforward example of a government expenditure that would be recorded in the GDP accounts.
(c) Even though the funds used to purchase the hotel are from illegal activities, the actual purchase would be recorded in the investment component of the GDP accounts.

(d) The $1,000 purchase of nails and lumber would be recorded in the GDP accounts. The carpenter's value added ($800) is not included since the carpenter did not report his income. The $800 represents an "underground" economy transaction.

(e) Although pollution costs are not recorded in the GDP accounts, the effects of pollution on market activity can appear in the GDP accounts. In this case, three lifeguards lost their jobs, and hence the income approach will indicate a decline in overall income (assuming that they were unemployed for a period of time after their dismissal).

(f) The income paid to welfare recipients is not included in the measure of GDP. However, if all were hired as municipal workers, their salaries would be included in the government expenditure component of aggregate expenditures.

(g) Abortion clinics, if financed by some level of government, would be included in the expenditure approach in measuring GDP. However, all other things being equal, their closure would decrease government expenditure. The purchases of abortion services from illegal, private clinics would presumably not be recorded in the GDP accounts.

Chapter 28

National Income and Aggregate Expenditure

Learning Objectives

After studying this chapter, you should be able to:

—determine the equilibrium level (and changes in it) under the assumption that the price level is constant

—understand the principal determinants of the major components of desired real aggregate expenditure

—distinguish between autonomous and induced expenditure, the latter including consumption and net exports

—understand the properties of a Keynesian consumption function—a relationship between desired real consumption expenditure and *current* real income

—distinguish between *shifts in* and *movements along* the aggregate expenditure function

—define and calculate the marginal propensity to spend and recognize its role in determining the value of the *simple* national income multiplier

—demonstrate how a disequilibrium level of income causes inventory adjustments that restore equilibrium

—determine the multiplier effect of a change in autonomous expenditures on the equilibrium level of real national income

Multiple-Choice Questions

1. Which of the following is *not* a component of aggregate expenditure?
    (a) investment
    (b) government expenditure on goods
    (c) personal taxes
    (d) exports

2. Which of the following is assumed to be induced?
   (a) consumption   (c) imports
   (b) personal taxes   (d) all of the above

3. The average propensity to consume out of disposable income is defined as
   (a) the ratio of total consumption expenditure to total national income
   (b) the ratio of total consumption expenditure to total disposable income
   (c) the ratio of the change in consumption expenditure to total disposable income
   (d) the ratio of the change in consumption expenditure to the change in total disposable income

4. For the Keynesian consumption function depicted in the text, it is likely that as disposable income rises, the APC value
   (a) falls   (c) is constant
   (b) rises   (d) is zero

5. Below the break-even level of disposable income, households
   (a) have a negative saving (dissaving)
   (b) consume less than their disposable income
   (c) save
   (d) spend an amount on goods and services equal to the value of their disposable income

6. If the marginal propensity to save out of disposable income is 0.25, then the marginal propensity to consume (MPC) is
   (a) 0.25   (c) 1.0
   (b) 0.75   (d) 0.33

7. If $Y_d = 0.8Y$ and consumption was always 80 percent of disposable income, then the marginal propensity to consume out of total income would be
   (a) 0.8   (c) 1.6
   (b) 0.2   (d) 0.64

8. Aggregate expenditure is equal to
   (a) $C + I + G + (X - M) +$ transfers
   (b) $C + I + G + (X - M)$
   (c) $C + I + G + X + M$
   (d) $C + I + G + (M - X)$

9. Equilibrium national income occurs when
   (a) $Y = C + I + G + (X - M)$
   (b) the average propensity to spend is 1
   (c) desired aggregate expenditure equals total output
   (d) all of the above

10. If desired aggregate expenditure exceeds real national income, there will be a tendency for
    (a) output and real income to contract
    (b) output and real income to expand
    (c) output and real income to remain constant
    (d) an equilibrium to exist in the economy

Questions 11 through 19 refer to the accompanying graph. Remember that the price level is assumed constant.

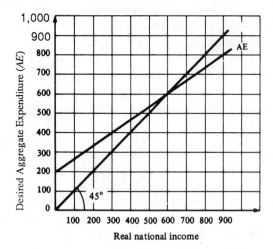

11. When real national income (Y) is 0, desired aggregate expenditure (AE) is
    (a) 600   (c) 200
    (b) equal to actual output   (d) 300

12. When real national income is 600, desired aggregate expenditure is
    (a) 600   (c) 300
    (b) less than income   (d) greater than income

13. If actual real national income were 400, desired aggregate expenditure would
    (a) exceed income, and hence output and income would likely contract
    (b) be less than income, and hence income would likely contract
    (c) exceed income, but equilibrium would exist
    (d) exceed income, and hence output and income would likely expand

14. When actual (measured) real national income is equal to 700, desired aggregate expenditure
    (a) is less than real income, and hence inventories are likely to fall unintentionally
    (b) is less than real income, and hence inventories are likely to rise unintentionally
    (c) is less than real income, but no change in inventory occurs
    (d) is equal to 700

15. According to the graph, the marginal propensity to spend is
    (a) ⅔ and constant
    (b) less than 1 but variable according to the level of income
    (c) ⅓ and constant
    (d) always equal to the average propensity to spend

16. The marginal propensity not to spend in this case is
    (a) 2/3   (c) 1
    (b) 1/3   (d) a variable fraction

17. The equilibrium level of real national income is
    (a) 500
    (c) in the range 400 to 500
    (b) 700
    (d) 600

18. At a real national income level of 300, desired aggregate expenditure equals 400, and the average propensity to spend is
    (a) 0.75
    (b) 2/3
    (c) less than the marginal propensity to spend
    (d) 4/3

19. At a real national income level of 600, the value of the average propensity to spend is
    (a) equal to the value of the marginal propensity to spend
    (b) unity
    (c) less than the value of the marginal propensity to spend
    (d) less than unity

20. The net export function typically slopes downward because
    (a) as Y increases, expenditure on imports increases, thereby decreasing net exports
    (b) as Y increases, exports fall
    (c) as relative prices rise, imports rise and exports fall, thereby reducing net exports
    (d) as Y increases, imports fall

21. A movement along an aggregate expenditure function
    (a) represents a change in prices at every level of national income
    (b) causes a change in the equilibrium level of national income
    (c) represents induced changes in expenditure caused by changes in national income
    (d) has no effect on the average propensity to spend

22. A change in the equilibrium level of national income is caused by
    (a) a shift in the aggregate expenditure function
    (b) only a movement along the aggregate expenditure function
    (c) an increase in output with aggregate expenditure remaining constant
    (d) a change in taxes caused by a change in national income

23. Increases in national income are predicted to be caused by increases in all but which of the following, other things remaining equal?
    (a) taxes
    (c) government expenditure
    (b) exports
    (d) investment

24. Decreases in national income are predicted to be caused by increases in all but which of the following, other things being equal?
    (a) the marginal propensity to save   (c) imports
    (b) tax rates   (d) exports

25. The *simple* multiplier measures
    (a) the extent to which national income will change in response to a change in autonomous expenditure at a constant price level
    (b) the rise in expenditure caused by a change in national income
    (c) the marginal propensity to spend
    (d) the extent to which national income will change in response to a change in autonomous expenditure at varying price levels

26. If expenditure in the economy did not depend on the level of national income, the value of the simple multiplier would be
    (a) zero   (c) infinite or undefined
    (b) unity   (d) −1

27. If the marginal propensity not to spend is 0.2, the simple multiplier is
    (a) 0.8   (c) 5.0
    (b) 2.0   (d) 1.25

28. Assuming constant prices and a marginal propensity to spend of 0.75, an increase in autonomous expenditure of $1 million should increase equilibrium national income by
    (a) $1 million   (c) $4 million
    (b) $250,000   (d) $750,000

Questions 29 through 35 refer to the accompanying graph. Assume that the price level remains constant.

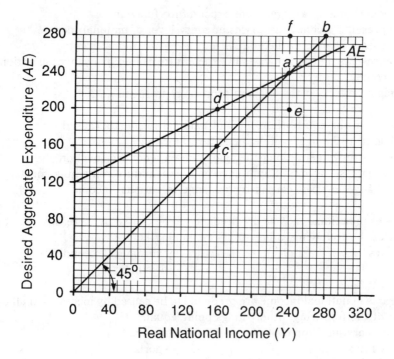

29. According to the graph, the level of desired autonomous expenditure is
    (a) 120
    (b) 280
    (c) 240
    (d) at point *b*

30. According to the aggregate expenditure curve labeled *AE*, the current equilibrium level of real national income is
    (a) 320
    (b) 240
    (c) 120
    (d) 280

31. The *AE* curve has a slope of
    (a) 0.5
    (b) 0.6
    (c) 2.0
    (d) 1.0

32. The value of the simple multiplier is therefore
    (a) 2.0
    (b) 2.5
    (c) 0.5
    (d) 0

33. Suppose that government expenditure decreased by 40 at *all* levels of real national income. The aggregate expenditure curve would
    (a) shift upward by 40 and intersect the 45° line at point *b*
    (b) shift downward by 40, but its slope would also decrease
    (c) shift downward by 40, have a slope of 0.5, and intersect the 45° line at point *c*
    (d) cause a movement along the *AE* curve from *a* to *d*

34. According to the new *AE* curve associated with question 33, if output remains temporarily at 240, desired expenditure is
    (a) 240 (at point *a*), and hence inventories remain unchanged
    (b) 200 (at point *e*), with the result that unplanned inventory accumulation is equal to 40
    (c) 280 (at point *f*), with the result that unplanned inventory reduction is equal to 40
    (d) 200, which is associated with point *d*

35. The decrease in government expenditure of 40 causes equilibrium real national income to
    (a) decrease in total by 40
    (b) increase in total by 80 to a new equilibrium level at 320
    (c) decrease in total by 80: 40 in government expenditure and another 40 in induced expenditure
    (d) decrease in total by 60: 40 in government expenditure and another 20 (0.5 × 40) in induced expenditure

Appendix Questions

The following questions are based on material in the appendix to this chapter. Read the appendix before answering them.

36. Suppose that a household purchases an automobile worth $30,000 in 1990 that for practical purposes is expected to last for six years. Which statement is true?
    (a) Actual consumption of the car in 1990 is about $5,000.
    (b) Consumption expenditure in 1990 is $30,000.
    (c) Actual consumption and consumption expenditure in 1990 are $30,000.
    (d) Both (a) and (b).

37. Which of the following is *not* a feature of the permanent-income theory or the life-cycle theory?
    (a) Both theories stress that actual consumption in a year is based on long-run expected income.
    (b) Both emphasize that any change in current income that is viewed as temporary may have only a small effect on permanent (or expected) income and hence on actual consumption.
    (c) A temporary increase in current income may cause households to increase saving or possibly to purchase more consumer durables.
    (d) Saving in any period is defined as income minus consumption expenditure.

38. Suppose that the government announced a temporary tax decrease. Which of the following statements is correct?
    (a) Keynesian consumption theory predicts that consumption expenditure increases since current disposable income increases.
    (b) The life-cycle and permanent-income theories suggest that households may increase their holdings of financial assets (save) rather than spend their increase in current disposable income.
    (c) The predictions of the life-cycle and permanent-income theories may be consistent with the Keynesian theory; increases in current disposable income increase purchases of consumer durables (consumption expenditure).
    (d) All of the above.

Exercises

1. The first two columns of the following schedule depict the relationship between desired consumption expenditure (C) and real disposable income (Y_d).

Y_d	C	APC	ΔY_d	ΔC	MPC	S
0	80	N.A.				−80
			100	50	0.50	
100	130	1.30				−30
			60	30	0.50	
160	___	1.00				___
			___	20	0.50	
200	180	___				20
			___	___	0.50	
400	___	0.70				120
			350			
750	455	___		___	___	___

(a) Fill in the missing values for the change in real disposable income (ΔY_d).

(b) Fill in the missing values for C using the formula $C = 80 + 0.5Y_d$.

(c) Using the definition for the average propensity to consume (APC), fill in the missing values for APC. What did you notice happened to the value of APC as the level of Y_d increased?

(d) Fill in the missing values for ΔC.

(e) Using the definition for MPC, calculate it for the income change from 400 to 750.

(f) Using the definition for saving $S = Y_d - C$, fill in the missing values in the table. Using the formula $\Delta S/\Delta Y_d$, prove that the marginal propensity to save is constant and equal to 0.5.

(g) What is the break-even level of real disposable income? What is the amount of saving at this level of Y_d?

(h) Plot both the desired consumption (as line C) and desired savings functions (as line S) in the grid. In addition, draw the 45° line and prove that this line intersects the consumption function at a level of Y_d for which $S = 0$.

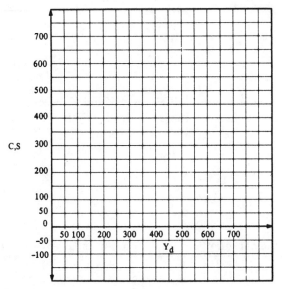

(i) Is desired consumption expenditure both autonomous and induced? Explain.

2. You are given the following information:

Y	Y_d	Desired C	APC	$S = Y_d - C$
100.0	70	100	1.43	−30
200.0	140	156	_____	−16
314.3	220	220	_____	0

(a) What relationship exists between Y and Y_d? Why is Y_d less than Y?

(b) Prove that the marginal propensity to consume out of real disposable income is constant and equal to 0.80.

(c) Calculate the marginal propensity to consume out of real income (Y).

(d) Calculate the values for APC out of real disposable income (the fourth column).

(e) What is the marginal propensity to save out of real disposable income?

(f) What is the break-even level of real disposable income? Total real national income?

3. Exercise 2 is based on specific mathematical relationships. The relationship between real income (Y) and real disposable income (Y_d) is $Y_d = 0.7Y$, and the consumption function is given by $C = 44 + 0.8Y_d$. The coefficient 0.8 is the slope of the consumption function (the MPC out of disposable income). You may wish to recheck your answers to exercise 2 using these equations.

(a) Suppose that Y = 400. Calculate the values for Y_d and C. Do the same for Y = 500 and Y = 600.

(b) Now assume that the relationship between Y and Y_d becomes $Y_d = 0.6Y$, but the consumption function remains the same. What factor might have caused the change? Recalculate the values of C and Y_d for levels of income of 400, 500, and 600. Compare these values with the values in (a).

(c) Suppose that the consumption function becomes $C = 44 + 0.9Y_d$ while the relationship between Y and Y_d given in (a) still holds ($Y_d = 0.7Y$). What is the value of the MPC out of real disposable income? Out of real total income? Calculate the values for C when Y has values of 400, 500, and 600.

4. This exercise involves real wealth and the consumption function. Suppose that an economy has a consumption function given by $C = 60 + 0.8Y + 0.1\,(W/P)$. The term W/P is the level of "real" wealth, W is the level of nominal wealth, and P is the price level. C represents desired consumption expenditure, and Y represents the level of real national income. Assume that the price level has a value of 1.0 and is constant and that the economy's total nominal wealth is 400. Therefore, in this case real and nominal wealth are both equal to 400.

   (a) Given that real wealth is 400, rewrite the expression for the consumption function.

   (b) Fill in the missing values in columns 2 and 4 in the following schedule.

(1)	(2)	(3)	(4)	(5)
	C	C	S	S
Y	$(W/P = 400)$	$(W/P = 2{,}400)$	$(W/P = 400)$	$(W/P = 2{,}400)$
	100	300	−100	−300
500	_____	700	_____	−200
1,000	900	1,100	+100	−100
1,500	_____	_____	_____	_____
2,000	1,700	1,900	+300	+100

   (c) Assume that the economy's real and nominal wealth increases from 400 to 2,400 (the price level remains at 1.0). Write the new consumption function, and fill in the missing values in columns 3 and 5.

   (d) As a result of the wealth increase, what happens to the consumption function? The saving function? Check your answers against the graph in the textbook.

5. As an economy expands in terms of real income, the balance of trade (or, for our purposes, net exports) typically falls. If $X - M$ is negative, a *deficit* in the balance of trade is said to exist. To explain this we present the following hypothetical schedule, where Y represents levels of real national income, X represents desired exports, and M represents desired imports.

Y	X	M	$X - M$
0	40	0	_____
100	40	10	_____
200	40	20	_____
400	40	40	_____
800	40	80	_____

   (a) Exports are assumed to be autonomous (independent of the level of Y). However, what specific relationship exists between M (imports) and Y? Identify some factors that explain the positive relationship between desired imports and real national income.

(b) Calculate the values for $X - M$. Does the balance of trade fall (become smaller) as Y increases?

(c) Plot the net export curve.

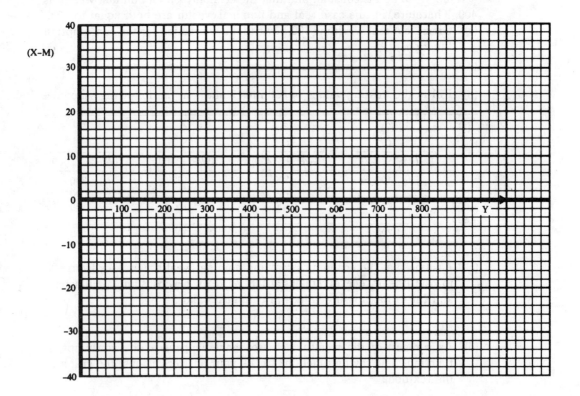

(d) Suppose that exports at each level of Y fell from 40 to 30. Recalculate the value of $X - M$ at each level of Y, and plot the new net export curve

(e) Identify three factors that might have caused exports to decline as in (d).

6. (a) The table shows the relationship between the various components of desired aggregate expenditure and real national income. Fill in the blanks and plot the values of total aggregate expenditure (AE) associated with levels of real national income (Y) on the accompanying grid.

Y	C	I	G	X – M	AE	ΔY	ΔAE
0	90	10	30	20	_____		
100	150	10	30	10	_____	_____	_____
200	210	10	30	0	_____	_____	_____
300	270	10	30	– 10	_____	_____	_____
400	330	10	30	– 20	_____	_____	_____

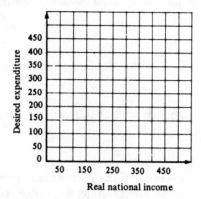

(b) The equilibrium level of national income is _____. Explain.

(c) Suppose that actual (measured) real national income was 400. What is the value of desired aggregate expenditure at that level? What does the residual amount $(Y - AE)$ represent? Is real national output likely to expand or contract in this situation? Explain.

(d) Calculate the values for ΔY and ΔAE and fill in the table in (a). Prove that the marginal propensity to spend is constant and equal to 0.50. The slope of the AE function you plotted should be 1/2.

(e) The marginal propensity not to spend is _____.

*7. This exercise involves an algebraic determination of equilibrium national income. You are given the following information about behavior in an economy: The consumption function is

$$C = 100 + 0.7Y_d \qquad (1)$$

The relationship between Y and Y_d is

$$Y_d = 0.8Y \qquad (2)$$

Investment expenditures are

$$I = 56 \qquad (3)$$

The net export function is

$$X - M = 10 - 0.1Y \qquad (4)$$

Government expenditures are

$$G = 50 \qquad (5)$$

(a) In the consumption function (Equation 1), what does the coefficient 0.7 mean?

(b) What components of aggregate expenditure depend on national income?

(c) Aggregate expenditure is the algebraic sum of the various components. Derive the algebraic expression for AE.

(d) Equilibrium national income is where $Y = AE$. This is the expression for the 45° line. Equate your expression for AE in (c) with Y. Solve for Y.

(e) Derive the marginal propensity to spend. (*Hint*: Substitute values for Y equal to 100 and 200 into the algebraic expression for AE and then calculate ΔY and ΔAE.)

(f) What is the value of the simple multiplier?

8. You are given the following information about an economy. The data labeled "Case A" represent the initial situation in the economy.

	Case A					Case B		Case C		Case D	
Y	C	I	G	X – M	AE	I	AE	X – M	AE	C	AE
0	10	50	10	10	80	60	90	−10	60	10	80
200	190	50	10	−10	240	60	_____	−30	_____	150	_____
300	280	50	10	−20	320	60	_____	−40	_____	220	_____
400	370	50	10	−30	400	60	_____	−50	_____	290	_____
450	415	50	10	−35	440	60	_____	−55	_____	325	_____

(a) For case A, determine the equilibrium level of real national income and the marginal propensity to spend.

(b) Graph the aggregate expenditure curve, and indicate the equilibrium level of real national income (case A).

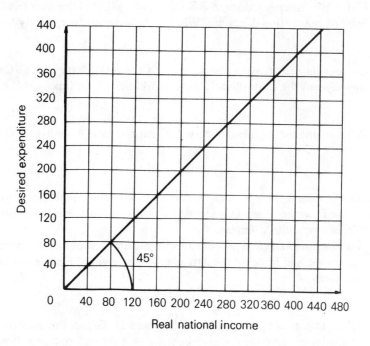

(c) Now assume that a change occurs in the economy so that case B holds. Case B is identical to case A except that investment *at every level of Y* increases from 50 to 60. Fill in the missing values in the table for *AE*, and plot the new aggregate expenditure curve. What has happened to the aggregate expenditure curve? (Compare case A with case B.)

(d) Using the *AE* curve for case B, what is the value of desired *AE* at a level of real national income of 400? What do you predict will happen to the equilibrium level of real national income in this situation? Explain.

(e) What is the equilibrium level of real national income for case B? What has been the total change in real national income (ΔY) between case A and B? Calculate the ratio $\Delta Y/\Delta I$ from A to B. What is the value of the simple multiplier?

(f) Calculate the value of the marginal propensity to spend (denoted as z in the text) for case B? Using the formula $K = 1/(1 - z)$, confirm your answer for the value of the simple multiplier in (e).

(g) The total change in income is composed of two parts: the change in the autonomous component of *AE* (ΔA), which in this case is ΔI, and the *induced* change in aggregate expenditure (ΔN). What is the value for ΔN? What was the change in consumption? The change in $X - M$?

9. Assume that case A is the initial situation but now net exports *at every level of income* fall such that $X - M$ has fallen by 20 at every level of Y. This is case C.
    (a) Fill in the missing values of AE for case C. What is the new equilibrium level of real national income? What is the marginal propensity to spend?

    (b) Comparing case A with case C, what is the total change in Y? Calculate the value of the multiplier. Calculate ΔA and ΔN [in this case $\Delta(X - M)$].

    (c) What happened to the AE curve? (Compare case A with case C.)

10. Assume that case A is the initial situation but that factors in the economy change so that case D applies. Case D is identical to case A except that the consumption function is now quite different.
    (a) Calculate the marginal propensities to consume out of national income for both cases, and indicate the nature of the behavioral change between the two cases.

    (b) Fill in the missing values of AE for case D. Graph the new aggregate expenditure curve on the grid in exercise 8 (b) and compare it with the one for case A.

    (c) Calculate the marginal propensity to spend for case D, and compare it with that for case A. Calculate the multiplier value, and compare it with the multiplier for case A.

    (d) What is the equilibrium level of real national income for case D?

*11. You are given the following equations:
     The consumption function is

     $$C = 30 + 0.9Y_d \qquad (1)$$

     The relationship between Y_d and Y is

     $$Y_d = 0.8Y \qquad (2)$$

     Investment expenditures are

     $$I = 40 \qquad (3)$$

     Government expenditures are

     $$G = 20 \qquad (4)$$

The net export function is

$$X - M = 20 - 0.12Y \tag{5}$$

The AE expenditure identity is

$$AE = C + I + G + (X - M) \tag{6}$$

The equilibrium condition is

$$AE = Y \tag{7}$$

(a) Substitute Equation 2 into Equation 1 and solve for C in terms of Y. Call this Equation 8.

(b) Substitute Equations 8, 3, 4 and 5 into the right-hand side of Equation 6. What is the value of the slope of the AE function ($\Delta AE/\Delta Y$)? This is the marginal propensity to spend.

(c) Using Equation 7, solve for the equilibrium level of Y.

(d) Now suppose that the federal government raised the personal income tax rate such that Equation 2 changed to $Y_d = 0.689Y$. Call this Equation 9.
    (i) Substitute Equation 9 into Equation 1 and solve for C in terms of Y. Call this Equation 10.

    (ii) Substitute Equations 10, 3, 4, and 5 into the right-hand side of Equation 6. What is the slope of this AE function? Compare it with the value you obtained in (b).

    (iii) Using Equation 7 and the new expression for the aggregate expenditure function, solve for the equilibrium level of Y. Compare this with your answer in (c).

(e) Calculate and compare the value of the simple multipliers before and after the tax rate increase.

Answers

Multiple-Choice Questions

1. (c)   2. (d)   3. (b)   4. (a)   5. (a)   6. (b)   7. (d)   8. (b)   9. (d)   10. (b)   11. (c)   12. (a)
13. (d)   14. (b)   15. (a)   16. (b)   17. (d)   18. (d)   19. (b)   20. (a)   21. (c)   22. (a)   23. (a)
24. (d)   25. (a)   26. (b)   27. (c)   28. (c)   29. (a)   30. (b)   31. (a)   32. (a)   33. (c)
34. (b)   35. (c)   36. (d)   37. (d)   38. (d)

Exercises

1. (a)   40, 200
   (b)   160, 280
   (c)   0.90, 0.61; the value of *APC* fell.
   (d)   100, 175
   (e)   0.50 =175/350
   (f)   0, 295. The marginal propensity to save is 0.50 and is constant. For an increase in Y_d from 0 to 100, saving increases from -80 to -30. The ratio of the changes is 0.50.
   (g)   160, at which $S = 0$
   (h)

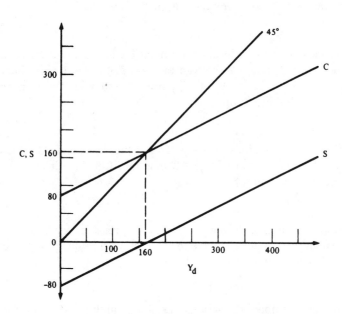

   (i)   Consumption expenditure is both autonomous and induced. It has an autonomous component because consumption is 80 when disposable income is zero. Since the marginal propensity to consume is 0.50, consumption is therefore induced as well.

2. (a) There is a positive relationship given by the expression $Y_d = 0.7Y$. It is less because taxes outweigh transfer payments.

   (b) $\Delta C/\Delta Y_d = 56/70$ and $64/80$, each of which equals 0.8.

   (c) $\Delta C/\Delta Y = 56/100 = 64/114.3 = 0.56$

   (d) $APC = 156/140 = 1.11$; $APC = 220/220 = 1.00$

   (e) $0.2 = 1 - 0.8$

   (f) When $C = Y_d$, which is 220; when $C = Y$, which is 100.

3. (a) When $Y = 400$, $Y_d = 280$ and $C = 268$; when $Y = 500$, $Y_d = 350$ and $C = 324$; when $Y = 600$, $Y_d = 420$ and $C = 380$.

   (b) The amount of income going to personal income taxes has likely increased. When $Y = 400$, $Y_d = 240$ and $C = 236$; when $Y = 500$, $Y_d = 300$ and $C = 284$; when $Y = 600$, $Y_d = 360$ and $C = 332$. For a given level of Y, both Y_d and C have fallen.

   (c) MPC out of Y_d is 0.9, while MPC out of total income is 0.63 (0.9×0.7). When $Y = 400$, 500, and 600, C values are 296, 359, and 422, respectively.

4. (a) When real wealth is 400, the consumption function becomes $C = 60 + 0.8Y + 0.1(400)$ or $C = 100 + 0.8Y$.

   (b) C is 500, 1,300.
       S is 0, +200.

   (c) The consumption function becomes $C = 60 + 0.8Y + 0.1(2,400)$ or $C = 300 + 0.8Y$.
       C is 1,500.
       S is 0.

   (d) The consumption function shifted up in a parallel fashion (an increase of 200 at every level of real national income). The saving function shifted down in a parallel fashion (a decrease of 200 at every level of real national income).

5. (a) Imports are positively related to national income by the expression $M = 0.1Y$. As national income rises, households buy more imported goods; firms, in order to produce more goods, require more imported inputs; and it is possible for governments and firms to import various machines, goods, and services as part of their investment and expenditure programs.

   (b) 40, 30, 20, 0, -40. Yes. because imports rise as income rises.

   (c)

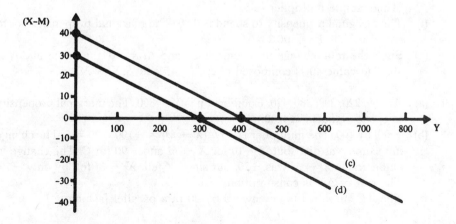

(d) $Y = 0$, $X - M = 30$; $Y = 100$, $X - M = 20$; $Y = 200$, $X - M = 10$; $Y = 300$, $X - M = 0$; $Y = 400$, $X - M = -10$; $Y = 800$, $X - M = -50$

(e) The domestic currency appreciated; foreign income fell; domestic inflation was higher than foreign inflation.

6. (a) AE values are 150, 200, 250, 300, 350. The AE curve has an intercept value of 150 (at $Y = 0$) and a constant slope of 0.5.

(b) Equilibrium is 300 because $AE = Y$.

(c) $AE = 350$ $(330 + 10 + 30 - 20)$. $Y - AE = 50$ is the amount of unintended inventory accumulation. Since there are costs associated with holding high levels of unplanned inventory, firms are likely to reduce production and lay off factors of production. As a consequence, real income falls.

(d) $\Delta Y = 100$, 100, 100, 100; $\Delta AE = 50$, 50, 50, 50; marginal propensity to spend $= 50/100 = 0.5$.

(e) The marginal propensity not to spend is equal to $1 - 0.5 = 0.5$.

*7. (a) The coefficient 0.7 is the marginal propensity to consume out of real disposable income.

(b) Net exports (because of imports) and consumption (through disposable income) depend on national income.

(c) $AE = 100 + 0.7 (0.8Y) + 56 + 50 + 10 - 0.1Y$, or $AE = 216 + 0.46Y$

(d) $216 + 0.46Y = Y$, or $Y = 400$

(e) When $Y = 100$, $AE = 262$; when $Y = 200$, $AE = 308$; hence $\Delta AE/\Delta Y = 46/100 = 0.46$.

(f) $K = 1/(1 - 0.46) = 1.85$

8. (a) $AE = Y$ at 400. The marginal propensity to spend is 0.80 and is constant $(\Delta AE = 160, \Delta Y = 200, \Delta AE/\Delta Y = 0.80)$.

(b) The AE curve has an intercept value of 80 on the vertical axis, has a slope of 0.80, and intersects the 45° line at an income level of 400.

(c) AE: 90, 250, 330, 410, 450. The AE curve shifts vertically upward by 10 in a parallel fashion.

(d) $AE = 410$ when $Y = 400$. Since AE is greater than national income, real income and employment will rise.

(e) $AE = Y$ at 450. The change in income is 50, and $\Delta Y/\Delta I = 5$. The value of the simple multiplier is 5.

(f) The marginal propensity to spend is 0.80. The marginal propensity not to spend is 0.20. $K = 1/0.2 = 5$.

(g) Since the total change in income is 50 and $\Delta I = 10$, the value of ΔN is 40. The value 40 is composed of $\Delta C = 45$ and $\Delta(X - M) = -5$.

9. (a) AE: 60, 220, 300, 380, 420. Equilibrium is $Y = 300$. The marginal propensity to spend remains at 0.80.

(b) Y fell by 100. The multiplier is $\Delta Y/\Delta(X - M) = -100/-20 = 5$. The change in income was distributed -10 for $X - M$ and -90 for C. The change in autonomous $X - M$ was -20, but since Y fell, $X - M$ fell by only -10. The rest of ΔN is consumption.

(c) The AE curve shifts downward by 20 in a parallel fashion.

10. (a) Case A: $MPC = 0.90$; case D: $MPC = 0.70$. Consumers have become more frugal; they are saving a higher proportion of national income.

(b) AE: 80, 200, 260, 320, 350. The new AE has an intercept of 80 on the vertical axis, has a slope of 0.60, and intersects the 45° line at $Y = 200$. The AE curve for case D is flatter than that for case A.

(c) The marginal propensity to spend for case D is 0.60, which is lower than 0.80 for case A. The multiplier for case D is therefore $1/(1 - 0.60) = 2.5$.

(d) $AE = Y$ when $Y = 200$.

*11. (a) $C = 30 + 0.9(0.8Y) = 30 + 0.72Y$: Equation 8

(b) $AE = 30 + 0.72Y + 40 + 20 + 20 - 0.12Y = 110 + 0.60Y$
The slope of the AE function is 0.60.

(c) $110 + 0.6Y = Y$ or $Y = 275$

(d) (i) $C = 30 + 0.9(0.689Y) = 30 + 0.62Y$ (approximately): Equation 10

(ii) $AE = 30 + 0.62Y + 40 + 20 + 20 - 0.12Y = 110 + 0.50Y$
The slope is 0.50 and hence the AE curve is flatter.

(iii) $Y = 110 + 0.50Y$ or $Y = 220$. National income has fallen from 275 to 220.

(e) 2.5 before, 2.0 after

National Income and the Price Level in the Short Run

Learning Objectives

After studying this chapter, you should be able to:

—explain why changes in the price level, by influencing consumption and net exports, cause the aggregate expenditure curve to shift

—derive a downward-sloping aggregate demand curve and recognize what factors cause this curve to shift

—explain why the simple multiplier gives the magnitude of the horizontal shift in the *AD* curve in response to the change in autonomous expenditure

—understand the economic factors that determine the slope of the short-run aggregate supply curve and demonstrate how changes in factor prices and productivity cause the *SRAS* curve to shift

—recognize that the effect of a demand shock on the equilibrium levels of price and national output depends on the slope of the *SRAS* curve

—explain why a demand shock has a smaller multiplier effect on output when the *SRAS* curve slopes upward

—demonstrate how supply shocks, especially changes in input prices and productivity, affect equilibrium national income and the price level

Multiple-Choice Questions

1. All other things being equal, an increase in the domestic price level will
   (a) increase the value of real wealth and hence cause an upward shift in the consumption function
   (b) decrease the value of real wealth and hence cause an upward shift in the consumption function
   (c) cause exports to increase, thereby causing the net export function to shift downward
   (d) decrease the value of real wealth and cause the consumption and aggregate expenditure functions to shift downward

2. All other things being equal, a decrease in the domestic price level will shift the net export function
    (a) downward, thus causing the aggregate expenditure function to shift downward
    (b) upward, thus causing the aggregate expenditure function to shift upward
    (c) upward, thus causing the aggregate expenditure function to shift downward
    (d) downward, thus causing the aggregate expenditure function to shift upward

3. The aggregate demand (AD) curve relates
    (a) real national income to desired expenditure for a given price level
    (b) nominal national income to the price level
    (c) equilibrium real national income to the price level
    (d) consumption expenditure to the price level

4. All other things being equal, a fall in the domestic price level causes
    (a) the aggregate expenditure curve to shift upward and hence leads to a movement downward and to the right along the AD curve
    (b) the aggregate expenditure curve to shift upward and hence leads to a movement upward and to the left along the AD curve
    (c) the AD curve to shift to the right and a movement upward and to the right along the AE curve
    (d) the AD and the AE curves to shift upward

5. An upward-sloping SRAS curve indicates
    (a) firms' willingness to supply more output if the output can be sold at higher prices
    (b) that expanding output means incurring higher unit costs and higher prices of output
    (c) that expanding output means higher factor prices and therefore higher output prices
    (d) both (a) and (b)

6. All other things being equal, the AD curve shifts to the right as a result of all but which of the following changes?
    (a) increased government expenditure
    (b) increased autonomous imports
    (c) increased autonomous exports
    (d) increased investment expenditure

7. If the SRAS curve is horizontal,
    (a) output can be increased at a constant price level
    (b) any increase in AD will cause real national income and the price level to increase
    (c) output is constant but the price level is variable
    (d) the economy is most likely operating beyond its potential level of real national income

8. If the current price level is below the short-run macroeconomic equilibrium level,
   (a) the desired output of firms is greater than the level of output consistent with expenditure decisions
   (b) desired aggregate expenditure is less than the amount of goods supplied in the short run
   (c) the desired output of firms is less than the level of output consistent with expenditure decisions
   (d) price will tend to adjust such that there will be movement downward and to the right along the *AD* curve

9. All other things being equal, an increase in desired investment expenditures will
   (a) shift the *AE* curve upward
   (b) shift the *AD* curve to the right
   (c) cause the equilibrium levels of real national income and price to increase if the economy operates in the intermediate range of the *SRAS* curve
   (d) all of the above

10. A rightward shift in the *SRAS* curve is brought about by
    (a) an increase in factor prices
    (b) decreases in productivity
    (c) increases in productivity and/or decreases in factor prices
    (d) decreases in factor supplies

11. With a given aggregate demand curve, a shift in the *SRAS* curve to the left will cause
    (a) increases in real national income and the price level in the short run
    (b) an increase in the price level but a decrease in real national income in the short run
    (c) a decrease in the price level but an increase in real national income
    (d) a decrease in potential real national income

Questions 12 through 19 refer to the following graphs.

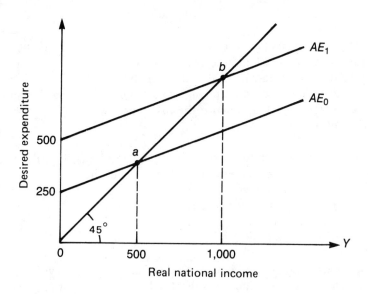

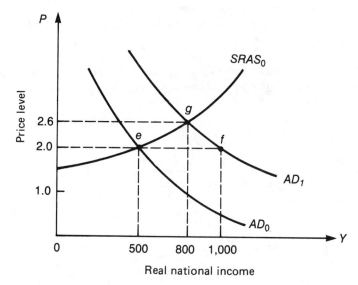

12. According to the curves AE_0 and AD_0, the equilibrium levels of price and real national income are, respectively,
    (a) 2.0 and 500
    (b) 2.6 and 800
    (c) 2.0 and 1,000
    (d) none of the above

13. Assuming that the AE curve shifts upward from AE_0 to AE_1 but the price level remains constant at its initial level, we can say that
    (a) autonomous expenditures must have increased by 250
    (b) real national income increases by 500
    (c) the aggregate demand curve shifts to the right so that $Y = 1,000$ at the price level 2.0
    (d) all of the above

14. Assuming that the price level remains at 2.0, the value of the simple multiplier is
    (a) 5.0   (c) 2.0
    (b) 0.5   (d) 4.0

15. Given the aggregate demand curve AD_1 and a price level of 2.0 (point *f*),
    (a) aggregate demand is less than aggregate supply
    (b) aggregate demand is equal to aggregate supply
    (c) firms are unwilling to produce enough to satisfy the existing demand at
         the existing price level, and hence the price level will rise
    (d) the price level is likely to fall

16. Given the increase in autonomous expenditure, moving from point *f* to point
    g represents the effect of an increase in the price level that
    (a) reduces both exports and real wealth
    (b) reduces exports but increases consumption
    (c) increases both exports and real wealth
    (d) increases exports and saving

17. The movement from point *f* to point *g* implies that the AE_1 curve
    (a) shifts downward until it intersects the 45° line at an output level of 800
    (b) shifts downward until it intersects the 45° line at an output level of 500
    (c) is the aggregate expenditure curve associated with a price level of 2.6
    (d) both (a) and (c)

18. Assuming that input prices do not change, the new short-run macroeconomic
    equilibrium as a result of the increase in autonomous expenditure will be
    (a) at point *g*
    (b) at an output level of 800
    (c) at a price level of 2.6
    (d) all of the above

19. The value of the multiplier after allowing for a price change is
    (a) 1.2   (c) 1.0
    (b) 2.0   (d) 4.0

Refer to the following graph when answering questions 20 through 23.

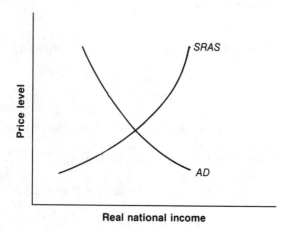

20. When consumers become worried about the future and decide to save more out of additional income,
    (a) the *AD* curve shifts leftward, causing national income and the price level to fall
    (b) the *AD* curve shifts rightward, causing national income and the price level to rise
    (c) the *SRAS* curve shifts rightward, causing national income to rise and the price level to fall
    (d) the *SRAS* curve shifts leftward, causing national income to fall and the price level to rise

21. The dominant short-run effect of an increase in desired investment is to
    (a) shift the *SRAS* curve to the left
    (b) shift the *SRAS* curve to the right
    (c) shift the *AD* curve to the left
    (d) shift the *AD* curve to the right

22. If the *AD* curve shifts to the right, we expect
    (a) the price level to increase and output to fall
    (b) the price level to increase and output to rise
    (c) unemployment to rise
    (d) productivity to fall

23. Rising oil prices resulted in stagflation in the Canadian economy in the 1970s because the *SRAS* curve
    (a) shifted leftward, causing output and the price level to rise
    (b) shifted rightward, causing output and the price level to fall
    (c) shifted leftward, causing output to fall and the price level to rise
    (d) shifted rightward, causing output to rise and the price level to fall

24. The multiplier value that allows for price changes will be equal to the value of the simple multiplier if the demand shock occurs in the
    (a) flat range of the *SRAS* curve
    (b) intermediate range of the *SRAS* curve
    (c) steep portion of the *SRAS* curve
    (d) range characterized by increasing unit costs

25. Under what circumstances would an aggregate demand increase result in virtually no increase in real income but a large increase in the price level?
    (a) if the demand shock occurred in the flat range of the *SRAS* curve
    (b) if the demand shock occurred in the intermediate range of the *SRAS* curve
    (c) if the demand shock occurred in the steep portion of the *SRAS* curve
    (d) if unit costs were constant before and after the demand shock

26. If autonomous investment increased, the multiplier would be zero if
    (a) price increases reduced consumption and net exports by the same amount as the increase in autonomous investment
    (b) the demand shock occurred in the vertical range of the *SRAS* curve
    (c) if the upward shift in the *AE* curve associated with the increase in investment was completely counteracted by the reduction in net exports and real wealth
    (d) all of the above

27. Assume that the *SRAS* curve slopes upward. After an economic shock, we observe that the price level is lower than before but real output has increased. Which one of the following events, by itself, could explain this observation?
    (a) an increase in input prices
    (b) an increase in factor productivity
    (c) an increase in exports
    (d) a reduction in investment expenditure

Exercises

1. This exercise involves the derivation of an aggregate demand curve from consumption theory. In making calculations, you should become more familiar with the basis for a downward-sloping *AD* curve. The exercise demonstrates that changes in price affect the level of real wealth, which in turn changes total consumption expenditure. You will also learn some of the factors that cause the *AD* curve to shift.

    Desired consumption (*C*) is shown at two different price levels, P_1 and P_2. The consumption function is given by the expression $C = 100 + 0.8Y + 0.1(W/P)$, where *W* represents the total nominal wealth in the economy. We assume that nominal wealth is 3,000. All other components of aggregate expenditure are lumped together in one column, labeled $I + G + X - M$. Entries in that column are assumed to be unaffected by the price level, but because imports are included in this combination, it is a negative function of real national income.

Y	C_1 for $P=1$	C_2 for $P=2$	$I + G + X - M$	AE_1 for $P=1$	AE_2 for $P=2$
0	400	250	1,200	1,600	1,450
2,500	2,400	2,250	700	3,100	2,950
2,875	_____	_____	625	_____	_____
3,250	_____	_____	550	_____	_____
3,625	_____	_____	475	_____	_____
4,000	_____	_____	400	_____	_____
4,375	_____	_____	325	_____	_____

(a) What is the value of real wealth when $P = 1$? When $P = 2$? Using these two values and the equation for the consumption function, confirm that at an income level of 2,500, consumption falls from 2,400 to 2,250. This should prove to you that an increase in the price level, by decreasing the value of real wealth, decreases consumption expenditures.

(b) Fill in the missing values for C_1, C_2, AE_1, and AE_2, assuming that the marginal propensities remain constant at all levels of national income.

(c) Plot the aggregate expenditure functions in the upper panel of the accompanying graph, and determine the equilibrium level of national income at each price level. Plot the two combinations of equilibrium price level and income (the AD curve) in the lower panel. Explain why the AD curve slopes downward.

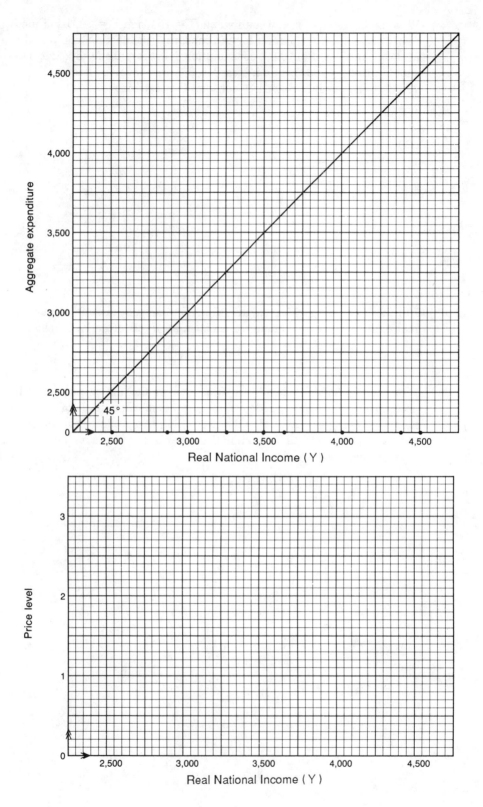

(d) Suppose that government spending rises at all levels of income by 150. Assuming a price level of 1, calculate the new values for AE_1, and plot the new aggregate expenditure curve (AE_d) in the upper panel. What is the new equilibrium value of national income?

(e) Assuming a price level of 2 and the 150 increase in government spending, calculate the new values for AE_2. Confirm that $AE_2 = 4,000$ when $Y = 4,000$.

(f) Using the combinations of equilibrium price and income in (d) and (e), plot the new AD curve in the lower panel.

(g) By inspecting the schedule of information at the beginning of this exercise, calculate the marginal propensity to spend. What is the value of the simple multiplier?

(h) You have demonstrated in (d) and (e) that at a given price level, the 150 increase in government spending increased equilibrium national income by 375. How does this value relate to the simple multiplier?

(i)   Confirm from your AD graph that the horizontal distance between the two AD curves at both price levels is equal to 375, which is equal to 150 times 2.5.

2. Another reason why the AD curve slopes downward is that a reduction in the domestic price level (assuming that the foreign price level remains constant) increases the domestic economy's competitiveness internationally, *ceteris paribus*. Thus net exports should increase if the domestic price level falls.

   This exercise has the same consumption function as exercise 1. However, now the component $X - M$ depends on relative prices (the ratio of the domestic price level to the foreign price level). For our present purposes, the foreign price is assumed to be equal to 1.0 and constant. Thus the relative price can be represented by the domestic price level, P. The nonconsumption items in aggregate expenditure are now determined by the equation

$$I + G + X - M = 1,500 - 0.2Y - 300P$$

There are two domestic price levels, $P = 1$ and $P = 2$.

(a)   Using the equation just given, fill in the entries for $I + G + X - M$ for both price levels. Then calculate AE_1 and AE_2 for all levels of income in the table.

Y	C_1	$(I + G + X - M)_1$	AE_1	C_2	$(I + G + X - M)_2$	AE_2
0	400	1,200	1,600	250	900	1,150
2,500	2,400	700	3,100	2,250	400	2,650
2,875	2,700	———	———	2,550	———	———
3,250	3,000	———	———	2,850	———	———
3,625	3,300	———	———	3,150	———	———
4,000	3,600	———	———	3,450	———	———
4,375	3,900	———	———	3,750	———	———

(b)   Plot the two aggregate expenditure functions (AE) in the upper panel of the graph on the next page, and determine the equilibrium level of national income at each price level (P).

(c)   Based on your answer to (b), plot the AD curve for this economy in the lower panel.

(d)   How can you characterize the slope of this AD curve compared to the one you derived in exercise 1?

(e)   Suppose that the expression for nonconsumption demand expenditures were $I + G + X - M = 1,500 - 0.2Y - 600P$. Without solving the model formally, how would you expect this change to affect the slope of the aggregate demand curve?

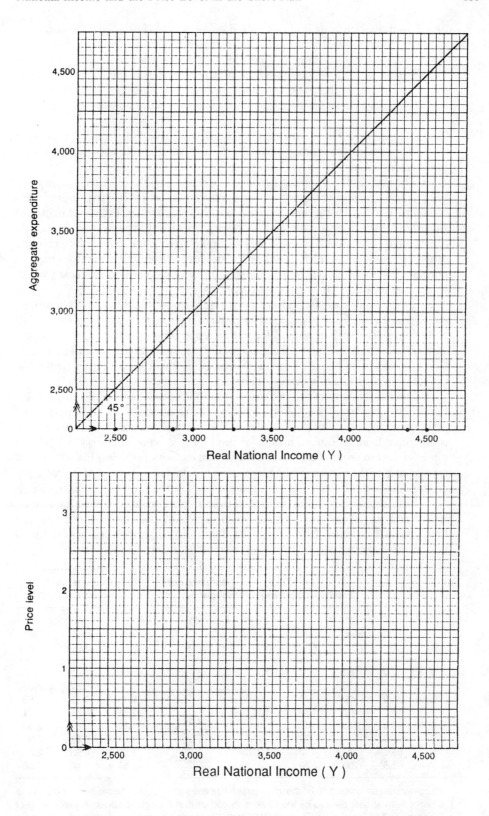

(f)   To summarize your findings, based on a common initial equilibrium price level and national income the more price responsive foreign demand is for domestically produced goods and the more price responsive domestic demand is for foreign goods, the (flatter, steeper) is the slope of the *AD* curve, all other things being equal. Also, the more responsive consumption is to changes in real wealth, the (flatter, steeper) is the slope of the *AD* curve.

*3.   This exercise involves an upward-sloping *SRAS* curve. Students who have not studied microeconomics may find it difficult. All students may wish to refer to Chapters 10 and 12 in the text.

The text explains that the *SRAS* curve represents the relationship between the price level and the supply of aggregate output when factor prices remain constant. The *SRAS* curve will have a positive slope when increases in output cause increases in unit costs and product prices even though input prices do not change. The *SRAS* curve tends to be relatively flat when the economy operates below its potential output level. However, production increases beyond normal capacity levels will be associated with large increases in unit costs, which in turn generate large price level increases.

The complete explanation of a positively sloped *SRAS* curve is complex; the aggregate relationship between output and the price level reflects the overall behavior of diverse firms that differ in market structure for products and inputs as well as in their objectives. This exercise deals with the concept of unit costs that increase in response to output increases by profit-maximizing firms that operate in competitive markets for inputs and products.

Short-run theory of competitive firms outlined in Chapters 10 and 12 yields the following principles: (1) A competitive firm's short-run supply curve is its marginal cost curve, which lies above the average variable cost curve; (2) a competitive firm maximizes profits (or minimizes short-term losses) by equating marginal cost to product price; and (3) short-run capacity is the level of output that corresponds to the minimum short-run average total cost. A firm that is producing at an output less than the point of minimum average total cost has excess capacity.

Consider a representative firm in the competitive sector. Assume that its total fixed costs (associated with a fixed capital stock) are $100 and that the firm pays $10 for each worker it hires. The following table provides detailed information about its production, employment of labor, and costs.

		Total cost (dollars)			Marginal cost (dollars per unit)	Average cost (dollars per unit)		
(1) Labor (L)	(2) Output (q)	(3) Fixed (TFC)	(4) Variable (TVC)	(5) Total (TC)	(6) (MC)*	(7) Fixed (AFC)	(8) Variable (AVC)	(9) Total (ATC)
0	0.0	100	0	100		—	—	—
1	15.0	100	10	110	0.67	6.67	0.67	7.33
2	34.0	100	20	120	0.53	2.94	0.59	3.53
3	48.0	100	30	130	0.71	2.08	0.62	2.71
4	60.0	100	40	140	0.83	1.67	0.67	2.33
5	62.0	100	50	150	5.00	1.61	0.81	2.42
6	63.0	100	60	160	10.00	1.59	0.95	2.54
7	63.5	100	70	170	20.00	1.57	1.10	2.68

*Marginal cost (in column 6) is shown between the lines of total cost because it refers to the *change* in total cost divided by the *change* in output that brought it about. An *MC* value of $0.71 is the $10 increase in *TC* (from $120 to $130) divided by the 14-unit increase in output from (34 to 48).

(a) What output level represents the firm's short-run capacity?

(b) Suppose that the firm considers increasing its production from 41 (the midpoint of the output range 34 to 48) to 54 (the midpoint of the output range 48 to 60). Will its marginal cost increase, decrease, or remain constant? What happens to the firm's average variable costs (unit variable costs)? Recalling that a firm equates product price with marginal cost, what change in price is required to induce the firm to increase its output from 41 to 54? Both output levels (41 and 54) are less than its capacity. Hence, when a firm has excess capacity, increases in output cause (large, small) increases in unit costs; therefore, its short-run supply curve is relatively (flat, steep).

(c) Why did marginal costs increase as output increased from 41 to 54? (*Hint:* What was the incremental contribution to output of hiring the third worker as output increased from 34 to 48 compared with the incremental contribution to output of hiring the fourth worker as output increased from 48 to 60?)

(d) Suppose that the firm considers increasing its output from 54 to 61 (the midpoint of the output range 60 to 62). Will its marginal costs increase, decrease, or remain constant? What happens to its average (unit) variable costs? What price will the firm require to maximize profits for the higher output? An output level of 61 is greater than the firm's short-run capacity. Hence for output levels that are higher than capacity, the firm's short-run supply curve is relatively (flat, steep).

(e) The text also explains that the SRAS curve will shift to the left if input prices increase. Prove that the representative firm's marginal and average variable costs increase at every output level if the wage rate increases from $10 per worker to $20 per worker. Continue to assume that fixed costs are $100.

(f) The SRAS curve will shift downward and to the right if factor productivity increases. Prove that the representative firm's marginal cost will decrease at every output level if labor productivity increases. New output levels refer to those after the productivity change. Continue to assume that the wage rate is $10 per worker.

Labor	Output Old	Output New	Total cost (dollars)	Marginal cost Old	Marginal cost New
0	0.0	0.0	100		
				0.67	_____
1	15.0	16.0	110		
				0.53	_____
2	34.0	36.0	120		
				0.71	_____
3	48.0	51.0	130		
				0.83	_____
4	60.0	64.0	140		
				5.00	_____
5	62.0	67.0	150		
				10.00	_____
6	63.0	69.0	160		
				20.00	_____
7	63.5	70.5	170		

4. The aggregate demand function is given by $P = 40 - 2Y$, and the short-run aggregate supply function is given by $P = 10 + Y$, where Y refers to real national income and P is the price level.

(a) Graph the AD curve and indicate both of the intercept values.

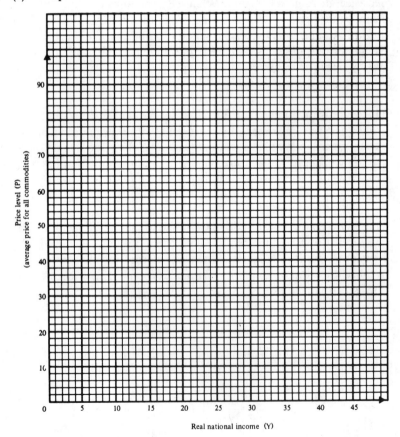

(b) Graph the $SRAS$ curve.

(c) Referring to the graph, what is the macroeconomic equilibrium (equilibrium levels of P and Y)? Prove algebraically that the intersection of the two equations yields these equilibrium values.

(d) Suppose that the expression for the AD curve became $P = 70 - 2Y$. Plot this expression in the graph, and discuss the changes that occurred to the levels of P and Y.

5. This exercise focuses on the value of the multiplier allowing for price changes. You are given the following information about an economy: The aggregate demand function is

$$P = \frac{60}{0.2Y - 25} \tag{1}$$

The short-run aggregate supply function is

$$P = 0.02Y \tag{2}$$

The AE function is

$$AE = 0.8Y + 25 + 0.1(W/P) \tag{3}$$

P represents the price level, Y represents real national income, and W is nominal wealth. The marginal propensity to spend is 0.8, and the nominal value of wealth is 600.

(a) Graph the AD and $SRAS$ curves.

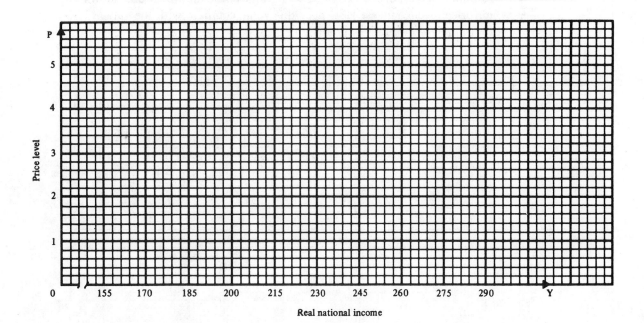

(b) According to the graph, what are the equilibrium values of P and Y?

(c) Using the equilibrium condition $Y = AE$, prove that your answer for the equilibrium value of Y (when $P = 4$) in (b) is confirmed.

(d) What is the value of the simple multiplier?

(e) Suppose that the AE function becomes $AE = 0.8Y + 10 + 0.1(W/P)$ because a component of autonomous expenditure decreases by 15. As a consequence, the AD function becomes $P = 60/(0.2Y - 10)$. When graphed, this expression lies to the left of the initial AD curve. If the price level remains at 4 for the time being, what is the new equilibrium level of Y according to the new AE function? (*Note:* This is not a permanent equilibrium value, as the next question in this exercise points out.)

(f) What is the quantity of output supplied at a price level of 4 according to the $SRAS$ function? What is the quantity demanded at a price level of 4 according to the new AD function?

(g) In the situation depicted in (f), the price level will fall. Prove that the new AD curve intersects the $SRAS$ curve at a price level of 3 and a real income level of 150.

(h) A fall in autonomous expenditure of 15 triggered a decline in the equilibrium level of Y of 50. What is the value of the multiplier that allows for price level changes? How does this value compare with the value of the simple multiplier? Explain.

6. Suppose that you are given the following values for the aggregate supply curve:

P	Aggregate supply	AD_a	AD_b	AD_c	AD_e	AD_f
1.0	0–50	___	___	___	___	___
1.2	70	___	___	___	___	___
1.4	80	___	___	___	___	___
1.6	85	___	___	___	___	___
1.8	85	___	___	___	___	___
2.0	85	___	___	___	___	___

(a) Assume that the aggregate expenditure function is $AE = 30 + 0.5Y - 5P$. Determine the appropriate entries for column AD_a and plot them on the accompanying graph, labeling the curve AD_a. (As a shortcut in deriving the AD curve without plotting the separate AE curves for each price level, note that equilibrium values of national income occur when $Y = 30 - 0.5Y - 5P$, and then simplify by combining the Y terms.) Also plot the AS curve. What is the equilibrium level of national income?

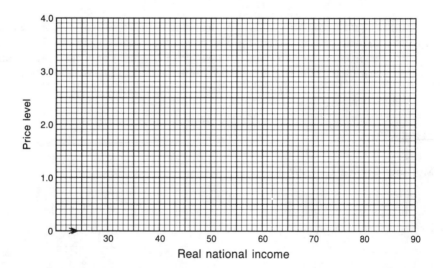

(b) Suppose that business confidence in the economy falls, investment declines by 10, and the AE function becomes $20 + 0.5Y - 5P$. Fill in the entries for the new AD curve under AD_b, and plot it on the graph. What is the new equilibrium level of national income?

(c) Suppose instead that business confidence rose, so that the AE function became $40 + 0.5Y - 5P$. Fill in the entries for the new AD curve (AD_c), and plot it on the graph. What is the new equilibrium level of national income?

(d) In (b) and (c), shifts in the AD curve by the same amount but in the opposite direction did not result in the same change in the absolute value of output. Explain why they did not.

(e) If the economy, instead, starts from a position where $AE = 47 + 0.5Y - 5P$, determine the appropriate AD curve entries (AD_e), plot them, and solve for the equilibrium level of income.

(f) Starting from a position where $AE = 47 + 0.5Y - 5P$, suppose that business confidence improves and investment rises by 10. What are the appropriate entries for the AD curve now (AD_f)? How does the resulting shift in the AD curve from (e) compare to the shift you determined from (a) to (c)? How does the change in equilibrium national income compare to what you found from (a) to (c)?

(g) From the various AD shifts you have examined, what can you conclude about the potential error from relying on the simple multiplier to predict changes in national income?

(h) Suppose that productivity in the economy rose with no offsetting increase in factor prices, so that the AS curve shifted downward by 0.2 at all points. Based on AD_c, how do the new price level (P) and national income (Y) compare to the solution you found in (c)? What seems to be the dominant effect of the productivity change in this economy?

Answers

Multiple-Choice Questions

1. (d) 2. (b) 3. (c) 4. (a) 5. (d) 6. (b) 7. (a) 8. (c) 9. (d) 10. (c) 11. (b) 12. (a)
13. (d) 14. (c) 15. (c) 16. (a) 17. (a) 18. (d) 19. (a) 20. (a) 21. (d) 22. (b)
23. (c) 24. (a) 25. (c) 26. (d) 27. (b)

Exercises

1. (a) Real wealth is 3,000 when $P = 1$ and 1,500 when $P = 2$.
   $C_1 = 100 + 0.8(2,500) + 0.1(3,000) = 2,400$ when $P = 1$.
   $C_2 = 100 + 0.8(2,500) + 0.1(1,500) = 2,250$ when $P = 2$.

   (b) The missing entries are as follows:

C_1	C_2	AE_1	AE_2
2,700	2,550	3,325	3,175
3,000	2,850	3,550	3,400
3,300	3,150	3,775	3,625
3,600	3,450	4,000	3,850
3,900	3,750	4,225	4,075

(c) When $P = 1$, equilibrium real income is 4,000. When $P = 2$, equilibrium real income is 3,625. As the price level falls, additional consumption occurs because real wealth increases. The increase in consumption generates an increase in real national income.

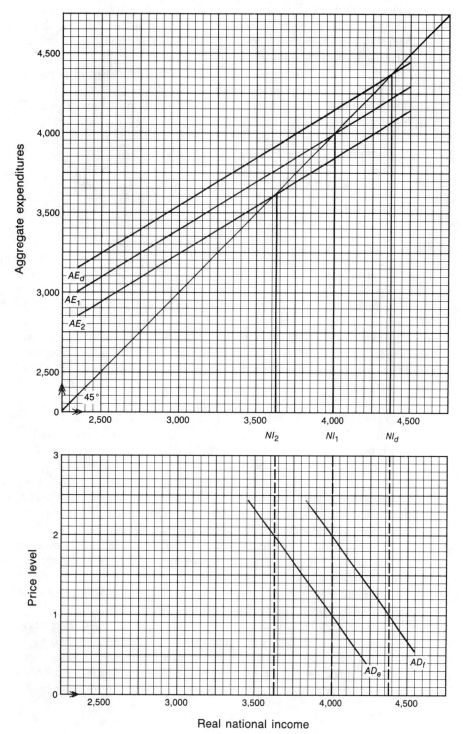

(d) The new values for AE_1 are 1,750, 3,250, 3,475, 3,700, 3,925, 4,150, 4,375. The new equilibrium value of Y is 4,375.

(e) The new values for AE_2 are 1,600, 3,100, 3,325, 3,500, 3,775, 4,000, 4,225. The new equilibrium of Y is 4,000.

(f) See the graph.

(g) The marginal propensity to spend is 0.6. This can be calculated by observing that AE_1 increased from 1,600 to 3,100 when Y increased from 0 to 2,500. The value of the simple multiplier is $1/(1 - 0.6) = 2.5$.

(h) The change in real income (375) is equal to the increases in government spending (150) times the simple multiplier (2.5).

(i) The horizontal distance between AE_e and AE_f at $P = 1$ and $P = 2$ is 375. See the graph.

2. (a) Missing entries are as follows:

$(I + G + X - M)_1$	$(I + G + X - M)_2$	AE_1	AE_2
625	325	3,325	2,875
550	250	3,550	3,100
475	175	3,775	3,325
400	100	4,000	3,550
325	25	4,225	3,775

(b) Equilibrium levels are 4,000 at $P = 1$ and 2,875 at $P = 2$.

(c) See graph on page 345.

(d) The slope of this AD curve is flatter than the AD curve in exercise 1.

(e) The larger the coefficient for the price term in the net export function (i.e., the more price-responsive net exports are), the flatter the AD curve.

(f) flatter, flatter

*3. (a) According to the schedule, the minimum ATC occurs at about 60 units.

(b) Marginal cost increases from 0.71 to 0.83. Average variable cost increases. Price must also rise to (at least) 0.83. Small; flat.

(c) The marginal productivity of labor falls for successive increments of workers; that is, the incremental contribution is falling. This can be shown by computing the ratio of the *change* in output associated with the *change* in labor. The third worker contributes 14 additional units of output; the fourth worker contributes only 12 additional units of output; the fifth worker contributes 2 additional units; and the sixth contributes only half a unit of output. Thus marginal and unit costs increase because of diminishing marginal productivity of labor.

(d) Its marginal cost increases from 0.83 to 5.00. Unit variable costs increase as well. Price must rise by (at least) 5.00. Steep.

(e) Total costs are now 100, 120, 140, 160, 180, 200, 220, and 240. The marginal costs are now 1.33, 1.05, 1.42, 1.66, 10.00, 20.00, and 40.00. Unit variable costs are now 1.33, 1.18, 1.25, 1.33, 1.61, 1.90, and 2.20.

(f) The new marginal costs are 0.63, 0.50, 0.67, 0.77, 3.33, 5.00, and 6.67. The firm's new marginal cost curve will be below the original marginal cost curve.

(c)

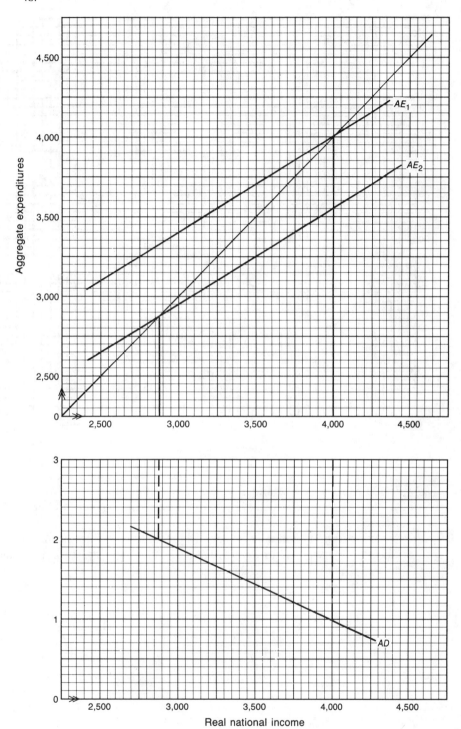

4.   (a) and (b)

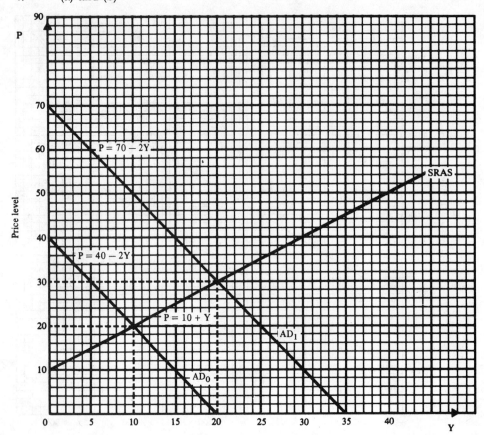

Real national income

(c)   Equilibrium is $P = 20$ and $Y = 10$. They can be solved algebraically by
      $40 - 2Y = 10 + Y$, which gives $Y = 10$. Substituting $Y = 10$ into either
      equation gives $P = 20$.

(d)   See the graph. The new equilibrium is $P = 30$ and $Y = 20$. A demand
      shock has caused real income to increase. The price level rises because
      the expansion in output causes unit costs to increase.

5. (a)

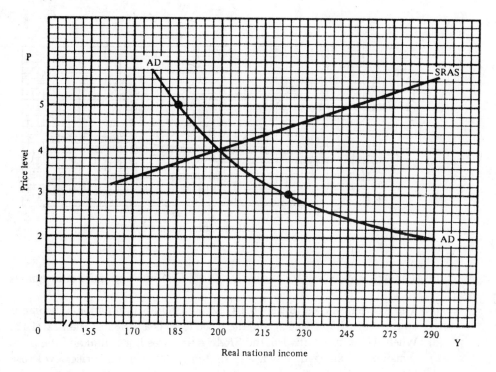

(b) The equilibrium levels are $P = 4$ and $Y = 200$.

(c) When $P = 4$, the value of real wealth is 150. Hence consumption expenditure plus the autonomous components of AE are $40 + 0.8Y$. $AE = Y$ at $Y = 200$.

(d) Since the marginal propensity to spend is 0.8, the value of the simple multiplier is 5.0.

(e) Equilibrium is given by $Y = 0.8Y + 10 + 15$ or $Y = 125$.

(f) At $P = 4$, the quantity of aggregate supply is 200. At $P = 4$, the quantity of aggregate demand is 125.

(g) For equilibrium, aggregate supply equals aggregate demand or $0.02Y = 60/(0.2Y - 10)$. Substituting $P = 3$ into the $SRAS$ equation, we obtain $Y = 150$. Moreover, when $P = 3$, $Y = 150$ according to the AD function.

(h) The value of the multiplier is $50/15 = 3.33$. This is smaller than the value of the simple multiplier, which in this case is 5.0. This is because the fall in the price level (from 4 to 3) increases the real value of wealth, thereby stimulating more consumption, and the domestic price level falls relative to foreign prices, thereby stimulating more exports and fewer imports.

6. (a) The AD_a entries are 50, 48, 46, 44, 42, 40. Equilibrium national income is 50.

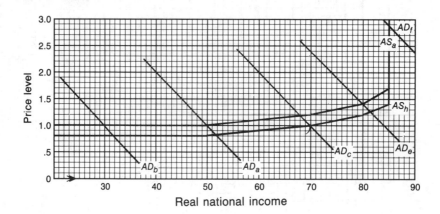

(b) The AD_b entries are 30, 28, 26, 24, 22, 20. Equilibrium national income is 30.
(c) The AD_c entries are 70, 68, 66, 64, 62, 60. Equilibrium national income is a little more than 68 (68.2), and the price level is a little less than 1.2 (1.18).
(d) When AD shifted leftward, the $SRAS$ curve was horizontal and the price remained unchanged. When AD shifted rightward, the price level rose because the $SRAS$ sloped upward, indicating that costs of production were higher at higher levels of output. The higher price reduces quantity demanded, and the increase in national income is smaller in absolute value than reported in (b).
(e) The AD entries are 84, 82, 80, 78, 76, 74. [(By extrapolation, AD is 70 at $P = 2.4$, a useful point in orienting the AD curve for (f)]. Equilibrium national income is 80, and the price level is 1.4.
(f) The AD entries are 90 at $P = 2.4$, 88 at $P = 2.6$, 86 at $P = 2.8$, 84 at $P = 3.0$. Equilibrium national income is 85, and the price level is 2.9. AD shifts by the same amount in each case (10 times the simple multiplier, or 20), but here real output increases only from 80 to 85.
(g) Applying the simple multiplier is least likely to result in errors in predicting changes in national income when the economy is operating in the relatively flat portion of the $SRAS$ curve. It becomes progressively less appropriate when the economy operates in the (relatively) steep portion of the $SRAS$ curve.
(h) The price level falls from 1.18 to 1.0, and equilibrium national income rises from 68 to 70. The primary effect of the productivity increase is to reduce the price level, which increases the purchasing power of a given amount of income.

Chapter 30

National Income and the Price Level in the Long Run

Learning Objectives

After studying this chapter, you should be able to:

—identify negative and positive output gaps by relating the economy's real potential GDP with the actual equilibrium income obtained from aggregate demand–aggregate supply analysis

—indicate how inflationary (negative) output gaps and recessionary (positive) output gaps create pressure for factor prices to change

—recognize the asymmetry of wage adjustments, with increases (during inflationary gaps) occurring much more rapidly than decreases (during recessionary gaps)

—understand that changes in unit labor costs depend on the relationship between the change in labor productivity and the change in the wage rate, since proportionately higher increases in wage rates compared to productivity increases increase unit labor costs

—explain how wage adjustments shift the *SRAS* curve

—indicate why, after all input prices have been adjusted to eliminate output gaps, the long-run aggregate supply (*LRAS*) curve will be vertical at the economy's potential level of output

—explain why prolonged recessionary gaps can result if wages are "sticky" in a downward direction

—suggest how supply-side economic policies are intended to affect the position of the *LRAS* curve

Multiple-Choice Questions

1. In an *AD-SRAS* diagram, a recessionary gap is shown by
   (a) the *AD* and *SRAS* curves intersecting at an output level that is to the right of potential GDP
   (b) The *SRAS, AD,* and *LRAS* curves intersecting at the same output level
   (c) the *AD* and *SRAS* curves intersecting at an output level that is to the left of potential GDP
   (d) the horizontal distance between the *AD* and *SRAS* curves for any price level

2. A recessionary gap is characterized by
   (a) an unemployment rate that is greater than the natural rate of unemployment
   (b) a tendency, albeit weak, for factor prices to fall
   (c) an unusually low demand for all factor inputs
   (d) all of the above

3. Starting from a position in which potential national income is constant and equal to actual income, an expansionary demand shock will result in
   (a) short-run increases in both the price level and real GDP
   (b) a short-run positive output gap, which creates pressure for factor price increases
   (c) a rightward shift in the *SRAS* curve as factor price increases
   (d) all of the above

4. The self-adjustment mechanism in the long run associated with any inflation caused by an expansionary demand shock refers to the tendency for
   (a) potential national income to adjust, thereby removing the inflationary gap
   (b) the supply of labor and capital to increase
   (c) factor prices increasing such that potential GDP and real factor prices are restored, thereby removing the inflationary gap
   (d) the price level to increase while factor prices remain unchanged

5. A decrease in aggregate demand will, in the long run, cause
   (a) the *SRAS* curve to shift to the left if factor prices are flexible
   (b) the *SRAS* curve to shift to the right if factor prices are rigid downward
   (c) persistent unemployment if factor prices are flexible
   (d) persistent unemployment if factor prices are sticky downward

6. When will there be strong pressure for wage increases to be higher than productivity increases?
   (a) when the economy is at potential real GDP
   (b) when there is a negative output gap
   (c) when there is an excess supply of labor
   (d) in the range of the Phillips curve that is to the left of potential GDP

7. The long-run aggregate supply (*LRAS*) curve relates the price level to real national income
   (a) in the vertical range of the *SRAS* curve where the economy is at its utmost limit of productive capacity
   (b) after all prices and input prices have been fully adjusted in response to any unemployment or overall labor shortages
   (c) when real factor prices vary in the long run
   (d) none of the above

8. With a vertical *LRAS* curve, output (national income) is
   (a) always at its potential level both in the short run and the long run
   (b) determined by the level of aggregate demand in the long run
   (c) determined solely by the conditions of supply in the long run, though the price level is determined by aggregate demand
   (d) always at its potential level in the short run but not necessarily in the long run

9. From an initial position in which potential and actual income are equal, which of the following causes a recessionary gap, *ceteris paribus*?
   (a) an increase in taxes
   (b) a sharp rise in investment expenditure
   (c) a decrease in imports
   (d) a decrease in desired saving at every level of real income

10. Which of the following is *not* likely to be associated with an inflationary gap?
    (a) rising output   (c) increasing unemployment
    (b) increasing demand for factors   (d) a rising price level

11. If wages were sufficiently flexible,
    (a) leftward shifts in *SRAS* could eliminate recessionary gaps
    (b) rightward shifts in *SRAS* could eliminate recessionary gaps
    (c) leftward shifts in *SRAS* could eliminate inflationary gaps
    (d) both (b) and (c)

12. Supply-side economics refers to policies that attempt to cure inflation and low growth in real national income by shifting the
    (a) *LRAS* curve to the right
    (b) *LRAS* curve to the left
    (c) *AD* curve to the left
    (d) *AD* curve more to the right than the corresponding shift of the *LRAS* curve

13. The *LRAS* curve is likely to shift rightward if
    (a) tax changes create incentives for more investment but less labor supply
    (b) the nation's supplies of all factors of production increase
    (c) tax decreases cause higher levels of aggregate demand
    (d) factor prices increase

14. Constant unit labor costs will prevail when
    (a) wages rise at the same rate as productivity
    (b) there is an inflationary gap
    (c) productivity rises at a higher rate than wages
    (d) factor supplies are constant and output increases beyond potential GDP

15. An economy moves from one position along a vertical *LRAS* curve to another *if*
    (a) workers are willing to accept a decline in real wages
    (b) prices and input costs have changed by the same percentage
    (c) labor and capital supplies have changed by the same percentage
    (d) both (b) and (c)

16. Most economists believe that
    (a) the *SRAS* curve shifts rapidly rightward when there is a recessionary gap
    (b) the *SRAS* curve shifts slowly rightward when there is an inflationary gap
    (c) the *SRAS* curve shifts more rapidly during an inflationary gap situation than it does during a recessionary gap period
    (d) potential GDP is highly variable in the short run

Questions 17 through 23 refer to the accompanying graph. The curves with the subscript 0 refer to the initial situation.

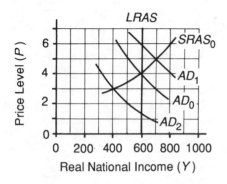

17. At the initial situation, given the *LRAS* curve,
    (a) we know that the economy has reached its potential real income level, and the price level is 4
    (b) potential income is greater than actual real income, although the equilibrium price level is 4
    (c) the economy is at a short-run equilibrium in terms of income and the price level but not input prices
    (d) the economy is in equilibrium, but factor use is above normal levels

18. Suppose that increases in exports shift the *AD* curve to AD_1. In the short run,
    (a) potential national income increases to 700 and the price level rises to 5
    (b) real national income increases by 100 and the price level increases to 5 due to increases in wage rates
    (c) a negative output gap of 100 is created, unit costs increase even though factor prices are constant, and the price level increases to 5
    (d) real national income increases by 200, factor prices remain constant, and hence the price level stays at 4

19. Given the increase in exports and the short-run reaction in question 18, we expect the following additional adjustments:
    (a) Wages and other factor prices begin to increase.
    (b) There will be pressure for prices to increase since factor unit costs rise at every level of real output.
    (c) As unit costs increase, the demand for factors falls.
    (d) All of the above.

20. Given the additional adjustment outlined in question 19, the long-run equilibrium after the export increase will be
    (a) a real income level of 600, higher nominal factor prices, and a price level of 6
    (b) a price level of 6 and real income of 800, due to an induced rightward shift of the AD curve
    (c) real income of 600, higher *real* factor prices, and a price level of 6
    (d) potential and real income equal to 700 and a price level of 5

21. Suppose that the AD curve shifted from AD_0 to AD_2 because of a decline in investment expenditure. The short-run impact of this contractionary demand shock is
    (a) a positive output gap of 200
    (b) falling unit costs but constant factor prices
    (c) an equilibrium price level of 3
    (d) all of the above

22. The situation described in question 21 will be temporary and short-lived if
    (a) factor prices remain constant
    (b) factor prices increase, thus increasing unit costs
    (c) the $SRAS$ curve shifts rapidly rightward because of lower factor prices
    (d) wage increases equal productivity increases

23. Given the investment decline, the situation described in question 21 will persist, possibly for a long period of time, if
    (a) some other autonomous expenditure component increases
    (b) factor prices remain constant or decrease very slowly
    (c) factor prices rise proportionately less than productivity
    (d) real factor prices fall

Exercises

1. Show graphically and explain the short-run and long-run adjustments that you expect from the following economic changes, given that the economy starts from a position where actual income equals potential income. Assume that the $LRAS$ curve is not affected by these events.
    (a) an increase in desired investment due to greater optimism over future profits
    (b) an increase in personal saving out of additional income due to the maturation of the baby-boom generation
    (c) an increase in the price of imported oil due to political instability in major producing regions
    (d) an increase in domestic grain production due to favorable weather conditions

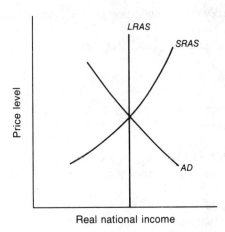

2. An economy has an *SRAS* function given by $P = 1 + 0.01Y$, presented here in schedule form, where P is the price level and Y is the level of real national income. The long-run aggregate supply curve is vertical at a real national income level of 1,000. Two schedules for the *AD* curve are presented, with case I being the initial situation.

				AD			
SRAS		LRAS		Case I		Case II	
Y	P	Y	P	Y	P	Y	P
0	1.0	1,000	1.0	0	111	0	116.5
500	6.0	1,000	6.0	500	61	500	66.5
1,000	11.0	1,000	11.0	1,000	11	1,000	16.5
1,050	11.5	1,000	16.5	1,050	6	1,050	11.5

(a) Taking case I for the *AD* curve, what are the equilibrium levels of P and Y? What is the value of the output gap?

(b) Assume that the *AD* curve shifts upward, represented by case II. If the *SRAS* curve does not change immediately, what are the new short-run equilibrium values for P and Y? What type of gap exists, and what is its magnitude?

(c) Given the shift of the *AD* curve, what do you predict will happen to factor prices in the long run? What will be the new equilibrium levels of P and Y in the long run? What will happen to the short-run output gap?

(d) Explain what is likely to happen to the *SRAS* curve in the long run. Rewrite the algebraic expression for it, assuming that the slope of the *SRAS* curve does not change.

3. A newly elected prime minister inherits the economic situation depicted here. Current potential real income is 1,800.

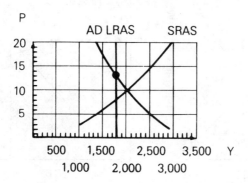

(a) Describe the economic situation that he inherited from the previous government.

(b) If the government does nothing, what is likely to happen to real national income and the price level in future time periods? Assume that aggregate demand (from the private sector) does not change.

(c) The new prime minister is a confirmed "supply-sider." His government initiates tax changes to increase both labor supply and the capital stock. Describe the general nature of the tax changes, and explain what this policy action is attempting to do.

(d) The opposition in the House of Commons vehemently objects to the government's policy. What arguments might they muster?

*4. An economy is currently operating at full employment (10 million workers) and at its potential level of GDP (1 billion). Initial equilibrium values of the price level and the nominal wage rate are 2 and 10, respectively. The aggregate labor demand and supply curves are drawn in panel (ii). Labor demand (D) is given by $P = (P/6)(40 - D)$. W refers to the price level and W to the nominal wage rate. Notice that the demand curve shifts when the price level changes. The labor supply curve is drawn with the assumption that workers expect a constant price level ($P = 2$) during the current contract. If the actual price level differs from the expected level, nominal wages at every level of employment will be adjusted in the next contract period. The initial situation in panel (ii) is point a.

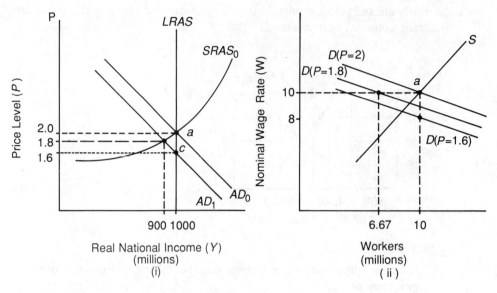

(a)   What is the current equilibrium real wage rate?

(b)   Now suppose that exports decline such that the aggregate demand curve becomes AD_1. As long as the nominal wage remains at $10 during the current contract period, what is the new short-run equilibrium in terms of panel (i)? What is the value of the output gap?

(c)   The decline in exports produces a lower price level ($P = 1.8$). Therefore, the labor demand curve shifts to the left. Assuming that the nominal wage remains at $10 during the current contract period (hence the labor supply curve does not shift), how many workers are employed? How many are unemployed? What is value of the real wage rate?

(d)   The scenario described in (b) and (c) will remain as long as the aggregate demand curve remains at AD_1 and the current contract with a nominal wage of $10 remains in force. According to panel (i), what equilibrium price level is required to achieve long-run equilibrium at point c?

(e)   As indicated in (d), the price level must fall to restore potential GDP. To achieve full employment, workers must take wage cuts at every level of employment in the next contract period. As they do so, the $SRAS$ curve in panel (i) shifts (rightward, leftward). In terms of panel (ii), as the price falls, the demand curve shifts leftward, and as workers take wage cuts, the supply curve shifts (leftward, rightward). What is the new equilibrium nominal wage rate that restores full employment and potential GDP? What is the value of the real wage rate?

Answers

Multiple-Choice Questions

1. (c) 2. (d) 3. (a) 4. (c) 5. (d) 6. (b) 7. (b) 8. (c) 9. (a) 10. (c) 11. (d) 12. (a)
13. (b) 14. (a) 15. (b) 16. (c) 17. (a) 18. (c) 19. (d) 20. (a) 21. (d) 22. (c) 23. (b)

Exercises

1. (a) The *AD* curve shifts rightward in the short run, resulting in greater output and higher prices. Higher prices likely cause wage demands to increase, causing an induced shift in the *SRAS* curve leftward and restoring the initial level of potential income at a higher price level.

    (b) The *AD* curve shifts leftward and rotates to become steeper as a result of an increase in the marginal propensity to save. A recessionary gap develops that puts downward pressure on wages and prices. If wages decline, the *SRAS* curve shifts rightward, restoring the initial level of potential income at a lower price level. Due to asymmetric adjustment in the labor market, the recessionary gap may remain for a considerable time.

    (c) The *SRAS* curve shifts leftward, resulting in higher prices and lower national income. Higher prices may induce a further leftward shift in the *SRAS*, as workers react to the fall in real wages. However, the recessionary gap exerts downward pressure on wages and prices. If wages decline, the *SRAS* curve shifts rightward, and the economy may eventually reach its potential income again.

    (d) The *SRAS* curve shifts rightward, resulting in lower prices and higher national income. Lower prices may induce a further rightward shift in the *SRAS*. However, the inflationary gap exerts upward pressure on wages and prices as hours of overtime rise and capacity utilization rates increase. Wages are likely to rise, shifting the *SRAS* curve leftward, and the economy returns to its long-run potential income.

2. (a) The equilibrium levels are $P = 11$ and $Y = 1,000$. The output gap is 0.
    (b) The new equilibrium levels are $P = 11.5$ and $Y = 1,050$. The output gap is a negative value (-50). This is known as an inflationary gap of 50.
    (c) Since the economy now tries to operate beyond its potential level, unusually high demand for factors will trigger increases in factor prices. As a consequence, the *SRAS* curve will shift to the left. In the long run, potential national income will be restored at $Y = 1,000$. According to the new *AD* curve (case II), $Y = 1,000$ is associated with a price level of 16.5. The short-run inflationary gap will be eliminated in the long run, but the long-run price level will be higher than that which resulted in the short run.
    (d) The new algebraic expression for the *SRAS* function is $P = 6.5 + 0.01Y$. Notice that when $Y = 1,000$, $P = 16.5$; these are the equilibrium values in the long run.

3. (a) The prime minister has inherited an inflationary gap of 200. Current equilibrium levels of real national income and price are 2,000 and 10, respectively.

   (b) If the government does nothing, the economy will adjust by itself. Factor prices will most likely increase, thereby shifting the *SRAS* curve to the left until it intersects the *LRAS* curve at $Y = 1,800$ and $P = 13$. As a result, the economy will have an even higher price level, but the inflationary gap will have been eliminated.

   (c) The prime minister's policies should involve lower tax rates, which stimulate increased labor supply, and more investment expenditure, which increases the capital stock. Thus potential real income is affected in the long run. If these policies are totally successful, the *LRAS* curve will shift to the right, perhaps to $Y = 2,000$ or beyond. Since equilibrium real national income equals the new potential level (2,000), the inflationary gap has been eliminated, and there will be no pressures for the *SRAS* curve to shift to the left.

   (d) The opposition should base their arguments on the fact that tax reductions will stimulate increases in *AD*. In the short run, there will be even higher pressures for prices and factor prices to increase. Moreover, the added pressures caused by *AD* increases may prevail for some time, since it is possible that the tax changes may take a long time to shift the *LRAS* curve to the right.

*4. (a) 5, which is the equal to 10/2.0.

   (b) $P = 1.8$ and $Y = 900$ million. There is a recessionary gap of 100 million.

   (c) 6.67 million workers are employed, but 10 million want employment at the wage rate of $10. Thus there are 3.33 million workers unemployed. The real wage is now 5.6 (10/1.8).

   (d) AD_1 intersects the *LRAS* curve at $P = 1.6$.

   (e) rightward; rightward. The supply curve of labor must shift rightward so that it intersects the labor demand curve labeled $D (P = 1.6)$ at a nominal wage of 8 and employment of 10 million. Notice that in the long run both the price level and the nominal wage rate fall by 20 percent. Hence the real wage rate of 5 (8/1.6) is restored.

Chapter 31

Business Cycles: The Ebb and Flow of Economic Activity

Learning Objectives

After studying this chapter, you should be able to:

—distinguish between the causes and implications of long-term growth in real income and those of short-term fluctuations in real GDP

—explain how fluctuations in GDP are related to shifts in aggregate demand and short-run aggregate supply curves

—describe factors that can cause shocks to consumption, government spending, net exports, and investment

—recognize the influence of the real interest rate on different components of investment

—indicate how fluctuations in the price of inputs (imported and domestic), productivity, and the exchange rate cause temporary shifts in the *SRAS* curve

—understand possible explanations of why fluctuations in income are transformed into business cycles

—recognize the accelerator principle as one reason why investment moves cyclically

—describe the international transmission of business cycles

—appreciate how fluctuations in business activity affect security markets and how fluctuations in security markets may have effects on real economic activity

Multiple-Choice Questions

1. Business cycles refer to
   (a) the upward trend in real GDP over time
   (b) temporary oscillations in GDP around potential GDP
   (c) changes in potential GDP over time
   (d) increases in securities prices during bull market periods

2. Which of the following would tend to shift the consumption function upward?
    (a) The real interest rate increases.
    (b) Prices are expected to fall in the future.
    (c) Income is redistributed from households with high marginal propensities to consume to households with low ones.
    (d) Government lowers income tax rates.

3. Which of the following would tend to decrease the exports of a particular country?
    (a) The real income of foreigners increases.
    (b) Foreigners' tastes change such that they prefer their own goods to this country's goods.
    (c) The external value of the domestic currency increases.
    (d) Both (b) and (c).

4. If you were measuring the total amount of investment expenditure, which of the following would you *not* include?
    (a) purchases of stock and bonds
    (b) changes in inventory
    (c) new residential construction
    (d) business fixed investment such as plant and equipment

5. Data series for many macroeconomic variables, such as real GDP, employment, and prices, are characterized by
    (a) large random changes followed by long periods of little change
    (b) a constant rate of growth over time
    (c) continual short-term fluctuations around a long-term trend
    (d) highly random behavior unrelated to other economic variables

6. Other things being equal, changes in inventories tend to vary
    (a) positively with changes in production and negatively with the real interest rate
    (b) positively with both changes in production and the real rate of interest
    (c) negatively with both changes in production and the real rate of interest
    (d) negatively with changes in production and positively with the real rate of interest

7. Other things being equal, investment in residential construction tends to vary
    (a) negatively with changes in average household income and positively with the real rate of interest
    (b) positively with changes in average household income and the real rate of interest
    (c) positively with changes in average household income and negatively with the real rate of interest
    (d) negatively with changes in average household income and the real rate of interest

8. In predicting expenditures on consumer durables, such as cars and appliances, economists expect that
   (a) rising interest rates will result in higher interest income and will thereby cause overall car sales to rise
   (b) rising interest rates will require larger monthly car payments and will thereby cause car sales to fall
   (c) car sales will be especially large in the trough of a business cycle
   (d) current purchases of durables will be especially large when most consumers expect durable prices to fall in the future

9. Suppose that individuals pay $8 annual interest per $100 borrowed and that the annual rate of inflation rises from 6 to 10 percent. Under these circumstances, borrowing for residential construction is likely to
   (a) rise, because the real interest rate is −2 percent, which provides a strong incentive for borrowers
   (b) fall, because the real interest rate is −18 percent, which represents a penalty against borrowing
   (c) remain unchanged, because borrowing for residential construction is based on the nominal rate of interest, not the real interest rate
   (d) fall, because the real interest rate has risen

10. The amount of investment by firms
    (a) is influenced by profit expectations and the real interest rate
    (b) has remained stable and predictable in Canada and thus is not a contributing factor to Canadian business cycles
    (c) is more stable and predictable than consumption
    (d) has little effect on the economy

11. Which of the following would *not* be a source of a short-run aggregate supply shock?
    (a) changes in input prices
    (b) changes in the foreign exchange rate
    (c) changes in desired investment
    (d) changes in the productivity of inputs

12. Imagine an economy that has been in a recovery following a depression. In its initial stages, it is likely to be characterized by all but which of the following?
    (a) increases in aggregate expenditure
    (b) rising incomes
    (c) favorable business and consumer expectations
    (d) large increases in the price level

13. In terms of macroeconomic theory, purchases of stocks and bonds constitute examples of
    (a) saving
    (b) consumption expenditure
    (c) investment
    (d) imports if the assets are issued by foreigners

14. Which of the following would tend to decrease the current price of a particular stock?
    (a) increases in the firm's expected earnings
    (b) expected increases in interest rates
    (c) expectations that the firm will increase dividend payments
    (d) a government announcement that it intends to purchase more of this firm's output

15. Other things being equal, a decline in U.S. GDP is likely to
    (a) increase U.S. imports from Canada
    (b) increase investment opportunities for firms which sell to U.S. customers
    (c) lead to a contraction in Canadian GDP since Canadian exports to the United States are likely to decline
    (d) have no impact on the Canadian economy as long as the U.S. dollar price of the Canadian dollar does not change

16. A once-and-for-all increase in exports that creates an inflationary gap may give rise to a cyclical output response, since
    (a) output increases with the rightward shift of the *AD* curve and then falls as increases in factor prices shift the *SRAS* curve leftward
    (b) increases in output trigger additional investment expenditure through the accelerator process
    (c) lags in the response of output to this demand increase may be spread out over a substantial period of time
    (d) all of the above

Appendix Questions

The following questions are based on material in the appendix to this chapter. Read the appendix before answering them.

17. The accelerator theory of the business cycle indicates that for net investment to be constant,
    (a) sales must be constant
    (b) sales must increase by a constant amount each year
    (c) interest rates must be constant
    (d) replacement investment must be zero

18. If three units of capital are required for every unit of output, then
    (a) the capital-output ratio is 1/3
    (b) the capital-output ratio is 3
    (c) six units of capital are required to produce three units of output
    (d) capital must cost more, relative to labor, per unit of output

19. The accelerator theory assumes
    (a) an increasing capital-output ratio, therefore capital deepening
    (b) an increasing capital-output ratio, therefore capital widening
    (c) a fixed capital-output ratio, therefore capital deepening
    (d) a fixed capital-output ratio, therefore capital widening

20. The multiplier and accelerator effects operating together
    (a) tend to cancel out
    (b) help to explain why movements of the economy tend to acquire momentum
    (c) make the amplitude of cycles less than they otherwise would be
    (d) tend to maintain growth perpetually

Exercises

1. The following two schedules relate desired capital stock to the interest rate.

Schedule A		Schedule B	
Capital stock	Interest rate (percent)	Capital stock	Interest rate (percent)
100	20	150	20
200	18	250	18
300	14	350	14
400	8	450	8
500	1	550	1

   (a) Inspect both schedules. Does a negative or a positive relationship exist between the desired capital stock and the rate of interest?

   (b) Assuming that schedule A applies, if the current rate of interest falls from 20 percent to 18 percent, what is the change in the desired capital stock? What net investment must occur to achieve this desired stock? Explain what factors would cause firms not to carry out this investment in a single year.

   (c) Suppose that the schedule suddenly changed to schedule B. With a current interest rate of 14 percent, what is the new magnitude of the desired capital stock? Does the change in the schedule imply new desired investment activity? Indicate two factors that may have caused the schedule to change.

2. A seller of shirts has had weekly sales of 100 and tries to keep inventory in stock equal to twice its weekly sales, adjusting weekly orders from the jobber according to the current week's sales. Complete the following table showing how actual inventory and orders from the store's supplier would change as weekly sales change.

Week	Weekly sales	Actual inventory, end of week	Inventory-sales ratio	Desired inventory	Desired inventory plus expected sales	Weekly orders for next week
1	100	200	2.0	200	300	100
2	100	200	2.0	200	300	100
3	110	190	1.7	220	330	140
4	110	220	____	____	____	____
5	120	210	____	____	____	____
6	120	240	____	____	____	____
7	110	250	____	____	____	____
8	110	220	____	____	____	____
9	100	230	____	____	____	____

(a) The range of weekly sales was from_____to_____.

(b) The range of weekly orders was from_____to_____.

(c) How do these findings illustrate the accelerator theory?

3. For some countries such as Canada and the United Kingdom, exports account for a large share of national income. For example, approximately 30 percent of Canada's national income is from exports, making Canada's economic activity critically dependent on foreigners' willingness to buy Canadian goods and services and allowing cycles in foreign economic activity to be transmitted to Canada. A major determinant of foreign imports is their national income, which itself can display cyclical activity.

You are given the following hypothetical relationship between foreign income and Canadian exports. Assume that the export multiplier on Canadian real national income is 2.

Year	Foreign income	Canadian exports	Change in Canadian income
1	100	10	
2	150	15	+10
3	200	20	____
4	180	18	____
5	100	10	____
6	100	10	____

(a) Deduce the relationship between foreign income and Canadian exports. List some factors that explain why foreign income levels might determine Canadian exports.

(b) Assume that exports change between two years and that the multiplier process works itself through by the end of the second year. On this basis, fill in the missing values for the change in Canadian national income.

(c) Has a business cycle been transmitted to Canada? Does it have the same basic characteristics as the foreign business cycle?

Appendix Exercises

The following exercises are based on material in the appendix to this chapter. Read the appendix before attempting these exercises.

4. This exercise illustrates the accelerator principle. The table shows the hypothetical situation for a firm that requires one machine for every 1,000 units of product it turns out annually. As it increases its output and sales in response to changing demand, show how its investment will be affected. Replacement for depreciation is one machine per year throughout.

Year	Annual output (units)	Units of capital needed	Additional machines required	Replacement machines	Total machines to be purchased (desired investment)
1	10,000	10	0	1	1
2	10,000	____	____	1	____
3	11,000	____	____	1	____
4	12,000	____	____	1	____
5	15,000	____	____	1	____
6	17,000	____	____	1	____
7	18,000	____	____	1	____
8	18,000	____	____	1	____

(a) Between year 2 and year 5, output increased by what percent?
(b) In the same period, the firm's desired investment increased by what percent?
(c) Plot the cyclical fluctuations in desired investment.

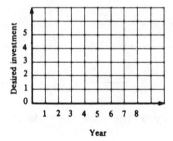

*5. This exercise explores the multiplier-accelerator interaction theory. The multiplier when combined with the accelerator may generate fluctuations in national income. For this model we have assumed (a) that the marginal propensity to consume is 0.5, (b) that consumption in time period t depends on the level of income one period past $(t - 1)$, (c) that the capital-output ratio, or what is often referred to as the accelerator coefficient, is constant and equal to 1, and (d) that investment in time period t depends on an autonomous amount, 100, plus the difference in income between $t - 1$ and $t - 2$.

These assumptions are expressed by the following equations:

$$C_t = 0.5Y_{t-1}$$

$$I_t = 100 + 1(Y_{t-1} - Y_{t-2})$$

Therefore, since $Y = C + I$,

$$Y_t = 0.5Y_{t-1} + 100 + 1(Y_{t-1} - Y_{t-2})$$

The economy is assumed to be at an equilibrium level of income of 200 in the current time period 0 and has been at that level for two previous periods, -2 and -1. In period 1 autonomous investment increases from 100 to 200 and stays at that level permanently.

The effect of this increase shows up in national income period 1 as simply an increase of 100. Why? Since consumption depends on the last period's income (period 0), and income is 200, the consumption level remains at a level of 100. Furthermore, there is no accelerator effect in period 1, since the difference between income in period 0 and period -1 (one period and two periods removed from period 1, respectively) is zero.

However, interesting things start to occur to national income thereafter. We have started the process by completing the entries until period 6.

(a) Fill in the missing values for periods 6 through 9 in the table.

Period	Consumption $C_t = 0.5Y_{t-1}$	Investment (I_t) Autonomous	Investment (I_t) Accelerator $1(Y_{t-1} - Y_{t-2})$	National income $Y_t = C_t + I_t$
-2	100.0	100	0.0	200.0
-1	100.0	100	0.0	200.0
0	100.0	100	0.0	200.0
1	100.0	200	0.0	300.0
2	150.0	200	100.0	450.0
3	225.0	200	150.0	575.0
4	287.5	200	125.0	612.5
5	306.3	200	37.5	543.8
6	_____	200	_____	_____
7	_____	200	_____	_____
8	_____	200	_____	_____
9	_____	200	_____	_____

(b) Identify by period the trough of the cycle, the peak, the expansion phase, and the recession phase.

(c) Did the accelerator process counteract or reinforce the multiplier process during the expansion phase? Did it counteract or reinforce the multiplier process during the recession phase?

(d) Assume that the autonomous element of investment is sensitive to the rate of interest. What changes in the level of the rate of interest might the government of this economy pursue in periods 2 to 4 and periods 5 to 8 to "smooth out" this business cycle?

Answers

Multiple-Choice Questions

1. (b)   2. (d)   3. (d)   4. (a)   5. (c)   6. (a)   7. (c)   8. (b)   9. (a)   10. (a)   11. (c)   12. (d)   13. (a)   14. (b)   15. (c)   16. (d)   17. (b)   18. (b)   19. (d)   20. (b)

Exercises

1. (a) negative
   (b) Desired capital stock increases from 100 to 200. Desired investment is 100. This investment may be spread over time if current availability of capital goods is restricted, if a larger immediate purchase is possible only at a higher price, or if installation of a larger number of machines becomes progressively more costly (as when less skilled workers must be hired or an existing plant must be shut down for a longer time).
   (c) Desired capital is 350. Yes, desired investment increases by 50. Profit expectations may have improved because of new innovations, or there are more optimistic forecasts about future sales.

2.

Week	Inventory-sales ratio	Desired inventory	Desired inventory plus expected sales	Weekly orders for next week
1	2	200	300	100
2	2	200	300	100
3	1.7	220	330	140
4	2	220	330	110
5	1.8	240	360	150
6	2	240	360	120
7	2.3	220	330	80
8	2	220	330	110
9	2.3	200	300	70

   (a) 100, 200
   (b) 70, 150
   (c) Orders for inventory (a form of investment) fluctuate more widely than sales. This variation in investment spending is a major factor behind economic fluctuations.

3. (a) Canadian exports are positively related to foreign national income. It appears that exports are 10 percent of foreign income. Foreign households will tend to buy more Canadian products when their incomes rise; foreign firms require more Canadian-produced inputs in order to expand their production.
   (b) Change in Canadian income: year 3: $2 \times 5 = 10$; year 4: $2 \times (-2) = -4$; year 5: $2 \times (-8) = -16$; year 6: 0
   (c) Clearly, a business cycle has been transmitted from abroad. The cycles of both economies are similar; they peak and trough in similar fashions.

4.

Year	Units of capital needed	Additional machines required	Replacement machines	Total machines to be purchased
1	10	0	1	1
2	10	0	1	1
3	11	1	1	2
4	12	1	1	2
5	15	3	1	4
6	17	2	1	3
7	18	1	1	2
8	18	0	1	1

(a) 50 percent

(c)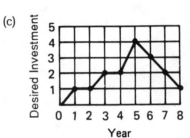

(b) 300 percent

*5. (a)

Period	C_t	Autonomous	Accelerator	Y_t
6	271.90	200	− 68.70	403.20
7	201.60	200	− 140.60	261.00
8	130.50	200	− 142.20	188.30
9	94.15	200	− 72.70	221.45

(b) Trough: period 8; peak: period 4; expansion phase: periods 1, 2, and 3; recession phase: periods 5, 6, and 7.

(c) Without the accelerator, the multiplier process would have increased Y by 200 [i.e., 100/(1 − 0.50)]. The accelerator process reinforced the multiplier during the expansion phase but caused a recessionary phase later on.

(d) During periods 2 to 4, the government should increase the interest rate to dampen investment. During periods 5 to 8, it should reduce the interest rate to increase investment.

Chapter 32

An Introduction to Fiscal Policy

Learning Objectives

After studying this chapter, you should be able to:

—describe the fiscal policy measures available to the government to influence aggregate demand

—explain the difference between discretionary fiscal policy and automatic stabilizers

—recognize why a government policy to keep the budget balanced may actually have destabilizing effects on the economy

—indicate why changes in the stance of fiscal policy are best shown by changes in the cyclically adjusted deficit

—distinguish the relevant lags in implementing fiscal policy that make fine-tuning the economy difficult

—understand why fiscal policies designed to offset abnormal aggregate demand and aggregate supply conditions must be reversible when more normal conditions again prevail

Multiple-Choice Questions

1. Fiscal policy refers to a government's
   (a) attempt to regulate prices
   (b) use of tax and expenditure policies to control the money supply
   (c) use of tax and expenditure policies to reach desired levels of national income
   (d) attempt to regulate pollution emissions

2. Assuming that private expenditure functions do not shift, an increase in the government's budget deficit due to a discretionary change in expenditures or tax rates
    (a) represents contractionary fiscal policy
    (b) would be an appropriate policy for closing an inflationary gap
    (c) will shift the aggregate demand curve to the right
    (d) will have no effect on aggregate demand

3. If there is currently an inflationary gap, an appropriate fiscal policy would be to
    (a) increase taxes
    (b) increase government spending on goods and services
    (c) decrease taxes
    (d) increase transfer payments

4. If the government increases personal income tax revenues by $5 billion and increases purchases of goods and services by the same amount, the most likely effect is
    (a) a net decrease in national income
    (b) a net increase in national income
    (c) no effect on national income
    (d) an increase in the value of the balanced budget multiplier

5. Consider an increase in government purchases of X dollars, a tax cut of X dollars, and a balanced budget increase in expenditure of X dollars as three alternative policies. Which will probably yield the largest increase in national income?
    (a) the expenditure increase
    (b) the tax cut
    (c) the balanced budget increase
    (d) They will all increase GDP by X dollars times the multiplier

6. The balanced budget multiplier
    (a) is larger than the multiplier for government expenditures
    (b) applies when additional tax receipts are equal to additional government expenditures
    (c) is the same numerical value as the multiplier for government expenditures
    (d) is the same numerical value as the multiplier for tax changes

7. Built-in stabilizers tend to
    (a) stimulate inflation
    (b) prolong recessions
    (c) reduce cyclical fluctuations
    (d) stabilize income but destabilize prices and employment

8. Which of the following is *not* a built-in stabilizer in the economy?
    (a) steeply progressive tax rates
    (b) government expenditures that vary positively with the level of national income
    (c) agricultural subsidies
    (d) unemployment insurance payments

9. If government transfer payments fall when national income expands, it can be said that these payments are
    (a) countercyclical, since they will rise relative to GDP when GDP is rising
    (b) procyclical, since they fall relative to GDP when GDP is rising
    (c) countercyclical, since they fall relative to GDP when GDP is rising
    (d) inconsistent with an upward-sloping consumption function

10. The rationale for calculating a "cyclically adjusted deficit" is that
    (a) aggregate demand will be deficient at high-employment levels of national income
    (b) the government's budget will be in deficit when there is an inflationary gap
    (c) government expenditures must exceed tax revenues at high-employment national income
    (d) the actual budget deficit may decline as the economy expands even though tax rates are unchanged

11. Which of the following would give the best measure of the stance of current discretionary fiscal policy?
    (a) present income tax rates
    (b) the size of the current government budget deficit or surplus
    (c) changes in the cyclically adjusted budget deficit
    (d) the change in tax revenue minus the change in government expenditure

12. The budget deficit function
    (a) relates tax revenue to national income
    (b) will shift if national income changes
    (c) will shift if increased national income generates more tax revenue
    (d) relates the budget deficit to national income

13. Induced changes in the government's actual budget balance due to changes in national income
    (a) are shown by shifts in the budget deficit function
    (b) result from discretionary changes in tax rates or expenditures
    (c) are shown by movements along the budget deficit function
    (d) cause shifts of the aggregate demand curve

14. An annually balanced federal government budget
    (a) is an idea supported by most economists because it would be easy to achieve
    (b) would create greater economic stability than one with deficits during slumps and surpluses during booms
    (c) is feasible from a political standpoint and desirable from an economic one
    (d) would avoid a rising future debt burden, but at the cost of destabilizing the economy

15. An attempt to reduce the national debt
    (a) would be an appropriate policy for attempting to cure a recession
    (b) requires a budget surplus and therefore would have a deflationary effect, other things being equal
    (c) would cause aggregate demand to rise by an amount equal to the debt reduction
    (d) transfers money from bondholders to taxpayers

16. Permanent-income theories imply that a one-year reduction in the personal income tax rate by 50 percent
    (a) will have little effect on permanent income and consumption
    (b) will have a major effect on current income and consumption
    (c) will tend to decrease personal saving
    (d) will tend to have a proportionally larger effect on expenditures for consumer nondurables than for durables

17. The paradox of thrift implies that in the short run,
    (a) increased saving allows greater capital formation and faster economic growth
    (b) increased saving reduces both aggregate demand and current GDP
    (c) reducing the cyclically adjusted budget deficit is an appropriate policy to stimulate the economy
    (d) individuals lack adequate incentives to save

18. A persistent recessionary gap may be removed by
    (a) a (slow) downward shift of the SRAS curve
    (b) a policy-induced increase in aggregate demand
    (c) a natural revival of private-sector aggregate demand
    (d) any of the above

19. A persistent inflationary gap may be removed by
    (a) a downward shift of the SRAS curve
    (b) a natural increase in private-sector demand
    (c) increases in tax rate
    (d) increases in transfer payments

Questions 20 to 25 relate to the accompanying graph. The current situation, which has persisted for some time, is shown by point *a*. The government spending multiplier is 5.0, the taxation multiplier is 4.0, and the balanced budget multiplier is 1.0. All multiplier values allow for price increases associated with policy changes.

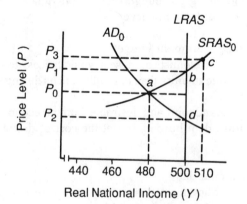

20. In the current situation, there is
    (a) an inflationary gap of 30
    (b) a positive output gap of 20
    (c) a negative output gap of 20
    (d) a positive output gap of 30

21. In the absence of any discretionary fiscal policy, potential GDP will be achieved
    if
    (a) investment expenditure decreases such that the new *AD* curve intersects
         the *LRAS* curve at point *b*
    (b) factor input prices decrease such that the *SRAS* curve shifts rightward to
         point *d* on the *AD* and *LRAS* curves
    (c) households increase their saving-to-income ratio in the short run such that
         the *AD* curve intersects the *LRAS* curve at point *b*
    (d) the external value of the domestic currency increases, shifting the *SRAS*
         curve rightward to point *d*

22. In the absence of any changes in private-sector spending, tax rates, or input
    prices, which of the following changes in government spending would exactly
    eliminate the current output gap?
    (a) an increase in government spending of 4
    (b) a decrease in government spending of 5
    (c) an increase in government spending of 5
    (d) an increase in government spending of 20

23. In the absence of any changes in autonomous private-sector spending,
    government spending, or input prices, which of the following tax changes would
    exactly eliminate the current output gap?
    (a) a tax reduction of 4, which creates a new equilibrium at point *d*
    (b) a tax reduction of 20, which creates a new equilibrium at point *b*
    (c) a tax reduction of 5, which creates a new equilibrium at point *d*
    (d) a tax reduction of 5, which creates a new equilibrium at point *b*

24. In the absence of any changes in autonomous private-sector spending or input
    prices, which of the following balanced budget policies would exactly eliminate
    the current output gap?
    (a) an equal increase of 5 in both government spending and taxes
    (b) an equal decrease of 5 in both government spending and taxes
    (c) an equal increase of 20 in both government spending and taxes
    (d) an equal decrease of 20 in both government spending and taxes

25. Starting from point *a*, which of the following (misguided) fiscal policies would
    create the inflationary gap situation depicted at point *c*?
    (a) an increase of 6 in government spending
    (b) a reduction of 7.5 in taxes
    (c) an equal increase of 30 in both government spending and taxes
    (d) all of the above

Exercises

1. A newly elected government inherits an inflationary gap. Record high export sales of one of the country's manufactured goods have created an inflationary gap of 12 billion. The recently appointed minister of finance seeks advice from her advisers. After careful study, they advise her to increase taxes permanently by 3 billion, keeping government spending at its current level. Their recommendation is based on the following assumptions:
    (a) The high level of export sales will continue, and potential GDP will remain at 1 trillion.
    (b) The taxation multiplier is 4.
    (c) Within the foreseeable future, input price increases are likely to be negligible.
    (d) Since the government has a large majority, policy changes can be made quickly with few execution lags. Moreover, the advisers are confident that the private sector will respond quickly to this policy change.
    The advisers have also been told by the chief economist in the ministry that both the export and government spending multipliers are 6.0.
    (a) Assuming that all information is correct, do you agree that the recommended policy will eliminate the inflationary gap? Explain.

    (b) The minister accepts the advice, the tax change becomes law, and the size of the output gap begins to decrease. However, shortly after the policy change, exports of one of the country's food products falls unexpectedly by 2.5 billion due to the introduction of a cheaper and higher-quality product by a foreign competitor. Assuming that input prices remain constant and that the chief economist's numbers are accurate, what will happen to the equilibrium level of GDP if no additional fiscal measures are introduced? What is the value of the output gap now?

    (c) The finance minister is severely criticized in Parliament. The prime minister insists that she reverse the government's fiscal stance and restore taxes to their original levels (that is, reduce them by 3 billion). Will this reversal in fiscal policy resolve the output gap problem described in (b)? Explain.

    (d) The finance minister threatens to resign. She argues that her credibility as minister is at stake. A reversal of policy would be political suicide for her. Moreover, her taxation increase was correct; unforeseen external factors caused the problem. She convinces the prime minister that the government's appropriate stance should be to retain the 3 billion increase in taxation but also increase government spending by 2.5 billion. Comment on this new policy stance.

2. A hypothetical economy, which has a horizontal (flat) *SRAS* curve, has expenditure behavior at various levels of real national income depicted in the following schedule. Its potential level of real national income is 220. The current personal income tax rate is 20 percent.

Y	C	I	G	(X − M)	Budget deficit $(G - T)$ (+ is deficit; − is surplus)
50	32	50	40	3	+30
100	64	50	40	−4	+20
150	96	50	40	−11	+10
200	128	50	40	−18	0
250	160	50	40	−25	−10

(a) If this economy is currently at equilibrium, what is the value of its national income? What is the government's budget deficit position? What is the value of the output gap? What is the value of its marginal propensity to spend? What is the value of its cyclically adjusted deficit?

(b) Assuming that the government's goal is to have full employment, what changes in its expenditure program would you recommend? You should assume that no private-sector autonomous expenditures are expected to change.

(c) If the government accepts your advice concerning expenditure changes, what will happen to its budget deficit position immediately? What will happen to is budget deficit position when the new equilibrium national income is attained? What is the value of its cyclically adjusted deficit (*CAD*) at the new equilibrium?

(d) Graph the economy's budget deficit function for (a). Then draw the new budget deficit function for (c).

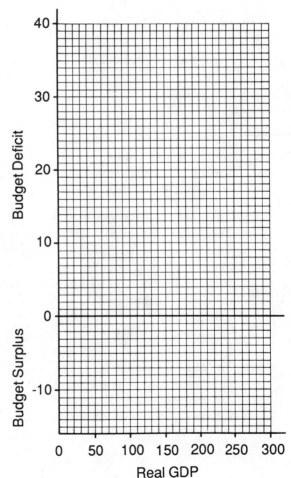

*3. An economy has a horizontal *SRAS* curve. Thus the price level will remain constant when the economy's GDP changes. Behavior in the economy is captured by the following equations.

Consumption is

$$C = a + bY_d \qquad (1)$$

where b is the marginal propensity to consume. Investment is

$$I = n \qquad (2)$$

Net exports are

$$X - M = x - mY \qquad (3)$$

where m is the marginal propensity to import. Government spending is

$$G = g \qquad (4)$$

Taxes are

$$T = h + tY \qquad (5)$$

where t is the marginal tax rate. Disposable income is

$$Y_d = Y - T \qquad (6)$$

(a) Prove that the equilibrium level of Y is given by the expression

$$Y = \frac{a + n + g + x - bh}{1 - b + bt + m}.$$

(b) The initial values are as follows:
The parameters are $b = 0.8$, $m = 0.04$, $t = 0.2$.
The autonomous terms are $a = 50$, $n = 18$, $g = 90$, $h = x = 10$.
Potential GDP (Y^*) is 405.
Prove that the current equilibrium level of Y is 400. What is the value of the current output gap?

(c) The general equation for the budget deficit is given by $B = G - T$ or, in this example, $B = g - h - tY$. At the initial values and the current equilibrium level of Y, prove that the government's budget position is balanced (i.e., $B = 0$). What is the value of the cyclically adjusted deficit?

(d) The government is determined to eliminate the output gap completely but is constrained by the country's constitution to have a balanced budget (i.e., $G = T$, or $g = h - tY$, or $B = 0$). It knows that if it increases G, total taxes (T) must increase by the same amount. Total taxes will increase if h is increased, if t is increased, or if GDP increases. Suppose that for political reasons the government wishes to keep the tax rate (t) constant. Thus any increase in g must be financed by a combination of increases in h and increases in taxation revenues caused by an increase in Y with a constant tax rate, t. What, therefore, is the necessary increase in G (and total taxes) to eliminate the gap?

   The answer to this question can be shown step by step. The first step involves recognizing that Y_d is now equal to $Y - g$. Why?

(e) Using the fact that $Y_d = Y - g$, reformulate the expression for the consumption function.

(f) Using the reformulated consumption function, prove that the new expression for the aggregate expenditure function is $(b - m)Y + [a + n + (1 - b)g + x]$.

(g) Prove that the new equilibrium expression for Y is $Y = [a + n + (1 - b)g + x]/(1 - b + m)$ and that the (balanced budget) government expenditure multiplier is $(1 - b)/(1 - b + m)$. Using initial parameter values, what is its numerical value?

(h) Given this numerical value for the multiplier and the value of the current output gap, what is the necessary increase in G?

(i) Given your answer to (h), what is the necessary increase in total taxes? Since t is constant by assumption and national income increases by 5 (thereby eliminating the output gap), what is the needed change in h (autonomous taxes)?

(j) Prove, with the numerical levels of g, h, and Y, that the government's actual budget is balanced ($B = 0$). But what is its cyclically adjusted deficit? This value should be different from that in (c), reflecting the change in the fiscal stance of government policy.

Answers

Multiple-Choice Questions

1. (c) 2. (c) 3. (a) 4. (b) 5. (a) 6. (b) 7. (c) 8. (b) 9. (c) 10. (d) 11. (c) 12. (d)
13. (c) 14. (d) 15. (b) 16. (a) 17. (b) 18. (d) 19. (c) 20. (b) 21. (b) 22. (a)
23. (d) 24. (c) 25. (d)

Exercises

1. (a) The inflationary gap of 12 will be completely eliminated if taxes are increased by 3 billion since the tax multiplier is 4.

   (b) GDP declines for two reasons. The increase in taxation will decrease GDP by 12 billion, and the decrease in exports will decrease GDP by 15 billion (2.5×6). The total decrease is therefore 27 billion. The economy's initial GDP level must have been 1,012. After the taxation and export changes, the new equilibrium level must be 27 billion less, or 985. Hence the recessionary gap is 15 billion.

   (c) No, a taxation cut of 3 billion will increase GDP by 12 billion, leaving a recessionary gap of 3 billion ($1,000 - 997$).

   (d) If nothing else happens, the minister's amended policy will restore potential GDP. As was discussed before, the taxation increase will eliminate the inflationary gap. The 2.5 billion increase in government spending will counteract the 2.5 billion reduction in food exports.

2. (a) Real national income = 200; it has a balanced budget; there is a recessionary gap of 20 ($220 - 200$); its marginal propensity to spend is 0.5, which can be obtained by calculating the change in total AE for changes in Y; the value of its cyclically adjusted deficit is a surplus of 4 (shown as -4), which is equal to 40 minus (0.2×220); the term 0.2 is the personal tax rate.

   (b) Since the marginal propensity to spend is 0.5, the government expenditure multiplier is 2.0. Thus an *increase* in government spending of 10 is required to eliminate the recessionary gap.

   (c) If G becomes 50 (an increase of 10), the immediate effect is to create a deficit of 10 at an income level of 200 [$50 - (0.2 \times 200)$]. However, the fiscal stimulus increases AD, and therefore real national income increases; tax revenues increase, such that at $Y = 220$, tax revenues are 44 and an actual budget deficit of 6 exists. In this case the actual budget deficit of 6 represents the value of the cyclically adjusted deficit. Notice that the CAD went from a surplus of 4 to a deficit of 6, and this is consistent with a deficit-creating fiscal policy stance.

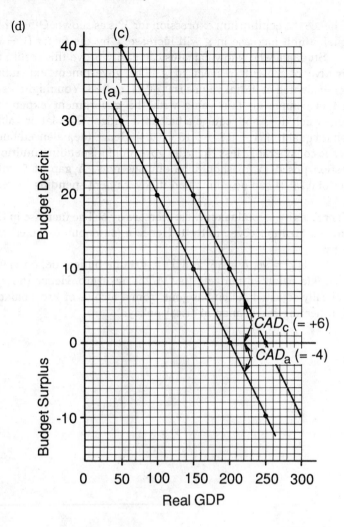

*3. (a) At equilibrium, $AE = Y$. The expression for the AE function is found by substituting the appropriate relationships into the equation $AE = C + I + G + (X - M)$. This gives $AE = (b - bt - m)Y + (a + n + g + x - bh)$. Equating Y to AE and solving for Y, we obtain the equation shown.

(b) $Y = (50 + 18 + 90 + 10 - 8)/0.4 = 400$. There is a recessionary gap of 5 $(405 - 400)$.

(c) The actual budget is balanced since $g = 90$, $h = 10$, $t = 0.2$, and $Y = 400$. The cyclically adjusted deficit is $90 - 10 - 0.2(405)$, which represents a surplus of 1 $(= -1)$.

(d) Disposable income is defined as income minus total taxes (net of transfers). The balanced budget requirement means that total taxes must equal government spending, or $g = h + tY$. Hence disposable income is $Y - g$.

(e) The consumption function becomes $C = a + b(Y - g)$.

(f) $AE = a + b(Y - g) + n + g + x - mY = (b - m)Y + [a + n + (1 - b)g + x]$.

(g) $AE = Y$; hence the equilibrium expression for Y is as shown. Other things being equal, a unit increase in g will increase Y by the factor $(1 - b)/(1 - b + m)$. Students who know calculus can easily prove this result; take the derivative of Y with respect to g. The government expenditure multiplier evaluated at initial values is 0.2/0.24, or 0.83. You might also be interested in comparing this value with the government expenditure multiplier, which does not require a balanced budget. The latter value is 2.5, which is equal to $1/(1 - 0.8 + 0.16 + 0.04)$. Hence the balanced budget multiplier is considerably less than the government spending multiplier.

(h)   The question posed in (d) should be obvious now. A gap of 5 with a multiplier of 0.2/0.24 can be eliminated if government spending increases by 6.

(i)   Since g increases by 6, total taxes must increase by 6. The increase in GDP of 5 increases taxation revenue by 1. Hence h (autonomous taxes) must increase by 5.

(j)   With new levels $g = 96$, $h = 15$, and $Y = 405$, the budget deficit is $96 - 15 - 81$, or 0 (a balanced budget). Its CAD is also zero. Hence the value of the cyclically adjusted deficit has gone from a surplus of 1 to a balanced position, reflecting the change in fiscal policy.

PART NINE

Money, Banking, and Monetary Policy

Chapter 33

The Nature of Money and Monetary Institutions

Learning Objectives

After studying this chapter, you should be able to:

—distinguish the various functions of money

—explain the historical development of fractionally backed money and fiat money

—understand the various functions of the Bank of Canada, the nation's central bank

—understand the structure of the banking system, which includes the Bank of Canada, Schedule A (chartered), B, and C banks, and other financial intermediaries such as trust companies and credit unions

—distinguish among target, required, and excess reserves in the context of a fractional reserve banking system

—explain the process by which the banking system can increase and decrease deposit money, given a set of assumptions regarding the target reserve ratio and cash drain from the banking system

—distinguish among money, money substitutes, and near money as well as among various types of deposit money

Multiple-Choice Questions

1. For money to serve as an efficient medium of exchange, it must have all but which of the following characteristics?
   (a) general acceptability
   (b) convertibility into precious metals
   (c) high value relative to its weight
   (d) divisibility

2. The value of money depends primarily on
   (a) the gold backing of the currency alone
   (b) the gold backing of both currency and deposits
   (c) its purchasing power
   (d) who issues it

3. To be a satisfactory store of value, money must have
   (a) a relatively stable value
   (b) a direct relationship to national income
   (c) a highly volatile value over time
   (d) no interest payments for holding it

4. "Debasing" the coinage had the effect of
   (a) causing prices to fall in the economy
   (b) causing inflation
   (c) increasing the purchasing power of each coin
   (d) a loss to the person issuing the coins

5. A fractionally backed paper money system exists when claims against banks' reserves
   (a) have 100 percent backing in precious metals such as gold
   (b) exceed the value of actual reserves
   (c) have a direct relationship to national income
   (d) have a fixed relationship to the quantity of coinage

6. Today, paper money in Canada is issued by
   (a) all Schedule A banks
   (b) the federal Department of Finance
   (c) Schedule A and Schedule B banks, including some trust companies
   (d) the central bank of Canada (the Bank of Canada)

7. All Canadian currency (coins and paper notes) is
   (a) fractionally backed by gold reserves
   (b) totally backed by gold
   (c) interest-bearing
   (d) fiat money

8. Which of the following is *not* an asset of a bank?
   (a) deposits of households
   (b) reserves
   (c) loans
   (d) Government of Canada securities

9. The reserve ratio is the fraction of a bank's
   (a) deposits that it must hold in the form of currency
   (b) deposits that it holds as reserves either in currency or as deposits with the Bank of Canada
   (c) assets that it holds in the form of reserves
   (d) reserves that it must hold in the form of deposits with the Bank of Canada

10. Which one of the following is *not* a function of the Bank of Canada?
    (a) providing banking services for the federal government
    (b) acting as a lender of last resort to the banks
    (c) controlling the supply of money and credit
    (d) lending to business firms

11. The deposits of banks at the Bank of Canada, which constitute their reserves, appear as
    (a) a liability on the Bank of Canada's balance sheet
    (b) an asset on the Bank of Canada's balance sheet
    (c) a liability on the balance sheet of the banks
    (d) a component of the item "purchase and resale agreements" on the Bank of Canada's balance sheet

12. Purchase and resale agreements (PRA) involve
    (a) sales and purchases of government securities among banks
    (b) sales and purchases of government securities between the Bank of Canada and the banks
    (c) sales of government securities by investment dealers to the Bank of Canada with agreement to repurchase them at a later date
    (d) sales of government securities by investment dealers to the Government of Canada with agreement to repurchase them at a later date

13. Which of the following is not an asset of the Bank of Canada?
    (a) Government of Canada deposits
    (b) Government of Canada securities
    (c) advances to banks
    (d) Government of Canada securities held under PRA

14. The process of creating deposit money by banks
    (a) is possible because of the fractional reserve system
    (b) is consciously undertaken by each bank
    (c) must occur if there are excess reserves
    (d) permits only small, gradual changes in the money supply

15. A reduction in bank reserves by payments of currency to foreigners will
    (a) always cause a multiple contraction in deposits
    (b) cause a multiple contraction in deposits only if there are no excess reserves
    (c) not affect domestic deposits
    (d) not affect the availability of domestic credit

16. If a bank currently holds $600 million in deposits and $40 million in reserves and has a target reserve ratio of 6 percent, this bank has
    (a) excess reserves of $4 million
    (b) required reserves of $4 million
    (c) target reserves of $2.4 million
    (d) target reserves of $40 million

17. If a bank must hold 4 percent of its deposits to satisfy the central bank's requirements but also wishes to hold an additional 3 percent of deposits to meet the needs of its customers, its target reserve ratio is
    (a) 1 percent
    (b) 4 percent, which is also equal to its required reserve ratio
    (c) 7 percent
    (d) 3 percent

18. Assuming a fixed target reserve ratio (v) of 10 percent in a banking system and no cash drain out of the banking system, a banking system that receives $1.00 in new reserves can increase new deposits *ultimately* by
    (a) $10.00, which is $1/v$ times $1.00
    (b) 10 cents, which is 10 percent of $1.00
    (c) the ratio $1/(1 - v)$, which in this case is approximately $1.11
    (d) $1.10, which is $(1 + v)$ times $1.00

19. The existence of a currency drain from the banking system will, other things being equal,
    (a) reduce the ability of the banking system to expand or contract the money supply
    (b) have no effect on the ability of the banking system to contract the money supply
    (c) have no effect on the ability of the banking system to expand the money supply
    (d) increase the ability of the banking system to expand or contract the money supply

Questions 20 through 23 refer to the following information about a banking system.

1. There is a banking system in which each bank has a fixed target reserve ratio of 5 percent.
2. There is no currency drain from the banking system, and all banks are assumed to hold no excess reserves for a prolonged period of time.
3. Banks experiencing excess (deficient) reserves respond by increasing (decreasing) loans.
4. The current status of the balance sheet of *all banks* is as follows:

All Banks

Assets		Liabilities	
Reserves:	$_____	Deposits:	$300 million
Loans:	$270 million		
Securities:	$_____		

20. If all banks initially had no excess reserves,
    (a) the reserves of the banks must have been $30 million
    (b) the holdings of securities by the banks must have been $15 million
    (c) the reserves of the banks must have been 5 percent of loans, or $13.5 million
    (d) the reserves of the banks must have been $300 million

21. If all banks initially had $16 million of actual reserves, then
    (a)   excess reserves are $15 million
    (b)   the banks have $1 million in deficient reserves (negative excess reserves)
    (c)   excess reserves are $1 million
    (d)   target reserves are equal to actual reserves

22. Assuming that the banking system begins with no excess reserves, a loss of
    $1 million of deposits from the system will *ultimately* lead to
    (a)   a reduction in the money supply of $19 million
    (b)   a reduction in the money supply of $500,000
    (c)   an increase in the money supply of $20 million
    (d)   deposit liabilities in the banking system of $280 million

23. Assuming that the banking system begins with no excess reserves, a gain of
    $1 million of deposits will *ultimately* lead to
    (a)   increased deposits of $20 million
    (b)   increased loans of $20 million
    (c)   increased loans of $1 million
    (d)   a $5 million increase in the money supply

24. The doctrine of the neutrality of money states that the quantity of money
    influences
    (a)   the level of money prices but has no effect on the real part of the economy
    (b)   the real part of the economy but has no effect on the money part of the
          economy
    (c)   both the real and money parts of the economy in an identical fashion
    (d)   neither the real nor the money part of the economy

25. Different definitions of the money supply include different types of deposits.
    The narrowly defined money supply, called M1, includes currency and
    (a)   term deposits
    (b)   demand deposits
    (c)   all deposits of Schedule A banks
    (d)   personal savings deposits

26. A money substitute is something that serves as a
    (a)   store of value
    (b)   unit of account
    (c)   temporary medium of exchange but not as a store of value
    (d)   temporary medium of exchange and also as a store of value

27. A rise of the Consumer Price Index from 100 to 110 would change the store
    of value represented by $1,000 in currency to
    (a) $1,100   (c) $909
    (b) $900   (d)   no change ($1,000)

Exercises

1. Indicate which of the three functions of money is demonstrated in each of the following transactions. Use the appropriate number: (1) medium of exchange, (2) store of value, (3) unit of account.

   (a) Farmer Brown puts cash in a mattress. _____
   (b) Storekeeper Jones adds up the total sales for the day. _____
   (c) Plumber Smith makes $500 per week. _____
   (d) Traveling salesperson Lee buys $100 of gasoline per week. _____
   (e) The Blacks buy a good oriental rug with the thought that it will keep its value for a long time. _____

2. Which of the following might be regarded in Canada as money, which as near money, and which as neither? Explain your answers briefly.
   (a) A share of stock in Bell Canada _____
   (b) A $10 Bank of Canada note _____
   (c) A Canada Savings Bond maturing in 1999 _____
   (d) A bank note issued by a Saskatchewan bank in 1897 _____
   (e) An ounce of gold in a Krugerrand (South African coinage provided for hoarders and speculators) _____
   (f) A savings account at a trust company _____
   (g) A demand deposit at the Bank of Nova Scotia _____

3. Arrange the following items on the proper side of a bank's balance sheet.
   (a) Demand deposits $5,000,000
   (b) Savings deposits   1,000,000
   (c) Currency in vaults   60,000
   (d) Deposits in the Bank of Canada   1,000,000
   (e) Loans to the public   4,000,000
   (f) Security holdings (Canadian government, provincial, municipal, and other)   1,500,000
   (g) Bank building and fixtures   360,000
   (h) Capital and surplus   920,000

Assets	Liabilities

4. We use "T-accounts," abbreviated balance sheets for a bank, to show changes in a bank's reserves, loans, and deposits. Make the entries on the following T-accounts, using + and − signs to show increase or decrease, for each of the following independent events. (Remember that all changes must balance.)

	Assets	Liabilities
(a) You deposit your paycheque of $100 at your bank.	Reserves: Loans and securities:	Deposits:
(b) A bank sells $10,000 of government bonds in the market to replenish its reserves.	Reserves: Loans and securities:	Deposits:
(c) A bank makes a loan of $5,000 to a local business and credits it to its chequing account.	Reserves: Loans and securities:	Deposits:
(d) A bank sells $50,000 of securities to the Bank of Canada and receives deposits in the Bank of Canada.	Reserves: Loans and securities:	Deposits:
(e) A business uses $5,000 of its demand deposit to pay off a loan from the same bank.	Reserves: Loans and securities:	Deposits:
(f) A bank orders $5,000 in currency from the Bank of Canada.	Reserves: Loans and securities:	Deposits:

5. Suppose that Bank A, a Canadian bank, begins with the T-account shown here. The target reserve ratio is assumed to be 10 percent. Joe Doe, a holder of a deposit in Bank A, withdraws $1,000 and deposits this amount in a commercial bank in a foreign country. Thus, $1,000 has been taken out of the Canadian banking system.

Bank A (initial situation)				Bank A (after the withdrawal)	
Reserves:	$10,000	Deposits:	$100,000	Reserves:	Deposits: $
Loans:	90,000			Loans:	

(a) What were Bank A's target reserves? Did it have excess reserves initially?
(b) Show the immediate effect of the withdrawal from Bank A.
(c) What is the status of Bank A's reserves now?
(d) Bank A reacts by calling in a loan that it had made to Mary Smith equal to the amount of its reserve deficiency. Mary repays the loan by writing a cheque on her account in Bank B, another Canadian bank that also has a fixed target reserve ratio of 10 percent. Bank B's initial T-account is shown next. Fill in the T-accounts for the effects of Bank A's receiving the payment from Mary and of Bank B's losing Mary's deposit.

Bank B (initial situation)		
Reserves: $ 5,000	Deposits: $ 50,000	
Loans: 45,000		

Bank B (after losing Mary's deposit)		
Reserves: $	Deposits: $	
Loans:		

Bank A (after receiving loan repayment)		
Reserves: $	Deposits: $	
Loans:		

(e) After this transaction, does Bank A have deficient reserves? Does Bank B?

(f) In fact, Bank B has a deficiency of reserves. It reacts by calling in a loan made to Peter Piper equal to the amount of the deficiency. Peter cashes in a deposit that he held in Bank C; that is, Bank C loses a deposit and Peter repays Bank B. Bank C's initial situation is shown next; its target reserve ratio is also 10 percent. Fill in the T-accounts for the effects of Bank B's receiving the loan repayment and Bank C's losing Peter's savings deposit.

Bank C (initial situation)		
Reserves: $ 7,000	Deposits: $ 70,000	
Loans: 63,000		

Bank C (after losing Peter's deposit)		
Reserves: $	Deposits: $	
Loans:		

Bank B (after receiving loan repayment)		
Reserves: $	Deposits: $	
Loans:		

(g) After this transaction, does Bank B have deficient reserves? Does bank C?

(h) After this transaction, the reduction in the money supply has been Joe's original withdrawal plus $_____ in other deposits. Loans have been reduced by $_____ .

(i) The process will continue until the total reduction in the money supply will be $_____ . The total reduction in loans will be $_____ .

6. Suppose that a foreign company withdraws money from its account in a foreign country, buys $1 million of Canadian currency, and deposits this sum into the Canadian banking system. The target reserve ratio for each bank is assumed to be 8 percent, and there is no currency drain from the banking system. The initial situation in the Canadian banking system is depicted as follows:

All Banks		
Reserves:	$ 72 million	Deposits: $900 million
Loans:	728 million	
Securities:	100 million	

(a) According to the initial scenario, target reserves are $ _____ and excess reserves are $ _____ .

(b) After the $1 million deposit, target reserves are $_____ and excess reserves are $_____ .

(c) Assuming that all excess reserves are used to expand loans, the final (increase, decrease) in the money supply will be _____ times the new $1 million deposit, which is equal to _____ .

(d) The final (increase, decrease) in loans will be $_____ .

7. Star Bank, a Schedule A Canadian bank that currently has $300 million dollars in deposits, has been operating with a target reserve ratio of 8 percent. Judy Kupferschmidt has just inherited the equivalent of $1 million Canadian from a relative living in Florida and deposits this sum in this bank.

(a) If the bank continued to operate on an 8 percent target reserve basis, what is the magnitude of its excess reserves after Judy's deposit?

(b) If other Canadian banks also had 8 percent target reserve ratios and there was no cash drain from the banking system, what might be the final change in the Canadian money supply?

(c) Suppose that Star Bank considers the risk of extending new loans from the excess reserves created by Judy's deposit to be too high. It decides to hold all of Judy's deposits in reserves. What is its new target reserve ratio, approximately? Will a multiple expansion in bank deposits occur?

(d) Assume that the scenario in (a) holds; Judy deposits $1 million in Star Bank. All Canadian banks, including Star, have a constant target reserve ratio of 8 percent. However, the Canadian public normally holds 2 percent of its money holdings in the form of currency (Bank of Canada notes and coins). If all banks used all of their excess reserves to extend loans, what would be the maximum possible change in the Canadian money supply?

Answers

Multiple-Choice Questions

1. (b) 2. (c) 3. (a) 4. (b) 5. (b) 6. (d) 7. (d) 8. (a) 9. (b) 10. (d) 11. (a) 12. (c) 13. (a) 14. (a) 15. (b) 16. (a) 17. (c) 18. (a) 19. (a) 20. (b) 21. (c) 22. (d) 23. (a) 24. (a) 25. (b) 26. (c) 27. (c)

Exercises

1. (a) 2; (b) 1 and 3; (c) 3; (d) 1; (e) 1, and the rug serves as function 2
2. (a) neither
   (b) money
   (c) near money; it is easily convertible to money
   (d) neither; once money but now a collector's item
   (e) neither, but readily convertible into money and considered by some to be a good store of value
   (f) near money
   (g) money

3.

Assets		Liabilities	
Currency in vaults	$ 60,000	Demand deposits	$5,000,000
Deposits in Bank of Canada	1,000,000	Savings deposits	1,000,000
Loans to public	4,000,000		
Security holdings	1,500,000		
Bank building and fixtures	360,000	Capital and surplus	920,000
	$6,920,000		$6,920,000

4. (a) reserves +$100; deposits +$100
   (b) reserves +$10,000; securities −$10,000
   (c) loans +$5,000; deposits +$5,000
   (d) reserves +$50,000; securities −$50,000
   (e) loans −$5,000; deposits −$5,000
   (f) total reserves unchanged; currency +$5,000; reserve deposits with the Bank of Canada, −$5,000

5. (a) Target reserves = $10,000; no
   (b) Deposits −$1,000 to $99,000; reserves −$1,000 to $9,000
   (c) Target reserves =$9,900; actual reserves =$9,000; hence its reserves are deficient by 900
   (d) Bank A: reserves +$900; loans −$900; Bank B: reserves −$900 to $4,100; deposits −$900 to $49,100.
   (e) Bank A does not, but Bank B has a deficiency of $810.
   (f) Bank B: reserves +$810; loans −$810; Bank C: reserves −$810 to $6,190; deposits −$810 to $69,190
   (g) No, but Bank C has a deficiency of $729.
   (h) −$900 + (−$810) + (−$729) = −$2,439; loans down by $1,710
   (i) $10,000; $9,000

6. (a) $72 million (0.08 × $900 million); 0
   (b) $72.08 million (0.08 × $901 million); $920,000
   (c) increase; 12.5 (1/0.08); $12.5 million
   (d) increase; $11.5 million (12.5 − 1.0)

7. (a) $920,000
   (b) $12.5 million (= 1/0.08 × $1 million)
   (c) Its initial reserve holdings were $24 million. After Judy's deposit, reserves are $25 million and total deposits are $301 million. Therefore, the new target reserve ratio is 8.3 percent. No; Star has no excess reserves that it lends out. Thus no other bank receives additional reserves.
   (d) $10 million increase. This is obtained by multiplying $1 million by 1/(0.08 + 0.02). The value 0.08 is the reserve ratio and 0.02 is the cash drain.

Chapter 34

The Role of Money
in Macroeconomics

Learning Objectives

After studying this chapter, you should be able to:

—explain the relationship between the market price of a bond and its interest rate

—identify three alternative motives for holding money

—explain the demand for money as a function of the interest rate, national income, and the price level

—distinguish between real and nominal money balances

—understand the transmission mechanism by which changes in the demand for and the supply of money affect aggregate demand

—understand the *monetary adjustment mechanism* by which an inflationay gap can be eliminated, provided that the nominal money supply is held constant

—explain why the slopes of the marginal efficiency of investment curve and the liquidity preference curve determine the effect that a change in the money supply has on national income

—understand that the effect of a monetary change on national income also depends on the slope of the *SRAS* curve and shifts in the *SRAS* curve triggered by changes in input prices

—explain the negative slope of an aggregate demand curve using the monetary adjustment mechanism

Multiple-Choice Questions

1. A bond that pays interest forever and never repays the principal is called a
   (a) perpetuity
   (b) fixed-term bond
   (c) preferred share
   (d) treasury bill

2. The present value of a bond is
   (a) always the same as its face value at some future maturity date
   (b) the interest rate per period to maturity
   (c) the specified value of the bond at maturity plus the interest in future value terms
   (d) the current value of a future stream of payments to which the bond represents a claim

3. The present value of a bond maturing at some future date
   (a) is negatively related to the interest rate
   (b) is positively related to the interest rate
   (c) depends entirely on the maturity date rather than the interest rate
   (d) is always equivalent to the face value of the bond

4. When the interest rate on an annual basis is 7 percent, the present value of a bond that promises to pay $114.49 one year hence is equal to
   (a) $1,635.57   (c) $107.00
   (b) $122.50   (d) by definition, $114.49

5. If Sue pays $95.238 for a one-year bond that promises to pay $100 at the end of the year, the interest rate on this bond, if Sue holds it to maturity, is
   (a) 5.24 percent   (c) 4.76 percent
   (b) 5.00 percent   (d) 9.52 percent

6. The amount of money held for transaction balances will
   (a) vary positively with national income measured in current prices
   (b) vary positively with interest rates
   (c) vary negatively with the value of national income
   (d) be larger with shorter intervals between paydays

7. Precautionary balances would be expected to increase if
   (a) business transactions were to become much less certain
   (b) interest rates increased
   (c) people were expecting securities prices to rise
   (d) prices and incomes fell

8. The speculative motive for holding money balances
   (a) applies to bonds but not other interest-earning assets
   (b) varies positively with national income
   (c) assumes that the opportunity cost of holding cash balances is zero
   (d) suggests that individuals will hold money in order to avoid or reduce the risk associated with fluctuations in the market prices of assets such as bonds

9. If there is an excess supply of money, households and firms will
   (a) sell bonds and add to their holdings of money, thereby causing the interest rate to fall
   (b) purchase bonds and reduce their holdings of money, thereby causing the interest rate to rise
   (c) purchase bonds and reduce their holdings of money, thereby causing the interest rate to fall and bond prices to rise
   (d) purchase bonds and reduce their holdings of money, thereby causing the price of bonds to fall

10. Suppose that the real and nominal value of M1 was $16.7 billion in 1975 and that prices doubled between 1975 and 1983. What would be the nominal value of M1 in 1983 that maintains a constant real supply of money over this period?
    (a) $8.35 billion
    (c) $16.7 billion
    (b) $33.4 billion
    (d) none of the above

11. Changes in interest rates caused by monetary disequilibrium
    (a) are usually of little consequence in influencing economic activity
    (b) provide the link between changes in the money supply and changes in aggregate demand
    (c) cause the liquidity preference function to shift, thus affecting desired investment expenditures
    (d) cause a change in the money supply, thereby affecting interest-sensitive expenditures

12. Other things being equal, a fall in the interest rate will cause
    (a) a shift in the *MEI* function to the left
    (b) a shift in the *MEI* function to the right
    (c) a movement down the *MEI* function
    (d) a movement up the *MEI* function

13. The marginal efficiency of investment curve illustrates the
    (a) positive relation between investment and the rate of interest
    (b) negative relation between investment and the rate of interest
    (c) negative relation between the capital stock and the rate of interest
    (d) positive relation between the capital stock and the rate of interest

14. A movement from excess demand for money balances to monetary equilibrium
    (a) tends to increase aggregate demand
    (b) has an unpredictable effect on aggregate demand
    (c) tends to decrease aggregate demand
    (d) will affect aggregate demand but not the interest rate

15. If the Bank of Canada increases the money supply, we would expect the
    (a) interest rate to fall, the *AE* curve to shift upward, and the *AD* curve to shift to the left
    (b) interest rate to fall, the *AE* curve to shift downward, and the *AD* curve to shift to the right
    (c) interest rate to fall, the *AE* curve to shift upward, and the *AD* curve to shift to the right
    (d) interest rate to fall, the *AE* curve to be unaffected, and the *AD* curve to become flatter

16. A rise in the price level, other things being equal, will tend to shift the *AE* function downward because of
    (a) reduced demand for money balances
    (b) a rise in the demand for money balances, which increases interest rates
    (c) an excess supply of money balances, which decreases interest rates
    (d) the fact that interest rates will fall

17. The monetary adjustment mechanism will eliminate an inflationary gap by
    (a) raising interest rates, reducing investment, and increasing aggregate expenditure
    (b) lowering interest rates, increasing investment, and increasing aggregate expenditure
    (c) raising interest rates, reducing investment, and moving leftward along the *AD* curve
    (d) raising interest rates, reducing investment, and shifting the *AD* curve

18. A given change in the money supply will exert a larger effect on real national income
    (a) the flatter the *LP* curve is and the steeper the *MEI* curve is
    (b) the flatter both the *LP* and *MEI* curves are
    (c) the steeper both the *LP* and *MEI* curves are
    (d) the steeper the *LP* curve is and the flatter the *MEI* curve is

19. A sufficiently large rise in the price level will eliminate an inflationary gap provided that
    (a) the nominal money supply remains constant
    (b) the nominal money supply increases
    (c) the Bank of Canada validates the inflation
    (d) government expenditures are financed by increases in the money supply

20. An inflation is said be *validated* when
    (a) the money supply increases at the same rate as the price level rises
    (b) the nominal supply decreases at the same rate as the price level rises
    (c) the monetary adjustment mechanism is unaffected by Bank of Canada policy
    (d) *Statistics Canada* releases the inflation data to the federal government

21. Bond X matures in 2 years and bond Y matures in 10 years. An increase in the interest rate
    (a) causes a larger percentage decline in the price of bond Y than in that of bond X
    (b) causes a smaller percentage increase in the price of bond Y than in that of bond X
    (c) causes the same percentage change in the price of both bonds
    (d) has no effect on the price of either bond

Questions 22 through 26 refer to the accompanying diagram. An initial equilibrium at point *a* is changed by an increase in the money supply. The new short-run equilibrium is shown by point *b*.

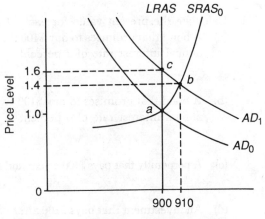

22. Point *b* represents
    (a) an inflationary gap of 10
    (b) a recessionary gap of 10
    (c) a positive output gap of 10
    (d) long-run equilibrium, since input prices will never change

23. The increase in the money supply shifted the *AD* curve to the right because
    (a) a decline in interest rates stimulated more investment expenditure
    (b) an excess demand for money was created in the money market; thus interest rates and investment expenditure will both increase
    (c) consumption expenditure increased as real GDP increased
    (d) none of the above

24. The gap situation depicted at point *b* is likely to cause further adjustment. Specifically, we would expect
    (a) input prices to rise
    (b) the *SRAS* curve to begin shifting leftward
    (c) the price level to increase beyond 1.4
    (d) all of the above

25. As the adjustment described in question 24 occurs, we would expect
    (a) the nominal demand for money to increase
    (b) the interest rate to rise as long as the central bank does not expand the money supply beyond the initial increase
    (c) a decrease in investment expenditure as interest rates increase
    (d) all of the above

26. As long as input price changes completely offset the price change, the long-run impact of the monetary expansion will be
    (a) at point *b*, since real wages do not change
    (b) increases in both real GDP and the price level
    (c) a price level of 1.6 and GDP of 900, or point *c*
    (d) at point *a*, since price increases causes the *AD* curve to shift leftward to its initial position

Exercises

1. Calculate the present value for each of the following assets:
   (a) A bond that promises to pay $100 three years from now and has a constant annual interest rate of 2 percent

   (b) A bond that promises to pay $100 two years from now and has a constant annual interest rate of 6 percent

   (c) A perpetuity that pays $100 a year and has an annual interest rate of 17 percent

   (d) An investment that pays $100 after one year, $150 after two years, and $80 after three years and has an annual interest rate of 10 percent

2. If you are not convinced that interest rates and present value are negatively related, perhaps this exercise will eliminate your doubt. The present value of a bond is often called the market price of the bond. Consider two bonds, A and B. Bond A promises to pay $120 one year hence, and bond B promises to pay $120 two years from now.

   (a) Calculate the present value for bond A when the interest rate is 8 percent. Calculate the present value for interest rates of 10 percent, 20 percent, and 25 percent. What happened to the market price when interest rates rose?

   (b) If you were told that the market price (present value) of bond A increased, what would you conclude is happening to the interest rate on bond A?

   (c) Calculate the present value for bond B for interest rates of 10 percent, 20 percent, and 25 percent.

   (d) Which of the two bonds had the larger percentage change in its price when the interest rate rose from 10 to 20 percent?

   (e) If the current rate of interest on both bonds were 20 percent, which bond would currently be selling for the higher market price? Why?

   (f) An individual who insists on receiving a 14 percent return on all assets would be prepared to pay what market price for bond A? For bond B?

3. Suppose that a household is paid $1,000 at the beginning of each month. The household spends all of its income on the purchase of goods and services each month. Furthermore, assume that these purchases are at a constant rate throughout the month. Consequently, payments and receipts are not perfectly synchronized.

   (a) What is the value of currency holdings at the beginning of the month? At the end of the first week? At the end of the third week? At the end of the month?

   (b) What is the magnitude of the *average* currency holdings over the month?

   (c) Suppose that the household's income increases to $1,200 and purchases of goods and services during a month are equal to this amount. What is the *average* currency holding?

(d) Suppose that the household is paid $1,000 over the month but in installments of $500 at the beginning of the month and $500 at the beginning of the third week. What is the magnitude of the *average* currency holdings per month?

4. Two liquidity preference curves are shown here.

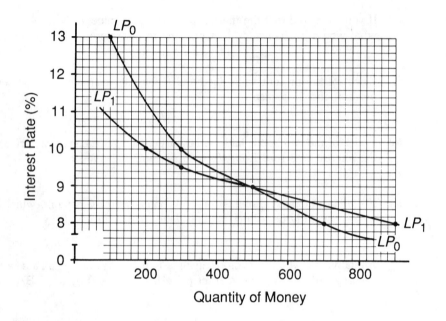

(a) Using your knowledge of the transactions and speculative motives for money, explain why the quantity of money demanded falls when interest rates rise.

(b) If the money supply is 500 and constant at all levels of interest rates, what interest rate is associated with monetary equilibrium? Plot the supply of money function in the graph, and indicate the monetary equilibrium interest rate.

(c) Suppose that the monetary authority decreased the money supply from 500 to 300. At an interest rate of 9 percent, what kind of situation exists in the money market? Would households and firms tend to buy or sell bonds? Explain. Predict what is likely to happen to bond prices and interest rates.

(d) As interest rates rise, what happens to the quantity of money demanded? Predict the new equilibrium level of interest rates first using LP_0 and then using LP_1.

(e) What increase in the money supply (from 500) would be necessary to achieve an equilibrium interest rate of 8 percent if LP_0 applies? If LP_1 applies? Comment on how the shape of the LP curve affects the effectiveness of monetary policy to achieve an interest rate target.

5. Explain and illustrate graphically an excess demand for money, and predict the effect on interest rates.

(a)

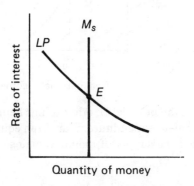

Quantity of money

(b) Explain and illustrate graphically an excess supply of money, and predict the effect on interest rates.

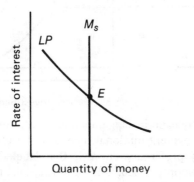

Quantity of money

(c) Predict the effect of an increase in the money supply by the Bank of Canada on the rate of interest and desired investment expenditure. Initial equilibrium is M_0, r_0, E_0, and I_0.

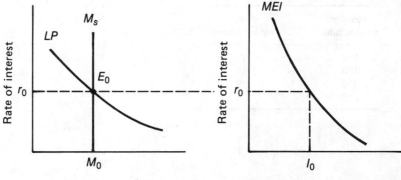

Quantity of money   Desired investment expenditure

(d) Assuming a constant price of p_0, show the effect of an increase in desired expenditure on the equilibrium level of real national income. Initial equilibrium is E_0 in both graphs.

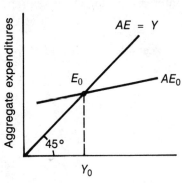

(e) Show the effect of an increase in the price level, other things being equal, on the rate of interest and investment expenditure. Start from equilibrium at E_0, r_0, and I_0, and assume that the supply of money remains constant.

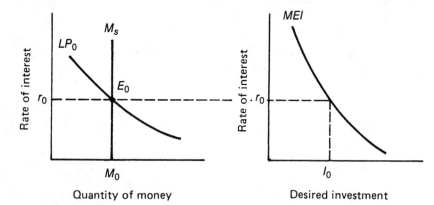

6. Suppose that the economy is currently experiencing unemployment. The central bank considers potential (full-employment) national income to be the policy objective. The economy's liquidity preference curve is that labeled LP_0 in exercise 4, and the current money supply is 500. Other information about the economy is described in points (i) through (vi).

   (i)   The marginal propensity to spend is 0.50.
   (ii)   The potential national income is 1,600.
   (iii) The MEI function is given by the following schedule:

Investment expenditure	Interest rate (percent)
160	13
180	11
200	9
210	8

(iv) Aggregate expenditures are depicted by the following schedule:

Y	C	I	G	X − M	AE
1,520	912	200	300	138	1,550
1,540	924	200	300	136	1,560
1,560	936	200	300	134	1,570
1,580	948	200	300	132	1,580
1,600	960	200	300	130	1,590

(v) The LP curve is not influenced by changes in the level of national income.
(vi) The $SRAS$ curve is horizontal at a price level of 2.0 for all levels of national income less than potential national income (1,600), at which level it becomes vertical.

The central bank sets its research department to work in order to establish accurate information about the current situation and to suggest what it should do in order to eliminate unemployment.
(a) Referring to the LP_0 curve in exercise 4, what is the current equilibrium level of the interest rate?

(b) Given the interest rate, what is the level of desired investment expenditure according to the MEI schedule?

(c) What is the current equilibrium value of real national income? What is the value of the output gap?

(d) What is the value of the simple multiplier? What change in autonomous expenditure is required for the economy to achieve the potential national income level without inflation?

Based on the information in (a) through (d), the research department is in a position to recommend policy changes for the central bank.
(e) Should the money supply be increased or decreased? Should the interest rate be increased or decreased?

(f) Changes in the money supply and the interest rate will change the level of investment. How much must investment be increased from its current level in order to achieve potential national income?

(g) To achieve this higher level of investment, what is the required level of the interest rate? (Refer to the MEI schedule.)

(h) Given the required level of the interest rate, what must the money supply be in order to achieve equilibrium in the money market at that interest rate? Refer to the LP_0 curve in exercise 4. What change in the current money supply is necessary?

Now suppose that the central bank is successful in lowering the interest rate and increasing investment by the appropriate magnitudes. It follows that real national income should increase by a multiple and attain a level of 1,600.

(i) Calculate the new level of consumption expenditure and calculate the aggregate level of expenditure at $Y = 1,600$. Is this an equilibrium situation?

(j) Illustrate the change in the AE and AD functions in the following graphs.

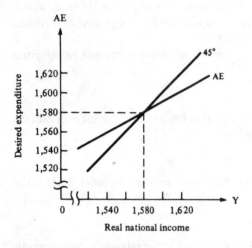 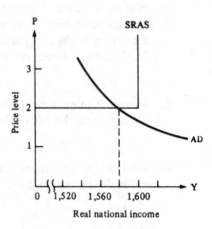

Appendix Exercise

The following exercise is based on the material in the appendix to this chapter. Read the appendix before attempting this exercise.

7. This exercise focuses on the shape of the aggregate demand curve and the monetary adjustment mechanism.

    The following two tables show the effects of changes in the price level on desired investment.

LP Schedule

Rate of interest (percent)	Quantity of money demanded	
	$P = 1$	$P = 2$
4	80	100
6	70	90
8	60	80
10	50	70
12	40	60
14	30	50

MEI Schedule

Rate of interest (percent)	Desired investment expenditure
10	180
11	179
12	177
13	174
14	170

Assume that the nominal supply of money is fixed at a value of 50.

(a) Assume that the price level is 1.0, what is the equilibrium interest rate? What is desired investment expenditure?

(b) Assume that the price level becomes 2.0. For a given level of real national income, what will happen to the demand for money? What will happen in the bond market? Explain.

(c) Using the LP schedule for $P = 2$, determine the new equilibrium interest rate.

(d) Given this change in the interest rate, what is the new level of desired investment expenditure?

The following table shows the effects of changes in desired investment (I) on real national income (Y).

Desired Y	Desired C	Desired I (interest = 10 percent)	AE (interest = 10 percent)	AE (interest = 14 percent)
340	170	180	350	_____
350	175	180	355	_____
360	180	180	360	_____
370	185	180	365	_____

(e) What is the equilibrium level of real national income (Y) associated with an interest rate of 10 percent and a price level of 1.0?

(f) Given the interest rate increase because of a doubling of the price level, what is the level of desired investment? Fill in the values for the new level of aggregate expenditure. What is the new equilibrium level of Y?

Now we synthesize the relationship between P and Y.

(g) Graph the *AD* curve, plotting the negative relationship between *P* and *Y* for this exercise. Use you answers to (e) and (f).

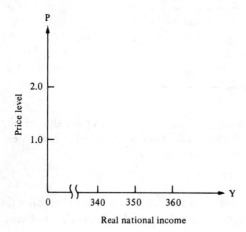

Real national income

Answers

Multiple-Choice Questions

1. (a)   2. (d)   3. (a)   4. (c)   5. (b)   6. (a)   7. (a)   8. (d)   9. (c)   10. (b)   11. (b)   12. (c)
13. (b)   14. (c)   15. (c)   16. (b)   17. (c)   18. (d)   19. (a)   20. (a)   21. (a)   22. (a)   23. (a)
24. (d)   25. (d)   26. (c)

Exercises

1. (a) $PV = \$100/(1 + 0.02)^3 = \$94.23$
   (b) $PV = \$100/(1 + 0.06)^2 = \$89.00$
   (c) $PV = \$100/0.17 = \$588.24$
   (d) $PV = \$100/(1.10) + \$150/(1.10)^2 + \$80/(1.10)^3$
        $PV = \$90.91 + \$123.97 + \$60.11 = \$274.99$
2. (a) PV at 8 percent is $\$120/(1.08) = \$111.11$
        PV at 10 percent is $\$120/(1.10) = \$109.09$
        PV at 20 percent is $\$120/(1.20) = \$100.00$
        PV at 25 percent is $\$120/(1.25) = \$96.00$
        As the interest rate increased, the market price (present value) of bond A fell.
   (b) Other things being equal, the interest rate must have been falling.
   (c) PV at 10 percent is $\$120/(1.10)^2 = \$99.17$
        PV at 20 percent is $\$120/(1.20)^2 = \$83.33$
        PV at 25 percent is $\$120/(1.25)^2 = \$76.80$
   (d) The price of bond A fell from \$109.09 to \$100.00, a 8.3 percent decrease. Bond B, having a longer maturity period, had a 16.0 percent decline in its price.
   (e) Bond A has the higher market price (compare \$100.00 with \$83.33). The further in the future that dollars are received, the lower the present value of those dollars, other things being equal. For bond A, \$120 was received one year from now, whereas bond B paid \$120 two years from now.
   (f) The person should be prepared to pay \$105.26 for bond A, \$92.34 for B.

3. (a) $1,000, $750, $250, $0
   (b) $1,000/2 = $500
   (c) $1,200/2 = $600
   (d) $500/2 = $250

4. (a) As the opportunity cost of money rises, people will tend to economize on their transactions demand for money. In addition, they are prepared to take more risk (and therefore buy more bonds) since the return on bonds has risen.
   (b) Demand (either LP_1 or LP_0) equals supply at 9 percent. The supply of money is a vertical line at 500.
   (c) At an interest rate of 9 percent, an excess demand for money exists. Households and firms would sell bonds to satisfy their excess demand for money. Hence bond prices would fall and interest rates would rise.
   (d) As interest rates rise, the quantity demanded falls until demand equals the lower value of the money supply. Interest rates would equal 10.0 percent for LP_0 and 9.5 percent for LP_1.
   (e) If LP_0 applies, the money supply must be 700. If LP_1 applies, the money supply must be 900. Monetary policy aimed at lowering interest rates would be more effective if LP_0 applied, since it takes only an increase in the money supply of 200 (700 − 500) rather than 400 (900 − 500) to reduce the interest rate by one percentage point.

5. (a) Excess demand for money at r_0; interest rates should rise to equilibrium at r and E.

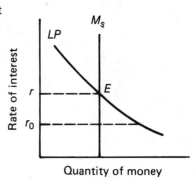

   (b) Excess supply of money at r_0; interest rates should fall to equilibrium at r and E.

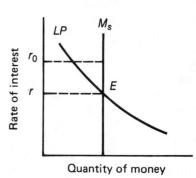

(c)   Interest rate drops from r_0 to r_1; investment expenditures rise from I_0 to I_1.

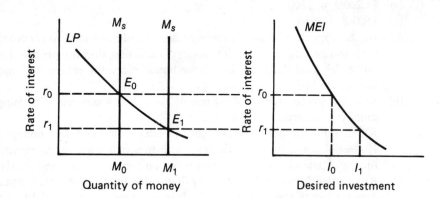

(d)   Upward shift in AE caused by more desired expenditure, also shifting AD outward; equilibrium income rises from Y_0 to Y_1.

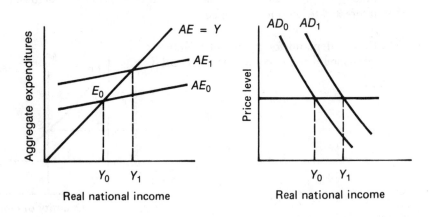

(e)   An increase in the price level increases demand for money (for transactions purposes primarily) from LP_0 to LP_1; this raises interest rates from r_0 to r_1 and lowers investment from I_0 to I_1.

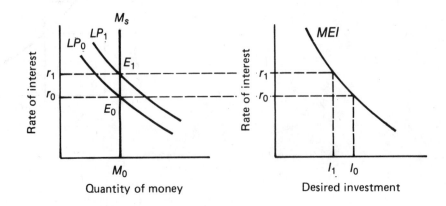

6. (a) 9 percent, at which demand is equal to supply
   (b) 200
   (c) When $Y = 1,580$, $AE = Y$. The output gap (recessionary gap) is $1,600 - 1,580 = +20$.
   (d) 2.0. Autonomous expenditure must increase by 10 to achieve an increase in Y of 20.
   (e) Since AE must increase, the interest rate must fall and hence the money supply must rise.
   (f) 10
   (g) The interest rate must fall from 9 percent to 8 percent.
   (h) According to the graph in exercise 4, the money supply must increase from 500 to 700, an increase of 200.
   (i) Consumption now equals 960, an increase of 12 ($20 \times MPC$ of 0.6). When $Y = 1,600$, $C = 960$ and $AE = Y$. This is equilibrium.
   (j)

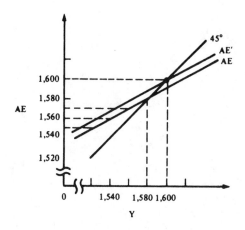 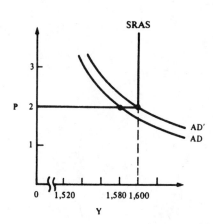

7. (a) Demand equals supply (50) at an interest rate of 10 percent. Desired investment expenditure is therefore 180.
   (b) If price increases, the LP shifts upward or rightward (the demand for money increases at every interest rate). Hence bonds will be sold, lowering their price. As a consequence, the interest rate increases.
   (c) The new equilibrium interest rate is 14 percent.
   (d) The new level of investment is 170.
   (e) $Y = AE$ at 360 (10 percent interest rate and $P = 1.0$).
   (f) Investment is now 170. AE: 340, 345, 350, 355. $AE = Y$ at 340. National income has fallen by 20.

(g)

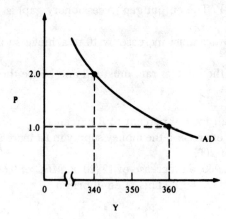

Chapter **35**

Monetary Policy

Learning Objectives

After studying this chapter, you should be able to:

—understand how the Bank of Canada can affect the reserves of the banking system by conducting open-market operations and by shifting government deposits between itself and the banking system

—explain other policy instruments such as moral suasion and the bank rate

—recognize that monetary policy in the short run is not capable of pursuing two objectives of pushing the price level and real GDP toward independently determined targets

—explain the distinctions among policy variables, policy instruments, and intermediate targets

—understand the distinction between monetary targeting (or monetary base control) and interest-rate targeting

—explain the various operating regimes available to a central bank

—explain why the full effects of monetary policy on economic activity may be subject to long and variable lags

—understand why shifts in the demand for money make intermediate targets unreliable indicators on which to base monetary policy

Multiple-Choice Questions

1. Open-market operations are
    (a) purchases and sales by the Bank of Canada of government securities in financial markets
    (b) sales of government securities by chartered banks to their customers
    (c) total purchases and sales of government securities in the bond market
    (d) changes in the interest rate charged by the Bank of Canada on loans to the banks

2. Which one of the following is *not* a policy instrument of the Bank of Canada?
   (a) raising the tax rate on interest income received from government bonds
   (b) moral suasion
   (c) transferring government deposits between itself and the banking system
   (d) open-market operations

3. If the Bank of Canada purchases bonds in the open market,
   (a) bank reserves will be reduced
   (b) bank reserves will be increased
   (c) the money supply will fall by a maximum of $1/v$ times the value of the purchase (v is the reserve ratio)
   (d) interest rates are likely to rise

4. If the Bank of Canada sold $10 million of securities in the open market,
   (a) reserves and securities in banks would each rise by $10 million
   (b) deposits and reserves of banks would initially fall by $10 million
   (c) the money supply would eventually increase by $1/v$ times the value of the sale (v is the reserve ratio)
   (d) deposits in the banking system would initially rise by $10 million

5. If the Bank of Canada purchases bonds in the open market, it is likely that
   (a) the price of bonds would fall and the interest rate would rise
   (b) both the price of bonds and the interest rate would rise
   (c) both the price of bonds and the interest rate would fall
   (d) the price of bonds would rise and the interest rate would fall

6. To eliminate an inflationary gap, the Bank of Canada might
   (a) sell bonds in the open market
   (b) purchase bonds in the open market
   (c) transfer government deposits into the banking system
   (d) increase the monetary base

7. The bank rate is defined as the interest rate
   (a) charged on preferred-customer loans by a bank
   (b) charged by banks for overdrafts of large corporations
   (c) at which the Bank of Canada makes loans to the banks
   (d) on three-month treasury bills

8. If the Bank of Canada transfers $10 million of government deposits from the banking system to itself,
   (a) reserves and government deposits in the banking system will increase by $10 million
   (b) reserves and government deposits in the Bank will increase by $10 million
   (c) reserves of the banks will fall by $10 million and government deposits in the Bank will increase by $10 million
   (d) the money supply is likely to increase by $1/v$ times the amount of the transfer

9. Generally recognized as a sign of a policy favoring tighter money is
   (a) the Bank increasing government deposits in the banking system
   (b) a rise in government bond purchases by the Bank of Canada
   (c) a rise in M1
   (d) a rise in the bank rate

10. If the Bank of Canada purchases government bonds in the open market,
    (a) an excess supply of money balances is created, higher bond prices will prevail, and aggregate expenditure will be higher than before
    (b) an excess demand for money balances is created, higher bond prices will prevail, and aggregate expenditure will be lower than before
    (c) an excess supply of money balances is created, lower bond prices will prevail, and aggregate expenditure will be higher than before
    (d) an excess demand for money balances is created, lower bond prices will prevail, and aggregate expenditure will be higher than before

11. If the Bank of Canada purchases government bonds in the open market,
    (a) the aggregate demand curve will shift to the right
    (b) the aggregate demand curve will shift to the left
    (c) the aggregate expenditure curve will shift downward and to the right
    (d) there will be a movement up the *MEI* curve

12. If the Bank of Canada chooses the interest-rate control approach to open-market operations, it
    (a) sets the price of bonds and the quantity of purchases and sales of bonds
    (b) sets the quantity of purchases and sales of bonds since the market will determine the equilibrium interest rate on bonds
    (c) sets the price at which it sells or buys bonds and allows the market to determine the quantity of purchases or sales
    (d) changes the bank rate without regard to its open-market policy

13. If the demand for money falls by a greater degree than the money supply is being restricted,
    (a) interest rates will fall
    (b) the quantity demanded for money will be greater than the quantity supplied
    (c) interest rates will rise
    (d) money supply expansion is necessary for achieving the initial target interest rate

14. An important implication of long and variable execution lags associated with monetary policy is that
    (a) national income can be easily fine-tuned with open-market operations
    (b) monetary policy is never capable of eliminating an inflationary gap
    (c) discretionary monetary policy may prove to be destabilizing
    (d) a stable monetary rule, regardless of demand instability, guarantees monetary stability

15. The experience of "monetary gradualism" in the period 1975–1980 in Canada indicated that
    (a) shifts in the demand for money were unimportant when setting a monetary growth rule
    (b) monetary growth rules ran into problems because of decreases in the demand for money
    (c) interest rates as the main intermediate target were reasonably easy to achieve
    (d) the demand for M1 was quite stable even though the demand for M2 was quite volatile

16. If the Bank of Canada were concerned about the potential effects of a deficit-reducing fiscal policy stance by the federal government, it might
    (a) purchase bonds in the open market
    (b) transfer government deposits out of the banking system
    (c) sell bonds in the open market with the intention of lowering interest rates
    (d) set a low monetary growth target

Answer questions 17 through 20 by referring to the accompanying graph.

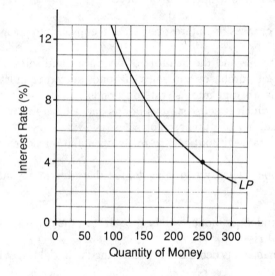

17. If the central bank chose an intermediate interest rate target of 12 percent,
    (a) both the money supply and the quantity of money demanded must be 100
    (b) it can set the monetary base at whatever level it wishes
    (c) a money supply of 150 would create an excess supply of bonds at an interest rate of 12 percent
    (d) both (a) and (c) are correct

18. If the money supply were 150 and the central bank's interest rate target were 12 percent, the central bank
    (a) need do nothing since a money supply of 150 achieves its interest-rate target
    (b) must sell bonds in the open market, thereby lowering bond prices
    (c) will lower the bank rate to indicate its intentions to decrease the supply of money
    (d) must increase government deposits in the banks in order to increase their reserves

19. If the central bank set a monetary supply target of 150, then according to the *LP* curve,
    (a) there would be an excess supply of money at an interest rate of 12 percent
    (b) there would be an excess supply of bonds at an interest rate of 4 percent
    (c) the equilibrium interest rate must be 8 percent
    (d) all of the above

20. If the central bank reduced its monetary supply target from 150 to 100,
    (a) it would have to increase its monetary base target
    (b) the equilibrium interest rate would rise from 8 to 12 percent, provided that the *LP* curve did not shift
    (c) it would have to increase the price of bonds by purchasing bonds in the bond market
    (d) it must have agreed to assist the federal government in financing additional spending

Answer questions 21 through 24 by referring to the following graph. The current situation is depicted at point *a*. Assume that both the *SRAS* and *LRAS* curves do not shift for the period under consideration.

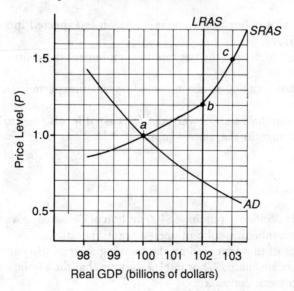

21. Which of the following combinations of policy objectives by a central bank are feasible in the short run?
    (a) a price level of 1.1 and real GDP of 100
    (b) potential GDP of 102 and a price level of 1.2
    (c) potential GDP and a price level of 1.0
    (d) all of the above are feasible if appropriate monetary base policies were adopted

22. Suppose that central bank policy is designed to eliminate the current output gap. Its monetary policy involves
    (a) a policy trade-off, since the elimination of the output gap is accompanied by an increase in the price level
    (b) either an increase in its monetary base target or a decrease in its interest-rate target
    (c) increasing the reserves of the banking system
    (d) all of the above

23. Information concerning the strength of the transmission mechanism indicates that every $500 million increase in the money supply increases real GDP by $1 billion. If the reserve ratio is 10 percent, the output gap will be completely eliminated if the central bank
    (a) increases reserves in the banking system by $100 million
    (b) increases the money supply by $500 million
    (c) increases the reserves in the banking system by $10 billion
    (d) none of the above

24. Given the policy outlined in question 23, which of the following might explain why the economy might achieve a short-run equilibrium at point c rather than point b?
    (a) The central bank's policy is accompanied by an unexpected increase in household saving.
    (b) The government increased the tax rate to complement the central bank's policy.
    (c) The central bank's policy is accompanied by an unexpected decline in export sales.
    (d) Actual import purchases are lower than forecasted levels used to design the required change in the money supply.

Exercises

1. The Bank of Canada decides to purchase $100 million of Canadian government securities from the nonbank public in open-market operations.
    (a) Show the effect of this first step on the banking system. (Be sure to use + and − to indicate changes, not totals.) Assume that the public holds all their money in bank deposits.

Bank of Canada		All Banks	
Assets	Liabilities	Assets	Liabilities
Securities:	Bank reserves:	Reserves:	Demand deposits:

(b) If the reserve ratio is 10 percent, it is now possible for deposits to increase by a total of _____ (including the original increase).

(c) What is likely to happen to the level of interest rates?

(d) Will the money supply necessarily increase by the full amount in (b)? Explain.

(e) What effect will the open-market operation have on the bank rate? Explain.

2. Suppose that each bank in the banking system has achieved its target reserve position. Now the Bank of Canada transfers a total of $300 million of government deposits from the banking system to itself.

(a) Show the effect of this transaction in the following balance sheets. Use + for an increase and − for a decrease.

Bank of Canada		Banking System	
	Government deposits:	Reserves:	Government deposits:
	Bank reserves:		

(b) Is the policy designed to combat a recessionary or an inflationary gap situation? Explain.

(c) If the reserve ratio is 5 percent, what is the possible *final* change in the money supply?

(d) Discuss the factors that determine the time it takes for the change in the money supply to eliminate the output gap problem.

3. Use the graphs to illustrate the effects of the following Bank of Canada monetary policies, and answer the questions.

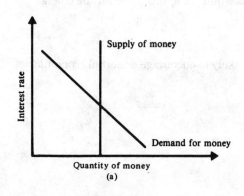

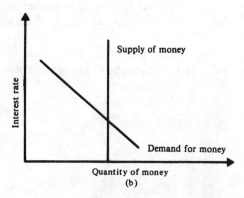

(a) Use graph (a) for this question. The Bank of Canada sells government securities.

Total reserves will (increase, decrease).

The money supply curve should shift to the _____ .

This policy is (expansionary, contractionary).

The quantity of money demanded will (increase, decrease).

Interest rates will tend to _____ .

(b) Use graph (b) for this question. The Bank of Canada transfers government deposits into the banks.

Excess reserves will initially (increase, decrease).

The money supply curve should shift to the _____ .

This policy is (expansionary, contractionary).

The quantity of money demanded will (increase, decrease).

Interest rates will tend to _____ .

(c) Use graph (a) for this question. The demand for money curve shifts farther to the left than the supply of money curve does.

Interest rates will tend to _____ .

Investment expenditure will tend to _____ .

National income will tend to _____ .

4. Suppose that the demand for money (liquidity preference) function was $D_M = 300 - 20r$, where D_M is the quantity of money demanded and r is the rate of interest in percentage terms. The supply of money is 100.

(a) What is the equilibrium value for the interest rate?

(b) Suppose, because of expansion in the economy, that the demand curve for money becomes $D_M = 400 - 20r$, but the supply of money remains at 100. If the interest remained at 10 percent, what situation exists in the money market? What is likely to happen to the equilibrium level of the interest rate in the future? Be specific.

(c) Given the circumstances described in (b) and assuming that the Bank of Canada was determined to maintain an interest-rate target of 10 percent, what change in the money supply would be required? Be specific.

(d) What type of open-market operations would be appropriate for the change in the money supply discussed in (c)?

(e) Is this type of open-market operation likely to encourage or curtail economic expansion?

5. Consider the same initial situation as in exercise 4. Now, however, money demand and supply are in terms of the M1 definition of money. The demand for M1 is $D_{M1} = 300 - 20r$. Moreover, the Bank of Canada is assumed to operate on the basis of an M1 target. Suppose that the Bank decreases its M1 target from 100 to 80, reflecting its wish to reduce investment expenditure to a level consistent with a particular lower level of real GDP.

(a) If the Bank accomplishes this intermediate target and the demand for money curve is stable, what is the new equilibrium interest rate? What factors determine the extent to which the change in the interest rate achieves the real GDP policy objective?

(b) Suppose that moneyholders find new ways to economize on their M1 requirements such that the demand for money function changes to $280 - 20r$. Assuming a new money supply of 80, what is the equilibrium interest rate?

(c) Although the Bank achieved its monetary target, is it likely to achieve its policy objective? Explain.

Answers

Multiple-Choice Questions

1. (a) 2. (a) 3. (b) 4. (b) 5. (d) 6. (a) 7. (c) 8. (c) 9. (d) 10. (a) 11. (a) 12. (c) 13. (a) 14. (c) 15. (b) 16. (a) 17. (a) 18. (b) 19. (d) 20. (b) 21. (b) 22. (d) 23. (a) 24. (d)

Exercises

1. (a)

Bank of Canada		All Banks	
Securities: +100	Bank reserves: +100	Reserves: +100	Deposits: +100

(b) $1 billion (10 × $100 million). The value 10 is obtained from 1/0.10.
(c) Other things being equal, interest rates are likely to fall because banks wish to make new loans and hence reduce the loan rate. All interest rates will fall because other institutions will want to be competitive with the banks.
(d) Excess reserves make money (demand deposit) creation possible. However, the actual effects on the money supply depend on the willingness and ability of banks to lend their excess reserves and whether there are any cash drains from the banking system.
(e) The treasury bill rate will fall. Since the bank rate is set at a premium of one-quarter of a percentage point over the three-month treasury bill rate, it is likely that the bank rate will fall as well.

2. (a) Bank of Canada: government deposits: + $300 million; bank reserves: −$300 million

Banking system: reserves −$300 million; government deposits: −$300 million

  (b) Since the Bank of Canada's policy reduces reserves in the banking system, the policy is directed to decreasing economic activity, which is an anti-inflationary policy. Assuming a stable demand for money function, interest rates will rise and investment will fall.

  (c) A $6 billion reduction. This is equal to $300 million times 1/0.05, where the value 0.05 is the reserve ratio.

  (d) A reduction in the money supply increases the interest rate. Firms would not necessarily revise their investment expenditures immediately. Moreover, when investment does decline, the effects on the induced components of aggregate expenditure may not be instantaneous; that is, the final effect of the multiplier process is achieved only after several time periods have elapsed.

3. (a) decrease; left; contractionary; decrease; rise
  (b) increase; right; expansionary; increase; fall
  (c) fall; increase; increase

4. (a) Equating demand with supply, we obtain an equilibrium level of the interest rate of 10 percent.

  (b) At an interest rate of 10 percent, there would be an excess demand for money. Firms and households would sell their bonds, thereby reducing bond prices and increasing the interest rate on bonds. Equating the new demand function with the money supply, we find that the new equilibrium level of the interest rate is 15 percent.

  (c) Since an excess demand for money exists at $r = 10$ percent with the new demand for money function, it follows that the Bank of Canada must increase the money supply in order to prevent interest rates from rising. Using the function $D_M = 400 − 20r$ and the fact that r must be equal to 10 (percent), D_M must equal 200. Since the demand for money must equal the supply of money and since the demand for money with a 10 percent rate of interest is 200, it follows that the supply of money must be increased from 100 to 200, an increase of 100.

  (d) The Bank of Canada should buy bonds in the open market to provide additional reserves for banks.

  (e) Given the increase in the demand for money with a fixed supply of money, the resulting interest-rate increase would have reduced some investment expenditure, thereby curtailing some of the economic expansion. However, with the Bank of Canada's interest-rate target policy and the expansionary open-market operation, economic expansion would be sustained or perhaps increased.

5. (a) The interest rate will increase from 10 percent to 11 percent. The effect
         on real GDP of the 1 percent increase in the interest rate will depend on
         (1) the slope of the *SRAS* curve, (2) the slope of the *MEI* curve, and (3)
         the size of the multiplier. The impact on *Y* will be large if the *SRAS* curve
         is relatively flat, the *MEI* curve is relatively flat, and the multiplier value
         is high.

    (b) The demand for money (liquidity preference) curve has shifted to the left.
         With a monetary target of 80, the equilibrium rate of interest is equal to
         its original level, 10 percent. This answer is obtained by equating 80 to
         the equation, $280 - 20r$.

    (c) The decrease in the demand for M1 has completely offset the reduction
         in the Bank's monetary target; the interest rate does not change. Thus the
         Bank is not likely to achieve its policy objective of reducing real GDP.

PART TEN

Issues and Controversies in Macroeconomics

Chapter 36

Inflation

Learning Objectives

After studying this chapter, you should be able to:

—distinguish between once-and-for-all and sustained inflation

—list several reasons for aggregate supply and demand shocks and explain how they cause inflation

—understand what is meant by monetary accommodation of a supply shock and validation of a demand shock

—explain the pressure on unit costs when actual unemployment is above, below, and at the NAIRU

—understand why expectational forces shift the *SRAS* curve

—explain why accelerating inflation will occur when there is a persistent inflationary gap and rising inflationary expectations

—understand that steady inflation at potential income results when the rate of monetary growth, the rate of wage increase, and the expected rate of inflation are all consistent with the actual inflation rate

—explain the three phases of breaking an entrenched inflation and why monetarists and Keynesians have differing views concerning the length of phase 2

—understand the role of incomes policies in breaking entrenched inflation

Multiple-Choice Questions

1. For any increase in the price level to be sustained,
   (a) there must be a supply shock
   (b) supply or demand shocks must be accompanied by increases in the money supply
   (c) both demand and supply shocks must occur simultaneously
   (d) the Bank of Canada must be increasing the money supply at the same rate as the growth in real national income

2. Monetary accommodation of an isolated supply shock
   (a) serves to moderate the price level increase
   (b) causes the initial rise in the price level to be followed by a further rise
   (c) forces the economy into an extended recession
   (d) causes a higher level of unemployment than would have been the case

3. Wage-cost push inflation emanating from labor markets is a type of
   (a) inflation caused by demand shocks
   (b) equilibrium
   (c) recurring supply shock inflation
   (d) nonlimiting inflationary process without monetary accommodation

4. If an isolated supply shock is not accommodated by monetary policy, the consequence will be
   (a) a rise in output
   (b) accelerating inflation
   (c) another supply shock
   (d) creation or expansion of a recessionary gap

5. All but which of the following will result with monetary validation of a single demand shock?
   (a) The AD curve shifts rightward, fueled by monetary policy.
   (b) Wages will rise, causing the $SRAS$ curve to shift leftward.
   (c) The price level will rise.
   (d) Real national income will fall.

6. Which one of the following could *not* be the initiating cause of demand shock inflation?
   (a) an increase in the money supply
   (b) an increase in exports
   (c) an increase in the prices of imported goods and services
   (d) an increase in investment expenditure

7. The phrase "validating the inflation" refers to
   (a) *Statistics Canada* providing inflation data to the minister of finance
   (b) the Bank of Canada changing the money supply in response to a supply shock
   (c) an inflationary process created by a balanced budget policy
   (d) the Bank of Canada changing the money supply in response to a demand shock

8. Which of the following will *not* occur if there is an increase in aggregate demand without monetary validation? Assume that the economy was initially at potential GDP.
   (a) Real national income will be restored to its potential level in the long run.
   (b) Both real national income and the price level will increase in the short run.
   (c) The $SRAS$ function will shift leftward because factor prices will eventually increase.
   (d) Both real national income and the price level will be higher in the long run.

9. Which of the following would contribute to rising wage rates and leftward shifts of the *SRAS* curves?
   (a) inflationary gaps
   (b) expectations of inflation
   (c) positive random shocks
   (d) all of the above

10. Which of the following events is *not* likely to cause the *SRAS* curve to shift leftward?
    (a) Productivity falls by 1 percent and wages rise by 1 percent.
    (b) Unit costs rise.
    (c) Productivity rises by 2 percent and wages rise by 3 percent.
    (d) Productivity rises by 4 percent and wages rise by 4 percent.

11. When the measured unemployment rate is below the NAIRU,
    (a) the *SRAS* curve will eventually shift leftward
    (b) demand forces put downward pressure on wages
    (c) potential real national income will rise
    (d) there is a recessionary gap situation

12. According to the acceleration hypothesis of inflation, when there are both an inflationary gap and monetary validation,
    (a) the monetary adjustment mechanism will bring inflation under control
    (b) expectations of inflation will be rising, and this will lead to increases in the actual rate of inflation
    (c) output will be held below its potential so that a recessionary gap occurs
    (d) the rate of inflation will accelerate even though inflationary expectations remain unchanged

13. A pure expectational inflation at a constant rate occurs when
    (a) there is excess demand for labor
    (b) the measured unemployment rate is higher than the NAIRU
    (c) there is no excess aggregate demand
    (d) the *LRAS* curve shifts to the right at a constant rate

14. If the Bank of Canada ceases to validate an entrenched inflation, we would expect
    (a) no further inflation
    (b) a persistent inflationary gap
    (c) stagflation until inflationary expectations are reversed
    (d) an immediate fall in the price level

15. Keynesians and monetarists would agree on all but which one of these statements about inflation?
    (a) Sustained price level increases require monetary accommodations or validation.
    (b) Expectations are an important consideration when devising policies to curb inflation.
    (c) The period of stagflation of an anti-inflationary process will always be of short duration.
    (d) An entrenched inflation requires demand contraction to remove the inflationary gap.

16. In which one of the following cases would an incomes policy be most successful in controlling inflation?
    (a) in conjunction with an expansionary monetary policy, to break entrenched inflation
    (b) in conjunction with a contractionary monetary policy, to break entrenched inflation
    (c) alone, as a permanent solution to demand inflation
    (d) alone, as a well-publicized substitute for contractionary monetary and fiscal policy

17. If labor and management expect 5 percent inflation, a recessionary gap is forecast to reduce (moderate) wage demands by 3 percent, and no random shocks are anticipated, a reasonable forecast for wage inflation might be
    (a) 8 percent, which will cause a rightward shift in the *SRAS* curve
    (b) 2 percent, which will cause a rightward shift in the *SRAS* curve
    (c) 8 percent, but the *SRAS* curve is unaffected since there are no random shocks
    (d) 2 percent, which will cause a leftward shift in the *SRAS* curve

Questions 18 through 21 refer to the following graph.

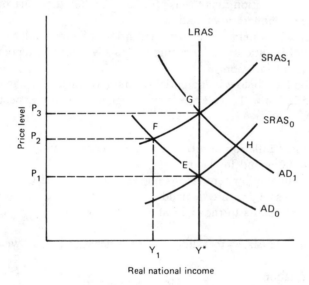

18. Starting from equilibrium at point *E*, if a supply shock shifts the *SRAS* curve from $SRAS_0$ to $SRAS_1$ and there is no monetary accommodation,
    (a) the recessionary gap puts downward pressure on wages and prices, slowly shifting *SRAS* back downward to $SRAS_0$
    (b) aggregate demand will increase from AD_0 to AD_1
    (c) the long-run equilibrium will be at point *G*
    (d) the long-run equilibrium will be at point *F*

19. Starting from equilibrium at point *E*, if the short-run aggregate supply curve shifts from $SRAS_0$ to $SRAS_1$ and there is complete monetary accommodation,
    (a) real national income would temporarily fall to Y_1, then be restabilized at Y^*
    (b) the aggregate demand curve would shift to the right to pass through point *G*
    (c) the price level will rise to P_3, assuming that no inflationary expectations are generated
    (d) all of the above

20. Starting from equilibrium at point E, the aggregate demand curve shifts from AD_0 to AD_1. If there is no monetary validation, long-run equilibrium will be at
    (a) point H, if no inflationary expectations are generated
    (b) point E, because the AD curve shifts leftward when the price level rises
    (c) point G, if no inflationary expectations are generated
    (d) point F, because the AD curve shifts leftward if inflationary expectations are generated

21. Starting from equilibrium at point E, the aggregate demand curve shifts from AD_0 to AD_1. If there is no monetary validation or accommodation,
    (a) the price level may temporarily increase to more than P_3 because of inflationary expectations
    (b) a recessionary gap may be temporarily created because of inflationary expectations
    (c) long-run equilibrium will be at point G, even though short-run inflationary expectations have been created
    (d) all of the above

Exercises

1. Briefly explain each concept and illustrate it on the graph.
   (a) Monetary accommodation of a single supply shock

   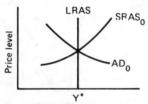

   (b) A single supply shock with no monetary accommodation

   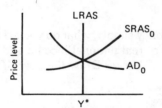

   (c) A demand shock with no monetary validation

   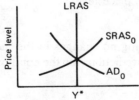

(d) Validated demand-shock inflation

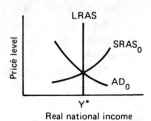

2. This exercise focuses on eliminating entrenched inflation. Suppose that an economy has for some time been experiencing inflation that has been validated by monetary policy. The starting point for this example is point A in the graph.

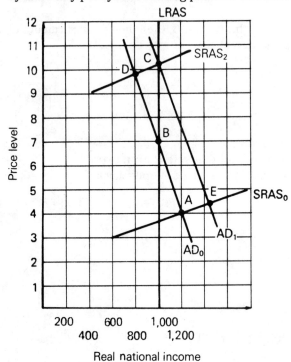

Real national income

(a) If the central bank stops expanding the money supply, what do you predict will happen during phase 1 to the levels of real national income and the price level? What will happen to the $SRAS$ curve? Draw the new $SRAS$ curve and label it $SRAS_1$.

(b) During phase 2, inflationary expectations are still present such that the $SRAS$ curve shifts to $SRAS_2$. Indicate the new (temporary) equilibrium point on the graph. What is the value of the recessionary gap? What are the values for real national income and the price level?

(c) After expectations are reversed, and assuming no changes in the money supply (AD remains at AD_0), what are your predictions for the equilibrium levels of real national income and price?

(d) Suppose in phase 3 that expectations are reversed *but* the central bank increases the money supply sufficiently to shift the *AD* curve to AD_1. What will be the equilibrium levels of real national income and price?

3. The following graph illustrates an initial equilibrium at point E with real national income Y_0 and price level P_0. Y^* is potential national income.

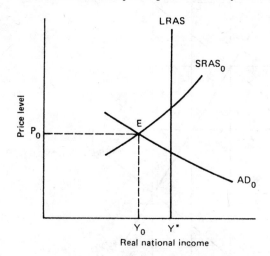

(a) If an increase in the money supply stimulated demand enough to achieve potential national income, draw the new aggregate demand curve and indicate the new price level.

(b) Suppose that the resulting rise in the price level in (a) caused expectations that inflation would occur in the future, and as a result, wages rose throughout the economy. Show on the graph what would happen to the *SRAS* curve. What will be the immediate consequence for real national income and the price level?

(c) If the supply shock that occurred in (b) was fully accommodated, what would happen to the aggregate demand curve? Illustrate on the graph.

4. Suppose that an economy has been experiencing accelerating inflation, a process
    that has involved central bank validation and accommodation of demand and
    supply shocks. In this exercise we trace out the consequences of reversing this
    process. Our analysis starts from the equilibrium shown by the intersection of
    AD_0 and $SRAS_0$. Potential national income is $3 trillion.

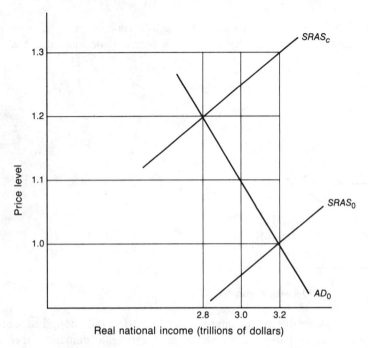

Real national income (trillions of dollars)

(a) Is there an inflationary or recessionary gap at the initial equilibrium? If
    so, how large is it?

(b) Show the shift in the $SRAS$ curve that would be necessary to restore real
    wages to the level consistent with the nonaccelerating inflationary rate of
    unemployment (NAIRU). What are the price level and real income at this
    point?

(c) Suppose that wages are increased not only to compensate for past inflation,
    thereby restoring the equilibrium level of real wages, but even further to
    offset the expected erosion of real wages as the rate of inflation is
    anticipated to increase. This situation is shown by $SRAS_c$. Is there an
    inflationary or a recessionary gap at this point? How large is it?

(d) If the central bank accommodates this shock, draw in the new AD curve
    that would be appropriate. What will be the new price level and national
    income?

(e) If the central bank decides not to accommodate this shock, under what
    circumstances will rising labor productivity help the economy reach
    potential real income again?

Answers

Multiple-Choice Questions

1. (b)   2. (b)   3. (c)   4. (d)   5. (d)   6. (c)   7. (d)   8. (d)   9. (d)   10. (d)   11. (a)   12. (b)
13. (c)   14. (c)   15. (c)   16. (b)   17. (d)   18. (a)   19. (d)   20. (c)   21. (d)

Exercises

1. (a)   Monetary accommodation of a single supply shock causes costs, the price level, and money supply all to move in the same direction. The supply shock is represented in the leftward shift of the $SRAS$ curve; monetary accommodation shifts the AD curve rightward. Equilibrium shifts from E_0 to E_2.

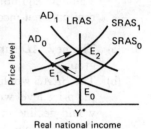

   (b)   The supply curve shifts to the left as a result of the supply shock, but without monetary accommodation, unemployment puts downward pressure on wages and costs, shifting the $SRAS$ curve back to $SRAS_0$.

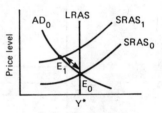

   (c)   The demand shock shifts the AD curve and creates an inflationary gap; this causes wages to rise, shifting the $SRAS$ curve to the left. The monetary adjustment mechanism causes movement along the AD curve, with the rise in price level eliminating the inflationary gap (at E_2).

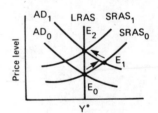

   (d)   The adjustment process in (c) is frustrated with monetary validation; increases in the money supply shift the AD curve to the right, and inflation is sustained. The economy moves along the vertical path indicated by the arrow.

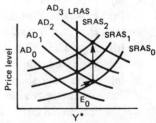

2. (a)   Under the combined influence of an inflationary gap and expectations of continued inflation, wages continue to rise, and the $SRAS$ curve thus continues to shift. In terms of the graph, the $SRAS$ curve shifts leftward to $SRAS_1$ and intersects the $LRAS$ curve at point B. At this point, real national income is at its potential level (1,000), and the price level is 7.

   (b)   Continuing price expectations shift the $SRAS$ curve up to $SRAS_2$. This curve intersects AD_0 at point D. A recessionary gap of 200 has been created. Real national income is 800, and the price level is 10.

(c) The recessionary gap is likely to reduce inflationary expectations and therefore wage rates. Hence the SRAS curve will tend to shift rightward (slowly) to point B ($SRAS_1$). There will be a movement along AD_0 from point D to point B, at which the price level is 7 and the economy is producing at its potential level.

(d) This question differs from (c) in that the central banking authority increases the money supply, perhaps to speed up the process of attaining potential national income. The AD curve shifts rightward with monetary expansion. The new equilibrium point is point C, at which the price level is 10 and real national income is 1,000.

3. (a) The new AD curve is AD_1 and the price level is P_1. (See accompanying graph.)

(b) The SRAS would shift to the left, for example, $SRAS_1$ in the graph, and the price level would rise further (along AD_1) to P_2. Real national income would decline to Y_1.

(c) The aggregate demand curve would shift to AD_2. (See graph.)

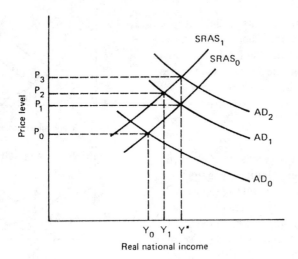

4. (a) $P = 1.0$, $Y = 3.2$; inflationary gap of $200 billion

(b) $P = 1.1$, $Y = 3.0$

(c) $P = 1.2$, $Y = 2.8$; recessionary gap of $200 billion

(d) $P = 1.25$, $Y = 3.0$. If the original demand shock that led to AD_0 were validated, the new equilibrium would be $P = 1.3$, $Y = 3.2$.

(e) If the wage shock is not accommodated, the real wage rate will rise. If labor productivity rises faster than nominal wages, unit labor costs will fall and the SRAS curve will shift rightward. A decline in unit labor costs due to a fall in nominal wages is less likely to occur.

Chapter 37

Employment and Unemployment

Learning Objectives

After studying this chapter, you should be able to:

—distinguish voluntary from involuntary unemployment

—describe the change in the composition of employment between the goods and service sectors and among the various subsectors within the service sector

—define frictional, structural, cyclical, real-wage, and search unemployment and indicate their relative importance during various periods in the Canadian economy

—understand the factors that determine each type of unemployment and identify the appropriate policy measures for dealing with each type

—explain the factors that can change the level of Canada's natural rate of unemployment (NAIRU)

—explain how the various types of unemployment can be measured in a vacancy-unemployment diagram

Multiple-Choice Questions

1. Voluntary unemployment
   (a) occurs when there is a job available but the unemployed person is unwilling to accept it at the existing wage
   (b) is of more concern to policymakers than involuntary unemployment
   (c) increases substantially during a deep recession
   (d) occurs when a person is willing to accept a job at the going wage rate but no such job can be found

2. Unemployment that occurs as a result of the normal turnover of labor as people move from job to job is called
   (a) involuntary unemployment
   (b) structural unemployment
   (c) cyclical unemployment
   (d) frictional unemployment

3. The existence of structural unemployment means that
   (a) there is an inadequate number of jobs in the economy
   (b) the building trades workers, particularly those in structural steel, are suffering high rates of unemployment
   (c) the composition of the demand for labor does not match the composition of available supply
   (d) cyclical unemployment must also be present

4. Search unemployment
   (a) may be a form of voluntary frictional unemployment
   (b) will tend to increase if search costs are low
   (c) occurs when members of the labor force look for more suitable jobs
   (d) all of the above

5. The unemployment rate is defined as the percentage of
   (a) unemployed to employed workers
   (b) the adult population that is unemployed
   (c) the labor force that is unemployed
   (d) the labor force that is collecting unemployment insurance

6. Which of the following does *not* usually explain the creation of structural unemployment?
   (a) economic adjustments created by changes in input mixes
   (b) changes in the composition of the labor force
   (c) disequilibrium structures of relative wages across markets
   (d) contractionary monetary policy

7. The unemployment that exists when there is a recessionary gap is called
   (a) structural unemployment   (c) natural unemployment
   (b) cyclical unemployment   (d) frictional unemployment

8. If an economy has achieved its NAIRU, it follows that
   (a) the measured unemployment rate is necessarily zero
   (b) any unemployment consists of frictional or structural unemployment or both
   (c) the value of the output gap is zero
   (d) both (b) and (c)

9. Real-wage unemployment will exist if the
   (a) real-wage rate is above the equilibrium real-wage rate
   (b) real-wage rate is below the equilibrium real-wage rate
   (c) aggregate demand for labor is equal to the aggregate supply of labor at a particular real-wage rate
   (d) real-wage rate index is not 100

10. The real product wage is defined as the
    (a) marginal product of labor times the real-wage rate
    (b) nominal cost of labor to the employer (excluding any taxes or fringe benefits) divided by the CPI
    (c) nominal cost of labor to the employer (including any taxes or fringe benefits) divided by the CPI
    (d) nominal cost of labor to the employer (including payroll taxes and fringe benefits) divided by the value of the output of labor in the same time period

11. The measured unemployment rate may underestimate the actual unemployment rate because
    (a) it includes people who have voluntarily withdrawn from the labor force
    (b) part-time workers are not counted as members of the labor force
    (c) it omits discouraged workers who have voluntarily withdrawn from the labor force
    (d) it omits those who are actively searching for work but who are unable to find work

12. Which of the following is *not* correct?
    (a) Unemployment insurance likely increases search unemployment.
    (b) It is neither possible nor perhaps desirable to reduce unemployment to zero.
    (c) Frictional unemployment in an economy such as Canada's is inevitable.
    (d) A rise in the real product wage caused by expansionary monetary policy will reduce unemployment.

13. A rise in the real product wage will, other things being equal, cause all of the following except
    (a) the shutdown of firms that are no longer able to cover their variable costs
    (b) an increase in unemployment
    (c) a tendency for firms to build new labor-intensive plants
    (d) investment in new, more capital-intensive production processes to be undertaken in the long run

14. Which of the following has *not* contributed to the increase in the NAIRU in Canada?
    (a) economic expansion in the late 1980s
    (b) changes in the composition of the labor force
    (c) increased wage and price rigidity, which serves to slow down economic adjustment
    (d) input price shocks from foreign sources

15. Which of the following policies would be appropriate for reducing the level of cyclical unemployment?
    (a) The Bank of Canada sells large volumes of government bonds in the open market.
    (b) The federal government increases personal income taxes.
    (c) The province of Alberta cuts back on its expenditures to education.
    (d) The city of Moncton increases its expenditures on public housing construction.

16. Which of the following would be appropriate for reducing structural unemployment?
    (a) more effective job training programs
    (b) increases in the minimum wage in all provinces
    (c) policies designed to promote more labor-saving technological change
    (d) none of the above

17. Which one of the following statements concerning demographic characteristics and unemployment rates is incorrect?
    (a) Young and inexperienced workers have higher unemployment rates than experienced workers.
    (b) In the recent past, there has been a large increase in the number of households with more than one income earner.
    (c) An increasing percentage of households with two earners tends to increase search unemployment.
    (d) An increasing number of inexperienced workers in the labor force decreases frictional and structural unemployment.

18. Which of the following does not accurately reflect the changes in the composition of employment in Canada over the past 25 years?
    (a) The highest annual growth rates in employment have been in the service sector.
    (b) The lowest annual growth rates in employment have been in primary industries.
    (c) Although annual growth rates in employment in the goods sector have been low, this sector continues to employ the largest share of workers.
    (d) Some of the highest annual growth rates in employment have been in the business, financial, health, and social services sectors.

19. Unemployment will increase if
    (a) the destruction of old jobs is greater than the creation of new jobs, assuming that the labor force does not change
    (b) the net creation of new jobs falls below the net increase in the size of the labor force
    (c) the destruction of old jobs is equal to the creation of new jobs and there is an increase in the labor force
    (d) all of the above

20. *Hysteresis* means that an increase in cyclical unemployment may
    (a) decrease the level of frictional and structural unemployment
    (b) increase the probability that new labor force participants will receive job training during and after a recession
    (c) increase the level of the NAIRU
    (d) both (a) and (b)

21. Efficiency wage theories suggest that
    (a) wages readily fall in response to excess supply in labor markets
    (b) employers may get a more efficient work force when labor is paid more than the minimum amount that would induce workers to work for them
    (c) wages must be competitively determined for workers to be efficient
    (d) workers are paid primarily on the basis of the efficiency of management and supervisors

Exercises

1. Classify the following situations as frictional unemployment, structural unemployment, search unemployment, real-wage unemployment, or cyclical unemployment, and briefly explain your choice.

   (a) An auto assembly worker is laid off because auto sales decrease during a slowdown in economic activity.

   (b) Firms lay off workers when real-wage costs increase due to higher unemployment insurance premiums paid by these firms.

   (c) An engineer refuses a job offer and decides to look for another job that has a higher rate of remuneration.

   (d) A social worker is laid off because the city of Toronto cancels one of its social welfare programs.

   (e) A brewery worker in Regina is laid off when the firm relocates its production to Saskatoon.

   (f) Stenographers are laid off as Vancouver firms introduce word processing equipment into their offices.

   (g) Systems analysts lose their jobs as firms curtail projects due to slumping sales.

2. The following graph depicts the demand and supply curves of labor in a particular industry. We assume that both curves depend on the real product wage rate. The current price of the output produced in this industry is $4 per unit, the wage rate is $9, and the other costs such as fringe benefits and payroll taxes (such as public health care and unemployment insurance) are $3 per worker.

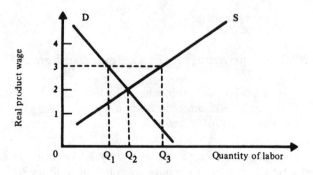

(a)   What is the current value of the real product wage rate?

(b)   Given the current real product wage rate, what situation exists in the labor market of this industry?

(c)   What policy recommendations might you make?

3.   What specific government policy would you recommend for each of the following causes of unemployment? Explain briefly.
(a)   Structural unemployment caused by sectoral shifts in demand

(b)   Cyclical unemployment

(c)   Longer search unemployment caused by generous unemployment insurance benefits

(d)   Real-wage unemployment

*4.   An economy has a constant labor force of 40 million participants and an unemployment-vacancy (uv) curve shown as uv_1.

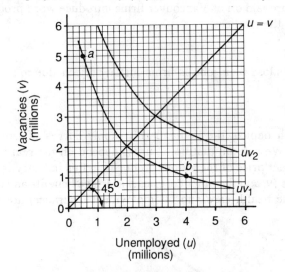

(a)   What is its NAIRU in percentage terms according to the graph? Explain.

(b)   If the economy is currently at point b, what is its total unemployment rate? Does this point depict an economic slump or a boom? Is there any cyclical or possibly real-wage unemployment?

(c)   What is the unemployment rate if the economy is operating at point a? Does this situation represent an economic boom or a slump?

(d) Suppose that the economy's *uv* curve shifted upward as shown in the graph by the curve uv_2. Explain what has happened to the NAIRU. What will be the measured unemployment rate if cyclical unemployment is 2 percent?

Answers

Multiple-Choice Questions

1. (a) 2. (d) 3. (c) 4. (d) 5. (c) 6. (d) 7. (b) 8. (d) 9. (a) 10. (d) 11. (c) 12. (d) 13. (c) 14. (a) 15. (d) 16. (a) 17. (d) 18. (c) 19. (d) 20. (c) 21. (b)

1. (a) Cyclical, because of the slowdown in economic activity.
   (b) Real-wage unemployment. Real product wage rates have been increased by the higher unemployment insurance premiums, and hence firms are forced to lay off workers, perhaps through plant shutdowns.
   (c) Search or voluntary frictional unemployment. The engineer refused a job because of the expectation of finding another job with a higher rate of remuneration.
   (d) Frictional if short-term, structural if the social worker is unable to find work after a prolonged search.
   (e) Frictional if short-term, structural if the brewery worker cannot find work in Regina or refused to move to Saskatoon.
   (f) Structural; stenographers may have to undergo retraining in order to acquire skills required by word processing equipment or other types of occupation. It would be frictional if the stenographers could find office work elsewhere.
   (g) If the reduction in sales is a result of a general economic recession, cyclical unemployment exists. Conversely, the sales reduction may be due to a sectoral shift away from these firms, in which case the unemployment is frictional if the system analysts find work elsewhere easily or structural if their unemployment is of long duration.

2. (a) The real product wage rate is ($9 + $3)/$4 = $3.
   (b) According to the graph, the equilibrium real product wage rate is $2. The current real product wage rate causes unemployment equal to $Q_3 - Q_1$.
   (c) A policy designed to lower costs, such as a decrease in nominal wages, might be appropriate. The reduction in the purchasing power of workers is not likely to have much effect on the demand curve for this industry's product.

3. (a) Retraining and relocation grants to make movement of labor easier; policies to improve information about existing and (possibly) future employment opportunities.
   (b) Expansionary fiscal and monetary policies.
   (c) Any policy changes are bound to be controversial. Current provisions may be enforced more strictly, or you may recommend changes in unemployment provisions such as reduced weeks or lower weekly benefits.
   (d) The real wage must be cut while aggregate demand is increased to counteract any deflationary pressure caused by the falling purchasing power of workers whose nominal wage rates are cut.

*4. (a) The *uv* curve intersects the 45° line at 2 million unemployed. Since total vacancies equal total unemployed at this intersection, the economy has no cyclical or real-wage unemployment. Thus its NAIRU is 5 percent (2/40 × 100 percent).

   (b) At point *b* there are 4 million unemployed workers and only 1 million vacancies. The economy is experiencing an economic slump. Its total unemployment rate is 10 percent. Since its NAIRU is 5 percent, cyclical and/or real-wage unemployment must be 2 million, or 5 percent of the labor force.

   (c) Point *a* represents an economic boom; vacancies far exceed the unemployed. The graph indicates that there are 500,000 unemployed workers, which represents an unemployment rate of 1.25 percent. Hence the measured unemployment rate is below the economy's NAIRU.

   (d) Structural and/or frictional unemployment must have increased. The new *uv* curve intersects the 45° line at 3 million. Hence the economy's NAIRU must now be 7.5 percent (3/40 × 100 percent). If cyclical unemployment is 2 percent, it is likely that the measured unemployment rate will be 9.5 percent.

Chapter 38

Economic Growth

Learning Objectives

After reading this chapter, you should be able to:

—distinguish between, on the one hand, once-and-for-all increases in real GDP caused by increases in aggregate demand and reductions in structural unemployment, and on the other hand, economic growth, which increases potential GDP due to changes in factor supplies or in the productivity of factors

—explain both the long-run and short-run effects of investment and saving on real national income

—recognize the cumulative nature of growth

—describe the income-raising potential of economic growth relative to that achieved either by removing inefficiencies or by redistributing the existing national income

—cite the factors that affect economic growth

—portray two different types of growth models: neo-classical models, which stress diminishing returns to capital and shifts in the *MEC* curve, and increasing returns models

—distinguish between embodied and disembodied technical change

—compare the costs, including the loss of current consumption, with the benefits of economic growth

—understand the repercussions of economic growth on resource depletion and the environment

Multiple-Choice Questions

1. Economic growth is best defined as
    (a) a rise in real national income as unemployment is reduced
    (b) fluctuations of GDP around its potential level
    (c) a rise in potential national income due to increases in factor supplies or in the productivity of factors
    (d) increases in real GDP as structural unemployment decreases

2. In the long run, an increase in saving, other things being equal, is likely to
    (a) cause the aggregate demand curve to shift to the left
    (b) cause real national income to fall
    (c) increase economic growth because more investment expenditure can be financed from these funds
    (d) reduce structural unemployment and therefore increase potential GDP

3. According to the "rule of 72," a growth in population of 2 percent per year means that population will double in approximately
    (a) 2 years   (c) 36 years
    (b) 72 years   (d) 260 years

4. Suppose that two countries have the same per capita output. Country A has an annual economic growth rate of 6 percent, while country B grows at 3 percent per year. According to the rule of 72, country A will have a per capita output four times as large as country B's in
    (a) 12 years   (c) 36 years
    (b) 24 years   (d) 48 years

5. The marginal efficiency of capital curve
    (a) relates the stock of capital to the price of an additional unit of capital
    (b) is generally assumed to slope downward as a consequence of the law of diminishing returns
    (c) relates investment to the rate of interest
    (d) both (a) and (b)

6. A contemporary view of the relationships among economic growth, increasing economic efficiency, and income redistribution is that
    (a) all three are interrelated
    (b) the income-raising potential of economic growth exceeds that of the other two
    (c) achieving one of them may have unfavorable effects on the others
    (d) all of the above

7. Neo-Classical growth theory, which assumes capital accumulation *without* innovation and learning, predicts that
    (a) the capital-output ratio will fall over the course of time
    (b) growth opportunities increase because the marginal efficiency of capital increases for successive increments in the capital stock
    (c) more and more investment opportunities appear over time
    (d) growth opportunities decline as successive increases in capital accumulation become less and less productive as investment opportunities are used up

8. A neo-Classical growth theory *with* innovation and learning predicts that
   (a) constant economic growth is possible if investment opportunities are created but at a slower rate than they are used up
   (b) despite large amounts of capital accumulation, the marginal efficiency of capital may remain constant or even increase as new investment opportunities are created
   (c) economic growth potential must decline even if innovation and learning shift the *MEC* curve outward over time
   (d) the marginal efficiency of capital is subject to increasing returns, not diminishing returns

9. Which of the following is *not* a feature of the increasing returns theory of economic growth?
   (a) Firms that first develop new investment opportunities receive low initial rates of return because of high fixed costs.
   (b) Investors who follow "pioneer" investors face increasing costs and therefore increasing returns.
   (c) Once a technological breakthrough has been made, new investors garner high rates of return since this technology is usually available to them.
   (d) Once a pioneer firm has resolved any product flaws or any customer resistance to a new product, new investors can receive high rates of return.

10. An *embodied* technical change is one that
   (a) improves the quality of labor
   (b) involves increases in the productive capacity of capital goods
   (c) is concerned with improved techniques of managerial control
   (d) involves changes in the organization of production

11. Which of the following is least likely to increase the potential for economic growth?
   (a) population growth, which has the effect of reducing capital growth
   (b) improvements in health that reduce absenteeism and illness among labor force participants
   (c) increases in the capacity to develop and market new innovations in products and production processes
   (d) improvement in labor productivity generated by on-the-job training programs and/or a better-educated labor force

12. According to the Brundtland Commission, *sustainable development*
   (a) is development that meets the needs of the present without compromising the ability of future generations to meet their own needs
   (b) means that the environment imposes no limits on sustained economic growth
   (c) entails governments ignoring the detrimental effects of growth on the environment, thereby encouraging the private sector to expand capital as rapidly as possible
   (d) requires advanced countries to limit their donations of financial capital to third-world countries in order to guarantee sustainable development

13. Which of the following is least likely to be an appropriate government policy for sustaining an advanced industrial economy's competitive advantage?
    (a) revise government policy that has inhibited competition
    (b) change the tax system in order to promote consumption and to discourage saving
    (c) phase out traditional subsidization policies supporting industries that cannot compete in the long run
    (d) provide tax advantages to R&D activities that have the greatest potential of increasing the competitiveness of many industries

14. An increase in economic growth
    (a) will usually require a reduction in the proportion of current national income consumed
    (b) will require an economy to decrease its savings ratio
    (c) will be aided by high real interest rates
    (d) can be accomplished only by accumulating more and more capital

15. Which of the following would normally *not* be considered a benefit of economic growth?
    (a) raising living standards
    (b) increasing the inequality of income distribution
    (c) making it easier to achieve some types of income redistribution
    (d) technological changes, stimulated by economic growth, that produce substitutes for dwindling resource stocks and have the least detrimental environmental impact

16. For the economy as a whole, the primary opportunity cost of economic growth is
    (a) borne by future generations, whose living standards will be reduced
    (b) the reduction in living standards for the current generation of consumers
    (c) the increased poverty that inevitably results from economic growth
    (d) both (b) and (c)

17. All but which of the following have been sources of rapid economic growth in Korea and Japan?
    (a) improved production technology
    (b) policies to encourage investment in manufacturing and export-sensitive sectors
    (c) increases in the quality of labor
    (d) increases in the productivity of labor caused by a decreasing labor force

Exercises

1. Assume that the productivity of labor increases by 2.5 percent a year, the labor force increases by 1.75 percent a year, hours worked per member of the work force decline by 0.25 percent a year, and population increases by 1 percent a year.

   (a) Predict the annual increase in real national income.

   (b) Predict the annual increase in per capita real national income.

   (c) Predict the number of years to double real national income.

   (d) Predict the number of years to double per capita real national income.

2. Indicate how each of the following factors would probably affect standards of living as measured by real consumption per capita, now and a few years from now. Use + for an increase, − for a decrease, and U for no change or too uncertain to call (the first blank is for the current effect, the second for the future effect). Assume other things remaining constant and full employment of resources.

   (a) an increase in the birthrate _____ _____
   (b) a decrease in current saving _____ _____
   (c) a technological innovation reducing input requirements _____ _____
   (d) an increase in current expenditures for technical education financed by increased taxes _____ _____
   (e) a decrease in the working life span of the labor force _____ _____
   (f) an increase in labor force participation _____ _____

3. Suppose that an economy has a marginal efficiency of capital curve as shown here. The current (equilibrium) capital stock is 50, and potential real national income and current real national income are 300.

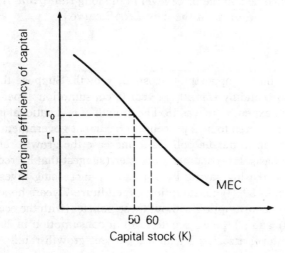

(a) Suppose that the capital stock increases to 60. Show this event in the graph in a way that is consistent with the neo-Classical growth model without innovation, and briefly explain your answer.

(b) Show this event in the graph in a way that is consistent with a neo-Classical growth model with innovation that assumes that investment occurs at exactly the same rate as investment opportunities.

(c) Suppose that the multiplier value (which allows for price changes) is 1.2. What are the likely changes in the equilibrium values of price and real national income in the short run? Use the accompanying graph in making your forecasts. The AD curve labeled AD_1 represents the new aggregate demand curve with a capital stock of 60.

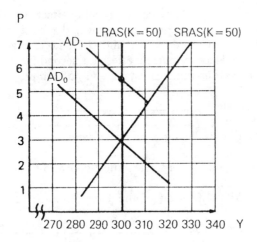

(d) Ignoring the distinction between growth with and without innovation, suppose that the 20 percent increase in the capital stock increases potential real national income by 10 percent. What are your predictions for the levels of real national income and the price level in the long run? (*Hint*: Assume that AD_1 is linear, and draw in the new $LRAS$ curve.)

4. This exercise focuses on the opportunity costs of growth. Suppose that the national income of an economy was 100 in year 0, consumption expenditure was 85, and investment expenditure was 15. The growth of real national income on an annual basis is expected to be 2 percent. The current government urges the citizens of this nation to pursue policies to increase the growth rate to 4 percent on an annual basis. Its economic forecasters suggest that by reducing consumption to 70 (increasing saving by 15) and by increasing investment expenditure to a level of 30, (1) consumption expenditure 7 years hence will be equal to that level of consumption without these policies (with the economy growing at 2 percent), and (2) the aggregate level of consumption in 20 years would be *double* the level associated with a 2 percent growth rate.

Annual Level of Consumption

Year	2 Percent growth	4 Percent growth	Cumulative (loss) or gain
0	85.0	70.0	(15.0)
1	86.7	72.9	(28.8)
2	88.5	75.8	(41.5)
3	90.3	78.9	(52.9)
4	92.1	82.1	(62.9)
7	97.8	92.6	(83.3)
8	99.7	96.4	(86.6)
9	101.8	100.3	(88.1)
10	103.8	104.4	(87.5)
17	119.4	138.2	(14.9)
18	121.8	143.8	7.1
20	126.8	155.8	61.5
30	154.9	232.4	
40	189.2	346.7	
50	231.1	517.2	

Your task is to confirm the accuracy of the government's economic forecasts by answering the following questions.

(a) What is the loss in consumption in year 4 because of the government's growth policy? What is the cumulative loss after four years?

(b) In what year will the level of consumption with a 4 percent growth rate equal the level of consumption with a 2 percent growth rate? Compare your answer with the government's assertion.

(c) In what year does this economy recoup all of the cumulative losses in forgone consumption?

(d) Is the government's assertion that this society will double its consumption level in 20 years correct?

Answers

Multiple-Choice Questions

1. (c)   2. (c)   3. (c)   4. (d)   5. (b)   6. (d)   7. (d)   8. (b)   9. (b)   10. (b)   11. (a)   12. (a)
13. (b)   14. (a)   15. (b)   16. (b)   17. (d)

Exercises

1. (a) 4 percent (2.5 + 1.75 − 0.25)
   (b) 3 percent (4 percent − 1 percent)
   (c) 18 = 72/4 (rule of 72)
   (d) 24 = 72/3 (rule of 72)

2. (a) −, U; increases the number of nonworking dependents in the population
       now; within a few years, little effect on standard of living but possibly
       increased output in the long run with increased labor supply
   (b) +, −; current increase in consumption; reduction in future output
   (c) U, +; current effect depends on investment required if "embodied"
   (d) −, +; contribution to intangible capital, increasing production in future
   (e) −, −; reduces proportion of productive population (immediate effect may
       be negligible, so U would also be acceptable)
   (f) +, +; more producers for a given population

3. (a) The neo-Classical view emphasizes the exploitation of existing opportunities
       with no "learning." Hence you would predict a movement down the MEC
       curve such that the marginal efficiency of capital falls to r_1 at a capital
       stock of 60.
   (b) The MEC curve would shift to the right. With the assumption that
       investment occurs at the same rate as investment opportunities, the
       marginal efficiency of capital would remain at r_0 at a capital stock of 60.
   (c) The increase in the capital stock (investment) is 10, and with a multiplier
       value of 1.2, real national income in the short run will increase to 312 (an
       increase of 12). According to the diagram, the new short-run price level
       is approximately 4.6.
   (d) The increase in the capital stock increases potential real national income
       by 30 (to a level of 330). Hence the $LRAS$ curve will shift to the right; it
       is a vertical line at $Y = 330$. By extending the AD_1 line down and to the
       right, you should forecast a new long-run equilibrium price level of 3.0.

4. (a) The loss in consumption is 10 (92.1 − 82.1); 62.9 is the cumulative loss.
   (b) According to the schedule, consumption (C) at 4 percent growth will equal
       C at 2 percent growth sometime in years 9 and 10. This is substantially
       longer than suggested by the government.
   (c) Sometime between the seventeenth and eighteenth years.
   (d) No; it is much later. According to the schedule, C at 4 percent growth is
       double C at 2 percent growth in approximately 45 years.
       (*Note*: All calculations assume annual compounding.)

Chapter 39

Government Budget Deficits

Learning Objectives

After studying this chapter, you should be able to:

—review recent trends in the federal government budget deficit, the deficit as a share of GDP, and the debt-to-GDP ratio

—understand that government deficits can be caused by large debt service payments created by the accumulation of national debt

—explain why deficits influence the economy through their short-run stabilizing or destabilizing role and through their potential to affect income and welfare adversely in the long run

—understand the two potential *crowding out* effects of deficits

—explain why the size of debt may hamper economic policy

—cite the economic and political economy implications of measures to reduce the budget deficit or control its growth

Multiple-Choice Questions

1. The value of the Canadian national debt as a share of GDP in the late 1980s was
   (a) slightly more than 50 percent
   (b) lower than its value in the 1960s
   (c) greater than its value during World War II
   (d) equal to the value of the federal government deficit as a share of GDP

2. The *primary budget balance* is defined as
   (a) the total federal deficit minus the value of outstanding debt
   (b) the total federal deficit generated by transfer payments to primary industries
   (c) the total federal deficit excluding debt service payments
   (d) the federal government budget position at potential national income

3. Compared with the 1970 period, debt service payments in the late 1980s
   (a) comprised a higher share of total government revenues
   (b) were a higher proportion of total government expenditures
   (c) represented a higher share of GDP
   (d) all of the above

4. Interest on the national debt as a share of GDP rose rapidly in the 1980s due to
   (a) increases in the interest rate
   (b) rapid growth in the total debt outstanding
   (c) an increase in the ratio of the budget deficit to GDP
   (d) all of the above

5. Some economists worry that the growing deficit is likely to result in higher inflation
   (a) as the government buys a disproportionately large share of total output
   (b) if the Bank of Canada increases its purchases of government securities by the amount of the deficit
   (c) if the Bank of Canada increases its sales of government securities by the amount of the deficit
   (d) if the Bank of Canada refuses to validate the deficit

6. One of the "crowding out" effects of a larger government budget deficit refers to the outcome of
   (a) higher interest rates and less investment
   (b) higher interest rates and more saving
   (c) lower interest rates and more investment
   (d) lower interest rates and less saving

7. An increase in the government budget deficit is more likely to reduce private investment when, other things being equal,
   (a) any additional income is earned by individuals with high marginal propensities to save
   (b) there is a recessionary gap
   (c) the economy is near full employment and saving is unlikely to increase
   (d) foreigners are eager to buy Canadian assets

8. If the capital stock falls as a result of a larger government budget deficit,
   (a) the current standard of living is likely to decline
   (b) the future standard of living is likely to decline
   (c) current national income declines
   (d) the concept of Ricardian neutrality holds

9. Even if the future capital stock is as large as it would have been in the absence of a deficit, future generations may be worse off if this situation is due to
   (a) greater foreign investment, which requires a future transfer to foreigners
   (b) greater personal saving, which means lower consumption
   (c) greater business saving, which means lower dividend payments to stockholders
   (d) all of the above

10. Other things being equal, a country's gross domestic product will exceed its gross national product when
    (a) its residents import more goods than they export
    (b) its capital equipment is fully depreciated
    (c) its potential output exceeds its actual output
    (d) net interest payments must be made to foreigners

11. Some economists are concerned that a large and growing budget deficit
    (a) reduces the government's flexibility to use fiscal policy as a stabilization tool
    (b) results in high interest payments, leaving less revenue for other public needs
    (c) requires higher taxes to make rising interest payments
    (d) all of the above

12. An annually balanced budget would be destabilizing because
    (a) it would lead to too large a government sector and greater economic inefficiency
    (b) it would lead to too small a government sector and inadequate provision of public goods
    (c) aggregate demand would grow faster at all stages of the business cycle
    (d) aggregate demand would be increased in expansions and reduced in contractions

13. Requiring the government budget to be balanced over the business cycle would be a difficult policy to implement because
    (a) studies have shown that the federal government consistently spends too little during recessionary periods
    (b) the federal government has traditionally chosen to use the cyclically adjusted deficit to evaluate fiscal policy
    (c) forecasting business cycles is difficult
    (d) all of the above

14. A deficit will crowd out net exports if
    (a) an interest rate increase causes the external value of the domestic currency to depreciate
    (b) there is a large outflow of international capital
    (c) the deficit attracts more foreign capital, thereby increasing the external value of the domestic currency
    (d) international capital flows are insensitive to interest-rate changes

15. Suppose that the current government deficit is $25 billion and total outstanding debt is $400 billion. If the annual inflation rate is 5 percent, the inflation-adjusted deficit is
    (a) $23.75 billion   (c) $26.25 billion
    (b) $5 billion   (d) $20 billion

16. If GDP grows over time, the goal of a stable debt-to-GDP ratio requires
    (a) a constant value of outstanding debt
    (b) a declining value of outstanding debt over time
    (c) budget deficits so that debt grows at the same rate as GDP
    (d) declining government deficits

17. Which of the following is likely to represent the view of a Keynesian concerning debt?
    (a) Balanced budgets are the only effective means of curtailing reckless spending.
    (b) A growing debt-to-GDP ratio is never a concern since the burden of debt is exactly offset by the interest payments that are made to holders of government bonds.
    (c) Changes in debt may be useful in dealing with short-term output gap situations.
    (d) Increases in debt (caused by increases in the cyclically adjusted deficit) are sound policies during economic expansions.

Exercises

1. This exercise focuses on the crowding-out effect in a closed economy. The country of Zed has a domestic market for financial funds (denominated in zees, abbreviated z). At present, all borrowing and lending occurs in the private sector. The government of Zed plays a completely passive role; it has no expenditures, owes no debt, and collects no tax. The supply of funds (S) in the private sector is given by the equation $S = 10 + 2r + 0.02Y$. The private-sector demand for funds (D) is $D = 60 - 4r$. Both curves represent demand and supply conditions each year; thus they are flow equations. Current GDP is 1,000.
    (a) At $Y = 1,000$, plot these two curves and determine the current equilibrium levels of the interest rate (r) and the total amount of borrowing (in zees) in the private sector.

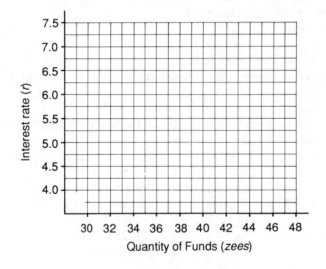

(b) Zed's government wishes to introduce some public programs that will cost
12z. This program will be financed entirely by issuing 12z of long-term
government bonds and selling them in the financial funds market. Hence
the new demand for funds is $D = 72 - 4r$, which is the sum of private
and public borrowing. No taxes are planned. Suppose that the spending
program has no effect on either real GDP or the price level. If the private-
sector supply curve for funds remains stable, determine the new equilibrium
levels for r and total borrowing either by plotting the new demand curve
or by solving algebraically.

(c) At the new equilibrium, what is the level of private-sector borrowing? How
does this compare with private-sector borrowing before the increase in
government borrowing? How much investment has been crowded out?

(d) At the beginning of the year, what is the deficit-to-GDP ratio? What is the
debt-to-GDP ratio? If no debt is redeemed at the end of the year, what debt
service payments will the government of Zed owe? What is its total deficit
at the end of the year?

(e) Suppose that the government spending caused real GDP to increase from
1,000 to 1,150. Derive the expression for the supply of funds equation at
the new GDP level. Why did the supply curve change? Now determine
the new equilibrium levels for the interest rate and borrowing by equating
the new supply curve with the demand curve, $D = 72 - 4r$.

(f) What quantity of private-sector borrowing will be crowded out now?

(g) What are the debt-to-GDP and deficit-to-GDP ratios now?

2. This exercise focuses on continuing deficits, debt accumulation, and debt service
payments. Consider the scenario outlined in exercise 1, parts (a) to (d), in which
Zed's government borrows 12 zees at an interest rate of 7 percent. Government
spending is assumed to have no effect on real GDP. At the end of the first year,
total debt is 12 zees. Zed must also pay for debt service payments of 0.84 zees.
It wishes to continue the public program it initiated in the first year and hence
must borrow 12 zees plus the accrued first year's interest obligations, 0.84 zees,
to finance the deficit in the second year. Tax revenues are still zero.
(a) Assuming that the private-sector demand and supply curves in the second
year are identical to those in the first year, what is the equation for the
total demand for funds in the second year? What is the equilibrium rate
of interest?

(b) What is the accumulated debt at the end of the second year? (Ignore the government's interest liability in the second year of the program.)

(c) At the end of the second year, what is the debt-to-GDP ratio? What proportion of the second-year deficit is the debt service payment?

(d) Zed's citizens make known their intentions to refuse to accept additional debt and demand that the government reduce total existing debt. What options does the government have to achieve a falling debt-to-GDP ratio? (Remember, this question assumes that GDP is not influenced by the government's deficit position.)

3. Can an annually balanced budget be a short-run destabilizing force in the economy? The proof to this proposition involves showing that private-sector shocks have a greater multiplier effect with a balanced budget requirement than without it. Consider the following behavioral equations for the economy of Soo.

$$C = 50 + 0.8(Y - T) \qquad\qquad I = 100$$
$$G = g \qquad\qquad\qquad\qquad\quad X - M = 10 - 0.04Y$$
$$T = 0.2Y \qquad\qquad\qquad\quad\ \text{Potential } Y = 800$$

(a) If $g = 160$, what is the current equilibrium level of Soo's real national income? What is the current budget balance for Soo's government? What is the current value of the output gap?

(b) Now assume that Soo's exports fall by 2 such that the new net export function is $8 - 0.04Y$. Assume also that the price level, the exchange rate, and the interest rate in Soo are unaffected by this change. Determine the new equilibrium levels of Y and the government's budget position. What was the value of the (simple) multiplier? What is the value of the output gap?

(c) Suppose that the conservative forces in Soo's government had been successful in implementing an annually balanced budget requirement before exports fell. Hence in each year g must equal $0.2Y$ (spending equals taxation revenue). Substitute $g = 0.2Y$ into the equation for G and prove that the equilibrium level of Y is 800.

(d) As before, exports fall by 2 such that the net export equation becomes $8 - 0.04Y$. Using the fact that $g = 0.2Y$, solve for the equilibrium level of Y. What is the value of g at the new equilibrium level of Y? What is the multiplier value now? What is the value of the output gap? How does this value compare with that of having no annually balanced budget requirement? Why are they different?

Answers

Multiple-Choice Questions

1. (a)   2. (c)   3. (d)   4. (d)   5. (b)   6. (a)   7. (c)   8. (b)   9. (a)   10. (d)   11. (d)   12. (d)
13. (c)   14. (c)   15. (b)   16. (c)   17. (c)

Exercises

1. (a) $r = 5$ percent and total borrowing (lending) $= 40$ zees.

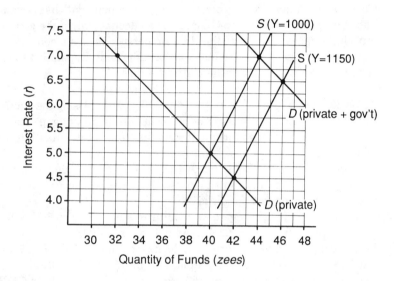

(b) $r = 7$ percent and total borrowing is 44 zees. $72 - 4r = 10 + 2r + 0.02(1,000)$; $r = 7$ percent

(c)   With the original demand curve for funds, private-sector borrowing at an interest rate of 7 percent would have been 32. We know that total borrowing at 7 percent is 44, 12 of which is government borrowing. Thus the crowding out of private-sector borrowing (investment) is $40 - 32$, or 8. Thus total borrowing increased by 4, which represents government borrowing of 12 minus the reduction in private-sector borrowing.

(d)   The deficit-to-GDP and debt-to-GDP ratios are both 1.2 percent. Since the interest rate is 7 percent, debt service payments are 0.84 zees. The total deficit is therefore 12.84 zees.

(e) $S = 10 + 2r + 0.02(1,150)$, or $S = 33 + 2r$. The supply of funds increased because saving increases with the expansion in GDP. The new equilibrium level is 6.5 percent for the interest rate, and total borrowing is 46 zees.

(f)   At an interest rate of 6.5 percent, private-sector borrowing with the original demand curve for funds $(60 - 4r)$ would have been 34. However, since total borrowing at an interest rate of 6.5 percent is 46 and government borrowing is 12, private borrowing is 34. Hence the crowding-out effect is now only 6 zees.

(g)   Both of them are 1.04 percent. Debt service payments at the end of the first year also will be lower than before.

2. (a) The government must borrow 12.84 zees at the beginning of the second year. Thus the total demand for funds equation is $72.84 - 4r$. Assuming that the supply curve is stable at $30 + 2r$, the new equilibrium interest rate is 7.14 percent. Notice that the need to borrow to finance the interest on the debt has increased the interest rate from 7 to 7.14 percent.

   (b) The accumulated debt is 12 (the deficit from the first year) plus 12.84 (the deficit from the second year, including the debt service payments), or 24.84 zees.

   (c) The debt-to-GDP ratio is 2.48 percent. The debt service payments are 6.5 percent of the second-year deficit.

   (d) To stop the deficit from growing, the government will likely cancel its public program. The debt-to-GDP ratio can decline only if the government introduces taxes to pay off the debt or persuades Zed's central bank to increase the money supply to help pay back the debt. Expanding the money supply is likely to cause inflation.

3. (a) $AE = 50 + 0.8(Y - 0.2Y) + 100 + 160 + 10 - 0.04Y$. Using the equilibrium condition $Y = AE$, we obtain $Y = 800$. There is no output gap. The budget is balanced since total government spending equals total taxation revenue of 160.

   (b) The new equilibrium GDP is 795. An export decline of 2 generated a decline in GDP of 5; hence the multiplier is 2.5. There is a recessionary gap of 5 and the government deficit is 1.0.

   (c) The expression for aggregate expenditure is now $50 + 0.8(Y - 0.2Y) + 100 + 0.2Y(= g) + 10 - 0.04Y$. As before, $Y = 800$.

   (d) With the decline in net exports of 2, the new equilibrium GDP is 790. Since total taxation revenue is 158, g must also be 158. The multiplier value is 5 since a decline in net exports of 2 created a reduction of 10 in GDP. The output gap is now 10, which is greater than in part (b), which required no balanced budget. The multiplier with an annually balanced budget requirement is larger because the recessionary gap automatically reduces tax revenue, which must be matched by an equal reduction in government spending. Thus, as the text suggests, an annually balanced budget serves as a *built-in destabilizer*.

Chapter 40

Macroeconomic Controversies

Learning Objectives

After studying this chapter, you should be able to:

—recognize that the disagreement over economic policy dealing with inflation, unemployment, and business cycles depends on differing views regarding the strength of self-correcting market forces and whether government policy improves macroeconomic performance

—distinguish between monetarists (usually identified with noninterventionist views) and Keynesians (usually identified with interventionist views)

—explain the noninterventionists' positions toward policies concerned with full employment, stable prices, and business cycles

—explain the interventionists' positions on these same macroeconomic policies

—understand the contributions of recent revisions to the monetarist and Keynesian models (new classical economics, real business cycle models, and new Keynesian macroeconomics models) in terms of the microeconomic underpinnings of macroeconomics and their implications for macroeconomic policy

Multiple-Choice Questions

1. Economists who advocate that the market system works well enough to preclude any significant constructive role for stabilization policy have been classified as
   (a) Keynesians
   (b) noninterventionists
   (c) post-Keynesians
   (d) interventionists

2. The *k-percent* rule
   (a) is supported by both interventionists and noninterventionists
   (b) calls for the money supply to grow at a constant rate even when there are short-run fluctuations in the demand for money
   (c) calls for the money supply to expand and contract as national income expands and contracts, respectively
   (d) is equivalent to the central bank following an intermediate interest-rate target

3. Which of the following does *not* represent a noninterventionist's view concerning the government's role in providing a stable environment in which the private sector can function?
   (a) the goal of stability in the budget balance
   (b) a "social contract" in which labor, management, and government agree on target wage changes
   (c) a steady growth rate in the money supply that does not vary with economic booms or slumps
   (d) avoiding continual changes in tax rates or government spending because both can create a climate of uncertainty that makes long-term planning difficult

4. Which of the following does *not* represent the views of an interventionist?
   (a) discretionary fiscal and monetary policies to offset significant inflationary and recessionary gaps
   (b) the wage-cost push theory of inflation
   (c) certain types of incomes policies
   (d) an avoidance of fine-tuning policies by government and its central bank

5. On which key feature of a macroeconomic model would monetarists and Keynesians agree?
   (a) In the long run, fluctuations in aggregate demand determine the level of real national income.
   (b) Changes in monetary and fiscal policies cannot give rise to short-run inflationary and recessionary gaps.
   (c) Deviations of national income from its potential level give rise to changes in wages and prices, which, if allowed to operate, will eventually restore full employment.
   (d) Changes in aggregate demand can affect real national income in the long run but not in the short run.

6. Which of the following represents a Keynesian's view concerning the causes of a business cycle?
   (a) Changes in private-sector spending cause short-run fluctuations in real national income.
   (b) Rapid increases and decreases in the money supply can be major sources of economic fluctuations.
   (c) Fluctuations in national income can cause fluctuations in the money supply if a central bank follows an interest-rate target policy.
   (d) All of the above.

7. On which of the following explanations for inflation would Keynesians and monetarists agree?
   (a) Temporary increases in consumption can cause inflation.
   (b) Supply shocks, without accommodation, will cause sustained inflation.
   (c) Sustained inflation requires a sustained expansion of the money supply.
   (d) All of the above.

8. Keynesians
   (a) believe that a recessionary gap will not be self-eliminating in the short run because prices and wages do not adjust downward very rapidly
   (b) do not believe that there is any correlation between changes in the money supply and changes in nominal national income
   (c) believe that the economy is inherently stable because consumption, investment, and net export functions are relatively stable
   (d) all of the above

9 A monetarist
   (a) believes that most unemployment can be considered voluntary
   (b) views most markets as competitive
   (c) believes that the automatic adjustment mechanism is sufficiently strong to ensure that a recessionary gap can be quickly rectified without government intervention
   (d) all of the above

10. The microeconomic model on which traditional Keynesian economics is based consists of
    (a) perfectly competitive markets and an excess supply of labor
    (b) imperfectly competitive markets but flexible prices
    (c) perfectly competitive markets and flexible prices
    (d) imperfectly competitive markets and fairly rigid prices

11. The theory of rational expectations suggests that individuals
    (a) look to current government macroeconomic policy to form their expectations of future inflation
    (b) understand how the economy works and form their expectations about economic behavior rationally
    (c) make random forecasting errors that are neither systematic nor persistent
    (d) all of the above

12. Which of the following is *not* a tenet of the new classical economics?
    (a) Systematic attempts to use monetary policy to stabilize the economy will lead to changes in real GDP.
    (b) Deviations from potential GDP occur only because firms and workers mistake changes in the price level for changes in relative prices.
    (c) Since forecasting errors of the price level are random and unsystematic, they do not permanently affect real economic activity.
    (d) Unsystematic monetary policy will cause people to make mistakes in their output and purchasing decisions and will therefore increase aggregate output fluctuations.

13. According to real business cycle models, cyclical fluctuations are caused by
    (a) changes in real aggregate expenditures such as investment and net exports
    (b) shifts in the *LRAS* curve due to supply shocks
    (c) shifts in the *AD* curve
    (d) all of the above

14. Which of the following explain wage and price rigidity according to new Keynesian macroeconomics?
    (a) Since firms face costs of changing prices, they will change prices at discrete intervals rather than constantly.
    (b) The economy consists of competitive firms that have flat cost curves.
    (c) Although the wages of union members (insiders) are variable, those of nonunion members (outsiders) are rigid.
    (d) Efficiency wage theory indicates that workers are paid the value of their marginal productivity, which tends to be constant in the short run.

15. The implication of rigid prices and wages is that
    (a) cyclical fluctuations in demand will cause employment and output to fluctuate
    (b) the automatic adjustment mechanism may take a long time to eliminate output gaps, particularly recessionary gaps
    (c) stabilizing fiscal and monetary policies may be required to eliminate output gaps
    (d) all of the above

Exercises

1. The text explains that Keynesians are usually identified with interventionist views and monetarists are identified with noninterventionist views. Using your judgment based on how the text develops the opposing positions, insert *M* for monetarist or *K* for Keynesian after each of the following statements.
   (a) Money supply growth should not respond to economic fluctuations. _____
   (b) Cyclical fluctuations in economic activity can be caused by fluctuations in private-sector expenditures. _____
   (c) Markup pricing characterizes few sectors in the Canadian economy. _____
   (d) Short-term decreases in real GDP and increases in the price level can be explained by wage-push factors. _____
   (e) Changes in the money supply may be responses to, rather than the cause of, changes in nominal national income. _____
   (f) Monetary policy is uncertain, variable, powerful, and lagged in its effects; therefore, it should be as neutral as possible. _____
   (g) All inflation is caused by excessive monetary expansion and would not occur without it. _____
   (h) Output gaps can be eliminated rapidly by changes in prices and input prices. _____
   (i) Since wages and prices tend to be rigid downward, a recessionary gap may persist for a prolonged time; expansionary fiscal policy should be used to eliminate the gap. _____
   (j) The major impact of fluctuations in aggregate demand is on output and employment rather than on the price level. _____
   (k) Investment expenditures are highly sensitive to interest-rate changes; monetary policy is therefore a powerful instrument. _____

2. Using your knowledge of how the text develops the opposing positions, insert *NCE* for new classical economics, *RBC* for real business cyclical model, or *NKE* for new Keynesian economics after each of the following statements.

   (a) Cyclical fluctuations can be caused by shifts in the *LRAS* curve.
   _____

   (b) Since firms pay efficiency wages, they may not adjust wages in response to changes in nominal demand. _____

   (c) The Lucas aggregate supply curve posits that national output will vary positively with the ratio of the actual to the expected price level.
   _____

   (d) Since firms are in a better position to bear the risk of economic fluctuations, they are prepared to enter into implicit contracts that give rise to wage rigidity and employment variability. _____

   (e) Short-term fluctuations are caused by unsystematic forecasting errors.
   _____

3. Suppose that a government's budget function is given by $B = tY - G$, where B is the budget position ($B = 0$ is a balanced budget). Current values are $G = 100$, $t = 0.2$, and $Y = 500$. Now suppose that a decline in net exports causes real GDP to fall to 490 but the price level does not change.

   (a) At current values, what is the government's budget position?

   (b) After the decrease in real GDP, what is the government's budget position?

   (c) If the government is committed to a balanced budget at all times, what change in government spending must occur (assuming that t remains constant)? What change in t (assuming that G remains constant) must it make?

   (d) Are the required changes in policy described in (c) procyclical or countercyclical? Would these changes be recommended by a noninterventionist or an interventionist?

   (e) What further economic adjustments would occur according to a noninterventionist?

4. This exercise focuses on the Keynesian view of the endogeneity of money supply and national income. Most economists agree that the money supply and national income move together through time, but the direction of causality is a matter of considerable debate. Suppose that the real demand for money equation is $D_M = 0.8Y - 2r$, where r is the interest rate. The current real money supply is 60 and real national income (Y) is 100.

   (a) What is the current rate of interest?

(b) Suppose that net exports increase such that real national income rises from 100 to 101. If interest rates were allowed to change, what is the new equilibrium level of the interest rate?

(c) Suppose that the central bank is committed to maintaining an interest rate of 10 percent. Given the situation described in (b), what change in the money supply is necessary? You should immediately recognize that the money supply has become endogenous; it has been changed because of the interest-rate target and the change in the demand for money.

5. Suppose that an economy has a real demand for money function given by D_M $= 100 + 2Y - 400r$ and a real stock of money equal to 100. Its potential level of real national income is 800, and equilibrium currently exists in all markets such that the interest rate in percentage terms (r) is 4.0.
    (a) What is the current equilibrium level of real national income (Y)?

    (b) Assume now that private investment expenditure falls, causing real national income to fall to a new equilibrium level of 790. What will happen to the demand for money? If monetary policy were passive what is the new level of the interest rate (to two decimal places)? What is the value of the output gap?

    (c) Although most Keynesians would probably prefer fiscal policy to solve this problem, what increase in the real money supply would Keynesians recommend to eliminate the output gap problem? You must assume that they believe that the interest rate must be lowered to 3.8.

    (d) Suppose that monetarists recommend for monetary expansion a stable 4 percent rule, which they believe is consistent with long-run growth prospects. Would this rate of monetary expansion be sufficient to restore the current level of potential real national income immediately? If not, what arguments might monetarists make to justify their policy stance? What counterarguments might Keynesians make?

Answers

Multiple-Choice Questions

1. (b) 2. (b) 3. (b) 4. (d) 5. (c) 6. (d) 7. (c) 8. (a) 9. (d) 10. (d) 11. (d) 12. (a)
13. (b) 14. (a) 15. (d)

Exercises

1. Some authorities may differ in their interpretation of Keynesian and monetarist views; our classifications are as follows:
   (a) M (b) K (c) M (d) K (e) K (f) M (g) M (h) M (i) K (j) K (k) M

2. (a) RBC (b) NKE (c) NCE (d) NKE (e) NCE

3. (a) At current values, the budget is balanced; $B = 0$.
   (b) Since real GDP falls by 10, tax revenue falls by 2. There is a budget deficit of 2.
   (c) Since the government is committed to a balanced budget, it must either decrease its spending by 2 or increase the tax rate from 0.2 to 0.2041 (100/490).
   (d) Both policies are procyclical since both will cause a larger recessionary gap. Balanced budgets are usually the preference of noninterventionists.
   (e) Although both policies are destabilizing, a noninterventionist believes that the recessionary gap will quickly trigger wage and price cuts that will eliminate the recessionary gap.

4. (a) The interest rate is currently 10 percent according to the equation.
   (b) The interest rate increases from 10.0 to 10.4 percent.
   (c) The money supply would have to increase from 60.0 to 60.8 in order to maintain an interest rate of 10 percent.

5. (a) Solving the equation $100 = 100 + 2Y - 400(4)$, we obtain $Y = 800$.
   (b) If real national income falls to 790, the demand for money will decrease because of lower transactions demand. Since the money supply has not changed, we solve the equation $100 = 100 + 2(790) - 400r$ and obtain a new equilibrium interest rate of 3.95. The decrease in investment has created a recessionary gap of 10.
   (c) If the interest rate must fall to 3.8 percent and real national income is restored to 800, the real money supply must increase to a level of 180 (an increase of 80).

(d) A 4 percent rule of monetary expansion would increase the real money supply to a new level of 104, which, although real income will increase, is inadequate to achieve potential real national income immediately. Monetarists would argue that the self-adjustment mechanisms (price and factor prices falling in a recessionary gap situation) will restore the economy to its potential level of national income. Although the Keynesian policy actually restores potential national income, at least in this hypothetical case, monetarists generally distrust stabilizing monetary policy because of the long and variable lags associated with this policy and the possible confusion and false expectations that it can potentially generate. Keynesians argue that self-adjustments work too slowly, with the result that unemployment will be too high for an unacceptably long period of time. Therefore, active discretionary government intervention is required.

PART ELEVEN

International Macroeconomics

Chapter 41

Exchange Rates and the Balance of Payments

Learning Objectives

After studying this chapter, you should be able to:

—understand that the exchange rate is the reciprocal of the external value of the domestic currency; if the exchange rate appreciates, the domestic currency depreciates

—explain why, for a small open economy, changes in the exchange rate cause changes in the domestic prices of traded goods

—explain the variety of international transactions that determine the demand for and supply of foreign currency

—understand that an exchange rate is set in a competitive market by the forces of demand and supply

—explain the economic factors that will cause changes in the equilibrium level of the exchange rate

—categorize various international payments and receipts as either current or capital account transactions

—understand what is meant by the official reserves account and how central bank actions affect this account

—understand that although the sum of the three accounts must be zero (an overall balance of payments), neither the current nor the capital accounts by themselves or added together need be balanced

—explain that an overall balance-of-payments deficit or surplus refers to the sum of the current and capital accounts, without reference to the official reserves account

Multiple-Choice Questions

1. An economy described as a small open economy
   (a) engages in no international trade because of its size
   (b) can influence the prices of traded goods by changing the supplies of these goods
   (c) allows free exchange of factors of production such as labor
   (d) is a price taker for goods it trades on the world market

2. The exchange rate refers to
   (a) the ratio of exports to imports
   (b) the amount of home currency that must be given up in order to obtain one unit of foreign currency
   (c) the rate at which one country exchanges gold with another
   (d) the volume of trading one currency in terms of all others

3. If one pound sterling trades for $1.50 Canadian,
   (a) the volume of trade must be in the ratio 1.00 to 1.50
   (b) the sterling price of a Canadian dollar is 67
   (c) one Canadian dollar exchanges for 0.67 pounds sterling
   (d) Canada will always have an excess of imports over exports as far as trade with Great Britain is concerned

4. If 20 Indian rupees trade for one Canadian dollar,
   (a) 20 Canadian dollars trade for one Indian rupee
   (b) the Canadian dollar price of rupees is 5 cents
   (c) parity exists between rupees and dollars
   (d) 50 Canadian cents trade for one rupee

5. If the Canadian dollar price of the U.S. dollar rises from 1.30 to 1.32,
   (a) the Canadian dollar has depreciated
   (b) the U.S. dollar has appreciated
   (c) the Canadian dollar has appreciated
   (d) both (a) and (b)

6. If the Canadian dollar price of Japanese yen changes from 0.008 to 0.005,
   (a) the yen has appreciated
   (b) the Canadian dollar has depreciated
   (c) the Canadian dollar has appreciated
   (d) both (a) and (b)

7. If a skiing trip to Aspen, Colorado, costs $3,000 (U.S.) and the Canadian dollar price of one U.S. dollar is $1.40,
   (a) Canadians must pay $2,142.86 in Canadian funds for this trip
   (b) Canadians must pay $3,000 in Canadian funds for this trip
   (c) Americans would pay the equivalent of $2,142.86 in Canadian funds for this trip
   (d) Canadians must pay $4,200 in Canadian funds for this trip

8. Suppose that the domestic country is a small open economy. An appreciation of the foreign currency, other things being equal,
   (a) lowers the domestic prices of traded goods
   (b) has no effect on the domestic prices of traded goods, since we are dealing with a small open economy
   (c) causes an appreciation of the domestic currency
   (d) raises the domestic prices of traded goods

9. For a small open economy, an appreciation of the domestic currency, other things being equal,
   (a) increases the domestic prices of traded goods
   (b) leads to a reduction in the quantity supplied and an increase in the quantity demanded for traded goods
   (c) is likely to increase the volume of exports and decrease the volume of imports
   (d) does not affect the prices of traded goods, since we are dealing with a small open economy

Questions 10 through 16 refer to the following graph. The two countries are Canada (the home country) and Japan. The currency of Japan is the yen.

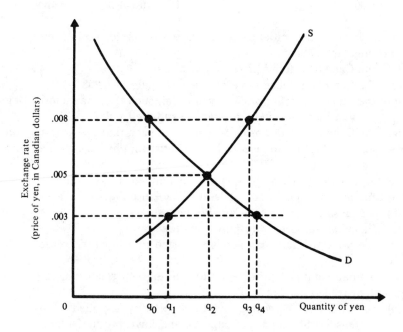

10. A movement down the vertical scale means that
    (a) the yen becomes more expensive
    (b) the Canadian dollar is depreciating relative to the yen
    (c) the yen is depreciating
    (d) the external value of the Canadian dollar is fixed

11. If the current exchange rate is 0.005,
    (a) $200 trades for one yen
    (b) 0.005 yen trades for one Canadian dollar
    (c) one yen trades for 0.005 Canadian dollars
    (d) the quantity demanded of yen is less than the quantity supplied

12. At an exchange rate of 0.008,
    (a) there is an excess demand of yen
    (b) there is an excess supply of yen
    (c) there is an excess supply of Canadian dollars
    (d) 0.008 yen trades for one Canadian dollar

13. At an exchange rate of 0.003,
    (a) the quantity demanded for yen is q_4 and the quantity supplied is q_1
    (b) the quantity demanded for yen is q_3 and the quantity supplied is q_1
    (c) there is an excess supply of yen of $q_4 - q_1$
    (d) there is an excess demand for Canadian dollars of $q_4 - q_1$

14. Given the demand and supply curves for yen, the equilibrium exchange rate allowing free market forces to prevail is
    (a) 0.003   (c) 0.005
    (b) 0.008   (d) impossible to predict

15. Assuming that the initial exchange rate is 0.008, forces in a free market for exchange are likely to cause
    (a) the Canadian dollar price of yen to rise
    (b) the Canadian dollar price of yen to remain at 0.008
    (c) the Canadian dollar price of yen to fall such that the quantity demanded for yen increases and the quantity supplied falls
    (d) the Canadian dollar price of yen to fall such that the quantity demanded for Canadian dollars rises and the quantity supplied of Canadian dollars falls

16. As the yen depreciates, the quantity demanded for yen increases because
    (a) the prices of Japanese goods in Canadian dollars decrease
    (b) Japanese imports from Canada increase
    (c) Canadian imports from Japan decrease
    (d) the prices of Canadian goods imported into Japan decrease

17. For a small country, appreciation of a foreign currency causes the domestic prices of traded goods to
    (a) rise, thereby increasing the total quantity supplied of traded goods, increasing the volume of exports, and lowering the volume of imports
    (b) fall, thereby increasing the total quantity supplied of traded goods, increasing the volume of exports, and lowering the volume of imports
    (c) rise, thereby increasing the total quantity supplied of traded goods, decreasing the volume of exports, and increasing the volume of imports
    (d) remain constant because we are dealing with a small open economy

18. A lower inflation rate in Canada than in Great Britain, other things being equal, is predicted to cause
    (a) the Canadian dollar price of sterling to rise
    (b) the sterling price of dollars to fall
    (c) the demand curve for sterling to shift to the right, as will the supply curve of sterling
    (d) the demand curve for sterling to shift to the left and the supply curve to shift to the right

19. A desire by Canadians to invest more in France than before, other things being equal, will cause
    (a) the French franc price of Canadian dollars to rise
    (b) the demand curve for francs to shift to the right
    (c) the supply curve for francs to shift to the right
    (d) both the demand and supply curves of francs to shift to the left

20. If short-term interest rates in Canada increase relative to short-term U.S. interest rates, other things being equal, then
    (a) capital flows from the United States to Canada are likely to increase and the U.S. dollar price of Canadian dollars is likely to rise
    (b) the U.S. dollar is likely to appreciate
    (c) the demand curve for U.S. dollars will shift to the right
    (d) the Canadian dollar will depreciate relative to the U.S. dollar

21. Which of the following is *not* likely to cause an appreciation of the Canadian dollar?
    (a) an increase in interest rates in Canada relative to rates elsewhere
    (b) a lower inflation rate in Canada relative to foreign rates
    (c) lower earnings expectations in Canada relative to those elsewhere
    (d) expectations of an appreciation of the Canadian dollar

22. If there is a current account deficit in Canada and no use of official reserves by the Bank of Canada, the sale of Canadian government bonds to foreigners will
    (a) increase the likelihood of a balance-of-payments deficit
    (b) increase the likelihood of a balance-of-payments surplus
    (c) offset totally the deficit on the current account, since the balance-of-payments accounts must balance
    (d) have no effect on the balance of payments, since this sale will not be recorded in the accounts

23. The current account includes all *but* which of the following transactions?
    (a) merchandise exports and imports
    (b) imports of services
    (c) short-term capital transfers
    (d) invisibles

Questions 24 through 32 refer to the balance-of-payment items listed here. Before attempting these questions, you should be familiar with the components of the capital and current accounts discussed in the text.

(a)	Long-term capital receipts		$ 1,305
(b)	Merchandise exports		17,785
(c)	Freight and shipping receipts		1,170
(d)	Freight and shipping payments	$ 1,147	
(e)	Short-term capital receipts	1,182	
(f)	Use of official reserves (increase)		777
(g)	Merchandise imports	15,556	
(h)	Long-term capital payments	814	
(i)	Short-term capital receipts	1,158	
(j)	Interest and dividend receipts	545	
(k)	Interest and dividend payments	1,613	
(l)	Other current account payments	721	
(m)	Net travel payments		201

24. The balance on merchandise trade is
    (a) a favorable balance of $33,341
    (b) a favorable balance of $2,229
    (c) a deficit (unfavorable balance) of $2,229
    (d) an unfavorable balance of $33,341

25. Which of the following is *not* an item in the current account?
    (a) item (m)   (c) item (e)
    (b) item (c)   (d) item (b)

26. The value of the current account balance is a
    (a) favorable balance (surplus) of $262
    (b) deficit (unfavorable balance) of $262
    (c) surplus of $1,508
    (d) favorable balance of $380

27. A surplus in the current account must be matched by
    (a) a deficit in the capital account   (c) either (a) or (b) or both
    (b) an increase in official reserves   (d) a surplus in the capital account

28. Which of the following is *not* a capital account item?
    (a) item (f)   (c) item (e)
    (b) item (i)   (d) item (h)

29. The value of the capital account balance is
    (a) an unfavorable balance (deficit) of $515
    (b) a favorable balance (surplus) of $515
    (c) an unfavorable balance (deficit) of $262
    (d) a favorable balance (surplus) of $262

30. In the situation shown by the information given, the sum of the current and capital accounts indicates that the balance of payments is in
    (a) a favorable (surplus) position of $777
    (b) an unfavorable (deficit) position of $777
    (c) a favorable (surplus) position of $253
    (d) an unfavorable (deficit) position of $530

31. The value of the balance-of-payments position in question 30 is reflected by the fact that the use of official reserves
    (a) increased by $777   (c) decreased by $530
    (b) decreased by $777   (d) increased by $253

32. If there had been no central bank intervention in the foreign exchange market, the situation described in question 30 would likely have led ultimately to
    (a) an appreciation in the external value of this country's currency
    (b) a depreciation in the external value of this country's currency
    (c) equilibrium in the balance of payments as the exchange rate changed
    (d) both (a) and (c)

Exercises

1. Suppose that the exchange rate between Canadian dollars and German marks is established in a free exchange market without any intervention by the Bank of Canada. For each of the following events, indicate whether the Canadian dollar price of marks will tend to appreciate, depreciate, or remain unchanged. Explain your answer briefly, and indicate whether the event is likely to affect the demand curve for marks (denoted by D), the supply curve of marks (denoted as S), or both.
   (a) Attendance of German rodeo fans at the Calgary Stampede doubles.

   (b) The rate of inflation in Canada increases relative to the German inflation rate.

   (c) Short-term interest rates rise in Germany relative to those in Canada.

   (d) Prolonged German economic expansion causes Canadian exports to Germany to increase from previous levels.

   (e) Germans buy several farms in southwestern Ontario.

   (f) Speculators anticipate a depreciation of the mark relative to the Canadian dollar.

2. Suppose that a small country produces soybeans. It imports manufactured goods, but these are not considered in this question. The price of soybeans is established in world markets at \$60 (U.S.) per ton. The current exchange rate is 10 units of this country's currency for every U.S. dollar. The domestic demand curve for soybeans is $Q_D = 10,000 - 5P$ and the domestic supply curve is $Q_S = 400 + 11P$, where P is the price of soybeans per ton in domestic currency. The demand and supply curves are shown on the graph.

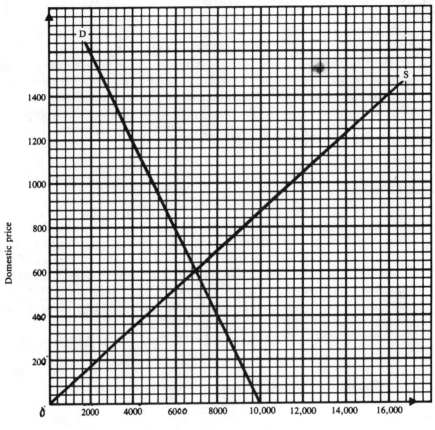

Quantity of soybeans (tons)

(a) What is the current domestic price of soybeans? How much is produced domestically? What quantity of soybeans would be exported (assuming that the domestic price is less than or equal to the world price)?

(b) Suppose that the world price of soybeans rises to \$100 (U.S.) per ton. What happens to the domestic price of soybeans in this country? At this price, what is the domestic quantity demanded? Quantity supplied? Does this country export or import soybeans? What quantity?

(c)   Now suppose that the exchange rate changes such that six units of domestic currency trade for one U.S. dollar. What has happened to the price of the dollar? What has happened to the external value of the domestic currency?

(d)   At this new exchange rate and a world price of soybeans of $100, what is the new domestic price of soybeans? What is the domestic quantity demanded at this new price? Quantity supplied? Quantity of exports? Compare your answers with those in (b).

3.   You are given the demand for and supply of U.S. dollars at alternative prices in terms of Canadian dollars. Assume that the U.S. dollar changes without intervention from any central bank. The curves labeled D_0 and S_0 represent the initial case. The other curves represent changes in economic conditions between the two countries. Use them to answer (b) to (d).

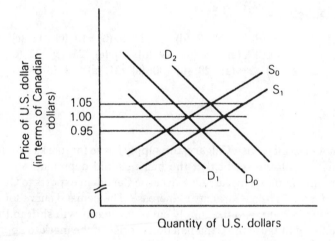

(a)   Determine the equilibrium Canadian dollar price of the U.S. dollar, assuming that D_0 and S_0 apply.

(b)   Suppose that there is a sizable increase in short-term capital flows from Canada to the United States, other things being equal. Which curves would shift and why? What will happen to the Canadian dollar price of the U.S. dollar?

(c)   Which curve or curves will shift if Canadians were to import significantly less from the United States? What will happen to the Canadian dollar price of the U.S. dollar?

(d)   Suppose that Canadian exports to the United States were to increase significantly, other things being equal. Predict the effect on the price of the U.S. dollar.

4. Assume a world with only two countries, Winn and Bert. Moreover, assume
    that the central bank in each country does not participate in the foreign exchange
    market. Two "pegs" (the currency of Winn) exchange for one "alas" (the currency
    of Bert). Winn sells 10,000 pegs' worth of autos to Bert, and Bert sells 8,000
    alases' worth of potash to Winn.
    (a) What is value of Winn's current account (valued in pegs)? What is the value
        of Bert's current account (valued in alases)? What is the value of Bert's
        current account valued in pegs?

    (b) Since there must be an overall balance in the international accounts in *each*
        country, what capital account transactions are likely to occur with the
        situation described in (a)?

Answers

Multiple-Choice Questions

1. (d)   2. (b)   3. (c)   4. (b)   5. (d)   6. (c)   7. (d)   8. (d)   9. (b)   10. (c)   11. (c)   12. (b)
13. (a)   14. (c)   15. (c)   16. (a)   17. (a)   18. (d)   19. (b)   20. (a)   21. (c)   22. (c)   23. (c)
24. (b)   25. (c)   26. (a)   27. (c)   28. (a)   29. (b)   30. (a)   31. (a)   32. (d)

Exercises

1. (a) When more Germans visit Calgary, the supply curve for marks should shift
         to the right, with the result that the mark should depreciate.
    (b) A greater inflation rate in Canada will cause Canadian exports to Germany
         to fall and imports from Germany to increase. The demand curve for marks
         will shift to the right, and the supply curve for marks will shift to the left.
         Both are likely to cause the Canadian dollar price of the mark to appreciate
         (the Canadian dollar depreciates).
    (c) Germany is likely to experience more capital inflows from Canada, and
         less international capital will flow from Germany to Canada. Hence both
         the demand and supply curves for marks are affected such that the mark
         will appreciate.
    (d) The supply curve for marks will shift to the right, and hence the mark
         will depreciate.
    (e) These transactions constitute capital outflows from Germany. The supply
         curve for marks will shift to the right, and hence the mark will depreciate.
    (f) The mark will depreciate. Both the demand and supply curves for marks
         will be affected.

2. (a) The domestic price is 600 per ton. Production is 7,000 tons. No soybeans would be exported.

   (b) The price of soybeans now rises to 1,000 per ton. Quantity demanded is now 5,000 tons, and quantity supplied is about 11,400 tons. This country now exports 6,400 tons.

   (c) The U.S. dollar has depreciated and the domestic currency has appreciated.

   (d) The domestic price of soybeans is again 600. Quantity demanded and quantity supplied are both 7,000 tons. Therefore, the country does not export soybeans. The increase in the international price of soybeans (which caused this country's exports to increase) has been completely offset by the appreciation of the domestic currency.

3. (a) One Canadian dollar trades for one U.S. dollar.

   (b) The demand curve for U.S. dollars will shift to the right (such as that labeled D_2). The U.S. dollar will appreciate and will equal 1.05 Canadian dollars.

   (c) The demand curve for U.S. dollars will shift to the left (such as that labeled D_1). The U.S. dollar will depreciate to a price of $0.95 Canadian.

   (d) The supply curve for U.S. dollars will shift to the right (such as that labeled S_1). The U.S. dollar will depreciate to a price of $0.95 Canadian.

4. (a) Winn's exports to Bert are worth 10,000 pegs. Winn imports the equivalent of 16,000 pegs of potash from Bert. Thus Winn has a unfavorable balance (deficit) of 6,000 pegs in terms of its current account. Bert's exports to Winn are worth 8,000 alases. Bert imports the equivalent of 5,000 alases of autos from Winn. Thus Bert has a favorable balance (surplus) of 3,000 alases in its current account. This is equivalent to 6,000 pegs.

   (b) Several scenarios are possible, but all will result in capital flows from Bert to Winn. For example, if the potash producers deposit their 6,000-peg surplus in banks in Winn, then Winn's international accounts will record a capital inflow (credit) of 6,000 pegs. Bert's international account will record a capital outflow (payment) of 3,000 alases. Winn's 6,000-peg current account deficit will be matched by the 6,000-peg capital account surplus. Bert's 3,000-alas current account surplus will be matched by the 3,000-alas capital account deficit.

Alternative Exchange Rate Systems

Learning Objectives

After reading this chapter, you should be able to:

—understand the necessary short-term actions by a central bank whose responsibility is to maintain the external value of the country's currency at some pegged level

—explain why the sufficiency of international reserves, changes in long-term trends in inflation and economic growth, and exchange speculation cause problems for an adjustable peg system

—explain how balance-of-payments adjustments occur under a flexible or floating exchange rate system

—distinguish between an adjustable peg system and a managed float system

—understand the concept of purchasing power parity and how it helps to identify the equilibrium level of an exchange rate

—explain why speculative behavior and exchange rate overshooting can cause major deviations in exchange rates from their purchasing power parity values and why these deviations cause problems for an economy

—understand current problems in exchange markets such as the adequacy of reserve supplies, the lack of an alternative to the U.S. dollar as a reserve currency, inconsistent exchange rate policies, and destabilizing exchange speculation

—recognize the role of international cooperation in responding to shocks in the world economy, regardless of the exchange rate system

Multiple-Choice Questions

1. If there is excess demand for a country's currency at some fixed external value, then a central bank, to maintain this pegged rate, must
   (a) buy its currency in the exchange market
   (b) wait until the demand and supply curves for this currency change such that no excess demand exists
   (c) sell its currency in the exchange market and therefore increase its holdings of official reserves
   (d) increase interest rates by selling government bonds

2. If there is an excess supply of a country's currency at some fixed external value,
   (a) it is likely that this country has a unfavorable position in its balance of payments
   (b) the central bank of this country will buy its currency in the foreign exchange market to maintain the pegged value
   (c) the country's official reserve holdings will fall
   (d) all of the above

3. Which of the following would *not* be an appropriate policy action for a country operating on a fixed exchange rate system and facing a long-term balance-of-payments deficit?
   (a) seeking permission to devalue its currency (lowering the pegged value)
   (b) increasing national income to promote more import purchases
   (c) restrictionary monetary policies to reduce the country's inflation rate substantially
   (d) legislating capital export restrictions

4. If speculators believe that a country's currency is undervalued at the current pegged value,
   (a) they will sell this currency and hold other currencies
   (b) they believe that the country's central bank will have to buy its currency in the foreign exchange market
   (c) their expectations are that the central bank will increase the par value, and so they increase their current holdings of this currency
   (d) they know that the country has been experiencing a long-term balance-of-payments deficit, and hence the par value will have to be lowered

5. A floating or flexible exchange rate system
   (a) is for all purposes the same as a fixed exchange rate system
   (b) allows fluctuations around some fixed rate, with IMF approval
   (c) allows the exchange rate to be determined by forces of demand and supply without central bank intervention
   (d) necessarily generates unstable exchange rate values

6. The "dirty" or managed float of currencies means that
   (a) currencies are officially pegged, but a large black market exists
   (b) the official price at which gold is being sold is allowed to fluctuate
   (c) currencies are officially floating but are being influenced from time to time by central bank policies
   (d) fixed rates are changed from time to time by the central bank

7. Suppose that country X holds 100 percent of its international reserves in U.S. dollars. If the United States devalues its dollar,
    (a) the value of country X's reserves will increase
    (b) country X will be in a better position to maintain a pegged U.S. dollar price of its currency
    (c) country X must continue to hold all its reserves in U.S. dollars
    (d) none of the above

8. Which of the following is likely to cause country Y to lower the pegged value of its currency?
    (a) Country Y has been experiencing a persistently higher inflation rate than its major trading partners.
    (b) Country Y's export shares have been eroded by the lack of product innovation.
    (c) Country Y, which is totally dependent on imported oil, faces continual oil price increases.
    (d) All of the above.

9. Suppose that country Z has experienced persistent deficits in its balance of payments. If it does not wish to change the external value of its currency, an appropriate domestic policy might consist of
    (a) an increase in its domestic money supply, which causes an increase in demand for its currency in international exchange markets
    (b) increased subsidies to domestic companies that import foreign goods
    (c) tax increases that reduce the ability of its citizens to buy imports
    (d) an expansionary government spending program that increases the external value of its currency above its purchasing power parity value

10. According to the purchasing power parity (PPP) hypothesis, if domestic inflation in country A exceeds that in country B by 10 percent, the price of B's currency expressed in A's currency
    (a) should increase by about 10 percent
    (b) should decrease by about 10 percent
    (c) should not change, since inflation rates are calculated on this basis of domestically produced goods and services
    (d) should not change, since the theory applies only to a fixed exchange rate system where currency values are pegged

11. Which of the following would tend to increase the external value of a currency above its PPP rate?
    (a) speculative behavior that involves selling this currency in large volumes
    (b) the country's central bank raising domestic interest rates above world levels
    (c) the country's central bank buying bonds on the open market
    (d) all of the above

12. Suppose that the PPP rate for a country's currency is U.S.$1.25 while its actual rate falls to U.S.$1.15. The actual rate would adjust to the PPP value if
    (a) the country's inflation rate rose relative to the U.S. inflation rate
    (b) speculators bought this currency with the expectation that the actual rate would adjust back to its PPP value
    (c) exchange speculators believed that the actual rate will continue to fall
    (d) none of the above

13. Suppose that a Canadian buys a one-year $100 U.S. bond, which has a 2 percent annual real rate of return, for $115 Canadian. When the bond matures in one year, she converts her U.S. proceeds into Canadian dollars at $1.12 Canadian per $1.00 U.S. Given this information, we know that
    (a) the Canadian dollar has depreciated
    (b) she made a 2 percent rate of return in terms of her initial Canadian-dollar investment
    (c) her rate of return is much greater than 2 percent since the Canadian dollar appreciated
    (d) she incurred a loss since her Canadian-dollar proceeds after one year are less than her original Canadian-dollar investment

14. If the PPP rate were $1.15 U.S. for the Canadian dollar and Bank of Canada policy creates a positive 3 percent annual differential between Canadian and American interest rates, then, all other things being equal, we would expect
    (a) international investors to buy Canadian assets
    (b) the Canadian-dollar price of the U.S. dollar to depreciate
    (c) international investors to be indifferent between lending money in Canada and elsewhere if they expect the Canadian dollar to depreciate at 3 percent per year to its PPP value
    (d) all of the above

15. Exchange rate overshooting caused by higher interest rates in country X than those in country Y will
    (a) cause country X's imports to fall
    (b) increase the competitiveness of country Y's export industries
    (c) cause economic expansion in country X
    (d) both (a) and (b)

Questions 16 through 20 refer to the accompanying graph.

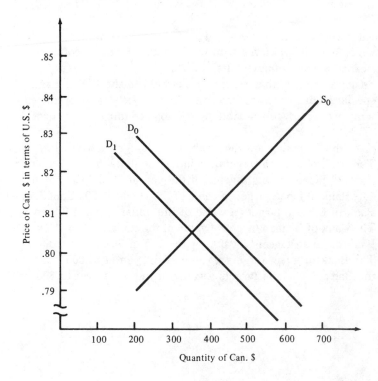

16. Referring to the curves D_0 and S_0 and assuming a floating exchange rate system, the price of the Canadian dollar in terms of U.S. dollars would be
(a) 400
(b) 0.81
(c) 1.81
(d) 1.23

17. If the demand curve shifts to the left to D_1, this might be explained by the fact that, other things being equal,
(a) Canadian export sales fell
(b) Canadian export sales rose
(c) imports to Canada rose
(d) imports to Canada fell

18. Because of the decrease in demand, the external value of the Canadian dollar is likely to
(a) remain unchanged because the supply curve did not shift
(b) rise above the initial equilibrium level
(c) fall to approximately $0.805 U.S.
(d) decrease temporarily but then revert to its initial equilibrium position

19. Assuming a demand curve of D_1, the Bank of Canada (pursuing a managed float) might try to maintain an external value of $0.81 for a short period of time by
(a) selling 100 Canadian dollars
(b) buying 5 Canadian dollars
(c) selling 50 Canadian dollars
(d) buying 100 Canadian dollars

20. If the PPP value and the actual value were 0.82 and 0.81, respectively, we might expect exchange speculators
(a) to sell Canadian dollars and buy U.S. dollars
(b) to gamble that the U.S. dollar will appreciate
(c) to buy Canadian dollars and sell U.S. dollars
(d) to take actions that cause the supply curve of Canadian dollars to shift to the right

21. Special drawing rights (SDRs) are
(a) supplementary reserves with the IMF that member countries can use to finance balance-of-payments deficits
(b) demand deposits that central banks hold in the World Bank
(c) special credits given to importers in less developed countries
(d) long-term reserves available to member countries in return for gold

22. Which of the following are inconsistent exchange rate policies?
(a) The Bank of Canada targets a value of the dollar worth 200 yen while the Bank of Japan targets a value of the yen at $0.005 Canadian.
(b) The Bank of Japan targets a value of the yen at $0.004 Canadian while the Bank of Canada targets a value of the dollar worth 250 yen.
(c) The Bank of Canada targets a value of the dollar worth 150 yen while the Bank of Japan targets a value of the yen at $0.008 Canadian.
(d) The Bank of Japan targets a value of the yen at $0.0033 Canadian while the Bank of Canada targets a value of the dollar worth 300 yen.

Exercises

1. The purchasing power parity hypothesis predicts that over the long run, exchange rates will reflect relative rates of domestic inflation. Test this hypothesis for the period 1967–1982 for the following five countries.

	United States	Canada	United Kingdom	West Germany	Japan
1982 CPI (1967 = 100)	290.0	304.0	517.8	196.5	304.2
Exchange rate (U.S. cents)					
1967	—	92.69	275.0	25.08	0.2763
1982	—	80.18	175.2	41.48	0.3981

What are the predicted PPP 1982 exchange rates? Compare these values with actual values.

    Canada _____

    United Kingdom _____

    West Germany _____

    Japan _____

[*Hint*: Use the formula (U.S. CPI/foreign CPI) (1967 exchange rate).]

2. Most observers would agree that the actual U.S. dollar price of the Canadian dollar was high relative to its PPP value in the 1989–1990 period. Estimates of the PPP vary, but suppose that the correct range is somewhere between 80 and 82 U.S. cents. The actual U.S.-dollar price of the Canadian dollar in early 1990 averaged around 85 cents. Explain how this deviation might have been caused by foreign exchange overshooting.

3. The graph represents the market for pounds sterling. The horizontal axis denotes million of pounds, and the vertical axis is the Canadian dollar price of pounds.

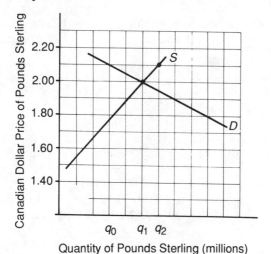

   (a) If exchange rates are flexible, what is the equilibrium dollar price of sterling?

   (b) Assume that the Bank of Canada chooses to have an unannounced target of $2.10 Canadian per pound sterling. What is its unannounced sterling price of dollars? What foreign exchange transactions must it do to maintain the targeted Canadian-dollar price of sterling? What will happen to its international reserve holdings?

   (c) What is likely to happen in the foreign exchange market if the Bank of England had an unannounced target of 0.48 pounds per Canadian dollar?

   (d) If future inflation rates were higher in Britain than in Canada, what would happen to the Canadian-dollar price of pounds if both banks had operated on a flexible exchange rate system?

4. A country has a demand curve for foreign currency given by $D = 6 - 2e$ and a supply curve given by $S = 0.5 + 3e$, where e is the price of the foreign currency in terms of the domestic currency and quantities are in millions.

   (a) If its policy had allowed the exchange rate to be determined freely on the exchange market, what would the equilibrium levels of e and the quantity of foreign currency have been?

   (b) Suppose that this equilibrium value also represents the PPP value. Now the country's central bank increases domestic interest rates relative to those in other countries with the result that the new demand curve is $D = 5.8 - 2e$ and the new supply curve is $S = 0.8 + 3e$. Explain why both the demand and supply curves for foreign currency changed, and predict the new short-term equilibrium exchange rate value. How does this value compare with the PPP value?

   (c) If the country's PPP value is not likely to change in the future, what is likely to happen to the value of e? Explain.

Answers

Multiple-Choice Questions

1. (c) 2. (d) 3. (b) 4. (c) 5. (c) 6. (c) 7. (d) 8. (d) 9. (c) 10. (a) 11. (b) 12. (b)
13. (d) 14. (d) 15. (b) 16. (b) 17. (a) 18. (c) 19. (d) 20. (c) 21. (a) 22. (c)

Exercises

1. Canada: 88.4; United Kingdom: 154.0; West Germany: 37.0; Japan: 0.2634. The depreciation of the Canadian dollar and the pound sterling and the appreciation of the mark are correctly (but not accurately) predicted.

2. As the text suggests, the Bank of Canada ran a restrictive monetary policy that created a 4 percent differential between Canadian and American interest rates. Such a large differential attracted a large inflow of international capital and increased the demand for Canadian dollars. Hence the Canadian dollar appreciated beyond its PPP value; the Bank of Canada policy overvalued the Canadian dollar relative to its PPP value. The high value of the Canadian dollar created problems for firms in Canadian export industries.

3. (a) $2.00 Canadian where $D = S$.
   (b) Its unannounced sterling price of dollars is $1/2.10 = 0.476$ (approximately). At a price of $2.10, there is an excess supply of pounds (and an excess demand for dollars). Thus the Bank must sell dollars and buy $q_2 - q_0$ pounds in the exchange market. The Bank's holdings of sterling (which may be held for reserves) will increase.
   (c) Probably confusion, increased speculation, and destabilized exchange markets. The unannounced Bank of England target is inconsistent with the Bank of Canada's target. The Bank of England's target of 0.48 pounds translates into a dollar price of pounds target of $2.08, which is different from the Bank of Canada's target of $2.10.
   (d) Britain's higher inflation rate would tend to decrease its exports to Canada and increase its imports from Canada. Hence the dollar price of sterling would fall over time and the sterling price of the Canadian dollar would rise. In terms of the graph, the demand curve for pounds sterling would shift to the left, and the supply curve of pounds sterling would shift to the right.

4. (a) Quantity demanded equals quantity supplied at $e = 1.1$; equilibrium quantity is 3.8 million.
   (b) An increase in the domestic interest rate will cause less capital outflows and more capital inflows. Less capital outflows decrease the demand for foreign currency and more capital inflows increase the supply of foreign currency. The new equilibrium exchange rate will be 1.0. Relative to the PPP value, foreign currency is undervalued while the domestic currency is overvalued.
   (c) Assuming that no additional interest rate differentials are created, we would expect the price of foreign currency to appreciate (domestic currency depreciates). This might occur through the activity of speculators who gamble that the undervalued foreign currency will rise to its PPP value in the future. Thus by selling domestic currency and buying foreign currency, speculators may cause the foreign currency to reach its PPP value.

Chapter 43

Macroeconomic Policy in an Open Economy

Learning Objectives

After studying this chapter, you should be able to:

—appreciate that conducting successful macroeconomic policy in an open economy is more complex than in a closed economy because additional policy targets exist and the effectiveness of macro policy instruments is altered

—understand what is meant by internal balance and external balance, the latter being either a net export target or a balance-of-payments target

—distinguish between expenditure-switching and expenditure-changing policies, understand how each affects the net export function, and recognize which policy choices are appropriate when conflicts exist between internal and external objectives

—indicate how a policy of sterilization affects the relationship between a balance-of-payments imbalance and the domestic money supply

—explain why external imbalances can be eliminated by exchange rate changes under a flexible exchange rate system

—understand why monetary policy is most effective under a flexible exchange rate system and why fiscal policy is most effective under a fixed exchange rate system when capital is highly mobile internationally

—appreciate the difficulty of conducting successful macroeconomic policies in Canada with various exchange rate regimes and during different domestic and international problems in the past few years

Multiple-Choice Questions

1. Which of the following cases represents a conflict in objectives?
   (a) a trade account deficit combined with an inflationary gap
   (b) a trade account surplus combined with a recessionary gap
   (c) an inflationary gap and a trade account surplus
   (d) none of the above

2. A country that has a trade account deficit and an inflationary gap may solve both problems if
   (a) government expenditure increases
   (b) taxes are increased
   (c) taxes are decreased
   (d) government expenditure is financed by an increase in the money supply

3. An expenditure-changing policy, assuming constant domestic prices
   (a) causes a movement along a given net export function
   (b) includes such measures as currency devaluation and import tariffs, which cause shifts in the net export function
   (c) will never generate conflicts between the objectives of internal and external balance
   (d) has no effect on net exports, since domestic absorption is always equal to real national income

4. An example of an expenditure-switching policy is
   (a) a reduction in the money supply
   (b) a cut in the personal income tax rate
   (c) an increase in defense expenditure
   (d) a tariff

5. A conflict arises when an expenditure-changing policy involves reduction of both
   (a) a recessionary gap and a trade account deficit
   (b) an inflationary gap and a trade account deficit
   (c) an inflationary gap and a trade account surplus
   (d) both (a) and (c)

6. Domestic absorption is defined as
   (a) $Y + (X - M)$ (c) $C + I + G$
   (b) $C + I + G + (X - M)$ (d) $C + I - (X - M)$

7. If a country has a trade account surplus,
   (a) domestic absorption is less than real national income
   (b) real national income is equal to domestic absorption
   (c) domestic absorption is greater than real national income
   (d) a conflict of objectives will exist if a recessionary gap exists, and expenditure-changing policies are to be used

8. If a country has a trade account deficit and an inflationary gap,
   (a) domestic absorption is above the current level of real national income
   (b) resources must be released from domestic usage to increase net exports
   (c) expenditure-reducing policies such as income tax increases should be implemented
   (d) all of the above

9. If an economy has an inflationary gap and a trade surplus, both internal and external balance may be attained by
   (a) an expenditure-switching policy that involves devaluation of the domestic currency
   (b) policies to induce a switch of expenditure from domestically produced goods to imported goods
   (c) a contractionary monetary policy combined with a contractionary fiscal policy
   (d) an expenditure-switching policy that involves export subsidies

10. An expenditure-switching policy that induces an increase in imports will
   (a) cause the net export function to shift to the left
   (b) cause the net export function to become positively sloped
   (c) shift the net export function to the right
   (d) generate a movement along a given net export function

11. The capital account is directly affected by an expansionary fiscal policy because
   (a) foreign-produced defense equipment may be purchased by the federal government
   (b) national income will increase and domestic households will travel abroad more frequently
   (c) a trade account surplus that is generated by the fiscal policy change must necessarily affect the capital account since the balance of payments must always balance
   (d) an increase in the rate of interest, assuming a fixed money supply, will trigger additional international capital inflows

12. To solve a capital account deficit in the balance of payments, the central bank should
   (a) reduce the bank rate
   (b) increase reserves in the banking system
   (c) transfer government deposits from itself to the banks
   (d) sell bonds in the open market

13. Other things being equal, a balance-of-payments surplus will lead to
   (a) a decrease in bank reserves
   (b) an increase in the domestic money supply
   (c) an increase in the domestic money supply, which will be followed by central bank sterilization policies such as open-market purchases of bonds
   (d) a capital account surplus since interest rates are likely to increase

14. The effectiveness of monetary policy to reduce a large recessionary gap when the country is committed to maintain a fixed exchange rate is
    (a) severely reduced because capital outflows (triggered by lower interest rates) will counteract the expansionary monetary policies
    (b) significantly increased because capital inflows will increase, thereby adding to the monetary expansion
    (c) as effective as monetary expansion under flexible exchange rates as long as capital flows are sensitive to interest rates
    (d) powerful because a central bank can indefinitely sterilize any balance-of-payments deficit that may result from an expansion in the money supply

15. The effectiveness of expansionary fiscal policy is enhanced under a fixed exchange rate system if
    (a) international capital flows are interest-sensitive
    (b) the money supply is not allowed to change
    (c) the central bank sells foreign currency in the foreign exchange market
    (d) the central bank buys foreign currency as a result of the capital account deficit caused by lower interest rates

16. Suppose that a country is operating under a flexible exchange rate and is experiencing a recessionary gap. An expansionary monetary policy, assuming that capital flows are interest-sensitive, will cause
    (a) an initial rise in imports, an inflow of capital into the country, and depreciation of the domestic currency
    (b) a capital account deficit and an appreciation of the domestic currency
    (c) a capital account deficit, depreciation of the domestic currency, and ultimate restoration of the balance of payments
    (d) a capital account surplus and appreciation of the domestic currency, followed by a current account deficit

17. Under a flexible exchange rate system, monetary policy
    (a) is unlikely to be as effective as under a fixed exchange rate system
    (b) exerts an important crowding-out effect on exports
    (c) is very effective because an initial monetary stimulus can be reinforced by changes in the exchange rate
    (d) requires the use of official reserves by the central bank

18. The crowding-out effect associated with expansionary fiscal policy in an open economy that operates on a flexible exchange system refers to
    (a) lower interest rates, which cause less saving and less capital outflows
    (b) fewer exports and more imports caused by an appreciation of the domestic currency
    (c) more consumption of domestically produced products at the expense of lower consumption of foreign-produced products
    (d) higher interest rates, which cause less domestic investment and more net exports

19. The fact that Canada was on a fixed exchange rate from 1962 to 1970
    (a) insulated Canada from the high rates of inflation in the United States
    (b) meant that monetary policy was more effective than it would have been
         on a floating exchange rate system
    (c) prevented authorities from avoiding the rising inflation rates experienced
         by Canada's major trading partners
    (d) both (a) and (b)

20. One way to manage a dirty float when there are pressures for the domestic
    currency to appreciate is
    (a) for the central bank to sell foreign exchange
    (b) to increase interest rates by selling bonds in the open market
    (c) to increase the money supply
    (d) to allow the exchange rate to appreciate but intervene if the process takes
         too long

Questions 21 through 25 refer to the accompanying graphs. Point *a* in panel (ii)
represents the initial situation in an economy, and the net export curve in panel (i)
is that labeled with a subscript of 0. Assume a fixed exchange rate system.

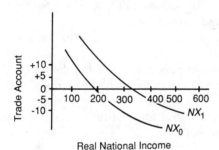

(i) Net Export Function

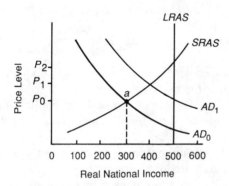

(ii) Determination of National Income

21. Initially, there is
    (a) a negative output gap of 200 and a trade deficit of 10
    (b) a positive output gap of 200 and a trade surplus of slightly less than 5
    (c) a negative output gap of 200 and a trade surplus of slightly less than 5
    (d) a positive output gap of 200 and a trade deficit of 10

22. Suppose that the government imposes a higher tariff on all imported goods. This is an example of
    (a) a devaluation policy
    (b) an expenditure-switching policy
    (c) an expenditure-changing policy
    (d) a restrictionary fiscal policy

23. With the new tariff in place, the *AD* curve shifts to the right, causing
    (a) the price level to increase from P_0 to P_1
    (b) the output gap to decline by 100
    (c) unit costs to increase
    (d) all of the above

24. The new net export function shown in panel (i) represents the effect of
    (a) lower imports due to the higher tariff
    (b) higher exports and lower imports because of the higher domestic price level
    (c) an increase in the marginal propensity to import
    (d) both (a) and (b)

25. The final effect of the tariff increase will be to
    (a) reduce the value of the initial output gap but increase the trade imbalance
    (b) decrease net exports
    (c) halve both the output gap and the trade imbalance
    (d) reduce the trade imbalance but increase the value of the output gap

Exercises

1. Assume that Canada, which is hypothetically considered to be on a fixed exchange system, experiences a balance-of-payments surplus because of increased sales of natural gas to the United States. Americans are assumed to pay Canadians in U.S. dollars, and the Canadian exporting firms wish to convert U.S. dollars into Canadian dollars. Suppose that the sale of natural gas is the equivalent of $40 million Canadian. Fill in the blanks in accordance with the following transactions.

Public (Canadian)

Assets	Liabilities
Foreign currency: _____	
Deposits: _____	

Chartered Banks

Assets	Liabilities
Reserves with Bank of Canada: _____	Deposits: _____

Bank of Canada

Assets	Liabilities
Foreign currency: _____	Deposits of banks: _____

(a) Americans pay Canadian exporting firms in U.S. dollars assumed to be the equivalent of $40 million Canadian. Canadian firms wish to convert this amount into deposits at Canadian banks. Show the effect of this transaction in the balance sheet of the public.

(b) Banks, having purchased the U.S. dollars from firms, wish to sell the $40 million to the Bank of Canada. How does the Bank of Canada pay for these U.S. dollars? Show this transaction in the Bank of Canada's balance sheet.

(c) Finally, after the Bank of Canada has purchased the U.S. dollars from the banks, show the effect on the chartered banks' balance sheet.

(d) What do you predict will finally happen to the level of deposits in the banking system if the target reserve ratio is 0.1 and there is no currency drain?

(e) You should have concluded that the money supply (deposits) increases by a multiple. If the Bank of Canada wishes to sterilize this increase, what should it do, buy or sell bonds to the banks? Explain.

2. The Republic of Can trades with other nations, but no international capital flows into or out of Can. The current price levels of goods produced in Can and in other countries are 2.0 and 1.0 (in foreign currency), respectively. The exchange rate is fixed at two units of Can's currency per unit of foreign currency. Hence the current terms of trade (R) is 1.0. The behavioral relationships in Can are as follows:

$C = 80 + 0.6Y$
$I + G = 40$
$X = 80 - 20R$
$M = 0.1Y + 30R$
Y_P (potential real national income) $= 310$

(a) Formulate the equation for AE and for domestic absorption (A). What is the marginal propensity to spend?

(b) Using the equilibrium condition $Y = AE$, calculate the equilibrium value of real national income (Y). At this level of Y, calculate the values of A and net exports.

(c) A recessionary gap of _____ exists in Can, although the balance of trade is balanced ($X - M = 0$). What specific expenditure-increasing policy with respect to G would you recommend in order to eliminate unemployment? (You may assume that Can's price level doesn't change.)

(d) Your expenditure-increasing policy has generated a trade-balance deficit of _____ when national income is at its potential level. At Y_P, domestic absorption is _____.

(e) To achieve both internal balance ($Y = Y_P$) and external balance ($X - M = 0$), an *expenditure-switching* policy must complement an expenditure-increasing policy. Specifically, since $X - M$ is negative at Y_P, the net export curve must be shifted (upward, downward) so that $X - M = 0$ at Y_P. To achieve external balance, it is clear that the value of R must be (increased, decreased). This may be accomplished by (increasing, decreasing), the external value of Can's currency in the foreign exchange market.

(f) Suppose that the government of Can devalues (decreases the external value of) its currency so that the exchange rate rises from 2.0 to 2.04 and at the same time increases government expenditures by 4 ($I + G = 44$). Will this combined policy achieve internal and external balance? What is the value of domestic absorption at the new equilibrium level of real national income?

3. A country with a fixed exchange rate is currently experiencing an inflationary gap as well as a surplus in its balance of payments. This initial situation is depicted as point *a* in panel (ii) and point *c* in panel (i). The government has two goals: eliminate the inflationary gap without causing cyclical unemployment and reduce the balance-of-trade surplus to an external balance situation.

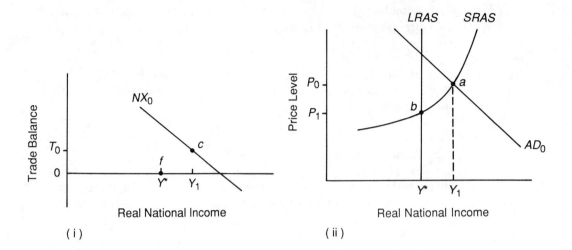

(i)   (ii)

(a) Explain the effects of a tax increase that shifts the AD curve to the left (passing through point b) on the trade balance. Ignoring the effects of price changes on the net export curve, show the new trade balance in panel (i) and label it point d. This policy has eliminated the inflationary gap and also has (increased, decreased, had no effect on) the trade balance.

(b) Instead of increasing taxes, the government decides to revalue the external value of its currency. This is an example of an (expenditure-switching, expenditure-reducing) policy. Assuming that both exports and imports are sufficiently sensitive to an exchange appreciation, the net export function will shift to the (right, left).

(c) If the revaluation were totally successful in achieving internal and external balance, the AD curve must have shifted to the (right, left) passing through point _____ and the net export curve must have shifted to the left passing through point _____.

(d) The shift in the net export curve represents two effects. The first involves the reduction in (exports, imports) and the increase in (exports, imports) due to the exchange revaluation. The second effect offsets some of the impact of the first. Specifically, a decrease in aggregate demand causes the price level to fall, and this should have the effect of (increasing, decreasing) net exports.

4. This exercise focuses on fixed exchange rates and the effectiveness of monetary and fiscal policy. Country T has a recessionary gap of 20; its potential real GDP is 820, and its current real GDP is 800. T's interest rate of 6 percent is equal to world interest rates. The central bank of T is committed to maintaining the external value of its currency at some pegged value. For the purpose of this exercise, assume stable prices in T and all other countries; thus relative prices remain constant. Moreover, assume that the expenditure multiplier is 2.0.

The central bank has reliable information about T's net export and capital account functions. Specifically, they are given by the following equations:

$$(X - M) = 22 - 0.02Y$$

and

$$K = -30 + 4r$$

where $X - M$ is the trade balance, Y is real GDP, K is the capital account balance, and r is the interest rate in percentage terms.

The government, which is under great pressure to solve the recessionary gap problem, considers using expansionary monetary policy to deal with the problem. You, as the governor of the central bank, are asked to present your comments and recommendations to the cabinet.

To ensure that your cabinet briefing is complete, you ask the central bank's economists to give you information about the current state of the economy, the effects of expansionary monetary policy on T's internal and external balance, and any problems that this policy might encounter. The following are the major points they make. You must respond to each of them in terms of whether you agree or disagree. Ask for any clarifications that need to be made.

(a) They point out that T's current trade balance is a surplus of 6. What is your response?

(b) They tell you that T's current capital account is in a deficit position of 6 and that combined with the trade balance, T has an external balance. What is your response?

(c) Previous research indicates that a money supply increase of 8 will decrease T's interest rate by 1 (percent) which in turn will increase domestic investment spending by 10. Using these numbers, they suggest that the recessionary gap could be eliminated if appropriate open-market operations increased the money supply by 8. What is your response? You ask for a clarification of the type of open-market operation they have in mind and why this policy will reduce T's interest rate.

(d) Assuming that the interest rate and GDP goals are achieved, they point out that T will have a balance-of-payments deficit of 4.4. What is your response?

(e) They warn you that the created deficit will necessitate central bank intervention in the exchange market, which will work against the original monetary stimulus. Moreover, sterilization is not feasible because official reserves amount only to about 4.5. What is your response?

(f) They advise against monetary expansion. The suggest that the government consider a fiscal expansion. This will solve the gap, create a surplus in the balance of payments, and allow the central bank to expand the money supply when it intervenes in the foreign exchange market. You agree, and you brief the cabinet with this advice. Provide a brief explanation for your recommending fiscal policy.

*5. A country that operates under a flexible exchange rate regime has a recessionary gap situation. The initial conditions in the economy are an interest rate of r_0, a balance in both the trade account and the capital account, and an exchange rate (the external value of its currency) of π_0. The government increases its expenditure in order to eliminate the recessionary gap without increasing the domestic price level. The effects of the economy are as follows: (1) the demand curve for money shifts to the right such that the interest rate increases to r_1; (2) although capital outflows are assumed to be unaffected, capital flows into this economy from other nations will increase; and (3) the external value of this country's currency appreciates to π_1.

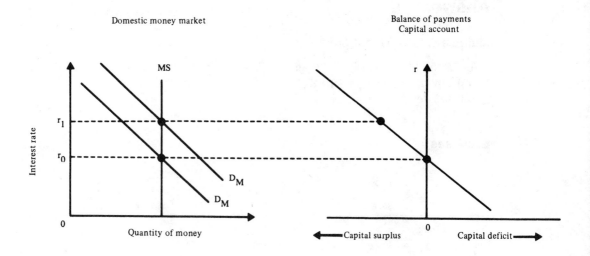

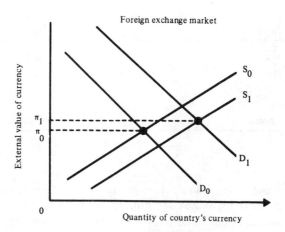

(a) Explain why the government's fiscal policy caused the demand curve for money to shift and the interest rate to increase.

(b) Why does the curve relating the interest rate and the capital account balance slope downward?

(c) Why is a capital account surplus generated by the government's action?

(d) Why did the supply curve for this country's currency in international markets shift to the right? Why did the demand curve for its currency shift to the right?

(e) At an exchange rate of π_0, with the demand and supply curves in the exchange market labeled D_1 and S_1, what situation exists for this country's balance of payments? What will happen to the external value of the currency?

(f) Outline some of the effects of the fiscal policy on the country's net export curve.

Answers

Multiple-Choice Questions

1. (c) 2. (b) 3. (a) 4. (d) 5. (d) 6. (c) 7. (a) 8. (d) 9. (b) 10. (a) 11. (d) 12. (d)
13. (b) 14. (a) 15. (a) 16. (c) 17. (c) 18. (b) 19. (c) 20. (c) 21. (d) 22. (b) 23. (d)
24. (a) 25. (c)

Exercises

1.

Public (Canadian)

Assets		Liabilities
Foreign currency:	− 40	
Deposits:	+ 40	

Chartered Banks

Assets		Liabilities	
Reserves with Bank of Canada:	+ 40	Deposits:	+ 40

Bank of Canada

Assets		Liabilities	
Foreign currency:	+ 40	Deposits of banks:	+ 40

(a) Once the public has sold the foreign currency to the banks, their holdings of foreign currency fall by $40 million and their holdings of deposits rise by $40 million. Hence the public has converted one asset into another.

(b) The Bank of Canada simply increases the reserves of the banks by $40 million. Recall that reserves are deposits with the Bank of Canada. The Bank's holdings of foreign exchange increase by $40 million, and the deposits of the banks in the Bank increase by $40 million.

(c) The reserves of the banks increase by $40 million, and the deposits of the public in the banks also increase by $40 million.

(d) The banks now have excess reserves. Target reserves (additional) are $4 million, and hence excess reserves are $36 million. The money supply will increase by $400 million ($40 million × 1/0.1).

(e) To prevent the money supply from increasing, the Bank of Canada should sell bonds to the banks or the public.

2. (a) $AE = C + I + G + (X − M) = 0.5Y + 150$; $A = C + I + G = 120 + 0.6Y$; the marginal propensity to spend is 0.5.

(b) $AE = Y$; or $0.5Y + 80 + 40 + (60 − 30) = Y$; $Y = 150/0.5 = 300$. Absorption (A) equals 300, and therefore net exports are zero.

(c) Recessionary gap is 10. Increase in G is necessary. With a multiplier of 2, the needed change is equal to one-half the value of the recessionary gap, or 5.

    (d) X still equals 60, but imports are now 0.1(310) + 30, or 61. Hence net exports are −1, a trade deficit. Domestic absorption is 311, which is equal to 125 + 0.6 (310).

    (e)   upward; decreased; decreasing

    (f)   Yes; exports will increase from 60.0 to 60.4. This is because the new terms of trade are 2/(2.04 × 1), which equals 0.98. Imports also increase from 60.0 to 60.4. This is because national income is 310 and the terms of trade are 0.98. Domestic absorption is also 310.

3. (a)   An increase in taxes decreases real GDP. Consumption of all goods (including imported goods) decreases. Although exports are unaffected, the decrease in imports *increases* net exports (or the trade balance). Point d is on the net export curve directly above Y^*. The *increase* in the trade balance is shown as a movement from point c to point d.

    (b)   expenditure-switching; left

    (c)   left; b; f

    (d)   exports; imports; increasing

4. (a)   You agree. Substituting $Y = 800$ into the net export equation, it is clear that there is a surplus on the trade balance of 6.

    (b)   You agree. Since the current rate of interest is 6 (percent), the capital account is in a deficit position of 6. This result is obtained from the capital account balance equation. The sum of the trade and capital accounts is zero, which represents an external balance.

    (c)   You agree. An increase in the money supply of 8 increases investment expenditure by 10. Since the expenditure multiplier is 2, real national income will increase from 800 to 820. They should tell you that the central bank must purchase bonds on the open market. By doing so, the price of bonds is bid up and the bond yield falls. Moreover, the interest rate should fall as domestic banks expand deposits and loans.

    (d)   After some analysis, you should agree. After GDP and the interest rate have changed, there will be a trade surplus of 5.6 and a capital account deficit of 10. Hence there will be a 4.4 deficit in the balance of payments.

    (e)   You agree. A balance-of-payments deficit creates an excess supply of the domestic currency and an excess demand for foreign currency on foreign exchange markets. To maintain a fixed exchange rate, T's central bank will have to buy its currency and sell off its reserves. This action will tend to decrease the money supply, which offsets the planned, initial monetary expansion. Moreover, sterilization seems out of the question since it would exhaust almost all of T's international reserves.

    (f)   After explaining the problems of using monetary policy to eliminate the recessionary gap, you should convince them that fiscal policy is potentially quite effective. An increase in government spending will increase both real GDP and the interest rate. Capital will be attracted to T. Although net exports will fall, a balance-of-payment surplus may result if the capital inflow is greater than the decrease in net exports. If this is correct, the central bank will sell domestic currency and add to its holdings of international reserves. As a result, T's money supply will increase, thereby reinforcing the expansionary effect of fiscal policy.

*5. (a) An expansionary fiscal policy increases real national income, which in turn increases the transactions demand for money. This causes the demand curve for money to shift to the right. Excess demand for money is created, and hence decision makers will sell bonds in order to obtain the additional money. This will lower the price of bonds and increase the interest rate.

(b) For high interest rates (relative to foreign rates), capital inflows should be large and capital outflows small, thereby creating a capital account surplus. For low interest rates, capital inflows will be small and capital outflows will be large, thus creating a deficit on the capital account.

(c) Since the interest rate has risen, more capital will flow into this country from other nations, thus creating a capital account surplus.

(d) Increased real national income will induce more imports (a movement along the net export function) and shift the supply curve for this country's currency to the right. Since capital outflows are assumed to be unaffected, increased capital flows will cause the demand curve for the domestic currency to shift to the right.

(e) Excess demand for this country's currency exists; the external value of the currency will therefore appreciate.

(f) The increase in real national income causes a movement down the net export function; the appreciation of the currency causes the net export function to shift downward (or to the left). This second effect is the crowding-out effect.